BRIAN MOYNAHAN
BEST-SELLING AUTHOR OF THE BRITISH CENTURY

The French Century

An Illustrated History of Modern France

Flammarion

Contents

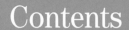

Page 1 from top to bottom
Marie Curie, Pétain,
Picasso, de Gaulle,
Jeanne Moreau, Sartre

Pages 2–3 "Après
le déluge, moi" …
the Mona Lisa *is rehung
in the Louvre after World
War II*

Pages 4–5 *The pioneer
aviator Alberto Santos-
Dumont attached an
engine to the front of a
balloon in 1898 and flew
it around the Eiffel
Tower. He landed outside
cafés on the boulevards
when the spirit moved
him, handing the
mooring rope to a waiter.*

Electricians replace light bulbs on the Eiffel Tower, 1937.

THE SIEGE OF PARIS (1870–71)

The only way out of Paris was by balloon; only carrier pigeons could get in, and the Prussian besiegers flew falcons to stop them. When Bismarck failed to starve Parisians into surrender – they ate salmis de rats *and "pieces of Pollux" from the slaughtered elephant at the zoo – he prescribed terror by shellfire (right, at Porte Maillot). After the Treaty of Frankfurt, his troops entered the city (below), its silent streets hung with black flags.*

THE COMMUNE (1871)

Civil war followed. The Paris Commune, arguably the world's first socialist government, supported by a volatile mixture of Jacobins, anticlericals, republican national guardsmen, the poor and the artist Gustave Courbet (top left), fought against the troops loyal to the national government in Versailles.

It was a desperate business, of lynchings, hostage-murder and summary executions, that created a deep and bitter divide between left and right. The semaine sanglante, the week of blood, began on May 22, when Versailles troops broke into the city. They were faced by barricades (below) and by the pétroleuses, Communard women armed with petrol bombs.

The Madeleine and the Opéra fell on the first day, and much of the Tuileries Palace (right) was destroyed. As the Versaillais advanced, the Communards butchered their hostages, including the archbishop. When his body was found, on May 28, the victorious Versaillais shot 147 captured Communards against a wall, the Mur des Fédérés, in the Père-Lachaise cemetery. It remains a shrine to the left.

More were killed over the week – perhaps 20,000 – than in the Terror of 1793. A national trauma had taken place. The poet Théophile Gautier wrote of "a silence of death" that reigned over the ruins, as profound as that in the necropolis of Thebes; no birdsong, no children's shouts, interrupted the "incurable sadness".

THE EXPOSITION UNIVERSELLE

Not since Renaissance Florence had a city enjoyed such an artistic and creative glow as turn-of-the-century Paris. The great Exposition, opened in 1900, stretched along both banks of the Seine and attracted fifty million visitors. It turned a profit, and the Grand and the Petit Palais were part of its legacy. Among its attractions were the Celestial Globe (far right), the Château d'Eau (right) and a fleet of tricycles (below). An Algerian souk, an African village and models of the temples of Angkor Wat were reminders that France was a great colonial power.

Below: A harshness lay behind the elegance of the race-goers of the Belle Époque. *The poor existed in the slums surrounding Paris. They included the* zoniers, *who lived in shacks and caravans, and eked out a feral existence picking through the city's rubbish. Opposite: The quaintness of washday on the Loire concealed backs and hands half-broken by toil.*

Native genius blossomed in all forms of transport. The Peugeot dynasty, André Citroën, the Renault brothers, and the marquis de Dion were the major car makers, their machines running on tyres invented by the Michelin brothers. The new pastime of touring by car – Marcel Proust chugged through Normandy – was largely invented by the French. So was the sport of motor racing, complete with pits (below, at a race in Boulogne), but using ordinary roads (as in a race at Dieppe, far right). Accidents were frequent. Louis Renault arrived at Bordeaux in the 1903 Paris–Madrid race (right) to be told that his brother Marcel had been killed in a crash.

FRANCE FLIES

Much of the glory of early flight, and many of its records, went to the French. Captain Ferdinand Ferber (right) landed his pioneering glider in Nice in 1902, while Jean Bécu got up speed (below) in Henri Fabre's hydroplane Canard *near Marseille in 1911. In 1909, Louis Blériot (left) flew across the Channel, only eight months after an aircraft had creaked up to a height of 100 metres. The pace was furious.*

Henri Farman, bicycle racer turned plane maker, became the world's first air passenger in history when the sculptor Léon Delagrange took him up at Issy in 1908. Louis Bréguet set a new record by taking eleven people aloft at Douai on March 23, 1911; the following day, Roger Sommer got airborne with a dozen aboard.

CHURCH AND STATE

The Church was savaged by republicans. The assault was vindictive, and politically reckless, for it entrenched old hatreds, and gave the faithful good reason to despise Marianne, the Republic's symbol, as "la Gueuse", the Whore. At first, it was petty malice. Naval ships were given provocatively republican names – Danton, Marseillaise *– in place of those of saints. Army officers who went to mass were secretly marked down for slow promotion. Then, in 1904, the right to teach was withdrawn from the religious orders. They had nurtured education since Charlemagne, but more than 2,500 Church schools were shut. Thousands of teaching priests and nuns, like these sisters of the Hôtel-Dieu in Paris (right), were driven into exile. "We have put out the lights in heaven," a government minister, René Viviani, exulted, "and no-one will turn them on again." Cynically, the priests and missionaries who brought learning to the colonies – like Monsignor Augouard (below) in the Congo – were allowed to stay on. Their teaching gave the secular imperialists in Paris the blanket of the* mission civilatrice.

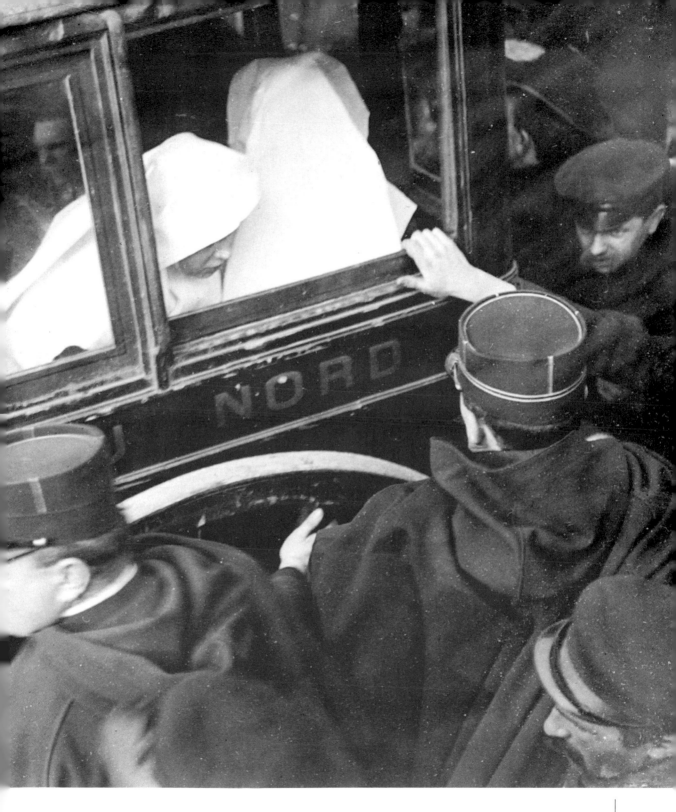

The big money in art went to docile chers maîtres long forgotten. The 840,000
francs paid to Jean Meissonier for 1812, his colossal canvas of the retreat
from Moscow, would have bought dozens of the early works of the artists here.
But Paris was an arts titan because it welcomed the poor, young and struggling,
French and foreign, and bathed them in a creative glow that existed nowhere
else. Here are snapshots of the beneficiaries: (below) Toulouse-Lautrec sleeps,
(facing page, clockwise) Henri Matisse, poverty-stricken, but still able to buy
a canvas by Cézanne, Pablo Picasso, Paul Gauguin, Pierre Bonnard of the Nabis,
the printmaker Félix Vallotton and Édouard Vuillard, another of the Nabis.

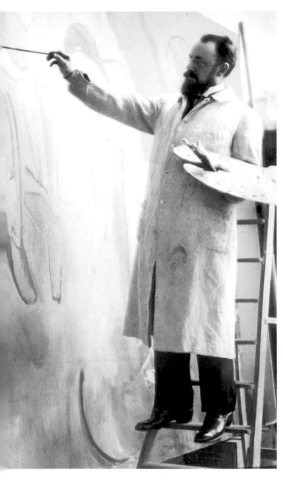

The French were brilliant creators of sporting spectaculars, among them the modern Olympic Games, the football World Cup and, of course, the Tour de France. It started as a publicity stunt for a publication devoted to the bicycle's great rival, the car. Henri Desgrange organised the first race in 1903 to drum up readers for his newspaper, l'Auto*. Sixty riders set off on a 2,500-kilometre, 19-day epic, with competitors riding through the night at times. It was won by Maurice Garin (below), nicknamed "the Chimney Sweep".*

1

Prelude

1789–1899

The French genius is, for the most part, supremely accessible. It has clarity and style. It travels well. So much so that the world has often absorbed it, words and all: a torrent of them – art nouveau, roman à clef, chef, chef d'oeuvre, avant-garde, décor, chic, cinema vérité, TGV – all used in the original.

But there are some habits of thought, deeply embedded, that the outsider finds baffling. They concern the past in particular. Few people have as rich a past as the French, and few guard it so jealously.

François Mitterrand, indeed, does so from beyond the grave. At the last gasp of his presidency, a dying man, he signed a secret agreement with the French National Archives under which the latter surrendered its right to authorise consultation or reproduction of his presidential papers. For a period of 60 years, no one was to be permitted to examine them without the written permission of Mitterrand's trustee.

To the outsider, it seems strange that he should be able to treat state papers as his personal *patrimoine*; but many of the French think of history as part of their inheritance.

They do so with as much self-flagellation as chauvinism. Often, or so it seems to the outsider, it is overdone. The self-recrimination over the 1940 catastrophe, for example, takes little heed of the truth of the remark made at the time by Field Marshal Ironside, the British commander, to an English politician who referred sarcastically to the French as "these bloody gallant allies". "I told him that we depended on the French army," Ironside said. "That we had no army and that therefore it was not right to say 'these bloody allies'. It was for them to say that of us."

Some areas, though, are *chasse gardée*, highly sensitive, a national preserve where the outsider and his questions are seen as trespassers. The law, like history, seems to be subject at times to special treatment. In most of its dealings, French law excels, and is secure and independent. Why does it seem less so, the closer it is to power? The presidential papers are a case in point. Why so little protest at the gagging of the state archive?

Other concepts that loom out of the past puzzle by their persistence. A century after Zola wrote "J'accuse", his words were projected onto the National Assembly. Is Dreyfus really still a stick with which to beat the right, one hundred years on? Why has the left-right divide in France – Lionel Jospin, the Socialist prime minister, declared that "la gauche était pour Dreyfus et la droite contre" – such long-lingering venom?

Is "intellectual" still synonymous with "left"? Why was it modish to be Marxist so much longer in France than anywhere else? Why does the word "republican" in France still have such resonance, quite unlike that in any of the world's other republics? Why did – do – people still "descend into the street", by the million? Is there not a whiff of the barricade when they do so?

And that is perhaps the point of linkage. These strangenesses, as they appear to the outsider, the heightened sense of the radical and the reactionary, stem from the Revolution.

The Revolution is the most sacred part of the *patrimoine*, shackled to national life, as the albatross hung from the neck of the Ancient Mariner, inescapable, malign; adoration of it bred barricades, and fear of it brought dark reaction. Nothing, not the passage of time, world wars, occupation, the passing of the Third and Fourth Republics, and the arrival of the Fifth, has weaned the French from the Revolution. It is a fundamental belief that it defines the nation; that it is the fount of human rights, of "republican" values, of democracy. But the Revolution defines nothing, least of all itself. It was many things to many men. If any single saying contains its pith, it is surely the remark Marie-Jeanne Roland made when she saw the wooden statue of Liberty as she was led to the scaffold in November 1793: "Oh liberty, what crimes are committed in thy name!" Her cry makes a mockery of the famous trinity of liberty, equality and fraternity. That these virtues were practised so fitfully during the Revolution owes much to the omission of a fourth and, in the context of good government, more important grace. No mention was made of justice, or its workaday and more important sister, legality. This absence does much to explain the follies and sadism of the Revolution. And it lingers on to this day, even – or, we might say, particularly – at the highest level, as many "affaires", kickbacks, interest-free loans and insider trading have shown.

Other uneasy traditions accompany this contempt for legality. July 14 is one. Bastille Day was declared the national holiday only in 1880, ninety-one years after the event it commemorated. There was good reason for the delay. Time enabled republicans to exaggerate the "storming" of the Bastille in the same way that Bolshevik propagandists were to fashion the "storming" of the Winter Palace in Petrograd from a bloodless and comical shambles. The reality was trivial, and treacherous. On July 14, 1789, a crowd of Parisians looted thousands of muskets from Les Invalides and crossed the river to besiege the Bastille and free its prisoners. The governor of the Bastille negotiated the surrender of his rundown fortress, on the promise of safe conduct for himself and his men. The prisoners were released. There were just seven of them, four of them forgers and one a "dessicated aristocrat".

The revolutionaries then murdered the men they had given their word to spare. Edward Rigby, an English physician who was walking along the rue Saint-Honoré, found himself caught up in a mob. "We then perceived two bloody heads raised on pikes," he wrote, "which were said to be the heads of the marquis de Launay, the governor of the Bastille, and of M. Flesselles, Prévôt des Marchands." It was, Rigby found, "a chilling and horrid sight". Bastille Day was later decked out with fabrications to conceal these unpleasantnesses. In the myth, scores of political prisoners stagger from their vile oubliettes, groaning with the sudden light and the weight of their fetters, to be led into freedom and fresh air by their fearless and gallant liberators.

Bastille Day was, of course, intended to give the country a unifying republican ideology. Besides its obvious flaw – that many families, who had lost ancestors in the Terror or in other massacres, had no reason to celebrate it – there were other subtler but still disturbing drawbacks. It glorified the action of a mob, and the descent of power into the street: it gave a national blessing to violent demonstration and sanctified sectarian and extra-parliamentary protest. The intimidating mass demonstration has remained a French art form; it draws its legitimacy from the elevation of the Revolution in the national consciousness, and its potency is such that, as recently as 1968, some dreamy students seemed on the verge of chasing the elected president into exile. By then, of course, France was on her Fifth Republic, evidence of the strange instability that the Revolution injected into this otherwise brilliant and coherent country.

In France, where the past can cast so long a shadow, the twentieth century is best approached with a quick gallop through the nineteenth. The First Republic had followed hard on the heels of the September massacre of 1792. This was the reverse of the Bastille; the mobs were set on murdering the inmates of the Paris prisons rather than liberating them. They dragged some 1,200 prisoners from their cells and beat, knifed or burnt them to death in the courtyards. On September 22, the monarchy was formally abolished and that day was declared the beginning of the Year 1 of the French Republic. A republican constitution was later presented in a great ceremony at the Altar of the Fatherland on the Champ-de-Mars, but it had a significant rider: that it should only be put into effect when peace was restored. It never was. This detail did not prevent Louis XVI facing trial for crimes against the people and then being guillotined in January 1793. The Terror that followed led to the execution of perhaps 20,000 people in Paris alone: it was the precursor of later waves of European ideological murder, in Soviet Russia, in Germany.

With the arrival of Napoleon Bonaparte, by way of a coup d'état in November 1799, the Revolution and the First Republic were effectively snuffed out. The general began as First Consul. On December 2, 1804, he was crowned emperor in Notre-Dame by a reluctant pope. France had its First Empire. Napoleon squandered its treasure and its young men. By March 1814, the Prussians were in Paris, shortly to be joined by the Russians. Napoleon was packed off to Elba, only to escape before his final defeat at Waterloo. Louis XVIII, "a gouty old gentleman", returned to his capital in the baggage of the Allies. The rue Napoleon became the rue de la Paix, and Bourbon statues were restored in the place des Vosges. Louis died on the throne, the last French king to do so. His successor, Charles X, was a thoroughgoing reactionary, with pretensions to rule by divine right. Sacrilege became a crime punishable by death; the Church, which had suffered much, showed little generosity on its return to pomp. The absolutist prince de Polignac was appointed first minister, a man who "carried proudly the burden of his family's prodigious unpopularity".

In July 1830 there were moves to restrict the press, which led to riots. A girl was hit in the forehead by a stray bullet from a soldier in the rue Saint-Honoré. A butcher's boy carried her body to the place des Victoires, where vengeance was vowed. On July 28, regiments of the National Guard defected. Republicans formed insurrection committees. The mob sacked the Tuileries, and started drinking its way through the great cellars, as full-scale battles broke out in Paris that evening. Charles refused to compromise. "I would rather hew wood", he grandly declared, "than be a king like the king of England." He could, he told Talleyrand, see "no middle way between the throne and the scaffold". To this, the cynical elder statesman retorted: "Your majesty forgets the post-chaise." And it was indeed in a carriage that Charles fled Paris, the last Bourbon in a dynasty created by Henri IV 240 years before.

The ageing marquis de Lafayette appeared on the balcony of the Hôtel de Ville on July 30. He proposed that Louis-Philippe, the duc d'Orléans, should become king of the French, not of France. The duke was duly acclaimed after he appeared on the balcony the next day, draped in a tricolour, and promising to guarantee the constitution. He had, so the historian Alexis de Tocqueville remarked, "no flaming passions, no ruinous weaknesses, no striking vices . . ." Like the banker he was, he aired himself in the Tuileries gardens in frock coat, top hat and with a green umbrella. His first minister, François Guizot, encapsulated his philosophy. Politics were a drudge that should be left to others. "Enrichissez-vous," he advised Paris businessmen. Some still hankered for a Bonaparte. The head of the dynasty was the emperor's nephew, Louis-Napoleon. He failed in a spluttering and ill-conceived coup d'état at Strasbourg in 1836, and was easily taken prisoner when he tried again at Boulogne in 1840. Oddly, Louis-Philippe did not mind a vague and nostalgic Bonapartism. He had the emperor's remains shipped back from St Helena in 1840, and reburied them in Les Invalides amid the greatest splendour. Odder still, Tsar Nicholas I presented the sarcophagus of red Finnish granite in which was lain the body of the man who had watched Moscow burn.

The barricades were back in February 1848. The government banned an outdoor banquet planned by the opposition. An angry crowd gathered on the boulevard des Capucines. A sergeant shot a rioter who was waving a burning torch in the face of his commanding officer. Other troops, hearing it, fired a volley into the crowd. Louis-Philippe dismissed the much hated François Guizot. It was too late. The July Monarchy blew away like gossamer. A mob broke into the Tuileries Palace and looted it, playing games in the gardens with the throne, and then burning it at the foot of the Colonne de Juillet that celebrated Louis-Philippe's accession. He and Queen Amélie – and with them the thousand-year-old French monarchy – fled Paris in disguise. The uprising was brief, victorious in three days, unplanned and unexpected. Few wished to overthrow the king. "This time a regime was not overthrown," de Tocqueville observed. "It was simply allowed to fall." A provisional republican government was appointed. In distant St Petersburg, nervously recalling the results of 1792, the tsar cried: "Gentlemen, saddle your horses. France is a republic once more!"

On May 15, a vast crowd marched from the place de la Bastille to the Palais Bourbon, the seat of the fledgling Second Republic's newly elected Chamber, too conservative for its liking. But this was too extremist for the National Guard, who broke them up. Full-scale insurrection then broke out in the poorer eastern part of Paris. Large numbers of troops from the provinces, with little affection for Parisians, were brought in by train to put down the rebels. General Louis Cavaignac, the war minister, a tough ex-governor-general of Algeria, was given carte blanche to restore order. In six days, over 4,000 were killed.

Louis-Napoleon, who had escaped from the Ham fortress to London in 1846, now stepped on the stage. He offered himself as a presidential candidate in a speech to the Assembly. He spoke hesitatingly with a German accent. Nonetheless, he outvoted Cavaignac by four to one, and became president. The new man had no intention of allowing the Second Republic to survive. "I am prepared to be baptised with the waters of universal suffrage, but I do not intend to live with my feet in a puddle," Louis-Napoleon said, or it was said that he said. His term as president was up in December 1851, and the constitution forbade his re-election. On the night of December 1, placards were posted across Paris urging people to support a coup to be carried out the next day. The following morning, 50,000 troops occupied the Imprimerie Nationale, the Palais Bourbon, newspaper offices and other key buildings. The Supreme Court ruled that Louis-Napoleon had acted illegally, and dismissed him, but there was little other resistance.

He declared himself First Consul, a stopgap that lasted a year. The following December, he somewhat confusingly proclaimed himself Emperor Napoleon III. (Napoleon I's four-year-old son had been proclaimed Napoleon II by loyalist Bonapartists in June 1815 after his father's abdication, but he was formally deposed after five days, to die young of tuberculosis.) Paris was transformed by Baron Haussmann's grand boulevards. Industrial production doubled as, in the north, a new and often beggared proletariat came out of the fields and farms to man the mines and steel mills. A modern banking system evolved with the founding of Crédit Lyonnais and Société Générale, helping to finance a railway boom and Ferdinand de Lesseps's Suez Canal, opened by his cousin, the Empress Eugénie, in 1869. The size of French colonies doubled, and, though the emperor's later plan to extend French influence to Mexico was a humiliating fiasco, he had acquired Nice and Savoy for France from the Italians in 1859. Nonetheless, from his exile on Guernsey, Victor Hugo fulminated against the emperor's petty authoritarianism – schoolteachers were forbidden to grow beards, and Baudelaire's *Les Fleurs du Mal* and Flaubert's *Madame Bovary* were brought to court for outraging public decency.

Napoleon III met his Waterloo at Sedan. Keen to restore ardour to the army, and deliberately provoked by Otto von Bismarck, the Prussian statesman, Napoleon foolishly declared war on Prussia in July 1870. He took assurances that the army was "ready down to the last gaiter button" at face value. The French had 270,000 men in the field by the end of July. The Prussians had twice that, with more arriving from their German allies. At the start of September, sick and exhausted, his troops surrounded at Sedan and besieged in Metz, the emperor surrendered. On September 4, the Chamber of Deputies declared him deposed and created a provisional government of national defence. That afternoon, Parisians demanded a republic.

"This is the third awakening and it is beautiful beyond fancy," wrote George Sand. "Hail to thee, Republic! Thou art in worthy hands, and a great people will march under thy banner after a bloody expiation." The "Ns" and the imperial eagles were chiselled off buildings. Victor Hugo returned from exile. And the Prussians arrived, as Bismarck, having failed to get the French to accept terms, laid siege to Paris. The only way out was by balloon; only carrier pigeons could get in, and the Prussians brought in falcons to deal with them. Parisians ate horses, dogs, cats and animals from the zoo: bear, deer, kangaroo, camel and "pieces of Pollux", from the slaughtered elephant. Elaborate dishes of *salmis de rats* were prepared at the grand Jockey Club.

The provisional government at length, on February 21, agreed terms with the new German empire. A lone German officer with an escort of Uhlans rode up the Champs-Élysées to the sandbagged Arc de Triomphe shortly after dawn on March 1. The avenue was deserted and buildings were draped in black flags. He was followed by 30,000 German troops marching to kettledrums. They had gone by the following morning, and Parisians purified the desecrated ground round the Arc with fire; but Napoleon's crushing defeat of the Prussians at Jena and Auerstadt was avenged, and France humiliated in the most formal and public manner.

Worse, much worse – civil war – followed. The new National Assembly moved itself out of Paris to Versailles, which became the seat of government. The city seethed with fury at this insult, and with mistrust and loathing for a government that had treated with the *boches*. Parisian national guardsmen seized 200 cannon from a government arsenal in Montmartre. On March 18, a detachment of government soldiers was sent to get them back. Many of the guns had been paid for by city workers, and a crowd drove off the troops and lynched two elderly generals, despite the best efforts of Georges Clemenceau, the mayor of Montmartre. Thiers ordered all officials and regular troops to leave Paris for Versailles. The rebels set up a rival power, the Commune de Paris, arguably the world's first socialist government, inside the Hôtel de Ville. Unarmed counter-demonstrators of the bourgeois Friends of Order were shot down on the rue de la Paix on March 22. Many of the better-off fled the city, leaving it in the hands of extremists and the poor. Bismarck now aided President Thiers by repatriating thousands of French prisoners of war to join the Versailles army, which was commanded by Marshal MacMahon, a veteran of colonial campaigns. Most of these troops were provincials, with little love for extremist Parisians. A bloodbath was in the making.

A sortie against Versailles on April 2 was easily blocked, and Gustave Flourens, a popular Communard leader, was taken prisoner and executed with a sabre. Two days later, Raoul Rigault, the Commune's procureur, began taking hostages. These included the archbishop of Paris, Monsignor Darboy, and other clergymen. Before dawn on May 22, anti-Communards in the city opened the Porte de Saint-Cloud, and MacMahon's men broke into the affluent western end of the city from the Bois de Boulogne. They were welcomed, and a number of national guardsmen surrendered. The following day, the Versaillais avenged the two generals who had been lynched in March. They rounded up 49 captured Communards at random, and shot them dead in the rue des Rosiers, where the generals had died. The Madeleine and the unfinished Opéra fell later that afternoon. In the evening, much of the Tuileries Palace was burned. The fine medieval Hôtel de Ville was burned on May 24. In an alley outside the prison of La Roquette, on the night of May 25, the Communards carried out their most infamous deed. They took out their hostages, including Monsignor Darboy, the archbishop, and executed them. The Versaillais extracted a terrible revenge as they pressed on through shattered streets to the Faubourg Saint-Antoine, the working-class cradle of revolution. The flamboyant marquis de Galliffet, one of the government commanders, embodied the barbarity of rich against poor. His mistress on his arm, twirling his mustachios, pointing out who should die, who live, making caustic jests, he told prisoners: "I am Galliffet. You people of Montmartre may think me cruel, but I am more cruel than you can imagine."

On May 26, Raoul Rigault was seized and shot. The Communards made a last stand in the Père-Lachaise cemetery, using the gravestones for cover. Resistance was all but over on May 28, when the unburied corpse of the dead archbishop was found. The Versaillais marched 147 captured Communards to the Père-Lachaise, and shot them against a wall known to this day as the Mur des Fédérés. And, to this day, the French left go in their thousands to lay wreaths at the wall at each anniversary of the massacre. Perhaps 20,000 were killed in the fighting and the fires over the *semaine sanglante*, more than in the Terror of 1793. Thiers was set on routing out all opposition, and a further 13,000 people were imprisoned or sent to penal camps. A national trauma had taken place. "The wholesale executions inflicted by the Versailles soldiery," the London *Times* reported, "the triumph, the glee, the ribaldry of the 'Party of Order' sicken the soul."

The physical recovery was stunningly rapid. An Exposition Universelle was held in 1878, to show the world how Paris had mended itself; tricolours flew legally for the first time since the Commune, and both Manet and Monet painted the bustle of crowds and flags. The Third Republic seemed to have got over its bloody birth. Thiers said that it survived as the regime that "divides us the least". Republicans were faced by Bonapartists and monarchists; typically, the latter were themselves split between *légitimistes*, who supported Henri, comte de Chambord and grandson of Charles X, and *orléanistes*, who wanted Louis-Philippe's grandson, the comte de Paris, to become king. A compromise was cobbled up whereby the childless comte de Chambord would first be king, to be succeeded by the comte de Paris. This was never put to the test: Chambord was so thoroughly obstinate, refusing to accept the tricolour, that monarchist sentiment rapidly ebbed. By 1875, a new republican constitution was in place, with a president, senate and a chamber, the president elected by the senate and the chamber, and the deputies elected by the – men only – people.

At first, at least, the Republic was remarkably unrepublican. MacMahon had succeeded Thiers as president. The marshal was an outright monarchist; his principal minister was the duc de Broglie, whose great-grandfather had commanded the army in July 1789. Gradually, though, the "Republic of Republicans" replaced the "Republic of Dukes". The symbols were put in place. "La Marseillaise" became the national anthem in 1879, and Bastille Day was adopted as the national festival in 1880, the year that a complete amnesty for the Communards came into force. Town halls were dressed up with busts of a woman in a Phrygian cap, "Marianne", the spirit of the Republic. Many squares, streets and avenues were baptised "de la République". And homage was paid to the other, older republic across the sea. Frédéric-Auguste Bartholdi finished his colossal statue of *Liberty Enlightening the World*, for which liberals had raised a public subscription, and, having first erected it in Paris, shipped it over the Atlantic to be set up at the entrance to New York harbour in 1886.

But a fragility persisted. The Republic mistrusted its capital. The seat of government remained at Versailles until returning warily to Paris in 1879. The city was not allowed to have its own mayor for more than a century, lest it find its own leaders again. The nation the Republic served, or parts of it, still hankered for a restored monarchy, or for another strong man in the Napoleonic tradition. This accounts for the strange phenomenon of General Georges Boulanger, a veteran of Algeria, Indochina and the Franco-Prussian war. He was the early protégé of a future political hero, Georges Clemenceau, but more suited to tragicomedy than a part in the destiny of a great nation. His bellicosity and his visibility – he and his horse cut dashing figures on his frequent outings along the boulevards – won him many admirers. The government, thoroughly alarmed, tried to bury him by sending him from Paris to command a corps in the provincial depths of Clermont-Ferrand.

He left the Gare de Lyon to tears and bouquets, leaning from the footplate of an engine swathed in banners announcing: "Il Reviendra". Back indeed he came the following year, buoyed up by crowds who wore his favourite flower in their buttonholes, red chrysanthemums, and who had his fleshy face on their dinner plates. The visit was unauthorised, so he was relieved of his army command, and his name removed from the army list. He was elected as a deputy for the Nord, resigning his seat when his proposals to revise the constitution failed to make progress.

His renown survived a duel in which his opponent, the minister-president Charles Floquet, a 60-year-old civilian, escaped unharmed and wounded the glamorous general in the neck. The crowds loved him for his promises to take revenge on the Germans for the defeats of 1870, while royalist and Bonapartist intriguers alike saw him as a useful instrument to bring down the Republic. Flush with funds, he announced that he was to stand for a Paris parliamentary seat.

On polling day, January 27, 1889, the discredited Third Republic was widely expected to be swept away by the nebulous forces of Boulangisme. Excited crowds flocked to the place de la Madeleine in the evening, as Boulanger and his aides celebrated his epic 80,000-vote majority in the Restaurant Durand. As he reached the coffee and cognac, the general's nerve failed him. There would, he said, be no coup d'état that evening. He would wait to see what happened. With that, he left the restaurant for the bed of his mistress, Mme de Bonnemains. Parisians, fickle themselves, realised that the general was little more than an empty gesture. A warrant was issued for Boulanger's arrest. On April Fool's Day, 1889, he fled to Brussels before it could be executed. He was tried for treason and sentenced to transportation in absentia. Boulangiste candidates fought the elections in the autumn, egged on by high-flying manifestos from their absent leader, but only 38 were elected. Histrionic to the last, Boulanger committed suicide at his mistress's grave in Brussels.

That this *opéra comique* took place at the same time as the second, brilliant 1889 Paris Exposition Universelle reveals the eccentricities of the French political psyche all too well. The day before Boulanger fled over the border, a party in top hats and formal tailcoats made the first official ascent of the Eiffel Tower, on foot, since the lifts were not yet ready. The prime minister gave up at the first platform, but Gustave Eiffel himself persisted to the top, where the Légion d'Honneur was pinned to him. The genius of a country that had so nearly given itself to a military buffoon had created the highest structure on earth, soaring 300 metres above the Champ-de-Mars, a work of the greatest skill and imagination that had consumed 2.5 million rivets, 7,300 tons of metal, a modest 15 million francs, and the labour of 300 steeplejacks for two years.

It was not to everyone's taste. A *protestation des artistes* objected to this "vertiginously ridiculous tower dominating Paris like a black, gigantic factory chimney", and demanded that it be pulled down. It was supposed to be dismantled after 20 years; it survived only because the large radio antenna that was later bolted to it was vital to French radio telegraphy. But the tower showed the flair that underpinned the nation, just as the Exposition itself, which took the burgeoning French empire as its theme, showed the country's natural reach and strength.

Its internal weakness remained the divide between left and right, which ran deeper than ideology. The left remembered the repression that had culminated in the slaughter of the Communards, while royalists had not forgotten the tumbrils, nor forgiven the Republic. They flew no tricolours on July 14. It was a day of mourning; ignoring the tumultuous crowds in the popular districts, the *beaux quartiers*, the Faubourg Saint-Germain and the grand new apartment blocks of the XVIe arrondissement greeted Bastille Day with closed shutters and drawn curtains.

The left responded with triumphal demonstrations in the place de la République, and mass marches to the graves of its martyrs. It nursed a consuming hatred of the clergy, whom it accused of militarism and anti-republicanism. "Le cléricalisme, voilà l'ennemi," cried Gambetta. Jules Ferry, mayor of Paris during the siege, kicked off the campaign against the Church as education minister by driving the Jesuits out of teaching and fostering state-run "schools without God". The republican school-teacher became a symbol in himself – so enthusiastic that the death rate for school-teacher volunteers in the Great War was to be higher than for any other social group – and an alternative focal point to the parish priest.

These allegiances had much to do with self-interest as well as tradition, of course, but they were – still often are – carefully dressed up with moral and philosophical principles. The left claimed a monopoly of the old revolutionary trinity of Liberty, Equality and Fraternity. The right stood for duty, *patrie*, faith and honour. The most notorious clash between them was the Dreyfus affair.

Alfred Dreyfus, a captain attached to the Deuxième Bureau of army intelligence, was arrested in October 1894. He was accused of passing documents to the Germans. A memo on the firing mechanism of a new French cannon, allegedly in his handwriting, had been found by a cleaner in the wastepaper basket of the German military attaché. He was found guilty by a military court, and publicly degraded at a humiliating ceremony in the courtyard of the École Militaire. Little boys in the trees shouted "The swine" when Dreyfus held his head up, and "The coward!" when he dropped it, as his sword was taken from him and his epaulettes were ripped from his shoulders. He was then shipped to South America to serve a life sentence in the French penal colony at Cayenne, known as Devil's Island.

There he might have rotted had not a new head of intelligence, Colonel Georges Picquart, suspected that a high-living officer, Major Esterhazy, had spied for the Germans to pay off his debts, forging documents to incriminate Dreyfus. In 1897 Picquart found himself posted to an infantry regiment in southern Tunisia for his pains. The army did not want a retrial. "Dreyfusards", convinced of his innocence, brought the affair into the press and parliament. The country split. To the right, the army was the "sacred ark" of the *patrie*, and neither it nor military justice should be called into question. Other, darker souls stressed that Dreyfus was Jewish. They pointed to the recent Panama Canal scandal, over which a Jewish financier had killed himself.

Esterhazy was brought to trial on January 10, 1898. He was acquitted the next day. On January 13, the newspaper *l'Aurore* ran a sensational headline, "J'Accuse", above an open letter by Émile Zola, a journalist whose brilliant novels had exposed the poverty of the industrial slums. "Truth itself and justice itself", Zola said with reason, "have been slapped in the face." He went on to transform the complex cover-up of an undoubted injustice into a classic political diatribe, in which he accused almost everyone involved of some personal or right-wing failing. He turned Dreyfus into the left's own archbishop-martyr. Zola was tried for criminal libel. The case lasted a fortnight, amid great tension. Soldiers demonstrated, and booed Zola, the Dreyfusards and Jews in general. The left responded by founding the League of the Rights of Man. Zola received the maximum sentence of one year, before escaping to England.

There is no doubt that Zola backed the right man. Dreyfus was innocent. Later in 1898, it was found that an intelligence officer, Major Hubert Henry, had forged documents and telegrams to discredit Dreyfus and Picquart. Henry was arrested, confessed and cut his throat in the fort at Mont-Valérian. Esterhazy fled to London, and was condemned in absentia to three years in prison. Early in 1899 President Félix Faure died suddenly, apparently in the arms of Mme Steinheil, his mistress. Émile Loubet, his successor, though personally gentle and conciliatory enough, was a staunch radical whose dislike of military extravaganza earned him the anger of the right. "Liguer les mécontents", gather the malcontents into a league, was an old technique of the *ultras*. The founder of the Ligue des Patriotes, Paul Déroulède, writer of the *Chants du soldat*, mined a rich seam when he attacked Loubet in speeches to his hyper-nationalist *ligueurs,* delivered in front of Joan of Arc's statue. The far right was as ready for street violence as the left – the nation had, after all, sanctified the Revolution – and Déroulède was eager to use it. He met with monarchists and other anti-republicans, and fashioned a coup with the apparent blessing of General Émile Zurlinden, the military governor of Paris. It was planned for February 23, the day of Faure's state funeral. Déroulède's patriots were to rally in the place de la Bastille, where they would join with Zurlinden's troops as they returned from the funeral procession. The combined force was then to march on the Élysée and throw out Loubet. The duc d'Orléans, pretender to the throne, returned incognito to Paris to be on hand.

Farce followed. The *ligueurs* went to the place de la République by mistake. The troops were led by a different general, Rôget. He refused Déroulède's plea to divert to the Élysée, though the desperate extremist hung onto his horse's bridle and refused to stop haranguing him until they reached the barracks, where the general had Déroulède arrested.

Further trouble unrolled over the summer. A right-winger whacked Loubet on the head with a walking stick at Auteuil racecourse on June 4. A week later, the leftists protested among the racegoers at Longchamp. Jules Guérin, another would-be coup maker, refused to submit to arrest after Dreyfusards were beaten up by his bruisers. He had given his patriotic league the masonic-sounding title of "Grand Occident de France – Rite Antijuif". Guérin retired to his headquarters on the rue Chabrol to sit out the police siege that followed. He was guarded by men from the slaughterhouses at La Villette; the doors and windows were covered with heavy bulletproof grilles, and he used a press in the basement to print leaflets calling on the French to rise up against Loubet and an infamous government that was at the beck and call of "cosmopolitan Jewry". They were sent out by mini hot-air balloon. The great patriot was, alas, taken for a clown. Diners rounded off an evening's entertainment with a visit to the rue Chabrol, where they mingled with English tourists despatched on special sightseeing trips by the ever-alert Thomas Cook. Newspaper advertisements claimed that the besieged *ultras* were drinking Pouges Saint-Léger mineral water, which "quenches the thirst, sharpens the appetite, and develops the strength needed to resist both the police and the heat". At length, the joke wore thin and Guérin gave up. He and Déroulède were sentenced for sedition.

The left celebrated its victory in November with a monster gala to inaugurate a sculpture of *The Triumph of the Republic* in the place de la Nation. The bronze showed Marianne, haughty, beautiful, atop a globe on a chariot drawn by two lions, with Labour and Justice pushing the wheels, and Peace at their side. As if that was not socialist symbolism enough, Jules Dalou, the sculptor, was a Communard who had been exiled.

A vast procession to the square was led by the editors of *La Petite République*, the socialist newspaper which had called for the gala, and by "shock troops" from the Red belt of Ivry and the XIIIe arrondissement. Loubet was there, and Jean Jaurès, founder of the Socialist Party, and the most loved figure of the left. He was born in the Tarn, his father a small landowner down on his luck, into a family with a naval tradition. His brother became an admiral; Jaurès, whose sharp intelligence and a scholarship took him through the elite École Normale Supérieure, was swept by a devotion to great causes into socialist and pacifist politics via a spell of teaching at the *lycée* in Albi. He was a sloppy dresser who scoffed his food, but he was gifted and kind, his speech eloquent, his instincts affectionate, and people responded to him. Red banners were permitted as long as something was written on them. They matched the chants of the crowd – "Vive Dreyfus . . . Zola . . . Jaurès!" – and people wore eglantines in their buttonholes, so that red swayed and foamed in a torrent. The police tried to remove the black flags of the anarchists. These were a waning force, better at publicity than action. They founded clubs with violent names, La Dynamite, La Révolte des Travailleurs, and described how to fashion home-made bombs in fiery papers called *L'Attaque*, *L'Affamé* and *Le Drapeau Noir*; they exploded few bombs, and it was six years since an Italian had carried out their most notorious deed, stabbing to death the French president, Marie François Carnot. The distinction between the procession and the spectators blurred; there was an air of imminent revolution, and the whole faubourg "went along in the darkness with a tremendous surge", applauding and chanting the slogan of *La Petite République*: "Neither . . . God . . . nor . . . Master."

The appeal court had quashed Dreyfus's sentence in June 1899; he was brought back to France on a cruiser at the end of the month, and was retried in front of another military court. This found him "guilty, but with extenuating circumstances", a mealy-mouthed verdict that was followed by a pardon – though he had done nothing that required a pardon. Two days later, General Galliffet, the war minister, issued an order of the day: "The incident is closed!"

But it was not. The Dreyfus affair gave the left a moral superiority, in its own eyes at least; it had rescued an innocent man from the bloody talons of the reactionaries. And it marked the century that was to come. On the night of January 13, 1998, to commemorate the centennial, an image of Zola's "J'Accuse" was projected in its entirety on the front of the National Assembly. It was, of course, a socialist prime minister, Lionel Jospin, who claimed the moral high ground for his own and rubbed conservative noses in the dirt during the debate in the chamber. The assembly's official ushers had to rush to protect him from angry deputies after he said piously that "the left was for Dreyfus and the right was against him"; at a commemoration at the Panthéon, Jospin quoted Zola to claim that "the profound causes of the country's blindness will not disappear in a single day".

Indeed they have not, and the Panthéon is itself an elegant symbol of the strains between Church and State, republicans and monarchists, believers and atheists. It was built in the eighteenth century by the architect Germain Soufflot as the church of Sainte-Geneviève. During the Revolution, it was unhallowed and rededicated as the Panthéon, a secular mausoleum for the storage of heroes. The Restoration restored it to the Catholic Church in 1814. It was reclaimed and resecularised again in the Revolution of 1830. The reaction regained it as a church in 1851. The Third Republic had secularized it again in time to receive the non-believing bones of Victor Hugo. The funeral oration provided a final twist. The Académie Française had intended it to be made by its director, the novelist Maxime Du Camp. He, however, was known as the "insulter of the Commune", and so a substitute, the dramatist Émile Augier, was drafted in.

It was, of course, in the Panthéon that artfully concealed cameras caught François Mitterrand as he came on pilgrimage a century later to celebrate the victory of the left, and the start of his presidency. Old splits and vendettas die hard in France . . .

2

Belle Époque

Émile Loubet, the president, opened the Exposition Universelle of 1900 on one of those brilliant April-in-Paris days that stir the buds and the blood. The Exposition covered the whole heart of the city, on a site so vast that pedestrians were speeded along at 5 mph by an electric-powered *trottoir roulant*. The Grand and the Petit Palais rose in glassy splendour. A colonial exhibition tumbled through the gardens that run down from the Trocadéro to the river. It had Hindu temples, Algerian souks, African huts, a model of the temples of Angkor Wat, newly revealed to the West, and Polynesian cabins. Jules Ferry, scourge of the Jesuits and hero of colonial expansion, had remarked that the belly dancer was the only imperial object to excite French passions; but, by reminding visitors of the grandeur of the empire, distant but colossal, the second largest on earth, the event kept minds off the loss of Alsace and Lorraine.

Industrial inventions, cannon, motor cars and an imitation California gold mine dug underground were on show across the river between the Pont d'Iéna and the Champ-de-Mars. The pavilions on the Quai des Nations on the Left Bank were reassuringly *folklorique*, and gave little hint of coming tensions. The Germans built a replica of a medieval town hall, relaxed and unmartial, though some observed that its spire was *über alles,* the highest of any building. The British housed themselves in a rambling Tudor manor house; the Italians had a great plaster impression of a Tuscan cathedral, the Turks a mosque, the Americans a florid domed creation.

Sideshows and amusements ran along the Right Bank. Gaiety and style ran riot, with troubadours in medieval costume strolling down recreated streets of "Old Paris", a giant Ferris wheel, a "House of Laughter", and screenings of "talking" films where the newfangled cinema projector showed scenes accompanied by sound from the marginally older phonograph. The film pioneer Grimion-Sanson went one better. His Cinéorama anticipated the widescreen and cinema in the round. A circular battery of ten projectors played onto a circular screen with the audience seated in a large wickerwork nacelle over the projector cabin. Grimion-Sanson showed film he had shot in flight with the aim of giving the spectators a "Balloon Trip across Europe and Africa" for one franc. Bags of ballast and ropes and anchors hung from the audience nacelle, as in a real balloon; unfortunately, the heat from the projectors was so intense that it was feared the nacelle might catch fire, and only three "flights" were completed.

Leading churchmen stayed away, in protest at the government's anticlericalism. So did the Prince of Wales. The Boer War was producing bouts of Anglophobia. Obscene caricatures of Queen Victoria in various poses with her ministers were doing the rounds. Monarchs were generally reluctant to be seen at a republican jamboree, the sovereigns of Sweden and Persia the only exceptions. It was, nonetheless, a resounding success. It pulled in 50,860,801 visitors – a minimum figure, for it was easy to slip in without a ticket – and it helped to cement the Republic. Marianne held her head high to the world, and needed to curtsey to no-one.

The nervous eye might have noticed that the Germans had more raw industrial muscle on display than the French. Electra, the "house of light" illuminated by the greatest concentration of electric bulbs on earth, was powered by a 3000 hp Siemens generator, and a working model of the *Deutschland*, the liner that currently held the blue riband on the North Atlantic, certainly dismayed French naval officers, fretful over their neighbours' new interest in the sea. The Japanese exhibits outstripped the Russians'. Given the importance of the Tsarist "steamroller" to France as a counterweight to the German army, this, too, was worrisome. France had now been at peace for three decades, however. The Paris Olympic Games were being held, the second of what would become the world's greatest sporting events, created by a young graduate from the Saint-Cyr military academy, baron Pierre de Coubertin. The first Metropolitan underground line opened in July. The incomparable Sarah Bernhardt was strapping her 55-year-old body into corsets to play Napoleon's doomed 22-year-old son in Rostand's *L'Aiglon* in her own theatre, a four-hour marathon that audiences cheered wildly; a French car broke the world speed record at Deauville, and forty thousand wines could be sampled at the Exposition. It even turned a profit. God seemed to be in a French heaven.

President Loubet was himself a phenomenon in both his person and his position. Switzerland being a confederation, he was, of course, the only European to preside over a republic. He was known for the warmth of the smiles that rippled through his broad white beard, and this geniality was justified by his own startling progress. He was the son of peasants from Marsanne, a down-at-heel little town among the dirt-poor farms of the Drôme to the east of the Rhône Valley. The excellent education system encouraged the bright and hard-working to get on, with a generous range of scholarships. Intelligence was held to balance out the shortfall in population. "What does it matter if France is no longer dominant in manpower," asked *Le Figaro*, "provided she continues to produce thinkers like Ampère and Pasteur?" Young Loubet profited from this. He did well at school, read law, married a tradesman's daughter, and became mayor of Montélimar. From that nougat-making town, he found his way to the Élysée palace.

It was inconceivable for a peasant to have become the prime minister of England or the chancellor of Germany, and his presidency reflected a certain egalitarianism and freedom. The French were not as in awe of their betters as other Europeans. They had no throne or court to impose morals or to stifle impulses; they were living an experiment, a lonely one, at least until the Russians joined them in 1917, and it left them touchy, febrile and open. The tone-setters were a mixed bag: writers, survivors from the much-battered noblesse, a lively and free-thinking press, politicians, senior officials – the short life-span of cabinets gave permanent officials great power – and professional men.

The high point of the Exposition for Loubet was the huge banquet to which he invited all the nation's 36,000 mayors in September. It was ironic to ask them to the only city in the land that had no mayor of its own – Paris was allowed no more than a municipal council – but 20,777 of them braved the often long and arduous journey.

They were proof that eternal rural France was reconciled to the Republic, and Loubet entertained them splendidly in two huge tents in the Tuileries gardens.

Many wore regional costumes, and spoke regional languages or dialects. These were used more than French in almost a third of the country (even today, a fifth of the population claim to speak a local tongue well, and 14 per cent fairly well). They included Bretons, Basques, Corsicans and Alsatians, as well as Provençals, Auvergnats and Gascons from the three distinct areas of Occitanie in the south. French-speaking was being boosted by compulsory lessons in schools and conscription into the army, but local pride remained a great and – since so many talents and powers and ideas drained into Paris – a vital strength. The law courts in Provence, Brittany and the Limousin were still using official interpreters in 1900.

It was only now that Monsieur Dupont was invented as the equivalent to the long-established John Bull across the Channel; putting him in a beret was still years away, for the beret was the mark of the Basques alone, until such a strong national craze developed that 23 million berets were made in 1932, almost one for every male in France. The French-speaking regions tended to be more prosperous. The social division along a line from Saint-Malo to Geneva was sharp. Those south of it were physically smaller and weaker than the northerners; they were less well-nourished, less educated, less law-abiding and more likely to evade taxes and military service.

If some people inside France did not speak the language, many outsiders did. As well as the elite of the still-expanding empire, they included the Russian and Polish aristocracy, the diplomatic corps, and educated Romanians, Greeks, Alexandrians and Levantines. Proceedings of the 130 congresses held during the Exposition on fire-fighting, vegetarianism, socialism, women's rights, for mathematicians, physicists, electrical engineers and physicians were in French. If English was now competing with it as a scientific lingua franca, however, Paris was unquestionably *the* city the world looked to for its entertainment and inspiration.

The pre-eminence of Paris went deeper than the sublime gloss of its artists, sculptors, composers, poets and writers. The city's lifestyle seemed so unattainably sophisticated that foreigners ruefully accepted the words that described it – *élan, panache, joie de vivre, belle époque* – to be untranslatable. The English even coined words like *bon viveur* that the French themselves never used. *Chic* and *haute couture* were French creations. So was *haute cuisine,* another expression that it is best – "high cooking" – not to play around with.

To nourish the mind, Paris had more newspapers – seventy dailies on sale, and weeklies and periodicals by the score – than anywhere else on earth. Each served a different shade of opinion, a slew of monarchists, socialists, Bonapartists, anarchists, radicals, clericalists and anticlericals. Physically, these malcontents went about their business in a city redesigned and rebuilt in large areas by the financier and town planner Baron Haussmann. Dark, narrow streets of broken cobbles were replaced by parks and elegant boulevards, whose street-level bustle and calm and stone-clad upper facades gave the city its air of lived-in grandeur. The recent installation of 350,000 electric streetlamps helped it live up to its reputation as the City of Light. It had outstanding engineers and scientists, with the Eiffel Tower as the most visible symbol of their handiwork. It was circumnavigated by an aviator whose reckless bravery was to astonish the Wright brothers. Alberto Santos-Dumont attached an engine to the front of his balloon in 1898, and performed aerial figures of eight and tours around the Tower. He replaced his balloon basket with a bicycle frame and saddle to save weight, and did not worry that only paper-thin fabric separated his hot and spitting petrol engine from the highly inflammable hydrogen in the balloon. He flew about Paris, descending into a boulevard and stopping outside a café when the spirit moved him, handing the mooring rope to a waiter. Street vendors sold gingerbread biscuits in the shape of his profile, and ladies of fashion wore veils appliquéd with airships.

Jean Charcot, who established the first neurology unit, at La Salpêtrière hospital, did not live to see the new century, but his pupils carried on his research into chronic and nervous diseases, Sigmund Freud among them. Louis Pasteur, the father of bacteriology, had also recently departed, but he had founded the Institut Pasteur to carry on his fight against disease. He had been professor of chemistry at the Sorbonne, the great university of Paris, the alma mater of Marie Curie, the young physicist who had recently isolated radium and coined the term "radioactivity", work for which she, her husband Pierre and Antoine Becquerel would shortly share one of the new Nobel prizes. The physicist friends of the Curies included Paul Langevin, noted for his work on the molecular structure of gases, Becquerel, who discovered the rays emitted from uranium salts, Gabriel Lippman, another Nobel laureate who produced the first coloured photograph of the spectrum, and Henri Poincaré, the mathematician who evolved many of the basic ideas in modern topology.

More than anywhere else, mass entertainment comes from Paris. Striptease was pioneered here, as well as nightclubs, crooners and chanteuses, cabaret, the revue or "spectacular" with "star turns", the "showgirl" and the chorus line, and seedier things, too, such as the trashy "yellow novel" and the pornographic film clip. The cancan and the revues at the Moulin Rouge gave Paris a global edge in popular song and dance that was vividly caught in the new poster art of Toulouse-Lautrec. The vocabulary of games of chance – or, more accurately, of very little chance, the odds being heavily stacked in favour of the *banquier* – reflected their French origins: *casino, croupier, roulette* and *vingt-et-un*.

The Lumière brothers had shot the world's first film in 1895, *La Sortie des usines Lumière*, showing the workers leaving their factory, a dull enough subject but one that proved that their camera and projector worked. They later hired the basement of the Grand Café in the boulevard des Capucines in Paris, and charged a franc to watch short clips of Lyon, horses and carriages, and a train arriving in a station. They took 35 francs the first day, but there were soon long queues outside and they were making 2,000 francs a day profit. Georges Méliès had worked as an illusionist in the Théâtre Robert-Houdin, the wellspring of modern conjuring. Méliès used the camera to create illusions and fantastical spectacles in films like *Escamotage d'une dame* (The Lady Vanishes), and *Voyage dans la lune* (A Trip to the Moon). Real commercial flair came in with Charles Pathé, who produced the cliffhanger series *The Perils of Pauline*, starring the popular French-based American Pearl White, and the first newsreels. By 1908, he controlled a third of the world film market; his cinema at Les Invalides had the world's largest screen and a 60-strong orchestra. Léon Gaumont demonstrated a film synchronised with a phonograph at the Académie des Sciences in 1910. His secretary, Alice Guy, directed his films for him, and soon had more than 300 to her credit.

The genres that came to dominate the cinema were being pioneered. Ferdinand Zecca, an ex-actor who directed for Pathé, shot the first version of the epic *Quo Vadis,* and made gritty dramas about everyday life such as *Les victimes d'alcoolisme*. Another Pathé director, Albert Capellani, adapted Zola's novel *Germinal* and made a three-and-a-half-hour version of Victor Hugo's *Les Misérables*. Victorin Jasset made detective thrillers. *Fantasmagorie*, the first animated film, was made by Émile Cohl in 1908. Louis Feuillade, would-be Catholic priest and former army sergeant, made a hugely successful series of films about the gentleman-crook *Fantômas* that has been aped on screen and television ever since. A music hall acrobat, André Deed, created the simpleton Boireau as the screen's first great figure of farce.

Much of the talent that fuelled the glittering metropolis came from elsewhere. The city had always sucked in ambitious young people from the provinces like a great whirlpool, a few to find glory, some to be spat out before slinking home, and some to drown in a downward spiral of drugs, disease and cheap alcohol. The writer André Gide described the first phase of this classic process when, as a 20-year-old, he found a room in the rue Monsieur-le-Prince with a friend. Its dusty window looked out over the dripping slate roofs towards Notre-Dame and the river, and it seemed a starship that would hurl them to the heavens. "We both dreamt of the life of a poor student in just such a room, with just enough money to be free to write, and with Paris at our feet," Gide recollected. "And of shutting oneself up in there with the dream of one's masterpiece, and only coming out again with it finished." This rite of passage took place in other great cities, of course. But there is a special ring to it in turn-of-the-century Paris, for the quality of those who came, and it remained a phenomenon for decades to come. An 18-year-old artist, Pablo Picasso, a prodigy in his Spanish childhood, "an angel and a devil" to his mother, arrived at the Gare d'Orsay off the Barcelona express in October 1900, and took a cheap room in a *maison de passe* – another of those untranslatable phrases, a subtler term than brothel, a place of assignation for whores and lovers – on the rue Caulaincourt. Hard on his heels a new poet arrived, christened Guillelmus (Wilhelm) Apollinaris de Kostrowitzky in Rome, now to be known as Guillaume Apollinaire.

At the top end – hotels like the Bristol, the Restaurant Richard-Lucas in the place de la Madeleine, new American bars like the Eureka – Paris was one of the most expensive cities on earth. But it was possible to live for very little on the lower slopes, and that made the city attainable to the young and impoverished. For just 70 francs, the cost of a week's room and board in a cheap hotel, they had a seven-day pass to a non-stop display of style and invention. It was easier, too, to get into France – and once in, to stay there – than almost anywhere else in Europe. In theory, political exiles were deported if they started meddling in local affairs. In practice, this was rare, and the artistic were generally left to themselves. Picasso, for example, spent the rest of his long life in France, including the German occupation, though his huge canvas of the bombing of Guernica was one of the most powerful of all anti-fascist images.

The Impressionists, and their ripping up of the conventions of colour and light, now seem the most obvious proof of this pre-eminence in the arts. At the time, though, it was the docile and unoriginal *chers maîtres* who won the big commissions and the prizes. The fashion was for huge canvases of historic events, *The Fall of Babylon*, *The Murder of Julius Caesar*, *The Funeral of an Ice-Age Chieftain*, painted in intricate detail as costume dramas. The best-loved painters, Édouard Détaille, Jean-Paul Laurens, Georges Rochegrosse, William Bouguereau, were seen as ornaments of French civilisation.

They were welcomed into high society, and inducted into the highest ranks of the Légion d'Honneur. Magazines ran photographs of their grandiose studios, and steel engravings of their works were snapped up by the thousand. The battle-scene painter Ernest Meissonier sold his famous *1812* for 840,000 francs a sum that would have bought Impressionist canvases by the dozen. Generals invited him to manoeuvres and staged cavalry charges to help his compositions; his assistants mocked up Napoleon's retreat from Moscow for *1812* with model soldiers, horses, guns and wagons covered in white powder to resemble snow.

It was a far, far cry from the artist as a wild man, a "bohemian", a tortured soul who did not illustrate a scene but tore it living from his own emotion. The word "impressionist" had been a term of abuse, first used to mock Monet's painting *Impression: Sunrise* in 1874. The Impressionists had held their own Salon des Refusés when their work was rejected by the official Paris Salon, and established work of glowing unmixed pigments in which they sought to convey light and atmosphere. Manet was gone now, the old father figure, whose *Déjeuner sur l'herbe* had raised early scandal with its nude female brazen among the clothed male picnickers. Van Gogh had completed his last painting in 1890, full of deep foreboding, *Wheatfields with Crows*, and then shot himself. Seurat was dead the following year, after finishing only seven canvases in his immensely intricate pointillist style; and Gauguin was in Tahiti, not far from death himself.

Others were much alive. In 1897 Camille Pissarro completed what was to be his most famous painting, *The Boulevard Montmartre at Night*. By 1900, Cézanne, who yearned that Impressionism become "something solid and durable like the art of the old masters", was at last beginning to win some recognition. Renoir still worked, his hands slowly giving way to arthritis, as Degas, his eyes failing, turned to sculpture, though on a very different scale to the work of Auguste Rodin. Monet was painting at Argenteuil. Henri Matisse, poverty-stricken but still able to buy a canvas by Cézanne, was working at the Académie Carrière.

Music, not always a French forte, was in full flow. Camille Saint-Saëns had seen his opera *Samson et Dalila* performed and had completed his *Carnaval des animaux*. He had been succeeded as organist at the Madeleine by Gabriel Fauré; Maurice Ravel, a beneficiary of Fauré's composition classes, had won praise in 1899 for his *Pavane pour une infante défunte* ("Pavane for a Dead Princess"). Claude Debussy, who had been inspired to write his *Prélude à l'après-midi d'un faune* by Stéphane Mallarmé's poem, was writing what was called "musical impressionism". He was about to complete his *Pelléas et Mélisande*. Erik Satie was introducing whimsy and atonality to serious music.

The old brilliance in literature – Balzac, Victor Hugo, Maupassant, Flaubert – was maintained by Zola, and Jules Verne lived still. The anarchy and shock of Rimbaud and Verlaine and Baudelaire fed through into Symbolist poets like Mallarmé and the playwright Alfred Jarry. The latter's play *Ubu Roi*, is a grotesque parody of Shakespeare whose first bellowed word is "Merdre!" – "shit" with an "r" added to round it out – and which portrays a fat, puppet-like, foul-mouthed king trying to win control of Poland through mass murder It deeply upset W. B. Yeats at its opening night, and it was a sensation. "You can smell Ubu everywhere," a critic wrote. "People fight for Ubu, and others want to disembowel them for it." Jarry developed a logic of absurdity, which he called *pataphysique*, and his work is now seen as a precursor to the theatre of the absurd; but he was an alcoholic, soon dead and forgotten but for that one exclamation. Theatre censorship had largely ended and the stage was booming with works from Edmond Rostand's historical romance *Cyrano de Bergerac* to Georges Feydeau's acutely observed farce *La Dame de chez Maxim's*. In philosophy, Henri Bergson was about to become professor at the Collège de France, there to restore to Paris some of the intellectual renown it had enjoyed with the eighteenth-century Enlightenment and Voltaire.

The heartland of Bohemia was the Latin Quarter on the Left Bank, downstream from Notre-Dame. It was the main student quarter, with a long tradition of unruly zest. Haussmann had pushed the boulevard Saint-Michel through its heart, pulling down crooked streets of medieval houses, but he had not killed it off. All the services an artistic temperament might need abounded here: cheap studios, cheap food, bars and cafés, absinthe, opium, girls, boys, and an abundance of kindred souls, poets, sculptors, musicians, writers for small magazines. Cafés were alive into the early hours, pungent with smoke and deafening with argument while the *soucoupes* stacked up on the marble tables to keep tally of the steady consumption of liquor. At the Café Voltaire, where a farewell was held for Gauguin before he left for Tahiti, Mallarmé held court; at the Taverne du Panthéon it was the dandy and novelist Jean de Tinan. In the basement of the Soleil d'Or in the place Saint-Michel, a soirée was held every second Saturday by Léon Deschamps, a poet who had founded a little art and literary review, *La Plume*. "All artists meet here to hear verses, to make music and to devise art," his magazine explained. "Politics are excluded from these meetings which are now attended by all the intellectual youth of Paris ... Everyone may come without an introduction, assured of a hearty welcome." The walls were decorated with sketches by Gauguin and portraits of writers for *La Plume*. As many as two hundred would cram in, Parnassians, Symbolists, Kabbalists, Anarchists, Brutalists, Decadents and more, to hear songs and poems recited to a piano on a rough wooden stage. Sometimes Paul Verlaine appeared for a few moments, half-destroyed by absinthe, like "a poor old street singer exposed for years to the wind and rain", a cane in his hand to balance him, with a yellow silk scarf like a slash of forgotten gaiety at his throat.

Another lively Paris was found far across the river. Scratch Las Vegas and you find Montmartre, the great cradle of showbiz, an Americanism that, ironically, French civil servants are now formally banned from using in favour of "industrie du spectacle". Drinking dens and *guingettes* had been stacked up in pre-revolutionary days among the working windmills high on *la butte sacrée*, the sacred hill on which the first bishop of Paris, Saint Denis, had been martyred; the *commune* of Montmartre was outside the city limits and the drink free of city taxes. Since then, Montmartre had been absorbed into the city. Atop the hill, the cupola of the Sacré-Coeur was being erected, to expiate the blood spilt in Paris during the 1871 Commune. Pleasure-seekers made do with lower Montmartre, where the punters massed through Pigalle and Clichy, alongside the pimps, pickpockets, prostitutes and con men who preyed on them.

The man who created brilliant spectacle from these seedy clip joints was an ex-butcher named Zidler, fashioning it from a riotous low-life dance, the chahut or cancan, and a disused dance hall, the Reine Blanche, which stood in a weed-infested garden facing the place Blanche in Pigalle. Zidler entrusted the décor to the painter Willette. The choice was inspired. Willette built a mock windmill with great red sails above the dance hall, and brought a redundant plaster elephant from the Exposition to grace the garden. The Moulin Rouge opened in 1889 to immense success. It was a pioneer of "variety", where stars ran through a whole gamut of acts – rubber-limbed contortionists, singers, comedians, crazy cyclists, acrobats, jugglers, knife-throwers – linked and introduced by a compère. The cancan provided the cream in this confection. It was more than a bubbly display of knickers and garters, deliciously naughty though such things were to the repressed Victorian English who sidled in to see it, as well as no doubt to the bread and butter customers, *curé*-dominated French provincials. It could be crude and harsh, a compelling mockery of those who watched it.

The dancer La Goulue (the Glutton) flashed her sweaty flesh in an invitation "brutal, blunt, without feminine grace, almost bestial" before exposing her bottom and ending with the *grand écart*, the splits. Her fellow dancer Grille-d'Égout (the Gutter Grill) had a stuck-out chin and protruding teeth that made her mouth seem to be "two bars in a pink-shadowed hole". With them came Valentin-le-Desossé, the boneless one, from an upright bourgeois family, the brother of a lawyer, intoxicated by the dance, his thin body making grotesque sharp lines. Sketching this famous trio, himself misshapen with his shortened legs and heavy upper body, no more than four feet six and walking heavily with a cane, in which he concealed a long, thin bottle of alcohol, was the young aristocrat Henri Toulouse-Lautrec, whose mastery of line, colour and movement helped to spawn poster art and immortalised the demi-monde of whores and dancers. ("I assure you Madame, I can drink safely . . . I am so close to the ground already.")

Performances were strikingly uninhibited and uncensored. Josef Pujol, Le Pétomane, was a farter of international fame. He had a repertoire of several tunes, including the Marseillaise, and he could blow out a candle at a range of one foot from his elegantly aimed posterior. No fakery was involved; doctors expressed their admiration of his "aspirating anus", and the king of the Belgians, prevented by his own censors from seeing him on stage in Brussels, made a special visit to see him.

The Prince of Wales took advantage of many pleasures denied him by his mother and polite society in Victorian England. A memento of his visits to Paris, a device coyly described as "the love chair of the future King" in the catalogue, was sold at auction in Paris in the 1980s; it resembled a miniature artificial rock-climbing frame, on which the prince and his lady companion could practise in safety many bodily contortions. The prince visited the Moulin Rouge incognito; he was, of course, recognised by all, but Parisians in those pre-paparazzi days were famously discreet. An exception was La Goulue, who, intoxicated with her own publicity, shouted to him: "Hey, Wales! You're paying for the champagne!" She left the Moulin Rouge abruptly. By 1900, she was performing in a lion cage and, aged and penniless, was soon dead. Another star, Jeanne la Folle, a flame-headed beauty with "an air of depraved virginity", so crazy about dancing that she performed free, also deserted, to go to the rival Folies Bergère. The supremacy of the Moulin Rouge was gone for good, but scarcely a spectacular on television or at Las Vegas is not in its debt.

Another invention was the café-concert, modest compared to the brocaded plush and sequins of the music halls, where popular singers were heard for the price of a few drinks. One of the most powerful was Jehan Rictus, a clochard who had slept on the streets, ill and tubercular-frail, who sang a powerful and poetic "Nocturne" in the voice of the slums:

> A chacun son tour le trottoir
> J'vais dans l'silence et le désert

Car l'jour les rues les plus brillantes
Les plus pétardier's et grouillantes
A Minoch' sent gu'des grans couloirs,
Des collidors à ciel ouvert.

[To each in his turn, the pavement
I walk in silence and in the desert
For in the day the grandest streets
At midnight are no more than vast hallways,
Corridors open to the sky.]

At Le Mirliton, Aristide Bruant sang of *clochards*, street gangs and whores, and mocked the fashionable customers who came slumming from the *beaux quartiers*. His finest songs were sung by Eugénie Buffet, who cast herself on the little *caf' conc'* stage as Pierreuse, the impoverished tart with the heart of gold.

One of the greatest and best-paid stars of the Moulin Rouge, Yvette Guilbert, went back to her roots in the poor faubourgs when she sang with intense theatricality at the little Divan Japonais. Edmond de Goncourt found her a "very great tragic actress who makes your heart seize with anguish", and she took London and New York by storm. It was said that her art lay in the "beautifying of the terrible", as in her haunting song "La Soulade" (the drink-sodden hag):

Dés le matin, on peut la voir
Sur le pavé, sur le trottoir
Cheminer, la mine haggarde

[At daybreak you can see her
On the cobbles, on the pavement
Trudging along, her face haggard]

These were a new type of song, of the slums, the walk to the scaffold and the guillotine, haunting and rebellious.

Striptease, too, was a Parisian invention of the age. It was first recorded, fresh, amateur and innocent, at the Bal des Quat' Arts, the annual pre-Lenten students' ball and carnival in February 1893. The revellers included artists' models and girlfriends. A makeshift beauty contest was held; a girl stripped off and climbed naked onto a table. Heartfelt applause soon turned to fury with the intervention of Senator Béranger, a fierce and self-appointed arbiter of morals. A fine was imposed on the organisers of the ball. It was met by riots and demonstrations in the Latin Quarter.

Police and students fought in the place de la Sorbonne; mobs hurled paving stones at the Préfecture de Police, troops were called in, shots fired, and a student was killed.

With a martyr on their side, the students won the day. The Paris prefect of police was sacked, and professional striptease appeared in 1894 at Le Divan Fayouac, a music hall aptly located on the rue des Martyrs. On a stage set like a boudoir with a bed, a fleshy lass called Yvette peeled off layer after layer of loose-fitting gowns until, leering at the audience, she was left in a shift. She then climbed into bed. Early striptease was coy, and stopped short of total nudity. In one famous act at the Casino de Paris, the lissom Angèle Hérald undressed to hunt down a flea in her underclothes.

Outright pornography was discreetly available. Specialist bars and clubs catered for homosexuals and lesbians; the masked balls held at the Paris Opéra were said to be "nothing else today than great festivals of pederasty". The *maisons de tolérance*, the licensed brothels, were renowned enough to be on the regular tourist circuit for rich visitors. Their clientele, so the writer Léo Taxil claimed, was made up of "the magistrature, the army, the navy, high finance, officials of the Republic, important men of business, members of the Jockey Club, foreign princes, visiting millionaires".

Crowds flocked to an exhibition of paintings of "Bars et Maisons closes" by the artist Georges Bottini in 1899. One brothel decked out its rooms in Russian, Italian, Spanish, Chinese, Indian and even Scottish décor. Another had a boudoir modelled on a ship's cabin, the walls draped with sails and rigging, and the bed hung like a hammock. The exclusive establishment at 14 rue de Montyon had genuine Louis XV chairs and a Salon des lords for its English patrons; Le Chabanais in the street of the same name, perhaps the most renowned brothel in Europe, had medallions painted by Toulouse-Lautrec in its Pompeian salon and, for "the English vice", the "prettiest torture chamber in Paris". The artist lived for a time at 6 rue des Moulins, where he sketched each of the girls; brothels advertised themselves by hanging large illumi- nated street numbers above the door, and Toulouse-Lautrec waggishly told his friends that he was staying at number six, "a very large number indeed." Downmarket clients were entertained in *brasseries des filles*, where the waitresses evaded the strict health regulations that covered the girls in the licensed houses.

All this helped to give the City of Light its darker reputation, as the city of smut. Edmond de Goncourt, novelist and founder of the Prix Goncourt, the most vener- ated of literary awards, complained in 1889 that "Paris is no longer Paris; it is a kind of free city in which all the thieves of the earth who have made their fortunes come to eat badly and to sleep with the flesh of someone who calls herself a Parisienne." That it was a "free city", of course, accounted for some of the visitors who made it the prime destination for the new tourist industry. But all capital cities cater for provincials and foreigners in search of a bit of fun. Paris did so with style and unashamed aplomb; a city like London, where underage girls were clandestinely exploited by the thousand, was closer perhaps to true depravity.

In part, at least, the reputation of Paris for decadence was based on affectation, or plain invention. It was fun to shock. Verlaine adored the word "decadence" for its own sake; it was "all shimmering with purple and gold . . . a blend of carnal spirits and sad flesh and . . . violent splendours." Rachide, an army officer's daughter who cropped her hair and wore men's clothes, enjoyed giving out visiting cards that described her as "Homme de Lettres". She wrote a novel of role reversal, *Monsieur Vénus*, where a women takes a fancy to a young worker and installs him in an apartment as her kept man. In his super-bestseller *Degeneration*, Max Nordau, a Hungarian physician in Paris, wrote that the city was the "confluence of degeneracy and hysteria" which had slipped from the permissive to the perverted. His research methods were a little dubious. The poet Adolphe Retté recalled that Nordau would sit as close as he could get to the Symbolists' table in their Left Bank café, and then "noted down our remarks whilst swallowing much absinthe. We were careful to prime him with the most amazing details." One claimed to be enslaved by "unnatural tastes", and another popped pellets of bread in his mouth, saying they were hashish and opium. All this was faithfully recorded by Nordau: the City of Light was not always all that it seemed.

Of the millions who made the pilgrimage to Paris as the city of artists, one of the flowers of Western civilisation, only a very few appreciated the genius that was incubating. One critic dismissed Debussy's *Pelléas et Mélisande* as "Péderaste et Médisance", the latter word meaning "scandalmonger". Another wrote of waiting for a tune that never came: "A succession of notes like the noise of the wind . . . I prefer the wind." The Paris Opéra refused to put it on – Debussy retorted waspishly that the Opéra building looked like a railway station outside and a Turkish bath inside – and he was fortunate that the Opéra Comique took the risk. Marcel Proust listened to it on the Théâtrophone, a service that transmitted live music and drama down a telephone line. He found that "the scent of roses in the score is so strong that I have asthma whenever I hear it." Proust would find it hard to get a publisher for his first novel, *Du côté de chez Swann:* "Words, words, so many words," one complained. He was reduced to bribing the editor of *Le Figaro* with a monogrammed Tiffany cigarette case to get him to run some extracts in the paper.

Money was not a problem for Proust. It was for others. The poet Paul Valéry lived and wrote in a room in a boarding house, his library an open suitcase, with a skeleton hanging on the wall to remind him to pierce to the bone. Matisse was too poor to be able to heat his studio, and wore a hat and overcoat as he worked. Picasso's room in Montmartre had little more than an old mattress on four legs in a corner and a little rusty cast-iron stove with a yellow bowl he washed in. Vlaminck was a racing cyclist and played gypsy music on a violin to keep body and soul together. Derain moonlighted as a professional boxer, and van Dongen sold newspapers. Maurice Utrillo, himself befriended by a kindly wine seller in Montmartre, thought his friend Amadeo Modigliani was the purest genius; but no one else agreed, and Utrillo kept him afloat until he foundered on drugs. But often an admirer would sooner or later ride to the rescue. For Matisse, it was the rich Russian Sergei Shchukin who commissioned two large panels of dancers for his

Moscow house and then bought three dozen canvases. Picasso was pulled out of near penury in 1906 by Ambroise Vollard, who paid him 2,000 francs for 30 canvases.

It was the genius of Paris to provide such life-savers, and another was needed now. The wonder years seemed to be running into the sands. Modish Post-Impressionists called themselves the Nabis, meaning "prophets" in Hebrew, and spread their Symbolist work across prints, book illustrations and posters. A sub-group, the Intimists, linked two painters who shared a studio and were strongly influenced by Gauguin and the passion for Japanese prints. Pierre Bonnard painted nudes, landscapes and interiors of exquisite subtlety and sensuality. Édouard Vuillard's flower pieces, theatre murals and interiors were also of great complexity and nuance.

The Nabis were not to set the world alight, however, and Art Nouveau's impact was always limited by the fact it was decorative rather than easel art. The term came from the Maison d'Art Nouveau in Paris. It was opened by the German art dealer Siegfried Bing, the leading dealer in Japanese art, inspired by Tiffany in New York. Bing used young artists to furnish his "palace of new ideas" with stained glass, pottery, furniture, tapestries, sculptures, lamps and glassware. It had walls of yellow ochre and olive-green bands, and an entrance hall of glass bricks. Critics slammed it as "made for rough cavemen", but Bing used brilliant craftsmen: the decorator Louis Majorelle, the painter and sculptor Victor Prouvé and Émile Gallé, the glass and vase maker, all from Nancy; and René Lalique, who decorated glass with relief figures of animals and flowers, and used enamels, pearls, precious and semi-precious stones and ivories to make brooches and diadems. Lightness and charm came from using the lines of flowers – the lily, iris and orchid above all – and with insects and birds abounding in colour, dragonflies, swallows, peacocks. The flowing lines and arabesques of Art Nouveau passed into fashion, in the tressed and tendrilled locks of the vermicelli hairstyle, and the passion for the curvaceous, S-shaped female form, displayed by Loie Fuller, the Rubenesque American dancer at the Folies Bergère, whose pirouetting figure glimpsed through floating veils was immortalised on ash trays, lampstands and film.

The style was passé soon enough. Hector Guimard's superb Métro entrances, each one unique, the steel and wrought iron lightened with glass, and the grilles shaped into plants, are now recognised as repositories of a veritable *style métro* and one of the glories of Paris. Guimard, architect, sculptor and artisan, died in obscurity in New York. Besides them, only Maxim's is left as a living shrine to Art Nouveau, and to the *cocottes* of the *belle époque* like the Belle Otero, mistress to the mighty, who danced fandangos on its tables. She was one of the *grandes horizontales* who, subtly graded into *belles-petites, tendresses, agenouillées* and *degrafées*, were obliged as apprentices to "conform to all the rules of snobbery, learn to ride, learn about sports, speak a few English expressions, learn the great families in the *Almanac de Gotha*".

Recovery started with the Fauves, the "wild beasts" led by Matisse. At the 1905 Salon d'Automne, paintings by members of Matisse's informal group were hung in a room with a quattrocento-style sculpture. The art critic Louis Vauxcelles compared the calm of the Renaissance man to the bold, frenzied colours of the paintings, and sighed: "Ah, Donatello chez les fauves." The name stuck. Matisse was inspired by the brilliance of the southern light he had found in the little fishing port of Collioure – "I worked as I felt," he said, "by colour alone" – and had just painted his famous *Woman with the Hat* with vermilion hair and green-patched cheeks. Clear, brilliant colour was characteristic of the Fauves – Matisse, Vlaminck, Raoul Dufy and André Derain. Georges Rouault painted clowns, prostitutes and religious figures in deep and glowing blues and blacks.

The Fauves were not as feral and savage as their name. The sharp and shocking infusion that changed all came from the boy, still not nineteen, who had got off the Barcelona train in 1900. The work by Pablo Picasso that had hung in the Spanish pavilion at the Exposition gave little hint of what was to come. It was a lugubrious academic work, titled *Last Moments*. A priest stood over a dying girl, a crucifix on the wall, the drama heightened by the light of a lamp, the scene stirred perhaps by the death of the artist's sister Conchita, or by Puccini's *La Bohème*, which had met with rapture and sensation when it opened in Barcelona.

It was a sentimental piece, and he painted over it, but it showed that Picasso was already a master of traditional technique. Within a year, his paintings *Longchamp* and *The Blue Room* showed that he had soaked in the Neo-Impressionists. Haunting pictures of the poor and despairing marked the evolution of his own style in his brief Blue Period, before he moved on to a cascade of paintings of harlequins, acrobats and circus life in his Pink Period.

Crude, compelling, self-consciously shocking, he painted *Les Demoiselles d'Avignon* in 1907. He was only 26, but he had changed the rules. "A painting is a sum of destruction," he once said, and he challenged reality to probe what is solid and what is not, looking beneath the surface at the different planes. Here were the roots of Cubism, creating the three-dimensional without using perspective. The Avignon girls were not innocents; they were prostitutes, angular, harsh, their faces like African masks of ferocity, painted in ochre, pink and blue. Life was not to be copied, decorated or emboldened in Fauvist colours; it was thrust into geometric shapes.

Its museums stocked with colonial exhibits, Paris introduced Picasso to African tribal art, and to Georges Braque. An orderly, respectable son of an interior decorator from Le Havre, married, an amateur flautist, temperamentally quite different to the Catalan, Braque was already painting landscapes in geometrical shapes. The two men pooled their ideas, as Braque put it, "like mountaineers roped together". They each chose to paint a girl, Braque with a mandolin, Picasso with a guitar, as the primitive mind might see her, by instinct and as patches of light and shade.

Braque knew from his father how to intimate rare woods and marble in paint; it was part of a decorator's stock in trade. He cut shapes from a wallpaper that copied oak panelling and then pasted them onto a charcoal drawing, to make a picture of a bowl of fruit and a wineglass on a wooden table against a panelled wall. As he and Picasso passed through phases of Cubism – analytic, synthetic, rococo – they used collage, bits of wire, newspaper cuttings and cigarette packets as media, together with paint.

They did dozens of these collages. "We tried to get rid of trompe l'œil to find a tromp l'esprit," Picasso said. "If a piece of newspaper can become a bottle, it gives us something to think about newspaper, and bottles too." A music-hall song score appeared in his *Ma Jolie* series of paintings. Braque had broken with Picasso by 1914; he continued exploring the techniques for still lifes, breaking subjects like a violin into fragments. Cubists were now a group, exhibiting at the Salon d'Automne. Fernand Léger was close to pure abstraction in pictures like *La Femme en Bleu*. Robert Delaunay, thought at the time to be the most important painter in Paris, used a method he called Orphism to break up the surface of his canvases into planes of pure colour. Piet Mondrian painted still lifes in which the patterns and planes took precedence over the subject.

The capital teemed with words as well as oils, a few of them English. The American lesbian Gertrude Stein, comfortably ensconced with her friend Alice B. Toklas, had her portrait painted by Picasso and wrote in prose that sometimes tried to ape the theories of abstract painting; less well off, the Irishman James Joyce wrote to his mother in 1903 to thank her for a postal order for 3s 4d, welcome indeed "as I had been without food for 42 hours". Most, of course, were French. Some 200 literary reviews appeared between 1900 and the war, published on a shoestring, running a few poems, short stories, criticisms and literary theories before the bailiffs moved in and they folded.

A great survivor was *La Nouvelle revue française*. It was founded by André Gide and Jean Schlumberger, and run from the latter's apartment by a business manager, Gaston Gallimard, who was to become a major publisher. The drive, zest and idealism came from Gide, a man of letters in the fullest sense, a writer of essays, poems, novels, biography, drama, memoirs, travelogues and criticism.

His parents, and his Scots governess, were Calvinists. His sense of this austere, stern, stripped-down faith was in tension with his homosexuality, his abandoning of restraints, and his shrine of pleasure. "My resolute paganism", he wrote, "remains soaked in the tears Christ has shed." He married his first cousin, Madeleine Rondeaux, but it was a *mariage blanc*, as the trip they made to North Africa together in 1900 confirmed to all but his innocent and unworldly bride. With his guide and protégé Athman, Gide travelled to the desert and found a paradise in its size and stillness. They went on to the oasis of Touggourt "in a sort of ecstasy of silent joy, of elation of the senses and the flesh". All this, and the boys who gave him such pleasure, saw his spirits and soul soar to such a height that he thought it a hosanna to the Lord.

On his return to Paris, he poured these un-Calvinistic ideas into his novel *L'Immoraliste*. Its hero is an archaeologist who, after losing his wife, goes back to North Africa and has an affair with a prostitute. It stirred up a hornet's nest of critics, and the fury of the clerics, but the publicity boosted its sales and Gide's reputation among the young. His next novel, *La Porte étroite*, the story of a young woman in love, added to his fame in 1909. Parts of it were run in the first issue of his *Nouvelle revue*. He built a house in Auteuil, the Villa Montmorency, which became a literary port of call down the years.

Gide's friend Paul Valéry was lapsing into a twenty-year silence. Others reflected a renaissance in Catholic thought; nothing, the secularists should have realised, revives a Church better than a good kicking. Francis Jammes, a poet from Tournay in the Pyrenees, wrote on nature and religion in works like *De l'angélus de l'aube à l'angélus du soir*; on reading his collection of poems *L'Église habillée en feuilles*, Gide claimed that it had made him "already completely a Catholic". If so, he did not remain one for long. The dramatist and poet Paul Claudel was a former freethinker who found himself suddenly flooded by a feeling of "the innocence and eternal infancy of God" whilst listening to vespers in Notre-Dame. He was posted as a consul to Fuzhou in China, where he had an affair with a married woman, "R", which he drew on in his play *Partage de Midi*. His other plays, like *L'Otage*, helped to re-establish Christianity as an artistic force. Unlike the Gide hero, who goes where his inner thoughts drive him, Claudel believed heroism was to bear witness to the truth, to Christ. Art and religion, Claudel said, had to be "at right angles, and their struggle feeds our life". This did not endear him to the consular service officials who employed him, on behalf of anticlerical governments, of course, and his own Christian compassion had its limits. He savaged Calvinists, and when his sister showed signs of madness, after the sculptor Rodin had abandoned her as his mistress and model, he packed her off to a provincial madhouse.

The most talented of popular writers was Gabrielle Colette. All Paris had read her *Claudine à l'école*, but they thought it was written by her husband Henri Gauthier-Villars, since they appeared under his pen-name of "Willy". He set her to work each day to write more Claudine books, pocketing the royalties and the fame. Cocteau noted the fleshy Willy, a moustachioed bully, whilst Colette was "thin, thin like a baby fox in cycling costume". She escaped him, and lived with the lesbian Mathilde de Morny, marquise de Belboeuf, the eccentric great-granddaughter of the Empress Josephine. Colette took to the stage, appearing in music hall, dancing and performing mime, mining the experience for her book *L'Envers du music-hall*. The intense physical sensuality of her work and her sense of drama made her work translate easily into films and musicals.

That an occasional scribbler for *Le Figaro*, a social gadfly and *malade imaginaire* always taking to his bed, was later to be considered the pick of a large bunch, would doubtless have amazed the other writers of his generation. At surface level,

Marcel Proust was indeed a sickly, precious, mother-fixated snob and dandy. A semi-invalid from nine, he suffered from asthma and taut-strung nerves that only his mother could calm. From her, he said, he got "a horror of falsehood, moral sensitivity and, especially, a sense of infinite goodness." His idea of unhappiness, he said when he was 14, was "being separated from my mother"; his *bête noire* was "people who are insensitive to what is good". He fluttered in a purple-lined pearl-grey frock coat with matching bowler hat, an orchid in his buttonhole, always with an invalid's fear of rejection and giving displeasure. His best friend, the composer and conductor Reynaldo Hahn, a fellow darling of the salons, said that he would tip all and sundry when leaving a café, and then spot a waiter in a corner, and rush back and give him a ridiculous tip, and say: "It must be so painful to be left out."

His mother died in 1905, when he was 34, two years after his father, a distinguished doctor. He was rich, and alone and vulnerable. A husband-and-wife manservant and cook looked after him. At first, he still travelled, but he gradually gave himself over to introspection. He had his apartment on the boulevard Haussmann soundproofed by lining it with cork to filter out the distraction of traffic; the windows were sealed against the scent of chestnut trees, which brought on attacks of asthma, and he lay in bed incessantly filling scores of notebooks. He was an insomniac, overdosing himself with soporifics, venturing out mainly at night, sometimes to go to the Ritz to ask the waiters and the maître d', Olivier, what the diners were talking about. He was not a snob, he was a watcher; every social station has its interest, he said, adding wryly that it could be as intriguing "to depict the manners of a queen as the behaviour of a dressmaker".

He had published his first book, *Les Plaisirs et les jours*, to complete indifference when he was 25. He now worked on his *À la recherche du temps perdu*, eventually to fill 13 volumes which, for some, make him the finest writer of the century, anywhere. He drew his characters, not outward description but by evoking the inner emotional life, the self that lives beneath the superficial consciousness. A person's most important ideas and actions could stem from the smallest and most insignificant moment. "An hour is not just an hour," he said. "It is a vase filled with scents, sounds, plans, atmospheres." Proust was a great enough technician – he wrote effortless pastiches of Balzac and Flaubert – to know that his first volume, *Du côté de chez Swann* (*Swann's Way*), was a masterpiece. Others did not. It was turned down flat by Gaston Gallimard and the *Nouvelle revue française*, before the young publisher Bernard Grasset agreed to take it on at Proust's expense.

Sarah Bernhardt was also *sui generis*, the greatest tragedienne of her long day, certainly, and perhaps the most versatile actress of any age. The illegitimate daughter of a Dutch courtesan, she had wished for a religious life until her mother was persuaded by the duc de Morny, half-brother of Napoleon III, to send her to the Conservatoire. She then gave herself to the stage, making her debut as a teenager in 1862. After a happy period playing Molière, Racine and Shakespeare at the Théâtre de l'Odéon, she returned to the Comédie Française. She stunned English audiences as Phèdre – she tore at the emotions in death scenes – and was brave enough to break with the all-powerful Comédie at home.

Some called her "Sarah Barnum", for there was something of the circus extravaganza to her flamboyance; but she took America by storm, visiting Thomas Edison at Menlo Park and recording the timbre of her splendid voice on the new phonograph machine. She was the husky mistress of *la voix d'amour* and, with her fiery temper, the master of *la voix de rage*. A foray into drugs saw her marry the addict Jacques Damala, a Greek actor, but the marriage soon fell apart and she recovered to play a series of star roles, in *Fédora, La Tosca* and *Cléopâtre*, created for her by the playwright Victorien Sardou. Playing Tosca in Rio, she fell from the net that should have caught her in her death plunge from the battlements. She would not allow the surgeon on the ship that took her from Rio to operate on her badly damaged right knee – she said he had dirty fingernails. It remained untreated, and had to be amputated in 1915. It was a measure of her fame that Barnum's circus offered her $10,000 for the right to exhibit the limb, and of her courage that she continued to perform on stage with all her old fire.

Glamour pictures were taken of her famously S-shaped body reclining on tiger skins, or on velvets and silks; but the age of the wasp waist, the large bosom and the flash of ankle was passing. Paul Poiret did away with the corset and launched the Empire line in 1906, with a high waist and a minimal bust, straight and simple, following it up with the hobble skirt, Turkish trousers and the first very high-heeled shoes. Other couturiers' colours, he said, were "nuances of nymph's thigh" – lilacs, blue hortensia, maize – soft and easy. Into this sheepcote he threw "a few rough wolves" – reds, greens, violet, orange. He was, in some ways, a forerunner of the modern merchandising Guccis and Diors. He made the first couturier's scent, calling it *Le fruit défendu*, although it smelt of peaches rather than the forbidden apple. He opened an interior-decorating business, and founded a group to stop New York department stores from copying Paris designs.

The very rich, Russians and the English prominent among them, wintered on the Côte d'Azur. The numbers and the resorts were still few. In 1905 Juan-les-Pins hardly existed, the writer Jacques Audiberti recalled. He went there as a six-year-old, in a sailor suit, gloves and beret. The avenues were laid out and the pine trees were there, together with the Grand Hotel and its restaurant, "but apart from that, there was nothing. Only this little boy and his mother." The rich summered on the English Channel, at Le Touquet, Deauville and Trouville.

Those below this category with some disposable time and money were a growing breed, and the first popular leisure magazines aimed at this new market – *Je sais tout, Lisez-moi, Nos Loisirs* – were appearing. The first Tour de France, a bicycle race transformed into an epic of endurance, was the happy result of a circulation war between sports newspapers. The French passion for cycling – they owned 3.5 million machines by 1914 – boosted sales of *Le Vélo*, one of the world's first sports newspapers. It was founded by Pierre Giffard, but he imprudently aligned the paper openly with the disgraced Dreyfus. This angered powerful backers like the marquis de Dion, a leading car and bicycle manufacturer, and the founder of the French automobile club. He founded a new paper, *L'Auto-Vélo*, edited by Henri Desgrange, to coincide with the Exposition and the Paris Olympics in 1900. *Le Vélo* held a Paris–Bordeaux race. Desgrange, a former racing cyclist, counter-attacked by organising the grandest, longest and toughest of races. Funded by de Dion and other industrialists, the first Tour de France pedalled off on July 1, 1903. It had only six stages, with riders having to battle on through the night. The winner, Maurice Garin, "the Chimney Sweep", was road cycling's first great champion.

Cheating riders and rioting spectators almost saw an end to the Tour in 1904 – riders took lifts in cars and even trains, and fans threw nails in front of riders they disliked – but it helped *L'Auto* thrive and *Le Vélo* gave up the sales battle, folding the same year. Desgrange honed the race, bringing in a points system and more stages to put an end to night riding, but it preserved its rough-and-tumble origins. Rivals were poisoned and leaders were disqualified for illegal bike changes. No outside help was allowed in breakdowns and punctures; when Eugène Christophe broke his forks in the Pyrenees, he was penalised because a lad had worked the bellows in the blacksmith's forge where Christophe made his own repairs. Desgrange introduced mountain stages, sending riders through freak snow in the Pyrenees in 1910 on a stage so vicious that the leader shouted out "Murderer!" as he reached the summit; in a publicity masterstroke, Desgrange dressed the leader in a yellow jersey, which matched the colour of the paper *L'Auto* was printed on.

Native genius was discovered in two other new forms of transport, the car and the aircraft. The Peugeot dynasty, originally in textiles, moved on to bikes and cars. André Citroën, the Renault brothers, and the marquis de Dion with his partner Georges Bouton, contributed to French car output, running on tyres manufactured by the Michelin brothers. Other former bicycle makers, Alexander Darracq and the ex-rider Fernand Charron, went on to build racing cars. Delahaye came into car making from farm machinery, Panhard-Levassor from woodworking. Léon Serpollet poured his considerable talent into the lost cause of steam cars.

A new pastime of touring by car, as Proust did in Normandy, and the sport of motor racing, were largely pioneered in France. Marcel Renault won the Paris–Vienna race of 1902 at a faster speed than the Arlberg express. He was killed in the Paris–Madrid a year later, but the 1,500 taxis that his brother Louis supplied to Paris in 1906 helped ensure a French victory on the Marne battlefields eight years on. By 1907, the first intercontinental race was organised, between Paris and Peking.

The French remained great pioneers of the sky. Their spirit of courage and enterprise was caught at an aviation meeting at Reims in 1909 by Gertrude Bacon, an intrepid visitor who was taken up in a Farman biplane. It looked like a box kite. Four long converging outrigger spars formed the fuselage, and the elevator projected far out in front. It had wooden sledge-runners for wheels, and the engine was mounted just behind the basket seat for the pilot. Miss Bacon was flown by Roger Sommer, who wedged her tightly between himself and the engine radiator, and warned her not to touch his arms. The ground was hard and bumpy; then, "suddenly there came a new, indescribable quality – a lift – a lightness – a life!"

The world's first dedicated aerodrome was Port-Aviation at Juvisy, south of Paris, which was blessed by the archbishop of Paris when it opened in 1907. Gabriel Voisin built an aircraft for the sculptor Léon Delagrange, which Gaumont filmed in flight, also in 1907. Henri Farman, himself a former bicycle racer who was never beaten in a tandem race with his brother, became the first aircraft passenger in history when Delagrange took him up at Issy in 1908; he later made the world's first night flight, at Châlons-sur-Marne. Paris was the first major city to have an aircraft fly over it, piloted by comte de Lambert in 1909; a more melancholy record was established the same year, when Eugène Lefebvre became the first pilot to be killed when his aircraft crashed at Juvisy.

"I do not say that the French cannot come," an English admiral said at the height of the Napoleonic wars. "I only say they cannot come by sea." Early in the morning of July 25, 1909, a Frenchman arrived near Dover by air. Louis Blériot described his flight in the *Daily Mail*, the newspaper that put up the prize money for the achievement. He cleared the French coast and soon left the naval destroyer that was to act as his safety ship far behind. It was making 20 knots, and he was going into the void at 35 knots. "Nothing to be seen, neither the torpedo-destroyer, nor France, nor England," he found. "I am alone, I can see nothing at all – *rien du tout*! For 10 minutes I am lost . . . I let the aeroplane take its own course . . . And then, 20 minutes after I have left the French coast, I see the green [sic] cliffs of Dover . . . I stop my motor, and instantly the machine falls straight upon the land . . . In two or three seconds, I am safe upon your shore. Soldiers in khaki run up, and a policeman. Two of my compatriots are on the spot. They kiss my cheeks."

To put Blériot's feat into its formidable context, remember that, safely above land, Wilbur Wright had become the first man to fly higher than a measly 100 metres only eight months before. Roland Garros, the first man to fly at 5,000 metres, also became the first man to cross the Mediterranean in 1913, from Saint-Raphaël to Bizerta. Aviation could help the French reach and map the vast and unknown spaces of North Africa and the empire they were still acquiring.

3

Before the Deluge

A wave of anti-Semitism at the turn of the century was deepened by the Dreyfus affair. Prejudice was whipped up by the press. When Jewish businessmen threatened to boycott the Exposition, *La Libre Parole* called for three cheers, on the grounds that the event could now be wholly French. But such irritants broke no bones, and it was perhaps inevitable that they should exist. The number of Jews living in France doubled to 100,000 in the years up to 1914, largely as a result of pogroms in tsarist Poland and the Ukraine. The arrivals were visibly Jewish, in their dress and manners, and doubtless met with the similar resistance to other newcomers, Italian or Portuguese. Established Jews were mostly accepted without strain or comment. Romain Rolland, the biographer and novelist, the composer Claude Debussy, and the poet and *haut bourgeois* novelist Paul Bourget married Jews. So did Dr Adrien Proust. His son Marcel, as he charted the nuances of society in his great novels, displayed not a trace of angst over his mother's Jewish origins. The Natanson brothers, publishers of *La Revue Blanche*, and the most important nurturers of artistic talent in the capital, were Jews; so were leading hostesses like Misia Sert, Geneviève Strauss, Ernesta Stern and the baronne Deslandes.

The Dreyfus affair would probably not have aroused such passions without the nationalism that had roused the country since the Franco-Prussian war. Anti-German feeling, which touched on the most profound issues of war and peace, was fuelled by the continuing humiliation of lost Alsace and Lorraine. Each July 14, in the place de la Concorde, a wreath of roses and orchids was laid in front of the stone figure of Strasbourg by mourners in black velvet suits and women in red skirts and silk aprons, with black ribbons falling from their hair. They wept as they sang: "Vous n'aurez pas l'Alsace et la Lorraine." On maps in French schoolrooms, the annexed territories were picked out in black crêpe. Wagner was not played at the Opéra. As for *perfide Albion,* only Bordeaux, eight hours distant from Paris by train, proud, self-sufficient and mindful of the importance of the English wine trade, was sympathetic to *les rosbifs*.

The other great question of the moment was the struggle between the Church and the radical Republic. It was, ironically, a politician of Genoese-Jewish extraction, Léon Gambetta, who had notoriously described clericalism as *l'ennemi*. It was said of President Loubet that he would no more mention "God" in a speech than he would dream of entering the German embassy. In 1900, a *congrégation*, the Assumptionist teaching order, deeply anti-Dreyfusard, was dissolved. Most Catholics were anti-Dreyfusard – Charles de Gaulle's father was a rare exception – and, though Pope Leo XIII had constrained the French clergy and monarchists to accept the Republic, many showed scant respect for liberal values. The secular left had good reason for resentment. Its pretensions to moral superiority, however, were destroyed by its pursuit of the religious. The prime minister, René Waldeck-Rousseau, a member of the new "republican nobility", a founder of the *Grand cercle républican* in Paris that gave republicans an equivalent to the great conservative social clubs, won a vote of confidence for the "defence of the secular state" in the summer. He spoke bitterly of Church funds as the "*congrégations*' billion", claiming that "too many monks are members of the *ligues* and too many monks are dabbling in business".

It was made compulsory in 1901 for all the teaching orders to be authorised by the state. The navy minister, Camille Pelletan, a journalist by trade, abolished the custom of flying flags at half-mast on Good Friday, and of naming some ships for saints; though the navy was still known as "La Royale", its ships were now to have the most provocative of republican names, such as *Danton* and *Marseillaise*. In 1903, Waldeck's successor Émile Combes, a provincial doctor turned radical politician, a goatee-bearded bigot, stepped up the pressure. He allowed General Louis André to connive with freemasons to spy on the religious habits of serving army officers. Those who went to Sunday mass were listed in a secret file marked "Carthage", whilst those who did not were listed as good republicans in a "Corinth" file, and only Corinthians got senior promotions. Combes personally presided at the unveiling of a statue to Ernest Renan in Brittany. Renan, an ex-seminarist, had cut and slashed at the supernatural aspects of Christ and Christian teaching in his controversial book *La Vie de Jésus*. His statue, with the goddess Minerva standing behind him, was taken as a deliberate freethinking insult to the deeply Catholic Breton soil on which it stood.

The real bombshell was lobbed in 1904. The right to teach was withdrawn from all *congrégations*. Religious orders, pioneers of education since Charlemagne, founders of the great medieval universities, were simply thrown out on their ear. A cynical amendment was voted to the bill. Novitiates on the staff of French schools in the colonies and abroad were allowed to stay on; without them, the *mission civilatrice* that Combes and his secular friends claimed as a justification of empire would have collapsed. Though Combes had gone when the secret of the Corinth and Carthage files was laid bare, formal separation of Church and state followed in 1905.

It was vindictive on an epic scale. More than 2,500 Church schools were shut down. Thousands of teaching priests and nuns left France in a spectacular exodus for Italy, Belgium and Switzerland. Religious processions were banned, and monasteries and convents expropriated. Rodin sculpted nudes in what had been a convent. At a stroke, almost a third of primary schools and a quarter of secondary schools were stripped of their teachers. There were plans to take over country churches and turn them into museums and village halls. Marcel Proust, touring Normandy from his summer base at the fashionable Grand Hôtel in Cabourg, fell in love with its ancient churches and wrote a passionate piece in *Le Figaro* calling for the government to leave them open for worship: they would only die, he said, when the sacrifice of the body and blood of Christ ceased to be celebrated.

The campaign was politically reckless, too. Catholics had been encouraged in the 1890s to accept *le ralliement* and work with the Republic. The anticlerical decrees of the new century stood this advice on its head. It became rare to find a good

Catholic who was warm to the Republic, whose symbol, Marianne, was now despised by many as "la Gueuse" (the Whore). Combes, a lapsed seminarist himself, was dubbed "Julian the Apostate". The traditional, respectable right was determined to defend the Church; beyond them were the Ligue des Patriotes and Action Française and their like, ready to use extra-parliamentary muscle.

Communes were given responsibility for Church resources. This involved making inventories – "counting the candlesticks" – which many of the faithful believed to be sacrilege. In Paris, in parts of the Haute-Loire, and other strongly Catholic areas, secular officials were physically barred from churches. Peasants in the Basque country and the Haut-Doubs defended their churches with pitchforks and bludgeons.

The anticlericals pointed happily to the decline of "superstition". In Limoges, the number of children not baptised shot up from 2 per cent in 1905 to 40 per cent in 1914, for example, and the number of civil marriages rose from 14 per cent to 60 per cent. René Viviani, the minister of work, crowed in triumph: "We have rescued men's consciences from belief! Where a poor fellow, exhausted by his day's work, knelt down, we have lifted him up, we have told him that behind the clouds there are only illusions. Together, with a magnificent gesture, we have put out the lights in heaven, and no-one will turn them on again." Far from feeling embarrassed by this claim to have switched off Christ like a light bulb, the government liked the speech so well that it had it placarded across the country. Romain Rolland, to become a Nobel laureate for his *Jean Christophe* novels, saw the deep wound it caused. The left thought that religion was no more than a material interest that could be bashed with impunity; they were blind to it as a faith "that is the lifeblood of half France – more than the lifeblood, since eternal life is held to be involved."

The secular left had thus aborted the birth of a mainstream, pro-republican Catholic party. It was a gross and unbalancing error, and it echoed down the century. The troubles were checked for the moment by Georges Clemenceau, as interior and prime minister. A doctor, a brilliant, restless journalist, founder of *L'Aurore*, a skilled horseman and a good shot much feared in duels, he was a republican of old stock who never forgot the hounding of his father under the Second Empire. He was anticlerical enough, but he was a practical and patriotic man – "before philosophising, one must *be*!" – and he saw the damage that was being done. "One does not have to kill men to count candlesticks," he said, banning the use of force in making church inventories.

Religion did not go away, of course. It revived under pressure. Some Catholics reverted to the old counter-revolution ideology of monarchy, faith, tradition, and a vision of that France which Talleyrand recalled when he said: "Those who were not alive before 1789 cannot imagine the gentle way of life." They joined Action Française, the extra-parliamentary *ligue* founded in 1905 by Charles Maurras, an emotional and vigorous populariser who transformed the ideology of monarchy from a lost cause into an effective anti-republican irritant.

A gentler Catholicism, too, appeared in *Le Sillon* (the Furrow) movement of Marc Sangnier. He sought to reconcile the faith and the Republic, and to promote fair wages and the right to strike. He started the *instituts populaires* as an alternative to the socialists' *universités populaires*, which would organise cheap outings for workers to museums and cathedrals. He formed workers' cooperatives making shoes and shirts. Five hundred study groups across France supported his ideas for a modern faith. The writer François Mauriac and his brother, Jean, a future priest, belonged to one in Bordeaux; Mauriac's first writings appeared in *Le Sillon*, which he sold on street corners. Sangnier declared that democracy was the only truly Catholic form of government. This was too much for Pope Pius X, who scored a spectacular own goal against Catholics of conscience by telling him to close his movement. But Sangnier made real gains – in 1912, a quarter of the elite *normaliens* were practising Catholics, an unthinkable number a few years before, and due largely to a Sillon study group at the college.

Charles Péguy had the last laugh on Viviani. A young friend of Jaurès, Péguy was like him a scholarship boy who had made it as a *normalien*, though by a tougher route: he was raised in a two-room thatched cottage in Orléans by his illiterate grandmother and widowed mother, helping them repair rush chairs to eke out a living before his intelligence and charm kicked in and took him off to Paris. The mix of Dreyfus, socialism, republicanism and atheism, or secularism, as it preferred to be known, was a brew so potent that it had led Péguy, a Christian, to turn his back on Jaurès for good. He first mortified the secular establishment by writing a poem, "The Mystery of the Charity of Joan of Arc", and entering it for the annual Académie Française prize. The poem had some weighty support, but the pillar of the atheist elite, the Sorbonne historian Ernest Lavisse, railed against Péguy as a Catholic anarchist with "holy water in his petrol bomb". Péguy retaliated by calling Lavisse a "fat gravedigger" and a serf of Sorbonne socialism. The Academicians, rattled, funked the issue by awarding no prize at all. Péguy's son was desperately sick with typhoid in 1912; when the boy recovered, Péguy kept his vow to go on a pilgrimage from Paris to Chartres. It took him three days to cover the 144 kilometres. He went the next year, too, convinced that France could only win harmony by returning to the Christian roots symbolised by its most beautiful cathedral. He was killed serving with his regiment on the Marne in the first days of the war in 1914; but the gesture of this finest of men was not forgotten. The young had begun making their own pilgrimage to Chartres; in their tens of thousands, they still do.

Rabid anticlericalism was only one manifestation of aggression. The pugnacity of the French was also evident in their beards and duelling, in both of which they were champions. The wannest office worker ran to a moustache; café waiters went on strike to win the right to wear beards, and the fully-fledged *à la rivière* or beaver could attain a depth of a foot. The most unlikely people – the pacifist Jean Jaures, the effete Marcel Proust – at least challenged or were challenged to duels. Georges

Clemenceau, always spoiling for a scrap – "If Germany wants war," he assured the British ambassador as early as 1905, "well then, fight we will!" – took part in twenty-two of them. After Pierre Curie was run down by a horse wagon, Marie Curie was accused by the wife of her fellow Nobel laureate, Paul Langevin, of having an affair with her husband. Raymond Poincaré, barrister-politician and later president of the Republic, represented Langevin to protect Marie. After three duels and much scandal, Langevin got a divorce.

Duels followed the code of etiquette from Chateaubriand's *Essai sur le Duel*, updated by the comte du Verger de Saint-Thomas. For Parisians, they took place just outside city limits, in the Bois de Vincennes or on the Longchamp racecourse. They were rarely fatal, though the marquis de Morès killed Captain Armand Mayer, a Jewish army officer, one of several duels fought over the Dreyfus affair. It was almost a rite of passage for journalists and editors to fight, as those they insulted in the public prints demanded satisfaction. The press was wild, savage, untamed. The laws of libel and defamation were hazy; newsprint was cheap, production costs low and opinions many.

One complainant, the wife of a senior minister, did without a duel or a libel case. She shot her husband's tormenter dead. The editor of *Le Figaro*, Gaston Calmette, let no chance slip to lambast Joseph Caillaux, the finance minister and a bogeyman of the right. Over a period of three months, Calmette published 138 articles and cartoons ridiculing the minister as a "German stooge" and a "socialist numbskull". He also threatened to publish personal letters belonging to the politician. Madame Caillaux, his second wife, feared that these would be love letters she had written to him when she was still his mistress. A woman of considerable courage and little brain, she had her chauffeur drive her to a gunsmith in her official de Dion-Bouton limousine. Here she bought a Browning pistol, which she hid in her muff. The chauffeur drove her to the *Figaro* offices, where she calmly killed Calmette. The jury did not believe that a woman could have it in her to kill in cold blood. They attributed her deed to temporary insanity, and acquitted her. The jury was all-male: women were not allowed to serve on them.

It was an oddity, in a place so proud of its revolution, that women played almost no part in politics. War tests all society, women and men, to the breaking point – striking women textile workers were to be the trigger for the Russian Revolution – but women's rights, stridently and sometimes violently demanded in England and America, were a curiously docile area. The *pétroleuses* of the Commune showed that they could rebel: a huge crowd attended the funeral of Louise Michel in 1905, the anarchist Vierge Rouge who had suffered captivity in distant New Caledonia, prison, and exile in London with dignity and generosity of spirit.

For the most part, though, the patriarchal Napoleonic Code kept women in a straitjacket, unable to vote, to hold public office, to act as witnesses in civil cases, to serve on juries or to take a job without the husband's consent. Their husbands legally owed them no more than "protection"; they owed their husband obedience, and their adultery was a crime, while for men it was a mere misdemeanour. A handful of reforms – divorce returned after its embargo by the Church; women won the right to spend their own earnings and to have eight weeks of unpaid maternity leave – had slipped in.

This was despite the fact more Frenchwomen worked than anywhere else in Europe – a possible contribution to the low birth rate – as primary schoolteachers, servants and clerks, and in textile sweatshops, but also as professional women. There were many go-ahead girls. They accounted for over a tenth of university students. The first woman joined the Paris bar in 1900, thanks in part to Marguerite Durand, a wealthy former actress who used her newspaper *La Fronde* in successful campaigns for women barristers and for the provision of chairs in shops where salesgirls could sit and relax. Significant numbers were physicians. The duchesse de Crussol d'Uzès, a fox-hunting, Boulanger-backing right-winger, was also a writer and sculptress, the founder of the Union of Female Painters, and the first woman to have a driving licence. The baronne Raymonde de Laroche became the world's first licensed woman pilot in 1910; the thoughtful pilot Madame Jeanne Pallier was one of the first of either sex to carry passengers.

The arguments against giving women the vote were thin indeed. One was that they were not full citizens, because they had not done their military service. To this they retorted that they paid their taxes and bought war loans, and that anyway "maternity is a daily battlefield". Another, used by Georges Clemenceau, was that they were besotted by religion and would foster clericalism. "To entrust the destiny of the government to the votes of women, influenced as they are from the sacristy," he said in 1909, "would be to return to the Middle Ages."

Support for the leading suffragette, Hubertine Auclert, was tepid nonetheless. She led marches, founded the Droit des Femmes and Suffrage des Femmes movements, and edited *La Citoyenne*, the first French suffragettes' paper. She earned her notoriety by trying to disrupt the elections of 1908. She strode into a Paris polling station, dressed in widow's weeds, and threw the ballot box on the ground. She denounced it as "the urn of lies", and lambasted the "unisexual suffrage" of the Republic, whilst grinding underfoot the evidence, the all-male voting slips. Her arrest sparked off few protests, however; only Norway and Iceland gave women the vote in Europe before the First World War, and it remained a dead issue in France for many years.

It was more difficult to keep workers in their place. The Confédération Générale du Travail, the CGT union, had been founded at the end of the old century. It represented only one worker in six, however, and the hard left was split between Jules Guesde's Parti Ouvrier Français, the semi-Marxist POF, and Paul Brousse's PSF, the Parti Socialiste Français. In 1905, the southerner Jean Jaurès, founder and editor of the socialist paper *l'Humanité*, welded the factions into a coherent force as the

SFIO, Section Française de l'Internationale Ouvrière. The socialists won a million votes and 51 seats in 1906; by 1914, their vote was up by a half and they had doubled the number of seats.

Militancy marked both sides in strikes. When workers building the Exposition and the Métro brought the construction industry in Paris to a halt, an army corps was quietly mobilised and brought into the city at night, so that the strikers awoke to find large numbers of troops patrolling the boulevards and the quaysides of the river. Tens of thousands of workers in cabinet-making, jewellery and building joined car makers on strike for an eight-hour day in 1906. Georges Clemenceau, once hard left and now premier, poacher turned gamekeeper, put it down with gusto, happy in his title of "le premier flic de France".

A wine glut caused near-rebellion in the Midi. The plains of the Bas-Languedoc had been converted by years of plenty into a vast vineyard, supporting rich villages with stone houses and handsome squares with plane trees. Overproduction, cheap Algerian imports and recovery from phylloxera devastated the growers in 1907. A café-owner in the Aude, Marcelin Albert, started an action committee. Every Sunday, the growers held huge meetings where banners in Occitan blamed Paris wine merchants and northern sugar-beet growers for making fraudulent wines to depress prices. Up to 700,000 people went to Montpellier to protest on June 9; it was certainly the largest demonstration seen in France, fed by fleets of specially chartered trains. The cardinal-archbishop of Montpellier, no friend of the priest-bashing cabinet in Paris, gladly opened his cathedral as a great dormitory. The growers burned down the police headquarters in Perpignan. Troops of the 17th Regiment of the Line, recruits from the Béziers area, refused to be used to repress their relatives.

This was mutiny. Clemenceau invited Albert to Paris for discussions. After they had talked, the premier pressed 200 francs onto his simple and unwary guest, to help with his travel expenses. Clemenceau then let it be known that the wine-growers' man had let himself be bought. He backed up this bit of skulduggery with a law suppressing fraud in the wine industry. The revolt in the Midi collapsed.

Troops did help Paris to survive the floods of January 1910, the worst for more than a century. The water rose to the beard of the famous zouave on the Pont de l'Alma. It was possible to scull along the boulevard Haussmann to the Gare Saint-Lazare. The Île de la Cité was totally submerged, and not a pavement was visible on the Île Saint-Louis. In the Gare d'Orsay, the waters were 5 metres deep by the platforms. When the wine-growers in Champagne rioted in 1911, the whole Marne *département* was placed under military occupation. Troops were called in, too, to keep the mail moving when postal workers struck.

The unions made some progress. A ten-hour day for women and children and an eight-hour shift in the mines were introduced. A mandatory one day of rest a week was a boon to exploited household servants and hotel staff. A new social insurance scheme was optional and underused, but two million workers had joined mutual aid societies by 1914. Real wages for urban workers had risen by almost a half since the beginning of the century.

When Étienne Clémentel arrived in his office on his first day as colonial minister in 1905, he gazed at the wall map above his desk with awe. "Les colonies," he sighed. "Je ne savais pas qu'il y en eût tant" ("I had no idea there were so many"). No minister had set foot in a colony in the dozen years since civilians had replaced military men in the post. The first to do so, Clémentel's successor Milliés-Lacroix, who paid Africa a fleeting visit, was thought so eccentric that Clemenceau nicknamed him "le Nègre".

The French empire was grand, and it was growing grander as Clémentel spoke. It was soon to embrace 12 million square kilometres, or almost 10 per cent of the land surface of the planet. Some of it was ancient. The tiny fishing islands of St.-Pierre-et-Miquelon lay off the coast of Newfoundland, the only remnants of Nouvelle France and the first attempt to carve out a colony, in seventeenth-century Canada. Further south, and much larger, were the Caribbean islands of Martinique and Guadeloupe and the South American mainland colony of Guyana. The latter was notorious for the penal settlement at Devil's Island. Martinique was sadder still. On May 8, 1902, a mass of fire swept down from the erupting heights of Mont Pelé onto St Pierre, killing 40,000 and obliterating the town and all but one of the ships in its harbour.

These were mere scraps against the immensity of French North Africa. This centred on Algeria, the first element of the new empire, acquired in the years from 1830 to 1847. To its east, Tunisia was dominated as a protectorate through various treaties, the first in 1881. Westward, Morocco retained its independence, for the moment at least. Though Algeria was heavily French settled, it was still a rough and ready place. A revolt had broken out in July 1900, when five Italians of the Foreign Legion were decapitated and a lieutenant of the Algerian *spahis* was speared to death. "Taxes, injustices and insults," *Le Temps* remarked, "that is about all the natives have." The London *Times* agreed. "The natives pay the majority of the taxes and receive little enough in exchange," it reported. "They are placed in a situation in which they must choose between resignation to utter misery or revolt."

Wilder still, below the Sahara, the bulging coast of West Africa had first been touched by Dieppe sailors in the sixteenth century. Géricault's painting of *The Raft of the Medusa*, which dominated the Salon of 1819 with its cargo of corpses, was based on the wreck of a ship three years before bringing soldiers and administrators to Senegal, just given back to France by the British. French West Africa was ruled from Dakar, given force and substance by the Tirailleurs Sénégalais, light infantry in red fezzes. Colonial types, fiery camel raiders, *pastis*-swilling planters and Foreign Legionnaires in dashing *képis* abounded in French children's comics. The most familiar native image to their parents, however, was probably the *tirailleur* who grinned at them from the cartons of Banania breakfast food. Further south, the small and fever-ridden town of Brazzaville on a pool of the Congo River served as the capital of French Equatorial Africa. The only French possession in East Africa was Djibouti, a strip of gravel and thorns at the entrance to the Red Sea that was dubbed French Somaliland from 1896. Its importance as a port increased after a railway was built through the baking mountains of the interior to Addis Ababa.

French possessions were scattered across the seas between Djibouti and the Pacific. French India, like French Canada, had been done for by the British, with the exception of Pondichery and Chandernagor, but Madagascar remained, if not finally pacified until a brutal skirmishing in 1896. Across the Indian Ocean, a governor-general in a fine palace in Hanoi administered a growing area of Indochina, though policing action against Chinese "Blue Flag" bandits in the north showed conquest to be still provisional, and the north-western corner of Cambodia was not taken from Siam until 1907. Money was made by the rubber planters, if not by the administration as a whole, which was weighed down with too many white *fonctionnaires*. It was made, too, by the Chinese for, as Tunisia was said to be an Italian colony ruled by Frenchmen, so Indochina was to a large extent a French-administered Chinese colony. The scattered possessions of French Oceania, and the islands and atolls of French Polynesia, were more peaceful. The larger territory of New Caledonia had spent much of its brief existence as a penal colony. Paul Gauguin was soon to die in the remote Marquesas, where Herman Melville had set his South Sea idyll, *Typee*, though Gauguin had done most of his painting on Tahiti. Finally, made barren by wind and ice, battered by the huge seas that roam between Cape Horn and Australia, lay uninhabited Kerguelen Island.

The odd crisis apart, the French paid their empire little attention. London proclaimed itself the heart of an empire with a plethora of statues and great buildings, but the only allegory in Paris to the *génie colonial* is a gilded statue of "la France civilatrice" overlooking a busy intersection in the XIIe arrondissement, and that was not sculpted until 1931. Most eyes were set on the *politique de clocher* (church steeple politics) at home, and on the "blue line of the Vosges". The loss of Alsace and Lorraine stirred the blood more than foreign adventures, and Jules Harmand, who defended imperialism with passion in his book *Domination et colonisation* in 1910, confessed that territory was taken either to protect existing colonies or because of "instinct and sentiment more than carefully thought out and debated reasons".

Yet, in spite of the lack of colonial enthusiasm, war with Britain had been narrowly avoided in 1898. The British reconquest of the Sudan from Muslim dervishes that year reopened the question of which power would control a trans-African route: the British on the north–south route from Cairo to Cape Town, or the French on the east–west axis, from Djibouti to Dakar. A key was control of Fashoda (Fachoda in French) on the White Nile. Jean-Baptiste Marchand, a fine soldier and explorer, took a small expedition of 150 officers and men across the fever-ridden, trackless and often swampy terrain between the Congo and the Nile. A relief column was supposedly wending its way to him across Abyssinia from Djibouti, but it proved to be a phantom. Marchand ran up the tricolour in Fashoda on July 10. British troops under

Herbert Kitchener were astonished to find it flying when they arrived on September 18. Europe braced itself for war. Marchand and Kitchener cracked a bottle of champagne and waited amiably for orders. Paris blinked first. Marchand, outnumbered twenty to one, withdrew on November 3. The French recognised British influence throughout the Nile basin. The British accepted French control in the immensity of the Saharan territories north and west of Lake Tchad, much of it yet to be conquered. The task occupied General Laperrine d'Hautpol and his squadrons of *méharistes*, his camel corps, until he was killed in 1920 whilst trying to cross the Sahara by aircraft.

North Africa, and in particular Algeria, was the exception in every sense. Algeria was closer, larger, richer and, above all, more settled by Europeans. By 1914, Algeria had 800,000 whites, all but 100,000 of them French, in a population of 4.8 million Muslims. Tunisia had 200,000 Europeans for 1.7 million Muslims; Morocco almost a 100,000 for 3 million Muslims. Algeria seemed to be a southward extension of France itself, with its three *départements* of Algiers, Constantine and Oran. As for Morocco, once France had decided to absorb it, its first resident general was General Hubert Lyautey. He was a fierce bundle of apparent contradictions, a Catholic monarchist serving an anticlerical republic, small in stature and grandiloquent in ideas, a thoughtful writer who was also a brilliant strategist and administrator, originally given command of the force guarding the Algerian–Moroccan frontier in the Sahara. He developed Casablanca as the fulcrum of French authority after the protectorate was declared in March 1912. By the end of September, he had occupied Marrakech and pushed on towards Algeria, occupying Taza the following May. It was a slow business – the French writ did not run in every corner of Morocco until 1934 – and complex, for this was an ancient state whose sultan was no petty offspring of an Ottoman placeman, like the bey of Tunis, but a descendant of the prophet and the *commandeur des croyants*. Lyautey had served under another great colonial governor, General Joseph Galliéni, whose dictum was to "govern with the Mandarin". He made sure that the sultan was respected, and toured the sharifian cities with him. The French presence was discreet but effective.

Black Africa made little impact; the British had taken the lion's share, the gold and diamond mines. "The numerous ships in our harbour give a little life to our pseudo-city of Dakar," the commandant of Senegal reported flatly, "but commerce is as usual of a hopeless nullity. Absolutely nothing but waffle-vendors." Indochina's well-educated and largely Catholic native elite made some impression in Paris, but it cannot be said that even it greatly occupied the French, for all the limpid beauty of its women and its river landscapes. *Soudanété* ("Sudanness"), a state of lethargy and indolence, ran through the empire. Albert Camus caught it neatly in the opening to *The Plague*: "Treeless, glamourless, soulless, the town of Oran ends up by seeming restful and, after a while, you go complacently to sleep there." The Transindochinois railway linking Hanoi to the south did not reach Hué until 1927 and Saigon until 1936.

For all that, the French injected stability, and hygiene and literacy into their territories. Indochina, for example, was a region long prey to famine, slavery, massacre and epidemics. Local doctors were trained at the Hanoi faculty of medicine. The Institut Pasteur at Nha Trang researched into plague, cholera and malaria. Motives were partly commercial, but idealism was present too. Albert Sarraut, a radical deputy from the Aude, declared that his principle as a governor-general in Indochina would be "the declaration of the rights of man as interpreted by St Vincent de Paul", the saint who had brought comfort to galley slaves and a foundling hospital to Paris two centuries before. Sarraut lived up to his promise to conduct *un exercise loyal et sincère du protectorat*. He sacked corrupt officials, or returned them to France, and required the others to learn Vietnamese, Chinese or Cambodian to a standard where they could do without interpreters. He encouraged education at all levels, financing it by creating state monopolies, or *régies*, in alcohol and salt, and overhauled the university at Hanoi to produce a local though generally Catholic elite.

In principle, at least, the French practised assimilation, in accord with the Revolutionary principle of "a nation one and indivisible". The ideal, as Arthur Girault, a professor at Poitiers, put it, was "an increasingly intimate union between the colonial and the metropolitan territory . . . The colonies are theoretically considered to be a simple extension of the soil of the mother country." Thus France was sometimes declared to be "a nation of 100 million". This was a convenient philosophy, of course. If the *France d'outre-mer* was no different to metropolitan France, give or take the intervening seawater, then there was no rhyme or reason for independence. In the self-confident, pre-war days, a man as left-leaning as Jean Jaurès was happy enough to accept the empire in practice, if he retained a few doubts in principle.

A few of the distant governed did object. A teacher named Ho Chi Minh left Indochina in 1911, to work as a cook on the ships between Hanoi and Marseille, and in a London restaurant. When he arrived in Paris, retouching prints as a photographer's assistant, he joined the French Socialist Party. He did so because its members were sympathetic to him personally, and to oppressed people in general. As yet, however, his ideas had not hardened into national liberation. "I understood neither what was a party," he wrote, "nor a trade union, nor what was socialism or communism." When he did learn, another facet of the French empire became clear: the extreme reluctance of the metropole to part with it.

The first murmurs of a coming cataclysm came out of Africa. It was over Morocco that the French and Germans started eyeing each other's throats again in 1905. The running sore, though, remained the loss of Alsace and Lorraine. Vineyards, forests and mines were gone. More than two million people were missing too, though some had fled the Germans for Paris, including the Dreyfus family, and tens of thousands had gone to Algeria.

"Think of it always," Gambetta said of the annexation. "Speak of it never." This was the motto adopted by Théophile Delcassé, foreign minister. He had been at university in Toulouse, hoping to become a dramatist, when the French armies surrendered at Sedan in 1870, and thereafter devoted himself to undoing the results. The death of the deputy for Foix, near Pamiers, gave Delcassé his chance. He married the rich widow and took her dead husband's seat in the Assembly. He looked to powerful allies for protection against Germany. Bismarck's resignation in 1890 had ended the diplomatic status quo in Europe. It was followed immediately by secret discussions between Russia and France, the two powers most suspicious of German might. Russia's ambitions in the Balkans were thwarted by the alliance of Austria-Hungary, her rival there, with Germany, while France was resentful of her lost provinces. The visit of a French squadron to the great Russian naval port at Kronstadt in July 1891 was the first public sign of this *entente*. The return courtesy visit of a Russian squadron to Toulon was a triumph. When they sailed, the Toulon crowds sang the Russian national anthem to them from the harbourside, renamed the Kronstadt Quay in their honour. The Franco-Russian alliance had followed in 1894. On paper, at least, sheer weight of numbers made the Russians seem invincible. Delcassé was at pains to keep them sweet. He made sure that President Loubet paid flattering attention to Russian exhibits at the 1900 Paris Exposition, taking a simulated trip on the Trans-Siberian Railway, where forests and onion-domed churches slipped past the carriage windows, painted on long canvases mounted on rollers. Loubet visited St Petersburg, and Nicholas II came to Paris.

The love affair between the egalitarian republic and the tsarist autocracy was strange, but real; the young poet Pierre Louÿs caught the fascination in a verse he wrote for his friend Debussy, who idolised Rimsky-Korsakov:

> O Claude-Achille Debussy
> En quel endroit de notre sphère
> Criez-vous: Vive la Russy!
> Comme tout bon Français doit faire?

It was driven by more than the mutual fear of Germany. The Russian aristocracy spoke French, wore French fashions, drank French wine, read French novels, and wintered on the Côte d'Azur. The phrase *la tournée des grands-ducs*, meaning to go on a spree like Russian grand-dukes, remains in the language to this day. It was their tips that enabled the doorman at Maxim's, Gérard, to retire to a château in the Pyrenees. Indeed, Russian revolutionaries shared this taste for things French: Leon Trotsky reminisced that he too read French novels whilst he languished in a tsarist prison, and he headed for Paris when he was exiled, a destination so common amongst his colleagues – Lenin among them – that the Russian secret police, the Okhrana, maintained their only foreign bureau in Paris. For their part, the French were the biggest investors in Russian industry and government bonds. "Russian Fives" figured in most portfolios.

Given that Germany would enjoy Austro-Hungarian and, it seemed then, Italian support in a new war, Delcassé looked to hedge his bets with a second ally. The British seemed ruled out, at least in 1900, by French hostility to the Boer War. The Fashoda Incident of 1898 also still grated. Then the obstacles to a cross-Channel rapprochement tumbled. Early in 1901 Queen Victoria died. The Kaiser's grandmother, and the widow of a German prince, she was not unsympathetic to the Reich, whereas her son Edward VII was a Francophile. The new king had loved France, and French actresses, since visiting Empress Eugénie's court as the 14-year-old Prince of Wales. When the Boer War ended in 1902, the British were also looking for a Continental ally, prepared to abandon their stance of "glorious isolation" from Europe. They saw the preservation of their empire as the main task of the coming century, and a friend might help.

France was the traditional enemy of many centuries standing, of course, and the Germans were a more likely partner. But they had begun building a large blue-water navy, a threat to which the islanders were hypersensitive, and they had begun acquiring their own empire. They had no interest in giving British imperialism a free hand, whereas the French already had colossal colonial holdings, and were looking thirstily for more in north-west Africa, a region of no interest to London.

The long-term implications of Delcassé's manoeuvres were immense. His colleagues did not realise this, and he did little to enlighten them. He was nicknamed "the gnome", and he was deeply secretive, working closely with the Cambon brothers, Paul, mastermind of the Tunisian protectorate and now ambassador to London, and Jules, former governor-general of Algeria and now Madrid ambassador, men of high quality. Backing came from the French Africa Committee, a powerful parliamentary lobby financed by banks, shipping lines and other interested parties, including the prospering Alsace-Lorrainers who had settled in Algeria. It was headed by Eugène-Napoléon Étienne, the burly deputy for Oran.

The first approach to London was made through Paul Cambon. The ambassador suggested that, in return for French friendship and recognition of British influence in Egypt, the British should give France carte blanche in Morocco. Something similar had happened in 1878, when Lord Salisbury as much as told the French that Britain would raise no objections to anything they might do in Tunisia if the French raised none over Britain's acquisition of Cyprus from the Ottoman Empire. The Moroccan deal, however, posed something of a problem. The independence of Morocco as a sovereign nation had been formally guaranteed at Madrid in 1880 by Germany, France, Britain and Spain, who had further agreed that commerce with the sultanate should be open to all comers. The British cabinet turned down Cambon's proposal. But Edward VII and Lord Lansdowne, the equally Francophile foreign secretary, were intrigued by the idea. The king was in a position to further it.

Portly and dashing, with a twinkle in his eye and a carnation in his buttonhole, he paid a state visit to Paris in May 1903. He spoke fluent French, and he had a friendly and sympathetic air. At the theatre, the old lecher kissed the hand of the actress Jeanne Grainer and told her: "I remember applauding you in London, Mademoiselle, where you represented all the grace and spirit of France." He said this in the foyer, and it whizzed round the theatre. When he returned to his box, the audience stood to cheer him. Another brilliant piece of public relations followed at the Hôtel de Ville. "I shall never forget my visit to your charming city," he said, "where I always feel as though I am at home." This, too, buzzed along the grapevine, and when he left the crowds cheered him: "Vive notre bon Teddy!" The warmth was real. When he died, Paris hackney drivers tied black bows on their whips.

London did not want Germany acquiring overseas ports, and Morocco had harbours on both the Atlantic and Mediterranean. Lansdowne indicated to Paul Cambon that he was willing to negotiate. Despite warnings, Delcassé did not discuss Morocco directly with Berlin. The Anglo-French convention was signed on April 8, 1904. It claimed that France had no desire to change the independent status of Morocco. She had Algerian territory bordering on Morocco, however, and the British agreed that France had an interest "to preserve order in [Morocco] and to provide assistance for the purpose of all administrative, economic, financial and military reforms which it may require." This was, of course, the imperial-speak formula for immediate commercial and ultimate military domination.

Delcassé moved fast. In June, French banks arranged a 62.5 million franc loan guaranteed by Moroccan customs duties, collection of which, independent state or not, was supervised by French officials. It was crystal clear what the terms of the loan meant. "It was my task to get the Sultan to swallow, without pain or at least without protest," wrote the comte de Saint-Aulaire, the diplomat in place, "an accord which signified the loss of his independence." By December, Delcassé had instructed Saint-René Taillandier, the French resident in Fez, to establish a French-run state bank, to begin a railway building programme, and to institute political reforms. Taillandier announced these "reforms" to the assembly of Moroccan notables. He claimed that they had the approval of the representatives of the other great powers in Tangiers. This was not so. The Germans had not been told, and Berlin was a signatory of the Madrid Convention that had guaranteed Morocco against the sleight of hand now being practised by the French.

The Entente Cordiale nonetheless now existed, though the Anglo-French Convention of 1904 was the only published declaration of the new friendship. An agreement signed by the two powers also stated that, in the event of the collapse of the sultan's authority, the part of Morocco opposite Gibraltar should be ceded to Spain. But this was kept secret. Secret, too, was a second treaty negotiated by the invisible Delcassé, this time with Madrid. It gave France four-fifths of Morocco and Spain the remainder if the sultanate was wound up.

Hearing of Taillandier's speech in Fez, the German chancellor, Prince Bernhard von Bülow, reacted with fury. He sent a message to the Kaiser, who was cruising aboard the imperial yacht *Hamburg*, asking him to land at Tangier and ride ostentatiously to the German legation – so that all would know of his imperial presence – and make it clear that Delcassé had been foolish to ignore Germany. Wilhelm agreed to do so, with some displeasure since he preferred being at sea. He stressed that he was visiting the sultan "as an independent ruler" of a "free Morocco" that he trusted would be open to all nations. Fretful stirrings came from the new partners, who guessed correctly that Bülow was trying to break up their new romance. *The Times* in London accused the Kaiser of a provocative act intended to bully the French out of the entente. The French press made much of Wilhelm going ashore with sword and cavalry boots, and accused him of "sabre-rattling" and insulting the French *mission civilatrice* in Africa.

But Delcassé had overstretched himself. Maurice Rouvier, the prime minister, was a cautious banker who did not wish to upset Berlin too vigorously. Wilhelm had called for an international conference to debate Morocco. Delcassé was opposed to it. Rouvier insisted. Delcassé resigned in June 1905, his reputation unblemished as the great patriot sacrificed to appease Berlin. In the event, though, Delcassé had his revenge. The conference was held at Algeciras in the first months of 1906. Germany was backed only by Austria-Hungary and Turkey. The French, supported by Russia, Britain, Spain and Italy, agreed to a few face-saving phrases, but were essentially left free to swell their influence in Morocco as it suited them. Thus was propagated the German notion of *Feinde ringsum*, of "enemies all around", with France, Russia and now Britain forming a malevolent circle around the Reich. It was highly dangerous, for a natural response to being trapped within a hostile ring is to lash out, but Morocco helped make that reaction understandable.

The Russians, however, were not all they seemed. In 1905, they were savaged on land in a brutal war against Japan. At sea, they lost the best part of a fleet in the worst naval disaster since Trafalgar. At home, revolution and near civil war threatened to bring down the autocracy. "Bloody Sunday", the day early in the year when troops opened fire on unarmed demonstrators outside the Winter Palace, had shown tsardom to be a strange bedfellow for a democratic republic.

The crisis passed. To keep the rouble and the Russian bond market afloat, French bankers were keen to give the country the best possible image. The Russian impresario Serge Diaghilev and France both benefited immensely from this interest. Diaghilev arrived in Paris in 1908, and within three weeks he met the great patroness Élisabeth de Greffulhe, to the mortification of Marcel Proust, who had waited three years for an invitation. Diaghilev wanted her and her husband to put up the 250,000 francs needed to transport an 80-strong ballet company from St Petersburg. Impressed by listening to him playing piano pieces "by Russian composers [they'd] never heard of", the de Greffulhes agreed to put together a consortium. It included

Basil Zaharoff, the "merchant of death", financier and arms supplier, the banker Henri de Rothschild, and the oil tycoon and aviation enthusiast Henri Deutsch de la Meurthe.

Ballet was in a sorry state in France. Women often danced male roles, and the few male dancers were so scorned as mere props for the ballerinas that a wag suggested they be replaced by bus conductors at three francs a night. Diaghilev was extravagant and painstaking. He commissioned the music and sets, and tracked down young Jean Cocteau to design the programmes. He brought back male dancers, handpicking the corps de ballet, too, and he used the finest choreographers, dancers, artists and composers: Fokine, Nijinsky, Balanchine, Massine, Picasso, Roussel, Satie, Stravinsky. Rich French talent helped build his Ballets Russes. He staged *Prélude à l'après-midi d'un faune* to Debussy's score, and Maurice Ravel wrote the score for his *Daphnis et Chloë*. In 1913 Nijinsky dancing in Stravinsky's *Rite of Spring* caused a riot on the first night in Paris, and his choreography had to be changed after a few performances to avoid further protests.

As artistic partners, the Russians proved compelling and long-lasting enough; but their fragility as military allies had been exposed. Britain, too, though an industrial and naval powerhouse, showed no signs whatever of raising an army large enough to count in a European war. The Peninsula and Waterloo were forgotten. It was admirals, not generals, who had the spending power across the Channel.

In 1911 there had been a reprise of the earlier Moroccan crisis. The Germans claimed the terms of the 1906 treaty of Algeciras were being ignored and they sent their gunboat *Panther* into Agadir harbour. Negotiations nearly broke down in September and Europe seemed posed on the brink of war, until the Germans backed down in return for a slice of the French Congo. In France itself, a distinct and, to the patriotic bourgeoisie, unpleasant internationalist and pacifist tang that seemed to bode ill in time of war was attached to the left. The anti-patriotic and anti-militarist element condemned the decision to extend conscription from two to three years in 1913. The CGT formally resolved that its members would not fight if war broke out. Jean Jaurès bitterly opposed the pact with reactionary, feudal and unstable Russia. He pinned his hopes on an accord between French and German socialists never to make war on each other. There were concerns, too, at the lack of industrial might. French investors were cautious, preferring the predictable income from bonds to the risks of holding equities. It was expensive for companies to raise money, and medium and small-sized family companies took precedence over the huge combines that marked German, British and American industry, which France now trailed. The very rich existed – the top 1 per cent had a 20 per cent share of national income – but in fewer numbers than in other industrialised countries.

The storm began to stir on the last Sunday of June in 1914. A young Serb threw a bomb at the motorcade in which the Archduke Franz Ferdinand, heir to the throne of Austria-Hungary, was being driven to lunch through the streets of Sarajevo in

Bosnia. The terrorist wanted the Austrians out of Bosnia, so that it could join Serbia. The bomb hit the back of the archduke's automobile and bounced off. He was not so lucky after lunch. Another Serb fired into the car: the dying archduke sat upright as his murdered wife fell across him, crying "Sopherl! Sopherl! Don't die. Live for our children!" This outrage was terrible enough, but it needed diplomatic incompetence and nationalist neurosis to then bring on the Great War.

Austria sent an ultimatum to the Serbs. The Russians, traditional protectors of their fellow Orthodox Slavs, growled with displeasure. The Germans warned St Petersburg not to go too far against their Austrian allies. A lethal game of alliances was now under way: Russia had to stand by Serbia, and France had to stand by Russia.

The French had no war aims beyond the recovery of Alsace and Lorraine. The Germans had already decided what they wanted: the further annexation from France of Briey, Longwy, Belfort, the western slope of the Vosges, and the French coast as far west as Boulogne; the annexation of Luxembourg and the subjugation of Belgium; the establishment of a European customs union, dominated by Germany and including France, Belgium, Holland, Denmark and Austria-Hungary; and the seizure of French and Belgian colonies in Africa. This great shopping list was drawn up because it seemed illogical to the Germans not to have one, but they went to war out of a frame of mind as well as policy. The peace had survived tensions before – in Morocco in 1905, at Agadir in 1911, in the Balkans in 1908, 1912 and 1913 – and the murder of an Austrian archduke did not cause war. A feeling, an intensity of nationalism, did.

"To be or not to be," Clemenceau had warned in 1905, "that is the problem which an implacable desire for supremacy poses for the first time since the Hundred Years War." He meant, of course, a German desire. The Germans naturally did not see it like that, and they quoted Hamlet, too. Wilhelm II complained in 1912 that other nations hated his, and that this antagonism was "not a question of high politics, but one of *race* . . . What is at issue is whether the German race is to be or not to be in Europe." That old obsession, of a *Deutschland gänzlich einzukreisen*, a Germany "totally surrounded", was driving events.

On July 16, President Poincaré and the prime minister, René Viviani, the old hammer of the clergy, set off from Dunkirk on the battleship *France* for a long-planned official visit to Russia. Waiting aboard the imperial yacht, Nicholas II told the French ambassador, Maurice Paléologue, that the Kaiser did not want war. "If you knew him as I do!" he said. "If you knew how much theatricality there is in his posing!" As the *France* steamed in, shore batteries fired salutes that merged with the thunder of the "Marseillaise".

A state banquet was held at the Peterhof Palace. The army, the great counter-weight to Germany, went through its paces at the annual summer review. The chatter among the assembled wives was of Paris fashions – wider skirts and no sleeves – and of the meaning of the elaborate military displays. "I wonder after all what an army is for," one said. "It's so immense, isn't it?" An officer replied. "Just a toy for kings and emperors to play with, Madame," he said. "Rather dangerous toys," she replied. The visit was relaxed. Poincaré thought war so dim a prospect that he prepared to leave for Sweden on another state visit. A telegram from Paris, however, urged him to cancel it. After four days, the *France* and its escorts sped westward, their wakes sparkling on calm and moonlit waters. Whilst they were still at sea, on July 28, Austria-Hungary declared war on Serbia. The following day, as they reached Dunkirk, Russia began partial mobilisation. The gathering of these vast conscript armies involved highly complex railway scheduling. Once a mobilisation was under way, it was difficult to reverse.

It was feared that French dissidents would call for strikes and marches against mobilisation. Pacifist deputies had parliamentary immunity. The leaders of the anti-militarist, anti-nationalist CGT did not. Their names appeared on Carnet B, a police list of dangerous troublemakers to be picked up in case of war. On the evening of July 29, warned of their imminent arrest by a story in *L'Intransigeant*, most of the union bigwigs fled to the houses of friends who were not on police files. On July 30, Russia mobilised fully.

The great advocate of peace, even at this desperate stage, was Jean Jaurès. He had urged a special socialist congress to use a general strike as a tactic against war. His contacts with German socialists convinced him that they would bring the railways to a halt rather than allow their comrades to be mobilised. For this, and for his criticisms of the tsarist autocracy, far-right newspapers attacked him as a traitor and German agent. A disturbed young man, Raoul Villain, took this nonsense for truth. On July 31, Jaurès denounced Russia for warmongering. That evening, Villain assassinated him at the Café de Commerce. Frantic with worry, the Paris police chief awaited an uprising. None came. At 1 a.m. on August 1, the interior minister Jean-Louis Malvy sent a telegram to prefects ordering no Carnet B arrests. His informers in the unions assured him that there would be no hindrances to mobilisation. The same day, Germany and Russia were at war.

France, committed to Russia, mobilised that day. She was perilously isolated. In London, 12 out of 18 cabinet ministers declared that they were against giving France any assurance of support in the event of war. The Entente Cordiale was a rapprochement, not a formal pact that obliged Britain to go to war if France was attacked. Winston Churchill, First Lord of the Admiralty, was alone in demanding that the fleet be mobilised. His request was denied. Germany declared war on France on August 3. Britain stayed out. She must not "run away from these obligations of honour and interest", said Sir Edward Grey, the foreign secretary. But she needed an excuse: the invasion of Belgium would suffice, since the British had been formally committed to defend Belgium since 1839. Early in the morning of August 4, Uhlans crossed the border into Belgium. London sent an ultimatum to Berlin, which expired at midnight.

Jaurès was buried that day. Speaking in front of the coffin, the CGT leader Léon Jouhaux said that he supported what was a war for republican liberty and justice against the tyrannies of the central powers. The German invasion gave the French left the moral basis to take part in the *union sacrée*, the great political coalition that represented the wartime unity of the French people. Jouhaux promised that the working class would do its duty. It did. In the evening, a mob of Berliners stoned the British embassy. "Rassenverrat!" they screamed. It was "race treason" for Britain's Anglo-Saxons to war with their Germanic cousins. All the elements were in place. The French expected much of the Russian steamroller, but there was little comfort closer at hand. The Belgian army was once a force to be reckoned with, a fifth the size of the French. That was in 1840. In 1914, it had a mere 200,000 men with 120 machine guns and no heavy artillery. Its Francophone officers, too, often got on with the Flemish rank and file no better than the Austrians with the Czechs. The British army was a seven-division midget compared to the Germans' 98 divisions. Sir Henry Wilson, then director of military operations, snorted when it was suggested that the part-time reservists of the Territorial Army could be shipped to France. "What amazing ignorance of war!" he said. "No officers, no transport, no mobility, no compulsion to go, no discipline, obsolete guns, no horses." A larger British army – the saying was that the existing seven divisions were "fifty too few" – might have dissuaded the Germans from attacking France at all. On August 8, just 80,000 men sailed for France, two corps to set against the German 1st Army of 320,000 men.

Where the British were strong was at sea. The Royal Navy was more than double the size of the German fleet. It could blockade Germany and begin to starve it; eventually it did, but this was inevitably a very long-term solution. Until it did, the French would have to rely on the distant Russians and on themselves. It was as well that they were the most militarised nation on earth. Eighty-five per cent of Frenchmen of military age were trained, as against only one in two Germans and Austro-Hungarians. The French army had 816,000 men before mobilisation of reserves, and 3.5 million after, the Germans 800,646 and 3.8 million. The German population, though, was 60 per cent greater.

There was no great appetite for the war. Young men in Paris and the big cities flung their hats in the air, and predominantly bourgeois onlookers cheered them, as in Berlin and St Petersburg, but such displays of patriotism were urban and fitful. The replies to questionnaires sent out by the education ministry told a very different story. The majority of the 300 *communes* surveyed in the Charente reported that the reaction to mobilisation was "stupefaction" followed by "surprise". The general response was negative in well over half the *communes*, and "calm and composed" in a fifth of cases. Less than a quarter manifested any patriotic fervour. The overriding sentiment was defensive. "France did not want war; she was attacked; we shall do our duty": this was the typical response.

A young lieutenant, Charles de Gaulle, caught the essence of the conflict at its outset. "What is this war, but a war of extermination?" he wrote to his mother. A man he would meet many years later, Winston Churchill, already a British government minister, was of the same mind. "This is no ordinary war," he wrote two months into the conflict, "but a struggle between nations of life or death. It raises tensions between races of the most horrible kind."

A tremendous solidarity swept the country. Clemenceau, the fiery anticlerical, kissed an abbé on both cheeks; the anti-militarist and anti-authority Anatole France tried to enlist at 70. There were few *embusqués* (shirkers), though among them was Gide's young publisher friend, Gaston Gallimard, who claimed to be ill with such fervour that he eventually became so. Braque rejoined his regiment. Matisse returned to Paris from the south but at 45 was declared too old to fight. Raoul Dufy drove a van for the army postal service. Lieutenant Charles Péguy, aged 41, was soon killed at the front; so was Henri Alain-Fournier, at 28 with only his great magical novel of adolescence, *Le Grand Meaulnes*, under his belt. Dreyfus's son Pierre fought in the first battles as a corporal, and ended the war as a captain; his father, repeatedly volunteering for the front, eventually took part as a gunner.

The troops were fed into Plan XVII, the *attaque brusquée* on Alsace-Lorraine devised by the chief of staff, Joseph Joffre, and agreed in May 1913. It took as gospel the adage that attack – by cavalry charge and close-order assault by infantry with fixed bayonets – was the best form of defence. It accepted the claim made by the artillery expert Hippolyte Langlois that the steady growth in the power of artillery "always facilitates the attack". A doctrine of *élan* was bred by the École de Guerre. "It is always necessary in battle", said Colonel de Grandmaison of the General Staff, "to do something that would be impossible for men in cold blood. Like marching under fire. That is only possible for men in a state of high excitement against men with low morale." Even the independent-minded young Charles de Gaulle, fresh from training at St Cyr, believed it. "Everywhere, always, one should have a single idea," he wrote. "To advance. As soon as the fighting starts everyone in the French army, the generals in command, the officers and the men have only one thing in their heads – advance, advancing to the attack, reaching the Germans, and running them through or making them run away."

An essential part of this formula – "reaching the Germans" – was usually impossible. They had 105- and 155-millimetre mobile artillery that outranged the excellent French 75s. Nonetheless, Plan XVII foresaw a quick victory won by a two-pronged attack on the German centre in Lorraine and north of Verdun. This would coincide with a big Russian attack on the sixteenth day of their mobilisation. Pummelled in the east, defeated in the west, the Germans would be forced to seek peace. Even on paper, this looks optimistic. In practice, it was worse. The terrain chosen for the assault was difficult, and German strength was badly underestimated. French intelligence allowed for 46 enemy divisions, where in fact they had 68, thanks to the mobilisation of their reserves.

The German military feared a prolonged campaign in the east against the Russians, and they planned for the French to be over and done with inside six weeks. The Schlieffen Plan aimed at a knockout blow – *Verbanquespiel* (going for broke) –

in the west. Count Schlieffen thought the French defence line from Belfort to Verdun to be impenetrable. It was thus to be sidestepped by an assault through Belgium, to be followed by a vast right-wheel flanking movement that would sweep south around Paris in a great arc that would encircle the enemy armies. *Vernichtung*, the annihilation of French forces, should be achieved in less than two months.

Helmuth Moltke, the chief of the general staff who tuned the Schlieffen Plan, had his doubts. He feared that the French campaign "cannot be won in one decisive battle, but will turn into a long and tedious struggle with a country that will not give up before the strength of its entire people has been broken". As he let loose the German offensive in August, he said that it meant "the mutual tearing to pieces by Europe's civilised nations . . . [and] . . . the destruction of civilisation in almost all Europe for decades to come."

Gott Mit Uns (God with us), it said on German belt buckles, and for the first month, so it seemed. One and a half million Germans crossed the Belgian border in the first days of August. By August 16, they were cutting across the Belgian plain. General Alexander von Kluck's 1st Army passed through Brussels on the 20th, and headed on to France. Joffre stuck doggedly to Plan XVII. If the Germans were strong in the north, they must be weak elsewhere. He attacked in Lorraine. When that failed, he struck further north. It was a massacre. The French cuirassiers wore shining breastplates that caught the enemy eye at a distance and did nothing to stop a bullet. The infantrymen were in red trousers – "le pantalon rouge, c'est la France" a pre-war minister of war had said – and blue jackets. They had no helmets, only kepis. The officers wore full uniform, some even white gloves. Their Saint-Etienne machine guns were fragile and jammed, and they had too few *crapouillots* (trench mortars). They fell back on the Meuse.

The "Old Contemptibles" of the British Expeditionary Force, raw off the cross-Channel ferries, checked but could not halt Kluck's advance among the bloodstained slagheaps of Mons. Kluck pressed on to within 50 kilometres of Paris. Memories of the siege of 1870 ensured a mass exodus. Joffre stayed calm. He read the crisis well: it would be best to abandon Paris and to concentrate his armies in the east. Joseph Gallieni, a veteran of 1870, and of campaigns in Africa and Tonkin, began organising the defence of the capital with scratch troops.

Mistakes now crept into the German side. The Russians had broken through into East Prussia. General Samsonov took the small town of Allenstein. His men thought themselves in Berlin and cheered. They were not. The Germans counter-attacked in the forests and sandy tracts. Samsonov lost 110,000 men in four days before shooting himself in shame. But the fear his brief foray aroused reached Moltke in the west. He transferred two corps from his right flank to the east, badly diluting German strength in a key position. So did Kluck. He was ordered to beseige Paris by moving south-west. He could not resist driving south-east to try and encircle the bulk of French forces.

On September 3, Gallieni saw from aerial reconnaissance that the Germans were swinging for the Marne east of Paris. "They offer us their flank!" he cried in relief. He ordered the French 6th Army to attack Kluck's right flank. What was more, by advancing more rapidly than Karl von Bülow's German 2nd Army, Kluck was exposing his left flank to the British, who had retreated exhausted but in good order between Mormant and Tournon. The allies now had 56 divisions in place to the Germans' 40. Gallieni persuaded Joffre to counter-attack, who in turn won over the British. If ever a man deserved to have a Métro station named after him, it is surely Joseph Simon Gallieni; perhaps poor Alexander Samsonov, whose sacrifice was so sweetly timed, should have earned one too.

Joffre requisitioned a thousand of the Renault brothers' little red taxis to speed volunteers to the Marne. "Soldiers! Your country's survival waits upon the outcome of this battle," Joffre told them and his words were flat fact. "Retreat would be unforgivable!" Gallieni, who had the idea of using taxis, was more laconic: "Eh bien, voilà au moins qui n'est pas banal" ("Oh well, at least it's not boring"). By September 6, the whole weight of the French army and the BEF had been thrown into the attack. The decisive day was September 8, when Louis Franchet d'Espérey's French 5th Army sliced through the gap between Kluck and Bülow at Ourcq, forcing a general retreat of the German right flank. On the left, the Germans tried hard to break through, and the French 3rd Army was in desperate straits near Verdun, but it hung on. Moltke admitted the game was up on September 10. He ordered a general withdrawal.

The Marne was a war-saving epic of nerve and good generalship, but it was not a war winner. The French and British had given almost their all. They were too dog-tired, and short of munitions, to win the "race to the sea", as each side tried to outflank the other in reaching the Channel. The Germans were able to dig in, on the hills of Champagne, on the Chemin des Dames and the old quarries of the Soissonnais, in well-sited positions on good ground. By Christmas 1914, a double line of trenches ran from Switzerland to the sea, over a distance of more than 700 kilometres. More than a tenth of French territory found itself on the German side of the line.

The war of movement was over. Attacking across open country against field artillery, machine guns and rifles capable of firing eighteen rounds a minute had proved a futile business. "All day they lie there," an officer wrote of the early slaughter, "being decimated, getting themselves killed next to the bodies of those killed earlier." The losses among French soldiers at the start of the war was unmatched by anything that was to come. In the first 45 days of the war, with 3.7 million men mobilised, the French lost 600,000, killed, wounded, missing or taken prisoner. In the first two and a half months, the known French dead reached 329,000. These figures are beyond comparison.

Adieu la Vie,
Adieu l'Amour

The losses of 1914 were masked by propaganda, but not wholly hidden. Too many refugees poured out of the German-occupied zone for that. "A dreadful cavalcade of old men and little children, wearing slippers and weighed down with bundles," an onlooker wrote. "An antheap changing its quarters." Panic was sown deliberately by the Germans – ancient and much-loved buildings destroyed, hostages taken and sometimes shot, houses set on fire – to persuade the elderly and women and children to flee. The more who left for free France, the fewer had to be fed.

Some 2.5 million people were left in the ten *départements* that were wholly or partly behind the German lines. The Alsatians and the Lorrainers were now joined by people from the Aisne, Nord and Marne. Towns like Lille, Lens, Valenciennes, Cambrai, St Quentin, Laon and Sedan shared the fate of Strasbourg. The modern *départements* of Meurthe-et-Moselle, Meuse and the Vosges, which had stayed French in 1870, were considered to be part of the Reich. But the Germans were suspicious of the whole region. Soldiers from here drafted into the German army were considered potential "enemies within" and were often sent to fight on the Russian front, and hundreds of prominent citizens – councillors, mayors and priests – were kept as hostages.

The north had been the industrial heartland. Four-fifths of pre-war steelmaking capacity was gone, and nine-tenths of textiles. Coal and electricity output was halved. Lille in July 1914 was a thriving city of half a million which, with the surrounding towns, Roubaix, Tourcoing, Croix, produced almost a fifth of the world's textiles. By September, it was a ghost town. All the men in the city aged between 20 and 48 were ordered to leave for Dunkirk at the beginning of the month. A vast throng departed for the coast. The city came under shellfire. Early in October, it was declared a "ville ouverte", abandoned to the enemy.

A baker of Péronne, a market town on the Somme, recorded the shock of falling to the enemy. Henri Douchet was wakened on a September morning at 5 a.m. by shells whistling overhead. The "desperate silence" that then fell on the town gave way to "an indefinable murmur . . . pierced by the sharp note of a trumpet sounding a few notes in a sad minor key . . . The noise grew, became overwhelming." The Germans had got into the northern suburbs, where they shot three women crossing the street. The troops had been fed stories of the *francs tireurs* guerrillas of the 1870 campaign, and the unarmed civilians they shot were always described as "snipers". At 5.30 a.m., Douchet reported, "An enormous wave, a tide of grey men shouting and waving, rushed into the town square. A simple-minded man was shot. Looting began, and the first fires. General von Arnim's 4th Army Corps had arrived."

There was a display of defiance – the mayor and his councillors and the local judge refused the German demand to lower the tricolour flying over the town hall, and the furious enemy tore it down – and then there followed the "long silence", the four years of occupation.

The Germans seized food from the outset. Pigs, beef, chicken, wine, hay, straw, corn, carts, harnesses and horses were taken from the farms. Detailed counts were made of livestock. No animal could be slaughtered or sold without permission. The Germans insisted that wild rabbits should be counted, and their skins and meat accounted for; it took some time for them to accept the impracticality of this order. In one typical *commune*, Le Cateau-Cambrésis, the German *Commandatur* demanded to be supplied with coal, butter, cheese, wheat, vegetables, and 140 pounds of beef and four sheep a day. At Christmas, the Germans took extra turkeys, geese, ducks and chickens. They demanded wine, and a dozen wreaths for monuments to fallen German soldiers. There was no bell ringing and no midnight mass. A 6 p.m. curfew was in force.

Hunger was universal. An average Lillois had eaten 600 grams of bread a day before the war. The Germans slashed the ration to 108 grams of poor-quality rye a day for adults and 70 for children. People did what they could to get by, of course. They hid grain and ground it in coffee mills and cattlefeed grinders. They falsified livestock lists and kept animals secretly. When German troops arrived as just such an off-record pig was being slaughtered, it was disguised as a dying grandparent, tenderly swathed in shawls and blankets, as sobbing relatives knelt beside it.

Starvation was nonetheless imminent by the spring of 1915. The American-led and largely Anglo-American-supplied Commission for Relief in Belgium offered to send food supplies to occupied France at this critical moment. The CRB was an extraordinary institution, galvanised by the energy of its chairman, Herbert Hoover. It was founded in October 1914 to aid the civilians of all nations at war. It had a fleet of ships and barges. Itself neutral, it signed agreements with combatants. By March 1915, it was shipping almost 100,000 tons of food a month to Belgium. Hoover declared that the CRB could "handle two million French people." The French government was reluctant – understandably so, since it was Germany's responsibility to feed those in the lands she had occupied – but at length agreed. The first great shipments of wheat, beans, rice, bacon, dried fish, condensed milk, cooking oil, rice and maize arrived in Valenciennes and Lille in April 1915. Britain and her empire, notably Canada, Australia and New Zealand, supplied 49 per cent of supplies, and the Americans 42 per cent, with much of the remainder coming from the Netherlands.

The system suited the Germans handsomely, of course. They plundered northern France of its food, and let the British and the Americans keep the French alive. Literally so. By January 1916, Lille had no potatoes, butter and eggs, and almost no vegetables or milk. The system was disrupted when the Germans began unrestricted submarine warfare, torpedoing the CRB ship *Euphrates* early in 1917 despite her German safe-conduct pass. The ships had now to be routed round the north of Scotland. But they still sailed. "Occupied France can be seen from all aspects as a vast concentration camp," Hoover said, "in which all forms of economic life are entirely suspended." He negotiated hard to ensure that relief continued after the United States entered the war.

"The Germans took everything," a French survey recorded after the war, "leaving only just enough to keep from starving to death those whom they forced to work for them." CRB supplies saved the rest from a hunger caused not by the war itself, for occupied France could have fed itself if allowed to, but by the pattern of depredation practised by the Germans.

Household goods, too, were "requisitioned", the official word for plunder. The objects taken from a house in Avesnes in early November 1914 set a pattern: inkwells, a broom, two lavatory buckets, two coffee pots, eight coffee spoons and sets of table silver and crockery, three forks, a coffee mill and two lamps. The occupiers were like light-fingered newly-weds, setting up home with stolen dressing tables, fur coats, armchairs, curtains, carpets, washstands, bicycles, barometers, pianos, even galoshes. By the end of 1916, Lille had no leather, and virtually no paper or personal linen. Only those aged 65 and over were allowed to keep their mattresses. The rest slept on bare bedsteads or on the floor. The men who inspected households to prepare inventories for requisitioning were perhaps the most despised of all the German forces. *Caporal Voleur* (Corporal Thief), the French called them, or *Monsieur Il Faut* (Mr You Must) or *Monsieur Fouine* (Mr Ferret).

Industries disappeared, too. "Every form of production which made the name of the city famous throughout the world," it was sadly remarked in Lille, "the fruits of its labour and the mark of its skill, disappeared bit by bit." In one textile factory, an up-to-the-minute machine was dismantled and taken to Germany. All 315 remaining looms were broken up with heavy hammers, a laborious task at the rate of six a day. Fifty or sixty explosions a day rocked the town, as civilians and prisoners under armed guard placed charges in workshops of all sorts. The great steelworks in Denain were destroyed. They had employed 4,000 men before the war.

This abnormal urge to destroy, this lust to force the enemy back into the dark ages, revealed a deep strain of malice that proved counterproductive. The Germans knew that word of their behaviour would get out. They themselves encouraged the flow of refugees – women, children, old people and those too ill to work, of course, not fit males of military age – who took the news to free France. No doubt they hoped that this would breed fear and defeatism. It had, in an indefinable but concrete way, quite the opposite effect. It persuaded the French that they were indeed fighting a war for national survival, and that the Germans wished to destroy them as a civilised and skilful people. It fostered the will to survive, and French fighting spirit.

The myriad of regulations in occupied France encouraged this fierce resistance among those who remained free. All clocks were set on German time. Doors had to be left unlocked night and day so that German soldiers could take shelter from shelling, even many miles from the front. Identity cards had to be carried at all times.

It was forbidden to bicycle without a permit. Travel between *communes* was forbidden without specific permission. Civilians were obliged on pain of arrest to take off their hats and remove their hands from their pockets when they passed a German officer. A man in Péronne took to carrying an empty suitcase in each hand to avoid this humiliation. The street names in Le Nouvion, in another petty irritation, were changed into German, so that the avenue de la Gare became Bahnhofstrasse. The inhabitants of Bucquoy, near Bapaume, were obliged to parade at 5 a.m. When insolence was suspected, the *commune* was called out at 1 a.m. A man of 93 who asked to be allowed to stay in bed was dragged out into the street by troops who told him that "fresh air is good for the dying". The parades had "no serious purpose", a sufferer remarked. "They took place solely to annoy." Men of mobilisable age, from seventeen to 50, and sometimes 60, had to report regularly to show that they had not escaped to free France. Some were sent to Germany to work. A third of the men in Douai were transported, and the male population of Chaulnes fell from 300 to 17. The official newspapers were German-controlled, but clandestine newssheets were printed with news gleaned from illicit radio sets.

Those who defied the Germans by keeping pigeons paid a terrible price. Northeastern France was grand pigeon fancier country. The men made up for the dirt and dark and heat of the steelworks and the mines by breeding birds that raced through the unfettered air. Lest they be used to carry messages, the Germans ordered that all of them be killed. Aline Carpentier recorded that her neighbours had handed over their pigeons as demanded; but when two or three birds later found their way back to the loft, they kept them. They were denounced to the Germans. Friends volunteered to pay a large voluntary fine. Without further ado, however, without trial and without charges being made, the Germans marched the pigeon fanciers to the main square and shot them.

Others undertook the perilous task of helping Allied soldiers and airmen to escape. A widow of great character in Lille, Marie-Jeanne Dentant, set up an escape network with a businessman, Georges Maertens, a territorial officer, Ernest Deconinck, and the wine broker Eugene Jacquet. A French officer on the run, Major Caron, also helped, together with the prefect, Félix Trépont, and Lille's deputy finance officer, Émile Vermeersch. By March 1915, when Caron escaped through Belgium to Holland, the network was helping at least two hundred men. Escapees were sent close to the Belgian border where local guides (*passeurs*) helped them slip over the frontier.

A very tall and rather infantile British pilot, Robert Mapplebeck, lost his engine and made a forced landing near Lille on March 11, 1915. He was handed to the escape group and was smuggled over the border. He was back with his squadron within a few days. Mapplebeck then flew over Lille and did some aerobatics to thank the citizens for his escape. He also dropped a letter attached to a long tricolour. It was marked for the attention of the German military governor, General von Heinrich.

It read: "12 April 1915. Lieutenant Mapplebeck presents his respects to the commandant of German forces in Lille and regrets that he was unable to make his acquaintance during his agreeable visit near Lille."

It was folly thus to goad the Germans. Mapplebeck had written a note about his few hours in the city which he had left in Jacquet's house. An informer, Louis Richard, betrayed the network to the Germans. Jacquet and his family were arrested, and Mapplebeck's incriminating manuscript was found stuffed down the side of an armchair. It told of his crash landing, and it named Jacquet and his wife, and Maertens, Deconinck and Sylvene Verhulst as helpers.

Twenty-seven men were arrested and locked up in the Lille citadel. Jacquet bravely claimed that he alone was responsible. He was sentenced to death with the three others named as helpers in the Mapplebeck note. They were shot on the ramparts of the city on September 22. Their memorial has the figure of a lad lying at their feet. This commemorates Léon Trulin, a boy who managed to get himself to England in June 1915. He convinced British intelligence officers that he could give them information. He returned to occupied France, and then went back to England with details of German troop strengths and movements. On his next trip, in October 1915, he was betrayed, captured with plans of trenches, airfields and ammunition dumps, and shot. He was 18.

Women were very active in the resistance. Louise de Bettignies, a talented girl from a Lille manufacturing family, made her way to Holland and on to England, where British intelligence ask her to set up a network of observers to pass on German movements. She returned to Lille in February 1915. She collected information on artillery batteries, ammunition dumps and regimental movements, and took it to Holland hidden in her skirt-hems, her coiffure and her umbrella. Railway level-crossing staff were the best contacts, providing details of troop movements and calculating German losses from the length of hospital trains. De Bettignies was arrested, and sentenced to death in March 1916. This was commuted to life imprisonment, and she died in Siegburg prison. "Neither asking nor accepting any reward, she organised and directed an extensive and most efficient service of intelligence," the Chief of the British General Staff, General Sir William Robertson, wrote of her, "by her ability, courage and devotion surmounting all obstacles."

By 1916, however, the Germans had mopped up most such resistance. The following year, all men between 16 and 45 were issued with red armbands – *brassards rouges* – carrying the initials ZAB, *Zivil Arbeiter Bataillon*, and forced to work. Many toiled on the defences of the Hindenburg Line, digging trenches and building blockhouses and light railways. Those who were deemed rude or idle were sent to ZAB6s, disciplinary labour gangs, who were given the most dangerous work, often exposed to Allied shellfire. "Frozen feet, mutilation, tuberculosis, from bad treatment and lack of food," a nurse in Cambrai noted of sick *brassards rouges*. "On some days we had nearly seven hundred such patients in our hospital."

The Hague Convention forbade the use of civilian labour for military work. When workers at Lambersart refused to make sandbags, the Germans banned all travel, imposed a 5 p.m. to 8 a.m. curfew, shut cafés and bars, and collected a fine of 375,000 francs to buy sandbags elsewhere. Many thousands of men were transported to Germany to work in huge camps, where they slept on bags of wood shavings in 200-man barracks, and broke stones for road building on rations of broth and a little bread.

Women, too, were ordered from their houses at bayonet point, taken to farms in their city clothes, barracked in stables and barns, and put to work in the fields. It needed the personal intervention of the king of Spain to stop these mass deportations. But children from eleven to thirteen were still rounded up illegally, issued with straw palliasses, and taken to the orchards to harvest apples and pears. By the end, the birth rate had fallen to zero in some places. The population of Lille fell to 129,000, and the city was recording fourteen deaths for each birth. The growth and weight of four-fifths of the 12–13 age group were abnormally small. A majority were classed as *débile*, weak and undernourished; the onset of puberty was delayed, and teachers found them mentally backward. Livestock all but disappeared. At Laon, a resident noted the departure of the last goat. Some *communes* had not a horse or mule left.

The sound of shellfire was welcomed in the occupied zone. It showed that the liberation remained possible. But at the front, the war was now conducted in the space between two trenches. Movement was easy enough behind the lines. If a section of line was threatened, large numbers of men could be switched to the critical area by train, truck or, as on the Marne, by taxi. But the front itself was a mass of immobilisers, trenches, blockhouses, wire, mud. It was astonishing, and it took a long time for staff officers to accept it as truth, that the most intense artillery barrage that could be laid down, from guns drawn up almost wheel to wheel, would fail to kill all those in the target area or remove all the barbed wire. Shocked, ears ringing, exhausted but alive, German machine gunners always emerged from their deep bunkers the moment the barrage lifted, to cut down the advancing infantry so that they fell in lines, one horrified observer said, as if tied together by a length of string.

All odds were stacked in favour of defence. *Élan* was replaced by a new watchword, attrition (*usure* in French, *Ermattungsstrategie* in German). Joffre spoke now of *grignotage*, the wearing down of the enemy, and of *l'épreuve de la durée*, the long haul. But there were more Germans to wear down than there were French. It was a matter of demographics. When it came to the depth of its pockets in terms of men, France was to beggar herself.

What was being done traumatised the nation. Figures are figures, indifferent to pity, but they tell a terrible tale. Serbian and Scottish regiments apart, nowhere was more lethal to be than in a French unit. France lost 16.8 per cent of those who were mobilised. More than one in five officers were killed or missing, a record shared by NCOs and men raised in the 5th Military Region at Orléans, which suffered the greatest regional losses, followed by Châlons-sur-Marne. The Germans lost 15.4 per cent and the British 11.8 per cent, though losses among Scottish infantry regiments reached 26 per cent.

All classes and professions in France suffered, though the need to keep industry and transport going meant that a smaller proportion of factory workers and railwaymen died than peasants, whose work was devolved to wives and children. The terrible losses in junior officers meant that the liberal professions suffered most.

Though he spoke of "nibbling" and not "breakthrough", Joffre still pined for movement. He sought it throughout 1915, in Champagne, in Woëvre, above all in Artois in May. Eighteen divisions tried and failed to take the high ground of Vimy Ridge near Arras. Joffre tried again in the autumn, after a three-day bombardment, the heaviest of the war. A three-kilometre dent in the German line cost 145,000 men. By the end of the year, 400,000 were killed or taken prisoner, or were missing – shell blasts vaporised men, as it were, so that the missing were not so much unaccounted for as removed without trace – for no gain of any significance. A sense of dread hung over the country at the hour when the postman called. Relatives were told that a man was dead by a white card with a black border; grey-blue cards were used for the missing. The women at the start of a street would look into the postman's bag. If there were no death or missing cards, they whooped and waved, while their silence engulfed the street in terror. The effect on morale was so severe that the government began to recruit tactful and dignified ladies to discreetly visit the homes of the dead and missing.

Joffre was not greatly worried by casualties. He claimed at his fine headquarters in Chantilly, home of the magical château and racecourse, that his offensives had achieved "brilliant tactical results". He sacrificed some generals as scapegoats: to this day, the French slang for the sack is *limoger*, for the fired officers were sent to Limoges to report for duty in the rear. Only the shortage of munitions, he claimed, had prevented a victory that would now be won with an offensive on the Somme.

The Germans had other ideas. General Erich von Falkenhayn planned to attack at Verdun, where the French line bulged into a large salient. His purpose was attrition. A limited attack would lead to the French cramming the salient with reinforcements, he expected, thus bringing them within range of his guns; he would then bleed them white. The Kaiser approved – the Crown Prince was to be a German commander in the battle – and planning for Operation Gericht (execution ground), began on Christmas Eve 1915.

He was wrong. His "limited attack" turned into the longest single battle in history. The Germans opened with a fierce bombardment in February 1916. The battle continued at least until November. The Germans called Verdun "the Mill", the grinder of men's bones. The Jesuit philosopher Pierre Teilhard de Chardin, who served as a stretcher-bearer, said that it turned the soldier into a *monade de guerre*, a "war monad", a depersonalised mollusc. It was a vision of the Inferno that cast a shadow to 1940 and beyond. "Everyone came to Verdun as if to receive some ultimate recognition there," the writer Paul Valéry said. "They seemed to go up the Voie Sacrée like some new form of offertory, to the most formidable altar that mankind has ever raised." He thought it was not a battle. Verdun was "a complete war in itself, inserted into the Great War." Even Maurice Barrès – the "nightingale of carnage" as the pacifist Romain Rolland called him – had second thoughts. He had assured his readers in *L'Écho de Paris* that the war would restore French vitality, but now he feared that France was not being regenerated by the teeming legions of the dead, but would join them in their eternal slumber. The howl of realism that the poet Henri Barbusse brought to the war in *Le Feu* – "Superhuman exhaustion, water up to your belly, mud, unspeakable filth, rotting faces and flesh in tatters . . ." – brought him the Prix Goncourt, the sobriquet "the Zola of the trenches" and sales of 200,000 copies.

A policy of strict unit rotation was in force, and because of it three-quarters of the whole French army on the western front marched up the narrow road from Bar-le-Duc to the salient. That helped to give Verdun a presence that, striking at the time and lingering long after, made it quite unlike any other battle. Barrès described this road, along which every soldier and cartridge had to pass, as the "Route Sacrée". It soon became known as the "Voie Sacrée", ringing with the very sorrow of the Via Dolorosa and Christ's Passion. Or so civilians called it. The troops found any mention of things "sacred" in their blistered and frightening world to be *bourrage de crâne*, head-stuffing, hogwash. Those who fought there said simply, *J'ai fait Verdun* or, without needing to name the place, *J'y étais* ("I was there").

It was a perpetual limbo of *mort de près*, death close at hand. Death, Maurice Genevoix wrote, was "a presence as real as a wasp that goes buzzing round your head, withdraws a little, comes back, makes your skin crawl with the brush of its wings, and which, at any moment, can sting, is going to sting." They persisted through comradeship. "I want only to talk about my men, my zouaves," wrote an officer in a colonial regiment. "In their midst, I felt surrounded by friends. For me, my unit was my family."

As they set out from Bar-le-Duc, they sang, "La route est longue jusqu'à Tipperary", or the bittersweet "Adieu la vie, adieu l'amour". They fell silent as they neared the zone of eternal smoke and dust and flares, and the constant din of shelling, for which they used the German word *Trommelfeuer* (drumfire). It was unnerving to pass the *revenants*, the survivors returning from the front. Lieutenant Pique de Mazenod recalled seeing a *revenant* standing up in a truck, his mouth pursed, his eyes glittering in their sockets. "He waved an emaciated arm to take in the horizon," the lieutenant wrote. "We knew that this mute gesture exposed a horror beyond words." Georges Gaudy, an NCO, wrote of "the pitiful flotsam from the great slaughter", their faces the colour of their greatcoats, silent, "past groaning" .

The town of Verdun lies on the Meuse, beneath 400-metre-high hills, the Hauts de Meuse, that command the eastern bank of the river and the insipid plain of the Woëvre. In 1914, the Hauts de Meuse were a natural barrier against the Germans, only sixty kilometres away in Metz, which they had occupied since 1870. The French fortified the hills with a complex of massive, deep-sunken forts. In the early fighting, the Germans crossed the Meuse 15 kilometres north of Verdun, and they held it again 35 kilometres to the south. Between those two points, the Verdun salient bulged into the German line. Salients are dangerous places. The Germans on the outer edge were vulnerable to a French build-up of forces which could strike them at any point. The French inside it were exposed to attack from several directions at once. They had, too, to funnel men and supplies through a narrow opening that could be shut by attacks on the wings, leaving them surrounded. The Germans assembled 1,200 guns, half of them heavies, with 2.5 million shells for a six-day bombardment. Crown Prince Friedrich Wilhelm, 34, commanded on the ground, a lanky man with a penchant for indiscreet affairs with Frenchwomen from the occupied zone, but intelligent enough to have tremors of doubt from the start.

He could call on seventeen divisions of some 300,000 men. The assault troops were hidden in underground barracks in deep forest, some holding a thousand men within a kilometre of French positions. This was a formidable force, but it was not enough to attack both wings of the salient simultaneously. The crown prince thus concentrated on the northern sector. Here he assembled 850 heavy guns, including 380-millimetre naval guns.

The French were much weaker than he realised. True, Verdun city was ringed with forts, the outer ring anchored by the two most formidable: Douaumont, a classic star-shaped fortress, and Vaux, on a plateau at the high point of 400 metres on the Hauts de Meuse. Their big 155-millimetre guns could be retracted under huge metal domes during a barrage, while galleries and rooms below could house garrisons of a thousand men. But because of the French philosophy of attack, the Verdun forts had been steadily downgraded. The French sensed something was wrong from February 12. Civilians started leaving the sector. The attack should have started that day, but snow and mist clung to the hills, and the Germans needed clear weather. Deserters came over telling the French of hospitals in Metz being cleared to be ready for mass casualties.

A full German bombardment opened at 7 a.m. on February 21. It was a clear, frosty morning, and French reconnaissance pilots reported that French units had disappeared into smoke and flame and a maelstrom of driven snow and tree branches. The rumble could be heard almost 150 kilometres away in the Vosges. Awful sights were commonplace. "Helmets full of blood," Captain Charles Delvert wrote, "rifles splashed with blood, a white shirt spotted with red. Near a tree a head . . ." A group of men near Raymond Joubert took a direct hit. "A great pile of earth," he recollected, "and sticking out of it, symmetrically, to a distance of about 40 centimetres, were legs, arms, hands and heads like the bloody cogs of some monstrous capstan."

After the barrage came the 140,000 field-grey men of the German 5th Army. They did not advance as swiftly as they hoped. They ran into sticking points, such as the Bois des Caures on the northern point of the salient, where Colonel Émile Driant, in his sixties, a deputy at the National Assembly, married to the daughter of General Boulanger, held out in a strongpoint. The Germans paid him the honour of deploying three army corps and firing ten thousand tons of shells in his direction.

Driant started the day with 1,200 light infantrymen from two battalions of Chasseurs à Pied. By 4 p.m., when the German batteries lengthened their range and the shells began to fall behind him, he had three hundred effectives left. The first Germans came with grenades and flamethrowers. Driant's men held. He visited them during the night. A renewed bombardment greeted the new dawn. It lifted at midday, and the German infantry reappeared. In the mid-afternoon, Driant told his remaining officers that they would soon be dead or prisoners, unless they tried to lead their men out. He was killed shortly after. Of his men, 118 reached safety in the village of Beaumont in the rear. They had robbed the crown prince of speed. It took him the best part of two days to get through two kilometres of ground at the Bois des Caures.

Among those deeply impressed by this was Heinz Guderian, a young intelligence officer. He was back in France in 1940 with a fleet of panzers. Charles de Gaulle was there, too, a company commander in the Douaumont sector. His regiment lost over half its strength in three days. He himself was posted missing. In fact, he was knocked unconscious and captured, and spent the rest of the war "buried alive" in a German prison camp. But he had learnt why the infantry reached the depths of despair. "It was caught every time between the certainty of a futile death within ten metres of the jumping-off trenches and the accusation of cowardice." Like Guderian, he became a prophet of tank warfare.

February 24 was a better day for the Germans. As he moved up, an infantry sergeant saw the remnants of General Chrétien's 30th Corps, the 30,000-odd men upon whom Friedrich Wilhelm's grey mass had fallen. "They were more desperate than men shipwrecked at sea, or lost in the desert, than men buried alive in a mine or a submarine," wrote Pierre Drieu La Rochelle, "because they knew that we were not saving them, and that they would return, after we had fallen, to this vast burial ground amid the iron rain."

On the 25th, the Germans took Fort de Douaumont, defended, not by the thousand men it could have housed, but by an elderly sergeant major and fifty territorials. Its guns were fired spasmodically by men with little training, no orders and no reinforcements. To their amazement, a few Germans were able to climb in through a casement without being shot at, and accepted the surrender of its bewildered occupants. In Germany, church bells pealed in celebration. The very stupidity of the loss of the fort made Verdun a national symbol: *il faut tenir*, we must hold out, and Douaumont must be avenged. There was no real French plan for Verdun, other than it must not be lost. Philippe Pétain now entered, a sharp-tongued, accomplished womaniser with chestnut hair and ice-blue eyes, the son of peasant farmers from the Pas-de-Calais, a man of simple tastes who, even as he accumulated generals' stars, preferred to wear the same *horizon bleu* as his men. He was also lucky. In 1914, he was a regimental colonel nearing retirement – he was 58, and he had already bought a modest house in Saint-Omer where he expected to see out his days – in an army still dominated by aristocrats and Catholic diehards. Pétain was a rarity, a good republican, and it speeded his promotion as scapegoats filled the ranks of the *limogés*.

He was also what was needed. He was very calm, a tic in his eyelid the only sign of pressure. He was excellent on detail. He was happy to defend: "Le feu tue", he said ("Firepower kills"). And he liked his men, and cared for them, and they knew it. He mourned the missing Charles de Gaulle, for example, as "an incomparable officer in all respects" who had died leading an attack as "the only solution he thought was compatible with military honour", and endorsed the recommendation that de Gaulle be awarded a posthumous Légion d'Honneur. He set up his headquarters at Souilly, on the Voie Sacrée, and when he had a spare moment, he stood on the steps of the town hall, and watched the men going up, and the *revenants*.

He introduced the system known as the *noria*, after endless bucket chains, or the *tourniquet* (turnstile). Ideally, each unit was rotated out of the front after eight days. It had its drawbacks. Moving into and out of the line was dangerous in itself; one infantry company left its barracks with 150 men, and was down to 30 when it reached the front. But it greatly helped morale, and so did Pétain's no-nonsense style. His order of the day on April 10 ended "*Courage, on les aura!*" "Take heart, we'll get them." It implied patience, determination and revenge, and – together with the other Verdun slogan, "*Ils ne passeront pas!*" – it caught the mood of the men and the nation.

The Germans attacked again along the whole Verdun sector in early April. They took the lower of the two summits of the crucial Mort-Homme hills, but the French took it back. German losses were now higher than the French, a poor outcome for a battle whose *raison d'être* was to bleed the enemy. Joffre, jealous of Pétain's soaring fame, kicked him upstairs as commander of the central sector, replacing him at Verdun with General Robert Nivelle. The Germans resumed a general offensive on June 1. They were quite literally on top of Fort de Vaux for much of the five days that Major Sylvain Raynal and his 600 men held out. Hand-to-hand fighting flared in the tunnels beneath the fort, and gas and flamethrowers were used against the battered defenders. "We were in near darkness, with the stench of the dead and the groans of the wounded, and the smoke from the grenades and the heat from the German flamethrowers made it difficult to breathe," a survivor, Adrien Artaud, recalled. "We had no water. We said nothing to each other. We waited for the end." A last carrier pigeon was sent from the fort. Shortage of water – the military position had long been hopeless – forced Raynal to surrender. He had lost 100 men. The Germans lost 2,600.

Nivelle, in a sign of worse to come, scrapped Pétain's policy of rotating units. Morale fell sharply. The divisions now locked into the salient were losing two, three, even four thousand men in each significant action. Pétain had allowed for the loss of a division every two days. Nivelle was losing two divisions every three days through his swaggering counter-attacks.

On June 12, the Germans were within spitting distance of victory. The distant Russians helped save the French, as they had at the Marne. General Brusilov broke through the Austro-Hungarians in Galicia, forcing them to beg the Germans for troops. Falkenhayn, fearing lest the Austrians be tossed out of the war, ordered the 5th Army to suspend its offensive at Verdun and sent three divisions east. By the time the 5th Army attacked again, the French had recovered their poise. The game was up for the Germans by the evening of June 23, when they accepted that no breakthrough was possible. The French counter-attacked at dawn the next day and regained most of the ground lost since the beginning of June. A week later, the British began to punch their full weight on the western front as their new divisions went into action on the Somme. A moment had passed.

Falkenhayn made another half-hearted attempt, with much use of gas. But he was soon relieved, replaced by Hindenburg and Ludendorff from the eastern front, shocked at the squandering of so many Germans on the naked and lacerated Hauts de Verdun. As the German pressure eased, the French planned a grander counter-offensive. Their tactics had improved. They recognised the need for better intelligence, for aerial photographs and raids to take prisoners. They saw, too, the importance of the platoon, and started small-group training, using leapfrogging and covering fire. Nivelle trained his infantry to advance behind a creeping artillery barrage. He attacked in October, and the Fort de Douaumont was once more almost empty when the French retook it.

By December 1916, when the battle was finished, the French army had taken 378,777 casualties – 61,283 killed, 216,337 wounded and 101,151 "missing", the euphemism for those dismembered by shellfire, entombed in mud, or rotted beyond recognition. The Germans had 143,000 dead in their 330,000 casualties. Both sides were, to all intents and purposes, back where they had been in February. How neatly the similarity between those two casualty figures – 378,000 and 330,000 – demonstrates the ghastliness of the Great War. Verdun was a super-battle that wounded or killed at an average rate of 2,600 a day, the adult male population of a fair-sized town, or 18,200 a week, thus disposing, week in, week out, of all the fit men in a city of over 100,000.

The French claimed it as a victory. So, in a way, it was, for the "if" – the consequence if they had lost – is enormous. French morale might have collapsed; Germany might not have been tempted into unrestricted U-boat warfare, and thus not provoked the Americans into the war. If the Germans had won Verdun, in short, they might have won the Great War and reduced France to the servility they had planned for her. But if Verdun helped the French to win the First World War, it also went a long way to losing them the Second. They poured their lifeblood into it. It was not their dearest battle – they lost men at a much faster rate in the opening months, and on the Somme between July and November 1916. Indeed, 1916 was not the worst year; that was 1915, with the attacks in the Champagne and Artois, when 335,000 died, compared with 218,000 for 1916. It cost them a tenth of all their dead, however, and it was the one that gelled in the imagination, because so many of them had fought there, because of the gigantic ossuary they built on the Douaumont hill, because of the monstrosity.

The determination of the men in battle had to be matched on the home front. Women were vital on the farms and in the arms plants. One in twenty of the workers in the metal industries of the Seine were women in 1914. By 1918, *munitionettes*, the affectionate name for the women who made shells, cartridges, grenades and flares, made up a third of the workforce. At Toulouse, the labour force in one explosives plant increased from 100 to 30,000, most of the newcomers being women. The arsenal at Rennes was manned largely by "the wives and daughters of servicemen."

Some saw them as *vaillantes héroines*: "The flames, the smoke and the fusing metal create a hazy throbbing atmosphere . . . There, scattered amid the men and shooting flames, are young women, grave, clad in leather, with a sculptured air." They took a less romantic view of themselves. They were paid less than men, at least a third less, for the same work. They were militant, and the sharp rise in the cost of living brought them out in several strikes in late 1916 and in 1917. Mostly, they won wage increases and concessions. Arms plants were making huge profits – Hotchkiss, with a share capital of 4 million francs at the start of the war, was making annual profits of 40 million francs by 1916 – and they could afford to pay better. The fact that half a million men had to be demobilised from the army in 1915 to return to work in strategic industries gave the women strong leverage. Pre-war labour legislation – the ten-hour day, no night work by women – was suspended in 1914, but pressure by *munitionettes* helped restore them in July 1917.

Plan XVII anticipated that the war would be over in a few months and that stockpiled munitions would be adequate. No mention was made of industrial mobilisation, and no specific military measures were taken to protect the great iron and steel regions of the north, which fell to the Germans. Despite this, industry was highly effective: the *belle époque*, so soft and pleasurable on the surface, had a steel backbone.

Industry was equal to the task. The socialist Albert Thomas proved an excellent capitalist as director of the national industrial programme. He was business-friendly, admired managers and entrepreneurs, and believed that initiative and energy should be well rewarded. He built up a strong team of technicians, men like Albert Claveille at transport, a former director of French railways, and Hugoniot, self-made, a telephone operator at fourteen, and a chief engineer to the Paris Métro at 29.

A huge effort was needed. Ten thousand 75-millimetre shells were being produced a day at the start of the war, but individual batteries were firing a thousand. Daily demand was put at 100,000 and rising. Workers were brought back from the front. Thomas paid well and promptly. André Citroën, for example, signed a contract in January 1915 to produce a million tons of 75-millimetre shrapnel shells at 24 francs apiece, to be made in a factory yet to be built. He got huge cash advances, 4.8 million francs for new machinery alone, and by the summer of 1915 the 100,000 a day target for 75-millimetre shells was all but met.

Industry created production groups, each led by a major "group leader", which received orders for the whole group and subcontracted them to other members. The Renault group, for example, included some of the grandest automobile names in the world: Delahaye, Delaunay-Belleville, de Dion-Bouton, de Dietrich, Panhard et Levassor.

Thomas told the workers that he remained a socialist, that he would help them to achieve "our ideals of justice and liberty" once the guns were silent, but for now they must give themselves "without stint to the salvation of the nation." Some were unconvinced. His own colleagues spoke of his "Creusot Socialism" – a snide reference to the great metal-bashing combine of that name – and spoke of his allegiance to "Messieurs Schneider et Renault."

Before stepping down in September 1917, when the SFIO left the government, Thomas had nonetheless transformed the munitions industry, swelling its workforce from 50,000 mainly state-employed workers to 1.6 million, more than two-thirds of them working for private companies. Their performance was sparkling, outstripping the British, no mean industrialists themselves, in the production of shells, rifles and artillery. In the air, Gnôme et Rhône, Renault and Salmson, with Hispano-Suizas made under licence, produced 90,000 aircraft engines, thrashing the British and Germans by a margin of two to one.

The "industrial union" created by Thomas was of profound future importance. He pleaded that it should be preserved in peace, "so that the industries grouped together in a great national organisation lend one another mutual support beyond all petty and harmful rivalries". This preference for cooperation over competition, and the close involvement of the state, was to become a characteristic of business and industry in France. State and state-owned enterprises coexist in a sector with private companies for, at least in principle, the mutual benefit of France. Thomas knew Renault well, and Gnôme et Rhône; Renault was to become the state's "group leader" in motor cars, whilst the engine-maker, renamed Snecma and also brought into state ownership, performed a similar role in aviation.

Another characteristic, a large and intrusive bureaucracy, was also gathering steam. It swelled by 25 per cent during the war, despite the need for men at the front and in factories. The bureaucrats developed a taste for planning in all its many forms – allocating labour, setting production targets, controlling prices, working conditions, welfare, labour relations – that they found hard to give up. This could be useful. A Direction of Inventions was set up in 1915; far from being dismantled in peace, it became the respected Centre National de la Recherche Scientifique. The lust for intervening in industry, however, and the bureaucrats' dream of "controlled capitalism", often led – still leads – to enterprise in France being smothered by paperwork and regulation.

As to the countryside, "a grim calm, a sense of the void" descended with the almost complete absence of young men. "Even fathers of families with three children went off to war," a woman in a small *commune* in the Haute-Loire recalled. "Almost half of them never came back." At harvest, "the saucy stories, the dancing in the shade of the trees to the clarinet or the oboe" had gone; all was quiet and subdued. A schoolmaster from the Yonne wrote of fields worked by "grey beards, white beards, bald heads, stooped backs, crooked hips, twisted bodies, halting legs." In a village in Isère, 53 men from a total population of 400, "the young, the strong, those who shouldered the weight of the work in the fields", had gone to the war. The village had changed its very appearance. The elderly, and the women and children, still produced food, at great toil but for good money. A dozen eggs, 80 centimes pre-war, were up to 2.20 francs by the end of 1916, and beef prices had doubled. Watching the congregation come out of mass at Saint-Lormel, an observer found it "just as in town . . . shortened skirts, knee-high boots, hats copied from the latest magazine. The traditional headdress was only worn by very old women", and "every young girl has a bicycle". In the Charente, it was said that families whom the war did not put into mourning were "truly well off"; but a glimpse at any village war memorial gives an idea of how many did wear black and how much was stripped from its soul.

Robert Nivelle was to keep many masons busy. A humble artillery colonel in 1914, he owed much to his reputation as the Verdun fort-stormer, and something to being a Protestant when republican politicians still muttered darkly of "Jesuit generals". Nivelle replaced Joffre as commander-in-chief in the last days of 1916, and was given command of the 1917 spring offensive. He was dashing. He spoke perfect English, and charmed British politicians, if not generals. He believed in the offensive spirit, the creeping barrage, and the use of the maximum number of troops in the first wave of an assault on the broadest front possible.

He chose a 50-kilometre front between Soissons and Reims for his attack. The sector was called the Chemin des Dames, an ancient road named for the sisters of Louis XV. The war minister, Louis Lyautey, the brilliant colonial administrator in Morocco, and a fine soldier, had no trust in the Nivelle plan. He called it *Kriegsspiel* (a war game). On April 3, stung by Germany's new strategy of unrestricted submarine warfare, the United States entered the war. Lyautey wanted to wait until sizeable numbers of American troops arrived. Pétain was the only military commander to share this scepticism, however, and the main attack went in on April 16.

The Chemin des Dames was one of the strongest points in the German line, and the Germans knew that the attack was coming. They bolstered their divisions in the sector from nine to 40, holding back the greater part of them safely out of the range of the 7,000 guns Nivelle had assembled. He remained so sure of success that he invited a group of parliamentarians to watch as the French left their trenches to fight an alert and well dug-in enemy in ice and fog. The German wire was largely intact, and so were the German machine-gunners and mortar crews. The creeping barrage frequently hit the advancing infantry it was designed to protect. By the second day, 120,000 French troops were casualties on the battlefield. The dressing stations and hospital trains could not cope. Ignoring the mounting disaster, Nivelle pressed on.

Units now began to mutiny, not while they were at the front – it was not a mutiny in that sense, but rather a "collective indiscipline", a protest strike against the way the war was being run – but in the rear. A battalion near Reims refused to march when ordered back to the line after only five days rest. Other battalions marched up bleating like sheep, sometimes waving Red flags, for the Russian Revolution had made its impression, and singing protest songs:

> Adieu la vie, adieu l'amour
> Adieu toutes les femmes
> (C)'est bien fini, (c)'est pour toujours
> De cette guerre infâme …
>
> C'est à Craonne, sur le plateau
> Qu'on doit laisser sa peau
> Car nous sommes tous condamnés
> C'est nous les sacrifiés.
>
> [Goodbye life, goodbye love,
> Goodbye all you girls,
> It's over, for always,
> In this vile war.
>
> It's at Craonne, on the plateau,
> That we'll leave our corpses,
> For we are condemned to die,
> We are the ones who are sacrificed.]

On May 3, the 21st Division, which had fought repeatedly at Verdun, refused to move to the front. The ringleaders were shot or transported: the division returned to the front on May 5, and was decimated. Individual infantrymen began to desert. The 120th Regiment refused to fight; when the 128th was ordered to shame it by attacking in its place, it too refused. Officers were being attacked in the Aisne by the third week of May. By the end of the month, men in eight divisions which had fought at the Chemin des Dames, or were being sent to do so, had mutinied.

The Nivelle offensive floundered on, and so did the trouble. Thirty to forty thousand men were affected. Most outbreaks started in rest camps or railway stations, and were spontaneous and short-lived. No attempts were made to fraternise with the enemy at the front; the Germans remained totally unaware of what was happening. The men defied orders because they had lost all confidence in Nivelle. His offensive was an act of pointless carnage, even by the standards of the time; by May 15 the French had suffered 187,000 casualties.

Some officers were so outraged and surprised by the disobedience that they thought it could only be spread by foreigners and civilians. Louis Franchet d'Espérey, the commander of Army Group North, wanted the whole country to be put under a state of siege, with foreign civilians expelled. The 10th Army commander, Dûchene, wrote of "a secret and more or less entrenched movement coming primarily from Paris, which seeks through these special circumstances – the events in Russia, the strikes in Paris, and so on – to win over the troops and demoralise them". Joseph Maistre, commander of the 6th Army, spoke of a sinister "leadership" among the mutineers. It was obvious there were leaders, he said, because of "the nearly complete absence of over-excitement and drunkenness – I note that the soldiers were obliged by their comrades to empty their canteens – in a word, obedience to instructions, which gave the revolt a character marked by organisation". Pétain, who was no red-faced blimp, also thought that "the movement has deep roots in the interior", with the "launching and exploitation of a pacifist propaganda campaign". The junior officers, however, saw no signs of any conspiracy. They found the demonstrations to be spontaneous and all-embracing rather than engineered by a few men. They identified leaders only when senior officers demanded that they do so, and then named men at random. The almost universal reply by men accused of plotting mutiny was: "J'ai suivi les camarades" (I followed the others).

Nivelle was packed off to command a corps in Algeria as governor-general. Pétain was appointed commander-in-chief, and used his patient skills as *le médecin de l'armée*. It was, Pétain always said, his finest achievement to bind the wounds. He calmed the army by judicious use of the carrot and a flick of the stick. He visited some ninety divisions, and spoke to individuals, reassuring them that there would be no more Nivelle-style offensives. The French would wait "for the Americans and the tank". He appealed to the stomach, old soldier that he was. The quality of the food, wine and cooks was improved; there were better lavatories and showers, more comfortable mattresses, and more leave. At the same time, 3,427 men were court-martialled. Of the 554 sentenced to death, 49 were shot, *pour encourager les autres.*

By June 20, the mutinies were no more than a bad memory. Pétain replaced the blood-drenched attempts to break through the German line with small lightning offensives aimed at wearing the enemy down. Tanks were used in close cooperation with infantry. Reconnaissance aircraft helped to achieve maximum surprise; as soon as they spotted a strong enemy reaction, the action was called off and renewed on a different stretch of the line. The Russian collapse enabled the Germans to outnumber the French in the west. Pétain anticipated their attacks by organising defence in depth. A lightly held front line disrupted the enemy, who was then held by the second defence line. These tactics were man-savers. Through them, Pétain won long-lasting and deeply-felt affection.

Problems on the home front also needed fixing. Red-tinged expectations had been built up by the Russian Revolution. Strikes had hit munitions plants since 1916, and they got worse. The police drew up a list of 2,500 troublemakers, but the interior minister, Louis Malvy, did nothing for fear of the street. He was driven from office, bringing down the Ribot government in September 1917. Ribot had refused to give passports to socialists who wanted to attend an International Socialist anti-war Meeting in Stockholm. The new premier, Paul Painlevé, was almost as great a defeatist as Malvy, and there was talk of peace with Germany and an end to the unnatural alliance with the old enemy, Britain. Painlevé lasted only until November. The Union Sacrée collapsed as the Socialists withdrew support.

President Poincaré now gave the government to the outsider of French politics, Georges Clemenceau, the radical leader, 76 years old and an active politician since the Commune, but a hard man who kept fit with daily Swedish drill, and a backer of total war who was prepared to turn on the Chamber to smash the appeasers. "We present ourselves to you with one thought," he said when he formed his cabinet. "Total war. No more pacifist campaigns, no more German intrigues, no treason, no semi-treason. Just war, war, and nothing but war." Malvy and Joseph Cailloux found themselves in front of the High Court "for treating with the enemy", as a result of extending peace feelers. Cailloux, the ex-finance minister whose wife had shot the editor of *Le Figaro*, was found guilty in 1920, though his sentence was commuted; Malvy was given five years' exile. Mata Hari, a glamorous dancer whose many lovers had included senior German as well as French officers, was shot, though possibly innocent, and certainly small fry. Clemenceau, the "Tiger", backed Pétain to the core. He put on helmet, greatcoat and boots to speak to soldiers at the front, and his adages – "War is too serious to be left to the army", "If I could pee like Lloyd George talks" – dazzled and reassured the nation.

He also pushed hard to get an inter-Allied military command, an important and belated move. Pétain remained as head of the French army, but another French general, Ferdinand Foch, was given overall command of Allied troops. Foch had dash, optimism and style. The British preferred him to the cautious and pessimistic Pétain, a slight that the latter may have stored away, to resurface in 1940.

Ludendorff was bundled into an offensive he knew was dangerous, because the Americans were coming, and the Germans would then be done for. They smashed into the British on March 21 in the Saint-Quentin sector. Before midday, the British had lost a fifth of their troops, and by midnight on the 22nd, helped by gas and fog, the Germans were close to annihilating the British 5th Army. The Ludendorff plan was to break the Allied line at the junction of the British and French forces. He hoped to knock the British line back on its pivot, to fall back towards the Channel coast, opening a corridor towards Paris. On March 24, the Germans brought terror to Paris. Explosions rocked the city, the first on the Quai de Seine, without aircraft flying overhead. A special Krupp-built "Paris Gun", a monster 35 metres long and weighing 138 tons, was firing shells at the rate of about two an hour from behind German lines. It was aimed at the Louvre, an act of cultural malice that gave substance to the legend of German barbarism; no shell ever landed on this sprawling target, but on Good Friday, March 29, a shell struck the church of Saint-Gervais during mass, killing 75 worshippers on the spot. In all, the terror shelling killed 256 Parisians, but it succeeded only in stiffening civilian morale.

The British lacked Pétain's defence in depth. They feared they might lose a million men as prisoners if they stayed on in France, and there was talk of a wholesale evacuation. But Ludendorff's losses were mounting – by the end of April they had reached 348,000, against 240,000 British and 90,000 French – and his attack was running out of steam. He failed to separate the British and French; it was a close-run thing, but they held on, while he achieved only exposed flanks, a longer front, crippling casualties and exhaustion.

In the summer, the Allies counter-attacked. On July 4, General Sir John Monash's Australians scored a brilliant success with tanks at Hamel. On the 18th, 15 French and four American divisions, with 500 tanks, broke the German line at Villers-Cotterets and drove them back ten kilometres. On August 8th, fourteen British and Dominion divisions under General Rawlinson, backed by over 400 tanks, again broke the German line near Amiens. Retreating Germans troops called the reinforcements they passed "scabs" who were prolonging the war. Ludendorff said in his memoirs that August 8 was "the black day of the German army in this war". Between July 30 and October 21, 1918, the British alone took 157,000 German prisoners. This was the first real evidence that the end was close. Fear and shame no longer prevented the Germans from surrendering. On October 17, the people of Lille came out of their cellars to find the Germans had gone. Scottish soldiers in the place de la République were showered with flowers. An aircraft landed on the central esplanade. Its pilot was Captain Carl Delesalle, the son of the mayor, who had flown in from Dunkirk to greet his father. Over the next few days, the visitors included Clemenceau, Poincaré and Winston Churchill. "Our joy is growing," a resident wrote a few days later. "We are getting used to happiness again."

The armistice was signed in a railway carriage fitted out as a command post, in the forests near Compiègne in the Oise. At the eleventh hour of the eleventh day of the eleventh month, the guns fell silent. That evening, Marthe Chenal of the Opéra Comique, in a robe of red, white and blue and a black Alsatian cap, sang "La Marseillaise" to the rapturous crowd from the steps of the Paris Opéra. On November 24, almost as sweet, French troops entered Strasbourg. The crowds cheered the tricolours. "That's the plebiscite for you," they said.

"My resolute paganism," wrote Gide (above), "remains soaked in the tears Christ has shed." His parents were Calvinists, and the tension between his sense of this austere and stern faith and his own abandonment of restraints added power to his essays, poems, novels and memoirs, and his travels to seek pleasure in North Africa.

LABOUR PROTESTS

It was not easy to govern France: the revolutionary habit of taking to the streets was deeply ingrained. Demonstrations by the wine growers of Champagne (below) escalated into riots in 1911, with the whole département of the Marne placed under military occupation. Growers in the Midi had earlier burned down the prefecture in Perpignan, whilst a locally recruited regiment refused to intervene.

Jean Jaurès, seen in full flow (right) at Saint Gervais in 1913, was the great figure of the left. A Dreyfusard, he founded the French Socialist Party and edited l'Humanité, its newspaper. He argued that war could be avoided if French and German socialists refused to fight one another. He was assassinated a few hours before his hopes were dashed by the onset of the Great War.

Alfred Cortot (right) was a double prodigy. As a pianist, he won first prize at the Paris Conservatoire at the age of 19, and he conducted the first Paris performance of Wagner's Götterdämmerung as a 25-year-old in 1902. The trio he founded with Jacques Thibaud and Pablo Casals gave a fresh brilliance to chamber music.

Gabriel Fauré (above left) was organist at the Madeleine and director of the Conservatoire. He composed with elegance and subtlety, ranging from his Requiem to the opera Pénélope. Claude Debussy (above right) is labelled the first of the modern composers. Camille Saint-Saëns (below) was also organist at the Madeleine and wrote a concerto for the instrument.

The early "Claudine" novels of Colette (far right) were published under the pen-name of her bullying first husband. After she left him in 1906, she lived with "Missy", the lesbian marquise de Belboeuf, scandalising audiences when they kissed in a pantomime at the Moulin Rouge. Colette's sensual and fluid novels made her dearly loved. She was the only Frenchwoman to have a state funeral, the Church having refused a religious burial.

To many, the work of Marcel Proust (left), redolent of France, was the finest fiction of the century to be written anywhere. France also soaked up foreigners – like the Surrealist poet Guillaume Apollinaire – Italian-born and of Polish descent (photographed above in Pablo Picasso's studio) – and made them its own.

Marie Curie (below) invented the term "radioactivity" and isolated radium with her husband Pierre Curie, winning a joint Nobel Prize for Physics in 1903 with Antoine Becquerel. After Pierre was run down by a horse wagon in 1906, she followed him as physics professor at the Sorbonne, isolating radium and later developing X-radiology. Alexis Carrel (left) was a Nobel medicine laureate in 1912 for his work on experimental surgery and the transplant of tissues and whole organs. He demonstrated that blood vessels could be kept in cold storage. He was later critized for his subsequent interest in eugenics.

"Dans les champs de l'observation," Louis Pasteur (below) remarked, "le hasard ne favorise que les esprits préparés" ("In observation, chance favours only the prepared mind"). The life of the father of modern bacteriology was majestic confirmation of this. His "germ theory" held that infectious disease was spread by micro-organisms. He developed prophylactic treatments for diphtheria, tubercular disease, cholera, plague and yellow fever, as well as rabies. The Institut Pasteur, founded in 1886, continues his work today.

It is strange that the Americanism "showbiz" is used for mass entertainment, since it was largely a French invention. Striptease was pioneered in Paris, along with showgirls (below) and chorus lines, the music hall and cancan at the Moulin Rouge (right), and nightclubs, chanteuses, cabarets and revues. The games of chance – or very little chance, the odds being stacked in favour of the banquier – played in casinos were equally French in origin. In the cinema, Charles Pathé produced the first newsreels and cliffhanger series like **The Perils of Pauline** *to such effect that by 1908 he controlled a third of the global film market.*

*"Alger la blanche" tumbled down steep hills to the port (left)
in white terraces, its hills dominated by Notre Dame d'Afrique
and the Hôtel Saint-Georges, above the Palais d'Été,
the governor-general's fine mansion. The city's boulevards
were elegant and Parisian, with wrought-iron balconies
and striped sunshades, and cool with high ceilings and parquet
floors. They seemed eternally French, but they stopped at the entry
to the Kasbah, the dark and teeming alleys of the ancient Muslim
quarter. The colonies were part enterprise and part imperium:
the railway in Morocco (below) was built by the Paribas bank.*

The union sacrée, *the great wartime union of the nation, embraced all manner of men and women. The joy with which Parisiennes saw the first men off to the front (left) gave way to sadness as the scale of casualties became known, but the pride remained. It helped to sustain these mothers queuing for food rations (below) and the* munitionettes, *the affectionate name for the girls who laboured in the arms plants, where they soon made up a third of the workforce. Even before the war, more French women worked than anywhere else in Europe; but even after it, despite their contribution, and the promises of 1789, they were still denied the vote.*

Three-quarters of the French army marched along the Voie sacrée *(right), the narrow road to the salient of Verdun, going up it, in the words of Paul Valéry, "like some new form of offertory, to the most formidable altar that mankind has ever raised". As a fresh lieutenant moved up with his unit, a returning* revenant, *eyes glittering in their sockets, his face the colour of his greatcoat, waved an emaciated arm in silent warning at the horizon. "We knew this mute gesture exposed a horror beyond words," the lieutenant wrote. The French hung on (overleaf), through the rugged persistence of Georges Clemenceau, prime minister and "Tiger" (above), and comradeship. "I only want to talk about my men, my zouaves," an officer wrote of his colonial troops (below). "In their midst, I felt protected. For me my unit was my family."*

THE MISERY OF WAR

Men were suspended in a limbo of mort de près, *death or maiming close at hand, or immolation in a trench (right) or blinded by gas (below). The Jesuit philosopher Pierre Teilhard de Chardin, who served as a stretcher bearer, said it turned the soldier into a "monade de guerre", a depersonalised mollusc. The poet Henri Barbusse caught its essence: "superhuman exhaustion, water up to your belly, mud, unspeakable filth, rotting faces and flesh in tatters".*

The war could not be tucked away as a Great Victory. It had cost more than a million dead, and three times that in wounded, whose grands mutilés *joined the widows as dependents of the state. Battlefields became deserts, "for mile after mile, and far out of sight", a report said of the Nord-Pas-de-Calais, "full of holes, churned up . . . in the fields, piles of metal and, above all, crosses, grouped on top of mounds or in ditches." The Germans left Lens (right) as a "premeditated deliberate ruin", reduced to twisted metal and tangled beams.*

The opening of an exhibition of Dadaist paintings by Max Ernst in Paris in 1921 (left). The writer André Breton hangs upside down while the poet Jacques Rigault holds him and the bicycle. Breton again helps publicise a fellow Dadaist, this time the Franco-Spanish artist Francis Picabia, in 1920 (below). Breton, along with several other Dadaists, turned to Surrealism – a word coined by Apollinaire, who believed that "prospectuses, posters, advertisements of all sorts" contained the "poetry of our epoch". Breton boasted of it as the "enemy of reason" and published the Surrealist Manifesto in 1924, though the movement was stronger in painting, with artists such as Magritte, Dalí, Max Ernst and Yves Tanguy, than in writing. Breton and the poet Louis Aragon later converted to communism in the – surreal – conviction that the Soviet Union was a haven of peace and righteousness.

PARIS ON PARADE

The talent let loose in Paris combined in the ballet
Parade. *The score was by Erik Satie (below) and
it was choreographed by Léonide Massine with a
scenario by Jean Cocteau. Picasso (seen right, on a
backdrop) designed the sets and also the costumes (left).*
Parade *caused a riot at its premiere in 1921. It gave the
composers grouped with Satie – they included Francis
Poulenc, writer of cool and translucent chamber music,
songs, opera and ballet – notoriety as Les Six. When Satie
lay dying in 1925, lacing his medicine with opium and
champagne, he chided his atheist friends: "Why attack God?
He may be as unhappy as we are."*

François Coty, reclusive anti-Semitic millionaire parfumeur *and*
bankroller of the far-right ligues *and* Croix de Feu, *could afford large*
advertisements for his book (below). A Corsican, he claimed to
be related to the Bonapartes and admired Napoleon and Mussolini
equally while excoriating the Third Republic. He bought Le Figaro
and set up the rabble-rousing rag L'Ami du peuple, *while keeping*
an arsenal of weaponry in the cellars of his château. His target,
the French Communist Party, held its inaugural rally in 1921 (right),
at which Ho Chi Minh was one of the speakers.

"Paris does not reproach the person bent on going to the devil," the American journalist
Harold Stearns observed. "It shrugs its shoulders and lets him go." It offered foreigners
spectacles: a watery fête de nuit at the Lido (below) or a transvestites' ball (two guests,
right and far right) at cheaper and cheaper prices as the franc steadily devalued. By 1927,
some 40,000 Americans were living in the city, finding it, as the poet e. e. cummings wrote,
a "divine section of eternity". Many were writers, and for a while Paris was the centre of
English, Irish and American literature.

JAZZ AND BANANAS

Black Americans, dancers and musicians, seen here at La Boule Blanche nightclub in 1930, had been in vogue since the revue **Paris qui Jazz** *had opened ten years before. Cocteau wrote of the jazz passion as "a kind of tamed catastrophe dancing on a hurricane of rhythms". The shimmy was the fashionable dance; "C'est la Faute au Shimmy", a hit song ran, blaming it for any moral lapse,*

from oversleeping to waking up with a stranger. Josephine Baker, in her famous banana skirt (below right), the star of La Revue Nègre, *was a phenomenon, a "pantheress with golden claws", who promenaded with a pet snake round her neck and a leopard on a lead. Her colour inspired the new habit of sunbathing, and her slicked down hair was aped as le Bakerfix.*

The sporting nation was in good heart. Suzanne Lenglen (below) won the singles and doubles five years running at Wimbledon (and the mixed doubles three times) before becoming one of the first tennis professionals. Playing against Jean Borotra (right), the Bouncing Basque, was an equally depressing prospect. With his fellow "musketeers" Lacoste, Cochet and Brugnon, he helped France win the Davis Cup six times on the trot.

Ever inventive, Henri Desgrange came up with the leader's yellow jersey to promote his Tour de France. He followed this with a 5,500-kilometre course in 1924. "The ideal Tour", he wrote, "would be one in which only one rider survived the ordeal." He came close to achieving it. One of the reporters on this "Tour de souffrance" had recently written on the overseas penal colonies. He found their hardships echoed by the race, and he dubbed the competitors "les forçats de la route", the convicts of the road.

A lawyer from Franche-Comté, Jules Rimet, conceived the first football World Cup competition in 1930. He had the solid gold trophy designed by the sculptor Lafleur. French sportsmen had design flair. The tennis player René Lacoste pioneered the now colossal and logo-loaded sportswear industry with his crocodile-blazoned tennis shirts.

Brilliance and originality teemed in cinema. Un Chien Andalou (below) was the great Surrealist film of 1928, made by Salvador Dalí and Luis Buñuel. Its images (a woman's eye sliced with a razor) were unrelated, disturbing, macabre, filled with the erotic symbolism of dreams. The brilliant young filmmaker Jean Vigo made his iconoclastic debut in 1929 with À propos de Nice (right). His next, Zéro de Conduite (Zero for Conduct), seized the anarchy of restless youth, but he was soon dead of leukaemia at 29.

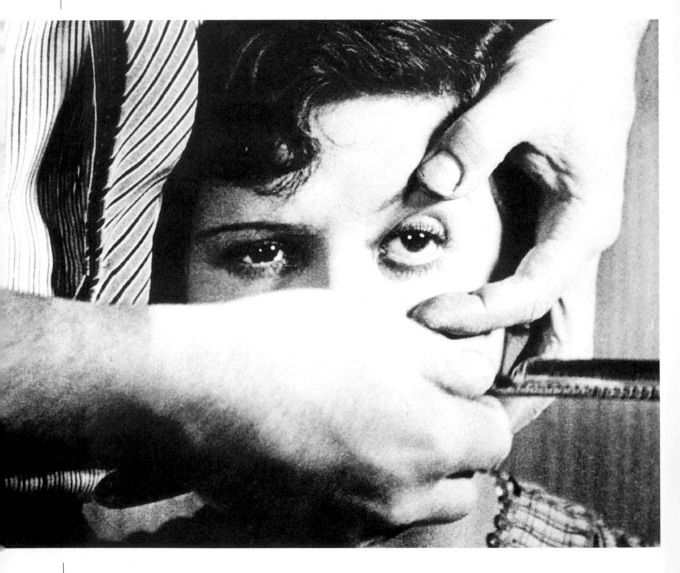

The shorter working week and longer paid holidays – the right
called Léon Blum, the Popular Front premier, the "minister for
laziness" – gave a new scale to leisure. The number of bicycles
rocketed to nine million as workers took to the roads with their
tents (facing page, top). "Elle fait de la bi-bi, de la bicyclette,"
sang Fernandel, "et ça fait mon bonheur."

The Channel resorts, once the preserve of the blazered and the boatered well-to-do, filled with day-trippers (bottom), and the new sport of sand yachting was tried out at Boulogne (below left). Over half the visitors interviewed on the Riviera had never seen the sea before. Not everyone approved. Chic shops in Nice put harsh notices in their windows – "Interdit aux congés payés" – and kept the new holidaymakers off the premises.

Art Deco (as at the Théâtre Pigalle below) flowered briefly around the Exposition Internationale des Arts Décoratifs et Industriels in 1925. It reworked old themes: the rich, throbbing colours and theatricality of the sets and costumes for Léon Bakst's Ballets Russes, and the sinuous patterns of Art Nouveau. But these were now crossed with the more austere lines deriving from modern architecture and the new engineering concept of streamlining.

Entr'acte

Paris remained raw and damp. It made do for heating on a slender ration of *boulets*, made of coal dust, peat and straw. It needed a cabinet minister to get a cartload of real coal to ease Rodin's last days as the sculptor lay dying of pneumonia. Hearses mingled with the crowds, laden with victims of a great influenza epidemic, and the abundance of women in black took the edge off the rejoicing.

This was not a war to be tucked away in the national memory under the file marked "Great Victories". It had cost more than the dead soldiers, whose names were now carved in long panels on village war memorials. Three million were wounded, a third of them so badly that they were unfit to return to normal life. These *grands mutilés* joined the widows as a drain on the state. To them must be added the 200,000 civilians dead in the fighting and the German occupation, and the wartime shortfall in births which the brief boom in "postponed" babies as the soldiers were demobilised did no more than dent, a loss that demographers put at a further 1.3 million. The Spanish flu devoured 166,000 more. The 90 *départements* of 1919, which now included 1.7 million returned Lorrainers and Alsatians, had fewer people than pre-war France.

Eight million acres of battlefield had been left a desert. "The very few trees which still stand are reduced to skeletons," a British visitor to the Somme observed. "In the fields, piles of metal, corrugated iron, or clumps of barbed wire . . . above all, crosses, grouped on the top of a mound, or in ditches."

The Germans had left Lens as a "premeditated deliberate ruin", reduced to a titanic pile of twisted iron and tangled beams. People found shelter in cellars, with no water, light or drainage. Stove-pipes sticking out of the ground were the only sign of their existence.

The villages around Verdun had gone from the face of the earth; the topsoil in the battle zone was so blasted and soured with explosives that it was fit only for thin forests. In the Meurthe-et-Moselle, 650,000 cubic metres of earth were needed merely to fill the trenches. Explosives had first to be removed. Chinese and Indochinese labour gangs were used for the work of recovery. Close to 850,000 buildings had been destroyed or badly damaged, so many that rebuilding was not completed until 1938.

Wrecked communities were helped by twinning, or "adoption". American, British, Canadian and Australian towns raised money and collected clothes for a French town. They also sent seed, young trees and much-needed breeding stock for the farms; a million sheep and goats in the occupied zone had fallen to 150,000; 900,000 cattle and oxen to 58,000. The war had worn away "something deeper than the renewable parts of a machine", Paul Valéry thought, and among the things it had wounded was the mind itself. "It has been cruelly wounded, it passes a mournful judgement on itself," he wrote in *La Crise de l'esprit*. "It doubts itself profoundly."

Civilisation, which had seemed so sturdy before the war, was shown to have the same fragility as a life. A shudder had run through the very marrow of Europe; she knew that "she was no longer herself", that she was losing a brilliant consciousness acquired through centuries of bearable calamities, won by thousands of men of the first rank, from innumerable backgrounds. Science, in which Europe had invested so much pride, was shamed "by the cruelty of its applications to armaments and warfare."

Worse, though, were the sterling moral qualities that had been used for mass slaughter. "The great virtues of the German people have begotten more evils, than idleness ever bred vices," Valéry said. "Conscientious labour, the most solid learning, the most serious discipline and application adapted to appalling ends."

Europe, no more than a promontory on the continent of Asia, had made itself the "brain of a vast body", the creative wellspring of the world. Valéry feared that this was now wrecked. Russians, Germans, Italians and Spanish abandoned themselves to dictatorships and violence. The French, alone of the great Continental powers, remained loyal to democracy. But Valéry was right. Something had given way. The nation that had produced Roland Garros, the epitome of European flair, courage and confidence, first man to fly across the Mediterranean, first fighter pilot and prison camp escapee, and that had so recently lost him, shot down in the dying weeks of the war, now suffered a nervous despondency, an escalating loss of certainties. Prisoners began returning from the German camps to the reception centre at the Grand Palais in Paris "no longer men but shadows clothed in torn rags, and so thin!" Civilians were shocked at their condition. With them came the Allied diplomats for the coming peace conference. The Americans sent 1,300 delegates, so many that the Hôtel Crillon could house only a fraction of them. The rest spilled over into Maxim's in the rue Royale and beyond. It was a reminder that, among the other unbidden results of the war, the global balance was shifting.

Work on the treaty started in January 1919 in the Quai d'Orsay. The French could hardly be blamed for wishing to lead the negotiations – they had suffered much more than the British, and incomparably more than the Americans – but it grated. "I never wanted to hold the conference in his bloody capital," Lloyd George muttered of Clemenceau. Woodrow Wilson's close adviser, the Texan-born diplomat Edward House, said he would rather have gone to a neutral city like Geneva, but "the old man" – Clemenceau was 78, with a wife 30 years his junior – "wept and protested so much that we gave way".

Harold Nicolson, an observant British diplomat, also had "a vivid impression of the growing hatred of the French for the Americans" whom he thought "annoyed" the Parisians. Not that the Americans were particularly enamoured with the British, whose policy, one of them complained, seemed to be to "bolster up the decadent races against the most efficient race in Europe", by which he meant respectively the French and the Germans. Clemenceau and Lloyd George were united in one thing: their dislike of the moralising Presbyterian professor from Princeton, Woodrow Wilson.

Clemenceau, the English economist John Maynard Keynes observed, was steeped in European cynicism and realpolitik. "He had one illusion, France," Keynes wrote, "and one disillusion, mankind, including Frenchmen and his colleagues not least." There was nothing very new to learn about the war and the end it was fought for, so Keynes had Clemenceau believe: the English had, as so often before, destroyed a trade rival and a "mighty chapter had been closed in the secular struggle between the glories of Germany and France". Prudence required some measure of lip service to the "ideals" of "foolish Americans and hypocritical Englishmen." But it would be stupid to believe that Wilson's famous "fourteen points" would inject any real moral principles into a world where rearranging the balance of power in one's own interest remained the norm.

Wilson was easy meat for a man so hardened by history. The American had arrived with his dream of a new world order at a time when Europe was dependent on Washington for food and finance. "Never had a philosopher held such weapons wherewithal to bind the princes of this world. His head and features were finely cut and exactly like his photographs," Keynes wrote of Wilson. "But this blind and deaf Don Quixote was entering a cavern where the swift and glittering blade was in the hands of the adversary . . . The President's slowness among the Europeans was noteworthy . . ." They were too swift, too agile for him, and faced by this terrible sterility, Wilson's "faith withered and dried up".

Security was Clemenceau's priority. He wanted to annex the Saar and establish the French military frontier along the Rhine. This involved a permanent occupation of the Rhineland and the west bank of the Rhine. Wilson and Lloyd George would not have it; though, a point often mislaid, the Germans had taken the better part of two rich French provinces for themselves after 1870, the merest skirmish compared to the Great War. The Germans had also imposed indemnities. Public opinion wanted these reversed, and with a vengeance.

The Germans must pay the costs of the war, the French held, not simply to replace what was destroyed, but also the pensions and indemnities paid to widows and the wounded. The finance minister, Louis-Lucien Klotz, whom Clemenceau described as "the only Jew who knows nothing about money", proposed levying a tax on capital to service the colossal debts run up during the war. The country would not stand for it. "Did we win the war?" a headline in *La Liberté* demanded early in 1919. "A plan for a tax on capital indeed! First of all German capital must be taxed!"

No one thought to ask the defeated Germans to the talks, though the French had been invited to the Congress of Vienna after Napoleon was beaten. Their delegation set off from Berlin on April 28, 1919 to receive the terms that the Allies had decided upon in their absence. They were to be given them, not in the Quai d'Orsay, where the victors had after much squabbling agreed them, but at Versailles. Louis XIV's great palace outside Paris had been the scene of modern Germany's greatest triumph, the humiliation of France and the proclamation of the Reich, in 1870–71. The roles were now reversed. It was the Germans who were to be humbled.

The process began as they passed through northern France. The railwaymen slowed their train down to 15 kph, so that they could reflect on the damage they had done. Reparations were set at a ruinous level; some of the wherewithawal to pay for them, notably the coal mines of the Saar and a large slice of West Prussia, was to be taken by the French and Poles. Many felt that no German government could possibly agree. A young American diplomat, William C. Bullitt, a future ambassador to France, explained that he preferred "to lie on the sands of the Riviera and watch the world go to hell", and resigned.

In Berlin, Philipp Scheidemann, the first chancellor of the new German republic, also resigned with his government. Foch ordered the French army to re-mobilise. Talk of an Allied march on Berlin followed. The new government of Gustav Bauer gave way.

A semicircular table was set up for the Allies in the Galerie des Glaces in the great palace. In front of it stood a small table for the signatories, half-jokingly called the "guillotine". Clemenceau used extreme economy of language. "Faites entrer les Allemands!" he commanded. The German delegation, in frock coats, ill at ease, came forward to sign. "La séance est levée," Clemenceau announced. Outside, guns fired in salute to tell Paris that the treaty – the second Treaty of Versailles, Clemenceau insisted, so different from the first – had been delivered. Paris was ill-humoured that day, June 28, a Saturday; the Communists brought the buses and Métro out on strike.

A temporary cenotaph was set up on Bastille Day in the Arc de Triomphe, dedicated "aux morts pour la Patrie." French troops paraded at the Arc for the first time since the site had been defiled by the Prussians in 1871. Led by the commander-in-chief, Pétain, astride a white charger, it took an hour for them to march past. Finally, nine spanking new French tanks clanked through the arch. The display of French might was comforting to watch, no doubt, and it was true that the French army was now the largest on earth. Clemenceau's gains – Alsace-Lorraine, a 15-year protectorate of the coal-rich Saarland, the demilitarisation of the west bank and a 50 kilometre-deep strip on the east bank of the Rhine, reparations, half-shares in Togo and Cameroon with the British, and the mandate of the new League of Nations in Syria and Lebanon – might seem little enough recompense for the holocaust.

But then the greatest gain, prayed for with such passion, was that it would not happen again: "Plus jamais ça!" The American writer Scott Fitzgerald rightly concluded: "This western-front business couldn't be done again, not for a long time. The young men think they could do it, but they couldn't. They could fight the first Marne again but not this. This took religion and years of plenty and the tremendous sureties and exact relation between the classes . . . You had to remember Christmas, and postcards of the Crown Prince and his fiancée, and little cafés in Valence and beer gardens in Unter den Linden and weddings at the mairie, and going to the Derby . . ."

There were to be no further massacres in the mud, not, at least for the French. "This war has marked us for generations," wrote Pierre de Mazenod. "It has left its imprint on our souls. All those inflamed nights at Verdun we shall rediscover one day in the eyes of our children."

And it was precisely there, with the children, that the French remained so desperately vulnerable. They did not have enough of them. The Germans had increased by 186 per cent in the last century, and the British by 150 per cent; the French were up by only 43 per cent, and in the new century they had been "more generous with their blood than their sperm", as one observer put it. "France must have lots of children," Clemenceau warned the Senate. "If not, you can put what you like into the treaty. France will be done for." Some effort was made. A law of 1920 laid down severe penalties for abortion and forbade all publicity for contraception. Family associations like the Ligue de la mère au foyer campaigned for women to stay at home and not to go out to work. A housewife of the year prize – the Concours de la meilleure ménagère – was awarded. A few industrialists, Romanet in Grenoble, the tyre maker Edouard Michelin, gave family bonuses to their workers, and the poorest parents were awarded small one-off birth grants. No regular family allowances were voted, however. A chronic lack of suitable housing was a major inhibitor for young families. Nothing was done to build low-rent lodgings until 1928, and mainly in the Paris region at that.

The population had to be propped up with immigrants once more. France was, after the United States, the great melting pot of footloose Europeans. Almost two million arrived in the 1920s, accounting for almost all the modest gain. Italians were again prominent, though now they worked less on southern farms and more in the industries of Paris, Lorraine and the north. Poles came in large numbers, half a million by 1928, shipped into the northern iron ore and coal mines on contracts made by French employers' associations with the Polish emigration office. "Free" immigrants also arrived, crowding into the poorest Paris arrondissements: Greeks, Armenians and Jews from the ghettos of central Europe. But the Germans knew, as they licked their wounds and brooded on their humiliations, that there were half as many more of them as there were French; and they produced seven times as much coal and four times as much steel. A tablet at Verdun recorded that the city had been besieged or damaged nine times between 450 and 1916. Stopping a tenth invasion from the east would depend as much on her allies as on France herself. There was only so much that the French could do, and defeating Germany single-handed was not one of them.

But the Allies were sour and out of sorts. The Anglo-American guarantee of automatic aid to France in the event of German aggression was dependent upon both countries ratifying the Versailles Treaty and the attached League of Nations Covenant. The American Senate refused to ratify either the Treaty or the Covenant. The British were not bound to help France alone. The guarantee fell through. In substance, if not in name, the Allies were now ex-Allies.

The ill-feeling was most obvious with reparations. Her security left in tatters by the US Senate, it was in French interests to weaken Germany and to delay her recovery as a great military power. Public opinion in Britain agreed with the French that the Germans should be "squeezed till the pips squeak". But the government, and the Americans, argued that French reparation demands were set dangerously high. The French ascribed this to Anglo-Saxon greed, in wanting a prosperous German market, and retorted that if they selfishly allowed the Germans to avoid their responsibilities, then France should not be expected to repay its huge debts to them. When the Americans and British stopped supporting the franc, in March 1919, it fell sharply. It had been rock steady since 1803, surviving Waterloo and the Commune with barely a shudder, but in 1919 it dipped to half its pre-war value, and by 1920 was down by four-fifths.

The row flickered on. In a brilliant, highly opinionated work, *The Economic Consequences of the Peace*, Keynes claimed that it was impossible for Germany to pay high reparations without embarking on a trade war against the allies to raise the money to pay them. Raymond Poincaré, the hard-line French president, resigned from the Allied reparations committee as the British position hardened. "The spectre of revision appears at every moment before our eyes," he said.

The British were hostile, too, to Marshal Foch's plan for a small German army manned by conscripts undergoing a few months' military service. The French rightly believed that this was the best way to prevent the Germans from creating a professional force whose expertise would underpin a new mass army if – when – they violated Versailles. The British had a different view, and it prevailed. The Germans were to have an army of 100,000 career volunteers, each serving for 12 years, the very basis for the powerful force the French wished to avoid.

The French were rightly worried that the League of Nations would achieve little without its own forces. Léon Bourgeois, a former Socialist premier who won the Nobel Prize for Peace in 1920 for his work in founding the League, promoted the French view that an international army should enforce League decisions. The Americans and British opposed it. The League was thus armed with no more than moral force and economic sanctions.

In the west, the Americans were all but gone, and the British were awkward allies, at best. Europe was of little concern compared to their empire. They kept their military spending to a minimum. From 1922, their budgets assumed that there would be no major war for at least ten years.

In the east, the Russians were gone. A French expeditionary force was sent to the Ukraine in March 1919 to help the Whites in the civil war; it failed to halt the Reds, and a mutiny in the French Black Sea fleet was led by a young warrant officer engineer, André Marty. It was a reminder that the French themselves were not immune to the temptations of Bolshevism – Marty helped to found the French Communist Party – and the victory of the right and the Bloc National in the 1919 elections was in part due to fear of the Reds, the "men with knives between their teeth".

The Petite Entente was the French attempt to reproduce the vanished Russian imperial steamroller as a counterweight to Germany. Its members were what some

Germans menacingly called *Saisonstaaten*, seasonal states that sprang up like hot-house plants at Versailles and were likely to perish at the first cold snap.

Poland was the cornerstone. In 1920, under Marshal Pilsudski, it drove the Reds back, 240 kilometres east of the frontier alotted at Versailles in 1919.

Having stung their Soviet neighbours, the Poles now angered the Germans. A plebiscite in Upper Silesia showed a majority in favour of rejoining Germany. The Poles, with French support, secured partition into a German and a Polish Silesia. A crucial ally, Poland was now a poor asset, devalued by the active hostility of both its big neighbours, and the mistrust of the British. As to the others in the entente, the Czechs were suspicious of the Poles. The alliance that France brokered between them was shallow and insincere. The Yugoslavs allied with the Romanians for fear of the Hungarians. Bucharest cosied up to Prague for the same reason.

Eastern Europe was a place of many cross-hatreds. It was economically weak, too, and France lacked the money to help it grow. The Paris market could not absorb Polish or Czech bonds, as it had once lapped up Russian Fives. The efforts Paris made were not welcomed by London, moreover, but were treated with deep suspicion. They were seen, not as purely defensive and laudable, but as efforts to extend French hegemony in Europe.

At home it had been clear for some time that President Paul Deschanel was a *baguette* or two short of a picnic. He had walked fully clothed into the lake at his country residence; he had also taken to tossing back the flowers in bouquets one by one to the girls who presented them to him, and held long conversations with trees. Then in May 1920 he fell out of a slow-moving tram and was found wandering on the track in his pyjamas. Alexandre Millerand replaced him as president the following September, and he was consigned to a sanatorium for nervous disorders.

The madness of President Deschanel, of course, no more meant that the nation itself was lunatic than had the better-known madness of George III of England. Whereas the latter was a mere dynastic fluke, however, Deschanel was chosen to be head of state. The coterie of ministers who installed him in the Élysée were indifferent to his state of mind, and to all his qualities bar one. He was not Clemenceau. Unlike the ferocious and mauling Tiger, who frightened them, Deschanel was malleable and morally flabby.

High politics was a perpetual game of musical chairs. The music stopped 40 times over the next twenty years, and each time a new government was formed as the same cast of characters scrambled for a seat in it. The shortest lasted three days; any that staggered beyond a twelvemonth was thought a titan. Aristide Briand was a cabinet minister 25 times, and prime minister eleven times. Raymond Poincaré darted from the finance ministry to the Quai, and on to the presidency and the premiership.

These were not little men – Briand had co-founded *L'Humanité*, Poincaré was a member of the Académie Française who wrote with verve on literature as well as politics – but the system made them seem so. It had no parties in the solid and established Anglo-American sense of Whigs and Tories; it was a creature of factions and intrigue.

The two men were dominant figures, and Germany the dominant theme. Poincaré was the French hard man, a believer in security through force if need be, convinced that the Germans were revanchist, and that the venal Americans and British would be delighted to see Germany revitalised, provided they had a slice of its market. Briand was a soft, eager and serious man whose face resembled "a composite of all the earnest animals in the zoo", the "apostle of peace" who sought rapprochement with Germany, feeling France to be too exhausted and isolated from the Anglo-Saxons to be martial in its demands.

A sum of 132 billion gold marks was finally arrived at by the reparations committee in April 1921. The Germans were to pay two billion marks a year, to which a sum equivalent to 26 per cent of their exports would be added. This was equivalent to them paying the victors 14 per cent of national revenue for thirty years. To do so, they would have to raise their exports by at least two thirds. It was, as Keynes had warned and the Germans now pleaded, impossible. Threatened with the occupation of the Ruhr, with the British and French in accord for once, Berlin crumbled and started payments.

The mark sagged. The dollar stood at 60 marks in May 1921, at 84 marks in August, and 268 by September. The French claimed that the devaluation was a deliberate ploy to get off the reparations hook. The British said it proved that Keynes was right. Briand, restored as prime minister in 1921, was half-inclined to agree. He started off toughly enough, promising to "grab the Germans by the throat" if they reneged, but found this impossible to maintain. "I practise the policy of our birth rate," he said in a telling phrase. Here, the tough laws against the *faiseuses d'anges*, the angel-making backstreet abortionists, were backed up by new state medals for fertility. Five children earned the mother a bronze, eight a silver, and, for those who broke the ten-barrier, gold. It availed nothing, and Briand got no credit for his frankness from a public that would not stand for concessions to the Germans. He resigned in January 1922.

As the mark went into free fall, Poincaré's new government refused to offer a moratorium, and threatened to occupy the Ruhr. The British disagreed, though Poincaré had every reason to be firm. Industrialists like the metals tycoon Hugo Stinnes were using low German wage rates to crucify the French iron and steel\ industry. German paramilitaries organised by General von Seekt were parading in defiance of the Versailles treaty. Inflation was dissolving internal debt and minimising taxation in Germany, and helping German goods win world markets. French business, restrained by Poincaré's strict budgets and taxes, could not compete. There was a moral point, too: if the British and Americans were unwilling to let the French default on their loans, why should they be soft to the Germans?

French and Belgian troops duly occupied the Ruhr in January 1923. The mark now disintegrated. In August, it was at 4,620,455 to the dollar. By December, it was at 4 trillion 200 billion. The German middle class was ruined. The French expelled thousands of troublemakers, many of them Prussian civil servants, and set up customs barriers between the occupied zone and the rest of Germany. The right dreamed of separating the whole of the Rhineland from Germany. "A Rhineland detached from Prussia and Bavaria means peace," the old patriot Maurice Barrès wrote shortly before his death in December 1923.

The month before, seizing on public anger with the Treaty of Versailles and the occupation, Adolf Hitler attempted to overthrow the Bavarian government with support from General Ludendorff's extremists. The Munich police opened fire on the Nazi columns. Sixteen storm troopers were killed. Hermann Goering was seriously injured, and Hitler was imprisoned, but it was a warning of things to come.

Over time, the French tired with the occupation and the tax rises used to pay for it. "Poincaré la guerre," the prime minister's opponents shouted, or "Poincaruhr." He lost the 1924 elections to the left-wing Cartel des Gauches coalition. His successor, the Radical-Socialist Édouard Herriot, bowed to Anglo-American pressure and accepted a much reduced reparations plan. A bone was tossed to the French, with the inclusion of a "prosperity index" under which German payments would increase if the country boomed. The troops were withdrawn from the Ruhr.

From now, a policy of accommodation with Germany was followed. It was not yet appeasement: Germany was still too weak to make demands. A watershed was nonetheless passed when the *poilus* pulled out of the Ruhr. A Keynesian sentiment became pervasive, which blamed Versailles and reparations for nurturing the German sense of grievance and outrage that ultimately created Hitler.

But it is also arguable that Keynes and his followers created the climate of appeasement that enabled Hitler to flourish. German non-compliance with Versailles began as soon as the ink was dry; whilst Poincaré played tough, the Germans tucked Hitler and other fanatics away in prison, and in any event only a small proportion of the greatly scaled down reparations was ever collected. The monster sprang from the Anglo-American kid glove, not from the French iron fist. That was the counter-opinion, put with bitter force by Étienne Mantoux in *The Carthaginian Peace, or the Economic Consequences of Mr Keynes*. It was published in 1946. By then, Keynes was dead; so too was Mantoux, killed fighting the Nazis.

At home, the franc slid; so did the Cartel des Gauches, to the extent of seven cabinets in two years. Poincaré was back in 1926, tough and vigorous, slashing government spending, raising taxes and winning back the confidence of financiers. He had stabilised the franc by 1928, if at a fifth of its pre-war value; ill health, and not defeat, forced him from office in 1929.

Briand served both the Cartel and Poincaré as foreign minister. He pursued rapprochement with energy and success. At Locarno in 1925, amid much joy and hope, the French, Belgians and Germans promised not to alter by force the mutual frontiers laid down at Versailles. They agreed to refer any dispute between them to the League of Nations. France thus gained a freely negotiated and signed settlement of Alsace-Lorraine, and the Germans a guarantee that there would be no more Ruhr-style occupations. In January 1926, French troops evacuated Cologne ahead of schedule as a first step in total withdrawal from the Rhineland. That September, France sponsored German entry into the League of Nations. "Away with rifles, machine guns and cannon!" Briand declared. "Make room for conciliation, arbitration and peace!" He and Gustav Stresemann, his German opposite number, shared the Nobel peace prize.

Rare goodwill flowed between the fractious allies. The French debts to Britain and America were consolidated, at £799 million and $4,025 million, large enough sums, but to be repaid at low interest rates over 62 years. The Kellogg-Briand Pact seemed further proof of blossoming fraternity. It was signed by the US secretary of state and the foreign minister in February 1928, and was extended to the British, Germans, Soviets and others. All declared that they "condemn recourse to war for the settlement of international differences." War was outlawed "as an instrument of national policy". Conflicts were to be resolved "by peaceful means only".

The French were already committed to a defensive strategy. Military service was slashed to 18 months, and then to a year. A harsh critic might find faults. The lessons of 1918 – mobility, tanks, breakthrough, victory – were ignored by elderly commanders who remembered the Verdun virtues of grim defence. Young officers found promotion blocked in the shrinking, age-heavy army. Inflation whittled away pay. Many resigned. Those who were left were barrack-bound, bitter and sometimes far right.

But it seemed churlish to say so, for this was the high water mark of peace.

The industrial dynamic was not gone, but it was uneven. Some did well out of reparations, for it was thought almost patriotic to over-egg claims for damages, since "the Boche will pay". The sugar baron Béghin, a big producer in the north, put together a lucrative empire with the 126 million Francs he received by adding the claims of smaller refineries he had taken over to his own losses. The big Kuhlmann chemicals combine used compensation to go on an acquisitions spree. Towns and villages were rebuilt very quickly. Some two million hectares of prime wheat-growing land that had been wrecked by the war in the plains north and east of Paris were back in production by 1925.

A new type of "neo-capitalism" was in fashion, in which vigorous state action combined with private enterprise along wartime lines to kick-start new development. That, at least, was the theory promoted in *La Revue des deux mondes* by Valéry Giscard d'Estaing's father, among others. Hybrid companies like the Compagnie

Nationale du Rhône and the Compagnie Française des Pétroles (CFP) mixed state and private investment. The state encouraged amalgamations and links, such as those between the giant Compagnie Générale d'Électricité and Alsthom, which was itself a merger of the Société Alsacienne de Constructions Mécaniques and Thomson-Houston. The major industrial interest groups, the Comités and Unions des Forges, des Produits Chimiques, des Houillères, des Industries Metallurgiques et Minières, created a powerful employers' organisation, the CGPF 'Confédération Générale de la Production Française' in 1919.

Spectacular growth was logged in a wide range of industries. Electricity production almost quadrupled between 1920 and 1928, with many hydro dams built in the Alps. Car manufacture was second only to the Americans, though the French had 5 per cent of global production, and the Americans 90 per cent. Many makers were too small – there were 150 of them in 1921 – but three giants built more than half the 250,000 cars produced in 1928.

The road-racing Louis Renault and the iron mongering Peugeots were joined by André Citroën, son of an Amsterdam diamond merchant, a brilliant engineer who had seen American mass production in action, and had used assembly line techniques in building an artillery shell factory during the war. He launched the Citroën A1, an economical, low-priced two seater, at the 1919 Paris motor show. Though he went for the mass market, Citroën was a pioneering engineer. His cars, like the famous 5CV of 1923 and the "all-steel" B1 two years later, teemed with innovation. He had a flair for publicity, too, and organised the "Black Rally" across the Sahara in 1922, and had his name lit in neon lights on the Eiffel Tower for the 1925 Art Deco exhibition. He was less gifted as a gambler, however, and lost so much money at the Deauville casino that he ultimately lost control of the business.

Some oil fields and the old Turkish Petroleum Company from the defunct Ottoman empire were now French controlled. The government set up CFP to exploit them in 1924. After the discovery of the Baba Gurgur field in 1927, another state-private hybrid, the Compagnie Française de Raffinage, was created to refine the oil. The big tyre-maker Michelin was another leader in the expanding motor sector, with rubber plantations in French Vietnam well placed to profit from the soaring demand for rubber.

A clause in the Versailles treaty enabled French chemicals companies to exploit German patents without paying royalties. The sector boomed. Saint-Gobain were involved in chemicals, oil refining, and cellulose and paper, as well as glass-making. Kuhlmann spread into fertilisers, copper sulphate and pyrites. Aalais, Frogues and Camargue, founded in 1925 for salt and its derivatives, blossomed into Péchiney and developed Alpine electro-metallurgy and aluminium production. The Motte and Gillet families created the giant Progil chemicals maker. Schneider expanded rapidly in iron, steel, bauxite and aluminium. The company played an important foreign policy role in maintaining subsidiaries in France's eastern allies, Poland, Romania and

Czechoslovakia, setting up a special bank to help finance industry in the region. These, and companies like Le Creusot, Dion et Bouton and Montlucon, spent on research and pioneered or kept up with technical advance.

The giants were few, however, and concentrated in Rhône-Alpes, the ports and the Paris region, which was transfused with much of the country's financial and industrial blood just as it dominated in politics and the arts. The centre, west and southwest were left pale and anaemic. The typical French company was small, family-owned, conservative, and leery and secretive towards banks, the stock exchange, tax men and other bureaucrats. Profits were often kept in cash rather than being reinvested.

A nervous conservatism was widespread. The rentiers, the often modest people who lived off savings in bonds, were more or less ruined. Inflation gnawed at the returns from domestic bonds, and foreign bonds like the Russian Fives became worthless when the Bolsheviks reneged on them. The fate of the *petite bourgeoisie* in Germany, thrown to the dogs by hyper-inflation, acted as a terrible warning to the shopkeeper and tradesman and small-time civil servant. They could not strike, like factory workers, or feed themselves, like peasants; their savings had melted away with inflation. They clung to their shabby-genteel status, wary of any reform that might improve the lot of those beneath them.

The far right dealt in tradition, in hard-faced nationalism, Catholicism and royalism. The Third Republic was ever "la Gueuse", the Whore. Charles Maurras's Action Française recruited students to harass Marxist professors and break up Communist meetings, and to compete with the rival Jeunesses Patriotes, founded by the Paris deputy Pierre Taittinger. This had fighting squads in the style of the old patriotic Ligues, and claimed 300,000 members by 1929.

The stridency of right-wing invective tended to obscure the fact that they were victims as well as perpetrators. In practice, the left was quite as violent as the right. Marius Plateau, a much decorated war hero and Action Française stalwart, was murdered by a woman anarchist in 1923. Another leading nationalist, Ernest Berger, also met his death at a woman's hands in 1925. In the intervening year, Communists murdered four members of the Jeunesses Patriotes in Montmartre.

An extraordinary saga surrounded Léon Daudet, a writer of powerful prose, son of the novelist Alphonse Daudet, and the editor of Action Française's newspaper. His 14-year-old son Philippe was found dead in a taxi with a bullet wound in 1925. An enquiry found the boy to have committed suicide, but Daudet maintained that he had been murdered, and accused the taxi driver of complicity. The driver sued for defamation. Police laid siege to Action Française's offices when they came to arrest Daudet, and the facts disappeared in a wave of sensationalism. Daudet was heavily fined and imprisoned. The tale took another twist when Daudet escaped from the Santé prison in 1927, after royalist friends had duped the prison governor into believing that he had been pardoned. He fled to Belgium.

The liberal right, anxious to distinguish itself from these pugnacious firebrands, had the curious habit of adopting left-sounding names. The Républicains de Gauche, the Indépendants de Gauche and the Alliance Démocratique made up the majority of the ruling right, not left, the power base of men like Poincaré, Briand, Laval and Reynaud. Their roots were in the provinces; they were cautious spenders, opposed to high taxes and state intervention. They were, however, split over foreign policy. Some, as we have seen with Poincaré, were nationalists who deeply mistrusted Germany, where others stood with Aristide Briand for peaceful reconciliation with the old enemy.

A more old-fashioned conservative force, Catholic, legitimist, uneasy with republican institutions, was found among the still pious peasants of the west and the southern regions of the Massif Central. Catholics were not the mindless bigots of anticlerical pamphleteers. Scholarship flourished under Jacques Maritain at the Insitut Catholique in Paris and Étienne Gilson at the Sorbonne. Action Française suffered a papal condemnation in 1926, on the grounds of extreme nationalism and cynical misappropriation of Catholic doctrine, and its newspaper was put on the index. The bishop of Lille came out in support of striking textile workers two years later. The employers – solid Church-going bourgeois – were shocked when Pius XI publicly backed the bishop. He was applauded by a new breed of left-leaning Catholic intellectuals, the novelist François Mauriac prominent among them.

In the centre were the Radicals, defenders of the "little man" and social reform, liberal interventionists in economic policy, supporters of the League of Nations and collective security abroad. The party had a solid base in the country. Édouard Herriot was the fireproof mayor of Lyon, and Albert and Maurice Sarraut were deeply ensconced in Languedoc. They were able to work with Socialists or with the pacifist wing of the liberal right, in principle at least. This, with their strong showing in the Chamber, made them indispensable to every coalition government. They were lukewarm to Socialist policy, however, and the Cartel des Gauches had proved itself a weak affair before Poincaré swept in and put it out of its misery.

The left got off to a poor post-war start. An attempt was made in 1920 to fashion a general strike from a walk-out on the railways by the powerful Fédération des Cheminots. It was a disaster. Support was well below expectation. Songs against *mercantis* (profiteers) might always raise a cheer, and people sang the praises of strikers in catchy little numbers like "Grève des Tramways de Lille", but France had no stomach for class war. The employers sacked 18,000 railwaymen, a fifth of the workforce. Union membership and morale slumped.

The Red victory in the Russian civil war inspired some, but served also to split the left at the Socialist Party's congress at Tours in December 1920. Moscow dictated rigid terms for membership of the Communist International. The entry price included total submission to the Comintern and Moscow – ditching the tricolour and the "Marseillaise", for example, for the Red flag and the "Internationale" – and the imposition of a monolithic party structure with strict discipline. Those who voted to join the Comintern founded the new French Communist Party at the congress. Léon Blum and the moderates of the Section Française de l'Internationale Ouvrière (SFIO), opposed them. In 1922, Trotsky demanded the expulsion of all party members who refused to quit the Ligue des Droits de l'Homme, which he lampooned as a centre of "petit-bourgeois ideology". The French party's secretary-general, Ludovic-Oscar Frossard, resigned at the start of 1923, taking the party's right wing with him.

The surviving rump fought all other parties and factions in its pursuit of Muscovite Bolshevism and class war. It picked up 8 per cent of the poll in the 1924 elections, and built up its long-term bastions in the Paris suburbs, the Cher and the Lot-et-Garonne, and the "red crescent" of the Massif Central.

The Communists treated the Cartel des Gauches with quite the same venom as the right. The Cartel itself was unloved and inept; it tried to ingratiate itself with fresh anticlericalism, but that vein had run dry, for opinion remembered that Catholic padres had served in the trenches, and the restoration of diplomatic relations with the Vatican in 1921 had bound up the old wounds. The Cartel's continued hostility to the Church was a reason why women continued to be denied the vote; the left was afraid that they would vote for pro-Church conservatives. Its naiveté helped corrode the franc when two clerks at the Banque de France were arrested and convicted for advising friends to sell their holdings in government bonds. The trial was widely reported, and the public, not being stupid, started dumping their own bonds.

Blum's SFIO was a self-consciously proletarian party – the inclusion of young bourgeois intellectuals made sure of that – which, despite its claim to be revolutionary, stopped short of the Communists and accepted the "positive" value of human rights and parliamentary reforms that would speed up the arrival of true socialism. It had many non-proletarian members – primary schoolteachers, postal workers, lower-grade civil servants, some small farmers, with Blum himself a lawyer – and the Communists derided them as "sociaux-traitres". For their part, the SFIO mocked their Bolshevik-dominated rivals as the "Moscoutaires".

There was little comradeship among the comrades.

In the arts, in fashion and joie de vivre, Paris remained supreme. True, rising rents in Montmartre had driven many to find a new haven in Montparnasse. Here, the three cafés round the Vavin crossroads – La Rotonde, Le Dôme and La Coupole – were the great meeting places for "les Montparnos".

The age retained a sense of tragedy. The Spanish flu did for Guillaume Apollinaire, survivor of a head wound in the trenches. Amadeo Modigliani died of tubercular meningitis, and neglect. He held a one-man show in 1918, but his nudes were judged to be too frank, and the exhibition was closed for indecency on the first day. He squandered the few francs he made from his portraits, whose elongated heads resembled African carvings, on hashish, cocaine and absinthe. When he died, early in 1920, part of his emaciated face was torn away by the death mask made by his friend Moïse Kisling. His young mistress, Jeanne Hébuterne, pregnant with their second child, was inconsolable. Her parents kept suicide watch, but she jumped from a fifth floor balcony to her death.

Picasso was rich enough now to live in bourgeois comfort in the rue de la Boétie, where his dealer, Paul Rosenberg, had his gallery round the corner. He honeymooned with the Ballets Russes dancer Olga Khokhlova in the swish Hôtel Lutitia on the boulevard Raspail. Still to make their way, the denizens of La Ruche, an old circular building from the 1900 Exposition divided into small studios on a derelict site in the XVe, lived in cheerful squalor. When Chaïm Soutine stole three herrings to use as still lifes, two rotted and rats made off with the third. He painted the carcasses in the next-door slaughterhouse with hammer force as bloodied deconstructions of once living things. Marc Chagall came, like Soutine, from imperial Russia, and used vivid blues, greens and yellows; his oxen were not butchered, but floated over the rooftops in dreamy scenes from Russian folklore. When Soutine came to call, throwing pebbles at his window to get his attention, Chagall turned his paintings to the wall for fear that Soutine would pollute them with his rancid overcoat.

Constantin Brancusi was once a shepherd boy in the Carpathians, and looked a "sort of peasant-saint", with shrewd piercing eyes and scraggy beard beneath a pudding-bowl hat, and a white spitz dog at his feet. He was so poor on his arrival that he was sacked from the choir of the Romanian Orthodox church in the avenue Jean-de-Beauvais for eating the sacramental bread to ease his hunger pains. He had worked in Rodin's atelier, and studied African carvings, and the influences showed in the direct simplicity of works like *The Prodigal Son*. Brancusi called it "sculpture for the blind", aiming to refine a subject to its very essence.

Dada was the novelty, a rootless import that travelled to New York and Cologne as well as Paris. The name was taken at random from a dictionary – "dada" was the nursery word for a rocking horse – and it grew out of absurdist performances at the Cabaret Voltaire in Zürich. It was an anti-art protest, or so its founders said, which put energy and change at a premium over aesthetic values. It was anxious to provoke – "machinery, massacre, skyscrapers, urinals, sexual orgies, revolutions" were its appointed subject matter – and self-consciously novel.

For eight years Marcel Duchamp laboured on a three-metre-high composition in glass and metal with the Dadaist title of *The Bride Stripped Bare by Her Bachelors Even*. He used what he called "ready-mades", creating the concept of the "found object" in which an ordinary product like a coffee mill is made artistic by virtue of its selection by an artist. Dada revelled in nonsense poetry where newspaper articles were cut into pieces at random and shaken up in a bag. The Romanian poet Tristan Tzara read out the words in the order they came out the bag to create the "poem", accompanied by castanets, cowbells and rattles. The next new movement took shape after André Breton and Louis Aragon published the Surrealist manifesto in 1924. Both had served as medical orderlies in hospitals for shell-shocked soldiers. They declared Surrealism to be the "enemy of reason". They dismissed Dada as an "intolerable tyranny" and set out to create what Breton called "pure psychic automatism". This was inspired by the subconscious, as explored by Freud, and the sense of the importance of dreams. Its major painters were Max Ernst, Joan Miró and Salvador Dalí, self-publicist and brilliant draughtsman, who had studied abnormal psychology and dream symbolism, and painted "paranoiac" and fanciful objects – a melted clock, a sculpted bone – in the landscapes of his Catalan boyhood with lucid realism.

Aragon wrote poetry, and a Surrealist novel, *Le Paysan de Paris*, in 1926, but he converted to communism in 1930 – a Surrealist decision in itself, for it followed a visit to the Soviet Union in 1930 just as the murder of the kulaks was getting into full swing – and thereafter he wrote a series of social-realistic novels. Prompted perhaps by his "pure psychic automatism", in which the artist put on paper whatever came into his head, free of reason, Breton, too, became a Communist, a move that was not to stop him sitting out the war in America.

Giorgio de Chirico, who greatly influenced the Surrealists, called his work *pittura metafisca*, in which mysterious imagery floated across the canvas, distorted, strangely lit, with tailors' dummies or plaster statues in place of people. In *The Uncertainty of the Poet*, a pile of bananas sat next to a plaster cast of a classical torso, whilst a train steamed across the deep background of the painting. Some critics thought that the bananas represented exoticism, and the torso was humanity and the train was travel, and that the painting captured the essence of the three. Others simply laughed.

A painting of a pipe, *The Treachery of Images*, has a Surrealist copy line beneath it, *Ceci n'est pas un pipe*, in René Magritte's best-known work. He started out as a commercial artist, and it showed in the meticulous and catalogue-like look of the pipe. His fantasies drift from dream to nightmare. A steam train pounds out of the middle of a fireplace, the clouds in a brilliant sky are loaves of bread. Yves Tanguy based his painting *The Invisibles* on André Breton's claim that there exist invisible animals that have escaped man's senses through camouflage, filling his canvas with strange creatures that hover over the barren landscapes of the mind like alien attack craft in a still from a sci-fi film. Joan Miró's dreamworld was filled with the strange hallucinations of his subconscious, fresh and vivacious and yet eerie, like cave paintings done on LSD.

The Cuban Wilfredo Lam, influenced like his friend Picasso by sculptures from tribal Africa and Oceania, brought a sense of voodoo to the surreal, with totems, brooding jungles, and dream-like but menacing figures with halloween masks and horse-faces in bamboo greens. Max Ernst, who worked with Miró on the decor for Diaghilev ballets, used *frottage*, a technique like brass-rubbing that creates an outline of what is beneath it. He did this with random objects, to bring a quality of chance to the surreal. The Surrealist purpose was to show that things are not as they seem, that conventional concepts of reality can be challenged. The line between the absurd and the merely ludicrous is a fine one. Salvador Dalí's immense talent kept him from sliding over it. In *Sleep*, a dreamer's head hovers above a landscape so delicately balanced on wooden props that the slightest breeze would wake him, the canvas awash with the sense of the fragility of rest and slumber.

It was difficult to pigeon-hole painters. Picasso deplored the habit, and was too elusive and changeable to fit any label for long. Artists like himself pioneered a style, he complained, and then others came and prettified it. Chaïm Soutine claimed to despise all his contemporaries, reserving his admiration for Rembrandt. He now ranged beyond slaughtered meat to paint powerful portraits of valets, bellhops, and the *Little Pastry Chef*, a nervous, highly charged figure with a slab-sided nose beneath his toque. The Swiss sculptor Alberto Giacometti took thin metal skeletons and added clay to them, and then cast them as restless, nervous, emaciated figures.

The Surrealists were thought to be cohesive enough for a group show to be held at the Galerie Pierre in 1925. It had work by Paul Klee, although he was then teaching at the Bauhaus in Germany, and his expressive, detailed semi-abstracts are highly personal and do not fit into any pattern. Picasso was shown with his Catalan friend, Joan Miró, though he had little time for the Surrealists. He dismissed the work of Max Ernst as resembling "a dove flying out of a stationmaster's arse". Miró had admired primitive Catalan art and Gaudí's extravagant architecture, but rushed into Surrealism after arriving in Paris in 1920, painting child-like dreams of people and animals in fantastical and flowing forms and patterned colours.

The American Man Ray set himself up as a photographer, painter, sculptor and film-maker in Paris. A galaxy of sitters passed through his tiny studio-darkroom: Gertrude Stein and Alice B. Toklas, Brancusi, Stravinsky. He photographed Tristan Tzara kissing the hand of Nancy Cunard, a self-willed shipping heiress whose independence was still found shocking in a girl. He photographed Mina Loy's naked back as a human cello, with thermometers as earrings, and strings and sound holes on her lower back to transform her flesh into an instrument. His sculpture *Inquiétude* featured a dismantled alarm clock in a glass case full of tobacco smoke. He began experimenting with filming after working with René Clair. Jean Cocteau, normally a drummer for anything new, shuddered at the Surrealists: "Ils sont tous les petits Nietzsches," he said. Cocteau was himself a human kaleidoscope, giddy with preening energy, perpetually precocious, an actor, director, artist, writer of scenarios and novels, critic and promoter of talent. As a boy, he was taken to the Comédie Française twice a week to see the classics, and brought up to think of literature and art as "a sport, an exercise like painting". His lawyer father killed himself when Cocteau was eight. He grew up close to his mother, obsessed with death and the myth of Oedipus.

The Twenties were his great decade, though he sparkled until his death in 1963. He had served as an ambulance driver in Misia Sert's private ambulance corps on the Belgian front, wearing a uniform designed by Coco Chanel. On his return, he struck up friendships with Picasso – "I admired his intelligence and clung to everything he said, for he spoke little" – and Giorgio de Chirico. He saw a new music flowing from the sounds of Paris, the medley of fairs, circuses and cabarets, with the resonance of steam engines, typewriters and sirens, and the energy of the American dance music that was sweeping the dance halls. "Enough of clouds, waves, aquariums, water-sprites, and nocturnal scents," he wrote in *Le Coq et l'arlequin* in 1919. "What we need is a music of the earth, everyday music."

The key work was Erik Satie's score for the ballet *Parade*, including parts for typewriter, machine gun and ship's siren. Cocteau produced the scenario, Picasso designed the sets and costumes, with choreography by Léonide Massine. It sparked off a riot at its premiere, and it provided the six composers who were grouped around Satie and Cocteau with a notoriety and reputation as a musical avant-garde that they welcomed. They became known as Les Six, though their compositions were many and varied.

A young war veteran, Francis Poulenc, wrote cool and translucent chamber music, as well as operas and the ballet *Les Biches*. Darius Milhaud had met the play-wright Paul Claudel whilst a wartime diplomat in Rio de Janeiro, and collaborated with him on the opera *Christopher Columbus*. He was to compose in a torrent – operas, incidental music for plays, jazz ballets, symphonies, and orchestral and choral works. Arthur Honneger, another member of Les Six, set himself up with his dramatic oratorio *King David* in 1921. Then came his *Pacific 231* in 1923, which followed Cocteau's ideas on using everyday sounds, here with the energy and drive of a Pacific-class locomotive rendered in music. Georges Auric became a master of the new art of film scores, working at his best with René Clair.

Les Six used the Salle Huyghens and the Théâtre du Vieux-Colombier as venues, with paintings and poetry readings often included in the performances. They dined with Milhaud in his apartment on Saturday evenings, and afterwards went out to fair-grounds to pick up sounds and cadences. They went, too, to a bar called Le Boeuf sur le Toit after an opera-bouffe dreamed up by Cocteau, with a score by Darius Milhaud, sets painted by Raoul Dufy, and performances by a troupe of acrobats from the Médrano circus. Milhaud and Cocteau had persuaded Moysès, the theatre world's pet barman, that if writers and artists could have their own cafés, then there should be a cabaret bar for musicians and composers. Dada artworks hung on the walls, with a creation by Picabia called *l'Oeil cacodylate* as the focal point; cacodylate were the salts used to treat venereal disease, and it was intended to shock. Milhaud played tunes by Cole Porter on the opening night, with Cocteau backing him on drums.

Les Six rubbed shoulders with Picasso, Diaghilev and René Clair, and a smooth singer and vaudeville actor, Maurice Chevalier, recently returned with a Croix de

Guerre from a German prison camp. They combined to write the music for Cocteau's *Les Mariés de la Tour Eiffel* in 1921 before eventually going on their separate, and successful, ways.

Satie was often to be seen in the Boeuf sur le Toit in stiff collar and bowler and with an umbrella. For all the charming melody and whimsy of his work, he was a lonely and often bitter man, sensitive to the least criticism. He appeared dully respectable, in his collar and tie, and striped shirt, cufflinks, waistcoat and pince-nez, but he was deeply eccentric. He had the police evict his mistress – she had, he told police, been "forcing her attentions on me" – and lived alone. He spent hours browsing in English bookshops, though he had no English. His compositions had strange names, as if they were bizarre puddings, *Valse au chocolat aux amandes*, *Trois morceaux en forme de poire*. In 1924, he wrote *Relâche* for Diaghilev's great rivals, Ballets Suédois, a Dadaist production with an entr'acte film by René Clair and Picabia. The prolonged booing, whistles, shouts and applause made it another scandalous triumph.

His health was giving way. He lived, but no one quite knew in what circumstances, in the suburb of Arceuil. From there, he rode into town on a trolleybus, often to attend the glittering salon of the princesse de Polignac, born Winnaretta Singer, a member of the fabulously wealthy sewing machine family. One evening early in January 1925 he lacked the strength to take the trolleybus home, his liver ruined by rotgut wine. Winnaretta paid for a private hospital room for him, where he laced his medicine with opium and champagne, and chided the friends at his bedside: "Why attack God? He may be as unhappy as we are."

Satie died in the summer, and his friends went to Arceuil to make an inventory of his possessions, as required by law. They found a single clammy room, with a squatter lavatory, and a bed and chair piled high with old suits, umbrellas and cigar boxes. The pedals of the shabby piano were tied up with chord; behind it, in a heap of unopened letters and packages, they found the score of a new ballet, *Jack in the Box*. Diaghilev produced it after his funeral, with sets by the Fauvist André Derain.

It was part of the genius of Paris itself, perhaps, that Cocteau should also have patronised Coco Chanel, a woman as supremely elegant as Satie was dowdy.

"The first war made me," she said. "In 1919 I woke up famous." Practical, simple clothes were a natural reaction to the war; the sinuous, highly coloured creations of the *belle époque* seemed garish and ornate, and the linear elegance of Chanel's clothes – "the straight line is the medium of expression" – were in perfect harmony with the times. They needed a slender figure to go with the bobbed hair and high hemlines, so a "slimming craze" was born.

She was born dirt poor in Saumur and was orphaned young, coming to Paris with her sister to work as a milliner. Slim, dark, vivacious and intelligent, her favours were shared on a town and country basis by two rich lovers. Étienne Balsan provided her with a Paris apartment. The Englishman "Boy" Capel, who entertained her at his hunting lodge, helped her start a millinery shop in the place Vendôme. Her flair for design was matched by a shrewd head for business. Her hats did her proud, but her heart was set on haute couture.

Poiret said that women were beautiful and architectural, "like the prow of a ship", until Chanel came along. Now, he said scornfully, they all looked like "undernourished telephone operators." She caught the new age better than he.

They clashed at the Exposition Internationale des Arts Décoratifs et Industriels that was held in Paris in 1925. Art Deco was a reworking of old themes: the rich, throbbing colours and theatricality that Léon Bakst had lavished on his sets and costumes for the Ballets Russes, the elongated patterns and sinuous lines of Art Nouveau, the gilt swirls of Louis XV furniture. The exhibition was a rather sotto voce affair. Bakst had died the year before, the Germans had no invitation, so there was no Bauhaus to see, and the Americans turned theirs down. Nevertheless, neon lighting was celebrated in the giant letters "Citroen" on the Eiffel Tower. Fountains of intricate glassware by René Lalique were also lit by neon; though in his mid-sixties, the artist-craftsman was still experimenting in glass. Sonia Delaunay used pure colours in waves pulsating with rhythm for paintings and much-copied textile designs. Émile Ruhlmann was the fashionable decorator of the time, and a pavilion based on a design for his town house showed off the new style in precious woods, ivory and tortoiseshell, in soft colour bursts of wallpapers and furnishings and ceramics, with screens and lamps of lacquer and silver-leaf and petalled glass.

Paul Poiret's clientele was ageing. The young were flocking to Chanel or to Jean Patou, with his sportswear and Joy perfume. Poiret counter-attacked, mooring three barges on the quayside of the exhibition. One was named *Amours*, and served as a nightclub-restaurant; *Délices* had a complete theatre aboard; *Orgues* was filled with his objets d'art, his furnishings and fabrics, and acted as his flagship, where he displayed himself with defiant confidence, as if all were for the best. It was not. He never mastered the post-war world, and the man who gave Western women the turban and harem pants slipped into impoverished obscurity.

Women were more liberated and independent. They smoked in public for the first time, and joined feminist societies. The heroine of *La Garçonne*, the best-selling novel of 1922, was a girl-boy who felt she could have a baby and live happy and free away from men, an idea so radical and shocking that the author, Victor Marguerite, whose normal fare was writing novels and histories of the Prussian war period in collaboration with his brother Paul, was expelled from the Légion d'Honneur.

Chanel freed such modern women from the corset and the wasp waist that exaggerated bosom and hips. Her first chemise dress of 1920 was followed by the collarless cardigan jacket. The vogue for costume jewellery and the evening scarf sprang from her base in the rue Cambon. So, too, did the "little black dress" that has retained its chic and sales appeal down the generations.

The peasant waif and wartime nurse became a rich and dazzling socialite. "Boy" Capel left her the then huge sum of £40,000 when he was killed in a car crash, and her business thrived. Chanel then became the patron-mistress of the Surrealist poet Pierre Reverdy, producing a volume of his poems illustrated with Picasso watercolours. She met Cocteau, and Picasso and his friend Max Jacob, a writer of satire and fantasy poems like "Le Cornet à dés" (The Dice Cup). Jacob was a Jew who had converted to mystic Catholicism, which was not to save him from the Holocaust. He persuaded Chanel of the Christ-like beauties of bobbed hair, which duly raced into fashion, bringing with it the cloche hat.

The heroine of Cocteau's *Antigone* in 1922 was closer-cropped still. The actress Genica Athanasiou shaved her head and plucked her eyebrows, appearing on stage quite bald. The production was crammed with talent. The music was by Arthur Honneger, the sets were designed by Picasso, Man Ray took photographs of the costumes by Chanel. "I asked Mlle Chanel for the costumes," Cocteau said, "because she is the greatest designer of our day and I cannot imagine the daughter of Oedipus badly dressed."

Chanel took other lovers. She passed through a brief Russian phase in design, with loose muzhik blouses embroidered in peasant style, and had Russian dalliances. She went into the perfume business with the son of the perfumer to the Russian court, and produced Chanel No 5 in its square-cut bottle, the largest-selling scent in history. She had an affair, too, with Igor Stravinsky. It was brief; small wonder, for Stravinsky pinned amulets and icons to his underclothes, and lived on a diet of raw potatoes dressed with oil and lemon. But she admired his music, and once gave Diaghilev 300,000 francs so that he could have a full orchestra in the pit for *The Rite of Spring*. Stravinsky had shown his brilliant flexibility during the war, creating the low-budget entertainment *The Soldier's Tale*. He returned to full ballet with *Pulcinella* in 1920, based on music by the eighteenth-century Italian Pergolese, and the opera-oratorio *Oedipus Rex*, based on Cocteau's version but sung in Latin for greater majesty.

Paris was filled with refugees from communist Russia. Ex-officers of the Imperial army drove taxis, waited at table, or, if still imposing in uniform and epaulettes, worked as hotel doormen. Princesses became childrens' governesses, or companions to the elderly. Prince Yusupov, another of Rasputin's murderers, dabbled as an art dealer until winning a record $375,000 in a defamation suit against a Hollywood studio. Charlatans came too. Dr Sergei Voronoff made his fortune by convincing the affluent elderly that he could rejuvenate them with monkey-gland injections. Tuberculosis was still a killer disease, which the émigré Ivan Manoukhin claimed he could cure by exposing the spleen to X-rays at his private clinic in the smart Passy district. Among the dying patients whom he defrauded was Katherine Mansfield.

Weakened by radiation sickness, she sought out another émigré, Georgei Ivanovich Gurdjieff, a striking figure with a shaved head above a flamboyant moustache. He and his disciples lived in a commune in a château near Fontainebleau, where she died.

There were charlatans in the arts, too. Surrealism crept into real life in the extraordinary case of the vanishing lady. Maria Lani arrived in Paris from Germany, or so she said, where she was a great star of screen and stage. No one has been painted by so many brilliant artists in so short a time as she – in charcoal, oils, water-colours, sketches and full-blown portraits and yet she remains ill-defined. Her essence was clearly powerful, for she swiftly captivated both high society and the world of arts, but it rests undisturbed. Her beauty was not breathtaking or even striking; it was regular, and rather plain, but her presence was clearly powerful and cascading, for she was the toast of the town in 1929, gowned and perfumed for nothing by the leading couturiers.

Though resting from her labours on the stage, she was graciously pleased to sit gratis for her new artist friends. Her agents, the Abramowitz brothers, floated the idea that portraits of her should be exhibited as a group at the Galerie Georges Bernheim in the last major vernissage of the 1920s. They did her proud.

Matisse painted her three times, as a sharp, incisive character, lively and alert. Rouault found her vulnerable and in some torment. To Braque, she was hiding behind a mask, to the critic George Waldemer, elegant and withdrawn. Jean Cocteau sketched her 14 times, and wrote the preface to the catalogue that the Abramowitz's had printed up. Soutine had her eyes suspicious and sad above an elegant black dress in his fine portrait. Foujita, Dufy, Vlaminck, Bonnard . . . she sat for them all, bar Picasso. The Abramowitz's tried hard. "I don't do portraits," he told them. Undeterred, they had some 50 portraits of her by a roll-call of established and coming names.

They sold some of them before the exhibition, and disappeared with the rest. Miss Lani herself, and her agents, were gone for good. It was found that she had been a stenographer in an office in Prague, and had never been on stage, though her acting ability was hardly in question. One Abramowitz was indeed a brother, though of hers and not the other, who was in fact her husband. As to the missing portraits, slowly, one by one, they appeared on the market and sold at escalating prices. The Soutine hangs now in the Museum of Modern Art in New York.

The foreigners who flocked to Paris found it more tempting and stimulating than ever. They made up 5.3 per cent of the population in 1921, Americans, drawn in by the ever-cheapening franc, in the van. By the end of the decade, they were within a whisker of 10 per cent. The city seemed a "divine section of eternity" to the American poet e. e. cummings; to his compatriot Ezra Pound, it was a place for brave souls who had "cast off sanctified stupidities and timidities". It was a centre of American litera-ture, perhaps *the* centre, and of Irish and English, too, an extraordinary achievement for a non-English speaking city. Little literary magazines in English opened and folded like so many flowers of a day: *Gargoyle, Broom, The Transatlantic Review*, or *This*

Quarter, whose brief existence was freighted with the heavyweight talents of James Joyce, Carl Sandberg, William Carlos Williams and Ernest Hemingway. Elliot Paul's experimental review *transition* drew heavily on artists as well, with covers by Miró, Picasso and Kandinsky as well as the ubiquitous Man Ray.

New arrivals found their way to Shakespeare and Company, the English bookshop and library on the rue de l'Odéon founded by Sylvia Beach, publisher of *Ulysses*, Joyce's much-persecuted masterpiece, and protector and chief loan-maker to expatriates. From there, in what was almost a rite of passage, the most privileged would be invited to call on Gertrude Stein in her studio on the rue de Fleurus, hung with works by Matisse, Derain, Gris and Braque, where she lived with her lover Alice B. Toklas, and sat beneath an unflattering portrait of herself by Picasso. It did not look like her, she complained. "It will," Picasso said.

"If you are lucky enough to have lived in Paris as a young man," Hemingway wrote, "then wherever you go for the rest of your life it stays with you, for Paris is a moveable feast." He had come to Europe as an ambulance driver on the Italian front. In Paris, he lived on cold leeks and vinegar and cheap wine in a shabby apartment, and wrote in the room on the rue Descartes where Verlaine was said to have died. He explored the city and its denizens: the six-day bicycle racers, who strained their bodies for a handful of francs, the boxers and acrobats, and the pensioners who whiled away their days with a rod and a net on the quays. As he began to make some money, Hemingway wrote at a table in the Closerie des Lilas, where writers had met since Baudelaire's day. George Orwell lived in squalor in the rue du Pot de Fer, around the corner, in 1928, working seventeen-hour days as a *plongeur*, washing up in hotel kitchens, the material for his *Down and Out in Paris and London* .

"Paris does not reproach the person bent on going to the devil," Harold Stearns, a wise racing writer for the *Chicago Tribune*, noted. "It shrugs its shoulders and lets him go." Paris helped to ruin Scott Fitzgerald, for he took to drink, and Zelda, his wife, to madness. He was honest about it. "I spoiled this city for myself," he wrote. "I didn't realise it, but the days came along one after another, and then two years were gone, and everything was gone, and I was gone."

American writers naturally made little enough impression on the French. American blacks, dancers and musicians, were another matter. The black revue *Paris qui Jazz* was the success of the year at the Casino de Paris in 1920. The shimmy joined the foxtrot and the tango as a "decadent" dance; moralists blamed the low birth rate on it, saying that dancing it left women too exhausted to conceive. Jean Cocteau wrote of the jazz phenomenon as "a kind of tamed catastrophe dancing on a hurricane of rhythms". Sidney Bechet toured with the Southern Syncopated Orchestra as a passion for jazz bands swept the country.

The jazz dancers of *La Revue Nègre*, a black American import of 1925, caused a sensation. The star was Josephine Baker, a caramel-coloured mulatto from St Louis of striking beauty and sensuality, with a lithe elegance and confidence that transfixed an audience. She appeared on stage in no more than a skirt of upturned bananas; she paraded down the Champs-Élysées with her pet snake Kiki worn around her neck, and her leopard Chiquita on a lead. The slicked-down spit curl on her forehead became a salon style, *le Bakerfix*; her colouring helped to inspire the new fashion for sunbathing. She sang, too, wistful and very French songs by Vincent Scotto: "La Petite Tonkinoise", "J'ai deux amours" and the haunting "Sous les ponts de Paris".

The most popular hostess was Bricktop, the orange-haired Ada Smith, in whose eponymous nightclub the rich and aristocratic danced the Charleston and the Black Bottom among the society gossips and hangers on. Cole Porter wrote the song "Miss Otis Regrets" for her. Baker started her own rival nightclub, Chez Josephine, but Bricktop survived into the next decade to welcome the Prince of Wales and his mistress Wallis Simpson.

The love affair with America had its strains and stresses. It was made compulsory for French nationals to make up half the number in any band, and some musicians merely sat there and never played a note. There was French anger at the American refusal to write off wartime debts, and cobblestones were thrown at tourist buses, while Americans were booed in the street.

A brief reconciliation followed the transatlantic flight by Charles Lindbergh. Two French pilots, Nungesser and Coli, had disappeared on their own attempt. Lindbergh, greeted by a crowd of 150,000 at Le Bourget, chanting "Lin-dee!", endeared himself by visiting Nungesser's widow. In the end, though, it was money that mattered most. At the beginning of October 1929, the dollar was worth 25.5 francs. The Paris branches of US brokerage houses were making heady profits as the expatriates took full advantage of the record levels of the New York stock market and the currency. On Black Tuesday, October 22, the market began to collapse. It hit bottom on November 13. By then, Paris cafés and hotels were already almost empty of Americans, and the brokerage houses were trying to cope with pleas for emergency funds for liner tickets home. The French called it *le krach*.

France itself remained unquestionably a great power, in every sense. Signs of the old scientific brilliance remained. A national office for research and inventions, the ancestor of today's redoubtable Centre National de la Recherche Scientifique, was set up in 1922. Marie Curie and Frédéric Joliot went on exploring the atom at the Institut du Radium. Jean Perrin won the 1926 Nobel prize for physics. The ducs de Broglie were a brilliant pair of independent scientists. Louis César, the sixth duc, famously researched X-ray spectra. His younger brother Louis Victor, the seventh duc, laid the foundation of wave mechanics. He published fundamental work on quantum theory in 1925, and won the Nobel Prize for Physics in 1929 for his pioneer work on the undulatory theory of matter.

Ideas in architecture and urban planning tumbled from Tony Garnier, the city architect of Lyon. In *Une cité industrielle*, he examined how modern materials like reinforced concrete could be used for social betterment. He put some of these utopian ideals into practice in the Grange Blanche hospital and the stadium at Lyons. Though he also had a building at the Arts Décoratifs exhibition in Paris in 1925, Garnier's designs never had a full airing.

Neither, in France at least, did those of Le Corbusier. Some might think this a blessing, for his technique of the "Modulor" – using standard-sized units whose proportions are based on the human figure – can seem sterile and soulless. He published *Aprés Cubisme* and the Purist manifesto with the painter Amédée Ozenfant in 1919, stressing simple, clean lines and strong basic shapes. He wrote on the interrelation between modern machines and architecture in his influential *Vers une architecture* in 1923. He had a building at the Arts Décoratifs exhibition, too, but he spent much of the 1920s designing tubular metal furniture, especially chairs.

The brilliance in cinema continued. The medium, with its pace, style, wit and clarity, suited the French genius. Abel Gance, the great innovator, used contrasts of landscape, machinery and faces to powerful effect in *La Roue* in 1923. His *Napoléon* of 1927, the first film shown at the Paris Opéra, used triple screens and mobile cameras. The avant-garde had Dadaist films like Man Ray's *Le Retour à la raison*. *Un Chien Andalou*, the great Surrealist film of 1928, was a series of unrelated but dramatic images put together by Luis Bunuel and Salvador Dalí.

Jean Borotra and Suzanne Lenglen triumphed at tennis. France won the Davis Cup. The Winter Olympics were held at Chamonix. Georges Carpentier became world boxing champion. In another form of sport, the tradition of the five-star *maison close* continued. The respectable investors in Le Sphinx, Martha Lemestre's upmarket house, included a bank; they earned a good return from her 60-odd *filles de joie*. The establishment was instantly recognisable by the stucco model of the Sphinx that gazed impassively above the front door. It was the first building in Paris to install air-conditioning.

The Tour de France had developed into one of the world's great sporting events. The promoter, Henri Desgrange, set out a 5,500-kilometre course for the 1924 race. "The ideal Tour," he wrote," would be one in which only one rider survived the ordeal," and he came close to achieving it. Riders could not change bikes, or anything else. What they started a stage with, they must end it with. This included clothes. A stage often started in the cool of the early morning before continuing into the blaze of a July afternoon. The defending champion in 1924 was Henri Pélissier, the only French winner between 1910 and 1930. He threw away a jersey as the sun began to climb, was heavily fined, and left the race in disgust to carry on a long and vitriolic newspaper feud with Desgrange.

The decade ended quietly. There was no feeling of crisis in 1929 which, with 1930, was a peak year of French prosperity. The gold reserves of the Banque de France soared from 29 billion francs to 55 billion. Poincaré was gone, but on health grounds, with what appeared a solid centre-right majority left behind him. Briand continued to preach rapprochement with Germany. The evacuation of the Rhineland began, and Briand proposed the idea of a European federation at the League of Nations. If that failed, then work on the defensive Maginot Line had begun. The Wall Street crash made little impact. When General Motors laid off workers at its French car and truck plants, Renault hired them all.

The observant could make out little distant clouds. The British had slipped back into their old imperial ways, with a big fleet and a small army, and the French economy, still largely rural, with four-fifths of the labour force working on the land, was hard-pressed to cope with the expense of La Patrie remaining on guard and alert. City water was unfit to drink, to the delight of the flourishing bottled-water companies. Gas meters leaked, the railway system was outdated, the power system weak.

Politics were dominated by rootless alliances and ill-disciplined factions, the majorities always fleeting and the public always cynical. The far right was about to throw up new figures, the perfume maker François Coty, Colonel de La Roque and the ex-veterans of his Croix de Feu. The extreme left despised the Republic with equal or greater venom. The Communist leader Maurice Thorez saw no distinction between bourgeois democracy and fascism. Like cholera and bubonic plague, he said, they were both fatal in the end.

The mainstream's coming men, André Tardieu and Pierre Laval, shared a certain shiftiness. The right adored Tardieu, but cartoonists saw him as a shark or a pike, a racketeer who had been a pre-war German agent. He was clever enough, a product of the École Normale Supérieure, but he had no time for parliamentary niceties, and sought a powerful state that would protect France against Communists and the left. He was president of the council, and minister of the interior, agriculture and war, a man who was addicted to flattery as well as power, and used secret funds to have the right-wing Ligues produce crowds to cheer him. Laval had a shady side, too. He was a millionaire now, but it was said that he had been buyable for the price of a good meal or a suit when he was an up-and-coming young Auvergnat.

Nonetheless, a decade on from the greatest war in history, the French had reason for quiet pleasure. They remained a parliamentary democracy. They had avoided the convulsions, bankruptcies, assassinations, civil strife and dictatorship that were infecting less happy parts of Europe.

6

Adrift in
the Thirties

The new decade started strong. Simone de Beauvoir felt that a golden age had arrived. "Peace seemed finally assured," she wrote. "The expansion of the German Nazi party was a mere fringe phenomenon, without any serious significance." The keel of the *Normandie* was laid in the shipyards of Saint-Nazaire in 1930. The great liner, a brilliant showcase for the engineers, architects and artists who worked on her, held the hope of a rich and expansive future. The slump bypassed France, for the moment at least; by Christmas, a mere 12,000 were registered as unemployed, where the Americans were counting in the millions. Indeed, some largesse was on offer. André Tardieu, a premier of robust and near-authoritarian views, cut taxes on property and company profits. Poorer souls benefited too. School fees were abolished at the *sixième* level, the precursor to free secondary education. A pension scheme for servicemen was completed, civil service benefits increased, and funds given to low-cost housing.

Five billion francs poured into public works like the Kembs barrage and the Alsace Grand Canal. The biggest of them all, the Maginot Line, named for the war minister, a much-decorated and severely wounded veteran, was authorised in January 1930. It enshrined the doctrine of defence in deep underground fortresses, whose railway lines, barracks, sports halls, clinics and cinemas lay snug and impregnable beneath the earth. All the lessons of the Great War were taken to heart, save one: it forgot the highly mobile aggression with which the tank had overwhelmed static defence lines in the final months of the war. The fortresses, too, and their interlocking fire, came to an end at Montmédy, near Verdun, and not on the Channel.

No matter. Briand, the Nobel peace laureate, remained foreign minister. Relations with Germany were cordial and untroubled. The last French occupation troops withdrew from the Rhineland on June 30, 1930. In the air, where it was felt that the real war of manoeuvre would be fought, French aviators were at the leading edge of progress. Mermoz completed the first airmail flight across the South Atlantic in 1930, and Costes and Bellonte flew their Bréguet on the first non-stop flight from Paris to New York, a journey into the wind that took them 37 hours. The airmail pilots braved darkness, storms, headwinds and engine failure in their fragile machines, without radio or navigation aids, flying the Aeropostale route from Toulouse down to Senegal, and over the ocean to Buenos Aires, then on over the dangerous downdraughts of the Andes to Santiago in Chile. They were heroes of the age. Antoine de Saint-Exupéry based fine and imaginative bestsellers, *Courrier sud* and *Vol de nuit*, on his exploits.

Overseas, the empire that reinforced the French claim to great power status was quiescent. The rebellious Berber Abd-el-Krim was exiled on Réunion; only in Indochina, where a schoolmaster called Nguyen Thai Hoc had founded a nationalist party, was there an audible call for independence. Other troublemakers wanted closer assimilation in France, not less. The cornerstone of a museum of the colonies was laid in the autumn of 1930. It was part of the giant Colonial Exposition which opened in Paris a few months later. Thirty-one million tickets were sold when it opened a few months later. Visitors wandered through a Sudanese village, a Laotian pagoda, and the Great Mosque from Djenné in Mali. They thrilled to an exhibit of cannibalism, where a dozen Canaques from New Caledonia sat in a dim hut, whilst torches flickered and a piece of smoking human flesh cooked on a fire. In fact, the flesh was beef, and the cannibals were mission-educated natives from the government printing works in Nouméa; but it served its purpose in linking imperialism with the *mission civilatrice*. The French showed more enthusiasm for visiting the Bois de Vincennes, the site of the exhibition, than in emigrating to the distant shores of *la Grande France*. A generous policy of naturalisation was needed to supply Spaniards to boost white numbers in Morocco and Oran, and Italians for Tunisia.

In science, Gustave Roussy established the Villejuif Cancer Institute. Henry Chrétien patented the Cinemascope film process, and the physicist René Barthélemy, of the École Supérieure d'Électricité, was soon to give the first public demonstration of television in France.

Sport was becoming big business. The PMU, the Pari-Mutual Urbain, was created in April 1930 to ensure that the state got its slice of the betting market. The big political newspapers began to run a minimum of a whole page of sport every day, where before they had made do with a quarter page. There was plenty to report. Sports car drivers raced balloonists. Unable to continue dancing at the Casino de Paris, after rupturing her knee fleeing an avalanche while skiing in the fashionable resort of Megève, the dashing Hélène Delangle turned herself into a car racing champion, driving her Bugatti 35 under the name of Hellé Nice. Crowds in the big football cities – Paris, Marseille, Montpellier – had grown ten times and more since the war. French teams were among the first to be openly professional, ending the sham of paid "amateurs". It took a Frenchman, too, to put football on a global stage. The first World Cup was held in 1930. It was the brainchild of a lawyer from Franche-Comté, Jules Rimet, the president of FIFA, the international football body. The tournament was hosted at his suggestion by Uruguay, the reigning Olympic champions. Lucien Laurent of France had the honour of scoring the first ever World Cup goal in the opening game, against Mexico, a game also distinguished by the referee, who brought the players back onto the field from the bath, having mistakenly blown for time six minutes early.

France won the Davis Cup for the fourth successive year in 1930; indeed, thanks to the "Four Musketeers", Borotra, Lacoste, Cochet and Brugnon, the world's premier tennis trophy remained in Paris for two years more. The ever restless Henri Desgrange kept the Tour de France on its toes. He greeted the new decade by scrapping manufacturers' teams in favour of national squads of eight riders, whom he picked, paid and mounted on identical bikes. He made up the shortfall in cash from the makers by creating a publicity caravan, and having the tour covered live on radio for the first time. In the 1920s, foreigners had won every race but one. French riders won the first five Tours of the 1930s. André Leducq, "le joyeux Dédé", and Antonin "le taciturn" Magne each won twice; when they rode their final Tour in 1938, they joined hands to finish the final stage in a grand gesture of comradeship and fair play.

A brilliant middle-distance runner, Jules Ladoumègue, though later to be drummed out of the Olympics as a professional, broke the world 1500 metre record. The weightlifter Charles Rigoulot was proudly known as "the world's strongest man". André Citroën organised the *Croisière jaune*, a 12,000-kilometre expedition by CV4s along the ancient Silk Route from Beirut to the China Sea. Women still had to have a father or husband's permission to apply for a passport, but it did not stop Maryse Hilsz flying from Paris to Saigon in her tiny Moth-Morane in 1930, the same year that Mme Bertrand-Fontaine became the first woman to be appointed as a hospital consultant.

In the cinema, the young filmmaker Jean Vigo made his iconoclastic debut with a private showing of *À propos de Nice*. René Clair released his first talkie, *Sous les toits de Paris*. Its hero was a *chanteur de la rue* in the little *bals musettes* and bistros of an old corner of Paris; these street singers were themselves threatened by the talkies, as well as by radio, and some audiences were hostile to the film's "repugnant population of *pierreuses*", the street walkers. As the posters boasted, though, it was *cent pourcent* French-speaking and singing, and it was said to be a welcome relief from Hollywood's cowboys and gangsters, and the "eternal vulgar detective chomping his cigar". Maurice Chevalier had jumped ship for Hollywood, but the colossal earnings of the ninth child of a Paris lacemaker – $600,000 in 1930 - were reported with much pride. At home, too, Marcel Pagnol was filming *Marius*, the first of his great Marseilles-based trilogy, and other great talents – Marcel Carné, Jean Renoir – were learning their trade.

The other arts were as vibrant as ever. Maurice Ravel performed his classic *Bolero*, while *Aubade*, with words and music by Poulenc, and choreographed by Georges Balanchine, premiered at the Théâtre des Champs-Elysées and Cocteau's *La Voix humaine* was playing at the Comedie Française. *Paris qui remue* opened at the Casino de Paris and it starred Josephine Baker, proclaiming her love for the city in the song "J'ai deux amours". Ray Ventura recorded the first album with jazz vocals sung in French.

A more casual and sporting style was mirrored in clothes. Bare arms, beach pyjamas, *robes sport*, *robes de villes* and cocktail dresses ate away at formality. Plus fours came off the golf course and onto the street; a society figure was shocked to find the minister of education "negligently dressed" in a pullover instead of a waistcoat in the Bibliothèque Nationale. The single combination replaced the chemise and petticoats. Corsets gave way to elastic girdles, and then to roll-ons. The *robe sirène*, the siren suit, was a revolution, with a length midway between afternoon and evening dress, allowing women to drift past nightfall without changing.

It was designed by a new genius of fashion. Elsa Schiaparelli was no beauty. Her eyes were deep-set and dark, her chin receded, and she had a scattering of moles on one cheek that reminded an astronomer of the Plough constellation. But she was bold and brilliant, a pioneer whose trademark was "hard chic". Her tongue was sharp, too. A shocked English girl in her place Vendôme salon noted that there was only a yard of material in a hugely expensive jacket. The reply was crushing: "How many yards of canvas are there in a Fragonard?"

She came into her own in 1930. She created the first evening dress that came with a jacket that year, the former a plain black sheath, the latter white crepe-de-chine. It was her most copied dress, which pleased her; she said it would hurt her not to be copied. She was the first designer to use visible zips on clothing, the same year, on the pockets of a beach jacket. She was the first, too, to use man-made fibres in couture, getting the manufacturers to crumple up their rayon fabric to give it stretch and drape, fifty years ahead of the rage for pleats and crinkles. Though Colette complained that the bathroom scale had become the "new oracle", and spinach and grapefruit diets were the rage – "grossir c'est mourir un peu" – flat chests were out of fashion. Schiaparelli launched the padded bra. Busts, and facelifts, were in.

"Schiap" thought herself grander than any mere frockmaker. Chanel described her as "that Italian artist who makes clothes", and she sought out kindred spirits. Man Ray photographed her hats. After Picasso painted a photograph of her hands to look like gloves, she made gloves that looked like hands, in white suede with red snakeskin fingernails stitched on them. Salvador Dalí painted a lobster tumbling down the skirt of a white silk gown of hers, surrounding it with painted parsley. He was angry that she would not let him season it with real mayonnaise. Another evening dress had a Cocteau design of two red-lipped faces about to kiss. Dalí worked with her on her renowned shoe hat, in black velvet with a heel in shocking pink. It was a colour she made her own, bold, striking, optimistic, like the new decade. Or so, superficially, it seemed.

There were other little telltales, warning that the *après-guerre* of the First World War might be sliding into the *avant-guerre* of the Second. Across the place Vendôme from Schiaparelli, the *parfumeur* Coty presided over his empire of odours. Born François Sportuno in Corsica, when he arrived in Paris he possessed little more than a nose of rare quality. He changed to his mother's maiden name and elaborated an ancestry that included the Bonapartes. Coty was sensitive to the most evanescent elements in a scent, and he combined a flair for creating exquisite perfumes with a genius for marketing them.

He worked first for Guerlain, and then set up on his own. "Perfume is a woman's love affair with herself," he said, and he capitalised on that insight to amass one of the greatest fortunes in France. At the end of a bitter divorce, he was ordered to make a settlement of 248 million francs for his ex-wife, the largest ever recorded. His money did not make him happy. Red-haired and reclusive, he was rarely seen in public.

He toiled in his laboratory on the Quai de Javel, blending new perfumes, which he packaged in Lalique-designed bottles, and he fretted in his Paris apartment or his château at Louveciennes over the decadence of France, nursing his hatred for the Third Republic and his adoration of Bonapartism and Mussolini. He was prepared to spend, profusely, on extremist politics. He bought a great newspaper, *Le Figaro*, and founded a rabble-rousing daily, *L'Ami du Peuple*, which seethed with his dislike for parliament and for Jews. He priced it at ten centimes, instead of the normal 25. He lavished funds, too, on the ultra-right Ligues. Coty, morose and ill at ease, was a man of the times.

The winner of the first Prix Populaire, Eugène Dabit, recognised this in his 1930 novel *Hôtel du Nord*. It was a tale of two lovers and a bungled suicide, set in a cheap hotel and bar alongside the Canal Saint-Martin in Paris. Dabit's parents had run such a hotel, and he had grown up amid the hard and broken lives of its customers, before serving as a gunner in the war. It had left him a *malade de guerre*; almost every night since he was demobilised, he said, "images of the front came back to haunt me and – a still worse nightmare – I dreamt that hostilities were starting again".

He smelled evil in the wind, in the way people drugged themselves with nostalgia, and averted their eyes from the future. "The illusion must end," he wrote. "War and revolution or fascism are before us. Life is not easy, sure and slow. Men are ever more beastly to each other, and more sick in their joys and hatreds." The present was bleak – "hard, violent and ugly" – and the coming generation was shallow and brutalised. "The young pretend that they are 'free,' he said, and he described them like proto-English skinheads, in their "pantalon à pattes d'éléphant", their flared trousers, with "scarves twisted round the nape of their shaven necks".

This sense of drifting to the extremes was mirrored in Julien Benda's piercing book *Le Trahison des clercs*. He accused thinkers of betraying calm speculation and philosophical neutrality. They had become politicised, he said, supporting Marxism or Fascism, doctrines riddled with class and race hatreds. Benda wanted to "restore the primacy of the spiritual". It was a task that he accurately judged as Herculean.

As tensions grew between the far left and the *ligues*, each side used fear of the other – the worker-slaying "fasciste", the bourgeois-baiting Red with "le couteau entre les dents" – to recruit its own bully boys. The Surrealists cosied up with the Reds. *Le Surréalisme au service de la Révolution*, a literary review edited by André Breton, appeared in July 1930, as militants helped to provoke riots between strikers, non-strikers and police in the textile and steel mills of the north. Its contributors put out a tract urging a boycott of the Colonial Exhibition. "La Grande France", they said, was a fraud perpetrated by the bourgeoisie; the reality was distant fusillades, and massacres from Annam to Morocco, for which the generals and administrators should be arrested immediately. Louis Aragon, the Surrealist poet-clown, who visited the Soviet Union and then converted to communism, wrote a series of "social-realistic" novels called *Le Monde réel*, though his own world – blind to the way in which his Soviet hosts were busily turning the countryside into a blend of prison camp and charnel house – remained wholly surreal.

For its part, the ultra-right was happy to rise to any provocation. In Bunuel's film *l'Âge d'or*, which opened at Studio 28 in December, bishops were hurled from windows, and Christ appeared as the hero of de Sade's *A Hundred Days in Sodom*. The cinema lobby was turned into a Surrealist gallery, with paintings, posters and photographs by Dalí, Max Ernst, Yves Tanguy, Joan Miró and Man Ray. Hard men from the Ligue Antijuive and Action Française duly slashed and defaced the artwork, tossed smoke bombs and attacked cinema-goers each evening until the Paris police *préfet* banned the film.

A new ultra-right paper, *Je suis partout*, appeared to keep Coty's *Ami* company. Its leading writers – Robert Brassilach, Pierre Drieu la Rochelle, Bertrand Jouvenet – were eventually to pay with their lives for their views, while Aragon, who had found Stalin's Russia so agreeable, lived on into honoured old age. That lay in the future, of course, but Drieu la Rochelle's fascination with violence was already of a mortal intensity. "Man need never have left the forest," he said in his book *The Young European*. "It is necessary to have killed with the hands in order to understand life. The only life men are capable of, I tell you again, is the spilling of blood: murder and coitus. All the rest is decadence." This bloodlust made up one the strands in the *ligues*; patriotism, royalism, capitalism, defence of Catholicism, contempt for communists, Jews and the Republic, in often confusing admixtures, were others. Coty's fellow-millionaire, the champagne magnate Pierre Taittinger, had founded his own blue-shirted Jeunesses Patriotes, by no means as fresh-faced and innocent as their name suggested. Charles Maurras and Action Française were as active as ever, and had spun off their own young royalist paramilitaries in the Camelots du Roi, kings of the street fighters.

The Croix de Feu, an organisation of ex-servicemen, was the largest group. Inevitably so, for France had six million veterans in 1930, and half of them, a quarter of the wholly male electorate, were members of veterans' associations. Most joined for benefits, not for auld lang syne. The Croix de Feu began as a non-political association of soldiers decorated for bravery, middle-aged men in berets who paraded solemnly with their medals and flags. Coty then started funding it, however, and it acquired a paramilitary edge, and a new leader. Colonel François de La Rocque was himself a veteran, much influenced by the brilliant colonial soldier-administrator Marshal Louis Lyautey. He had paid for service on the Western Front, and in the Rif war, with malaria and severe leg wounds. Like many officers, de La Rocque had retired early, frustrated by the slow pace of post-war promotion. He brought with him a flair for organisation, a shrewd eye for the morale of his men, and an ability to portray them as disciplined defenders of Christian civilisation.

Here, in the bitter hatreds between the extremes, were the makings of internal strife, of the civil war of the *clercs*. "The people to battle were not the Germans across the border," the pacifist leftist Henri Jeanson said, "but fellow French at home

– class enemies, fascists, industrialists, politicians, officers of the general staff." From the other side, the *ligueurs* railed at degenerate art, brothels, drugs, alcoholism, homosexuals, freemasons, Jews and moderates.

If the centre held its nerve, of course, it mattered little. The vicious squabble between Marx's friends and Mussolini's would be confined to the gutter, where it belonged. The times were abnormal, however, and they sapped confidence. The odd American writer still came, but odd they were. "Paris attracts the tortured, the hallucinated, the great maniacs of love," wrote Henry Miller, who arrived in 1930. "Here all the boundaries fade away and the world reveals itself for the mad slaughterhouse that it is." Miller, his wife June and the erotomaniac Anaïs Nin explored all avenues. The insatiable lesbian Natalie Barney, a rich American, noted 18 assignations in a single night. The English author Vita Sackville-West darkened her face, and dressed as a sailor with a bandage wrapped round her head; her lover Violet Trefusis called her "Julian".

Miller took his *Tropic of Cancer* to Sylvia Beach, to see if she would publish it, but Beach no longer had the funds to produce work that would be banned for obscenity in its home markets. American tourists no longer came to her shop. Had André Gide not started a rescue committee, Les Amis du Shakespeare & Company, with support from Paul Valéry, Hemingway, André Maurois and others, she would have been bankrupted.

And, if the American economy was suffering so, how long would France hold out? As long as a French cabinet? Camile Chautemps had been appointed premier on February 21, 1930. He was gone four days later. André Tardieu replaced him on March 2, but his cabinet survived only until December 4. Political instability was endemic; corruption, too, it began to seem. The collapse of the Banque Adam threw unwelcome light on the affairs of the man who ran it, Albert Oustric, a financier with a taste for high living and a contacts book filled with politicians' names. Among them was Raoul Peret, the Garde des Sceaux, the Republic's senior law officer. He was the highest-profile casualty of the press revelations – the undersecretaries of state for public works and fine arts were others, and the car maker Peugeot.

Across the Rhine, a monster was beginning to break surface that would test the French to the breaking point. The Germans had not celebrated as the last *poilu* quit the Rhineland at the end of June. Those who thought the evacuation to be "a generous gesture", the *Frankfurter Allgemeine* noted acidly, were met with "scornful silence". The Nazis increased their votes sevenfold in the German elections three months later, their seats in the Reichstag shooting up from 12 to 107. French military intelligence analysts had no illusions whatever of the implications. They thought it a "certainty" that Hitler would come to power and rearm.

Facing him in January 1931 was Pierre Laval, *Time* magazine Man of the Year in 1931. "Calm, masterful and popular", Laval beat Mahatma Gandhi to the title. The rise of the "man in the white tie", the son of a butcher from the Auvergne, was remarkable indeed. Aged 47 and previously Tardieu's minister of labour, *Time* found him to be "Worker, Driver, Leader" with a "tremendous will to rule". Faced by communist riots in Indochina, he criticised the repression that had led to the guillotining of 700 local communists over the past two years, and sent Paul Reynaud, the minister of colonies, to the Far East to "sympathetically examine native grievances". Laval obliged Briand, his old patron and now his foreign minister, to take a tougher line to prevent a customs union between Germany and Austria. On a visit to Washington, and dressed in his striped trousers, black jacket, white tie and suede-topped buttoned shoes, Laval famously wagged his finger at President Hoover whilst saying that France would not stand for the Americans thrusting forward a moratorium on German reparations "suddenly and brutally." The president, he said, could sacrifice the $275 million due to the US if he wished. But Hoover had no right to insist that France sacrifice its $97 million, the amount owing to it for the year.

On his return to Paris, Laval steered his fiscal programme though the Chamber. This included a $140 million programme of public works to relieve unemployment, then standing at 500,000 (it was three times that in Britain and had reached 7.2 million in the US), and a $12 million loan to French Line to complete its super-liner the *Normandie*.

Laval did not last long in 1932. He was gone in February. André Tardieu returned. In April, Hitler won 13 million votes in the German presidential elections. Hindenburg had 19 million, but it was clear who was the coming man. In May, President Doumer was shot dead by Paul Gorguloff, a deranged White Russian émigré. He was replaced by Albert Lebrun, a timid, pleasant, short-sighted nonentity. Tardieu was unable to hold his coalition together. Édouard Herriot formed a government on June 3. It was primarily Radical Socialist, negotiations with the Socialist SFIO having broke down, and its life expectancy was not good. At the beginning of July, the Germans finally got off the financial hook. After a last payment of 3 billion Reichsmarks, the Allies agreed to abolish reparations at the Lausanne Conference.

There were some diversions over the summer. Marcel Thil won the world middleweight championship, maintaining the French position as a world-class boxing power, after the American Gorilla Jones was disqualified for punching below the belt. The French won the Davis Cup for a sixth year running. André Leducq triumphed in the Tour. Gorguloff went to the guillotine.

Herriot pushed through disarmament proposals in the autumn, with backing from Léon Blum and the Socialists, but he was gone by Christmas. As long queues braved the cold outside the Casino de Paris to catch Josephine Baker in her new revue, *La Joie de Paris*, Joseph Paul-Boncour formed a new cabinet. By the end of January, Hitler had become chancellor. He arranged for the Reichstag building to be burnt in February, blaming this on a communist plot, and using it to force another election. Though the Nazis barely scraped a majority, Hitler used the Enabling Acts to seize absolute power. The monster was out of his cage.

He revealed his hatred for France on page one of *Mein Kampf*. Recollecting his childhood in Braunau-am-Inn, Hitler wrote that the town was steeped in the blood of the martyr Johannes Palm, executed in 1806 on French orders because he had "the misfortune to have loved Germany well". Palm was a local bookseller who was arrested for distributing a leaflet called "Germany's Deepest Humiliation". It bewailed the French occupation of Munich in 1800, and Napoleon's insistence that the Bavarians supply him with an army. Hitler went on to compare Palm to Leo Schlageter, shot by a French firing squad in May 1923 for blowing up a bridge in protest at the occupation of the Ruhr. He made it clear as crystal that the French were hereditary enemies of all true Germans, set now, as ever, on dismembering the Reich. But French politicians, fearful of alarming the electorate, did not dwell on Hitler's views. A French court ordered a word-for-word translation of *Mein Kampf* to be destroyed. It was replaced by a sanitised version from which the rabid Francophobia was largely, or, as in the case of his frequent references to his neighbour-enemy as "the French hydra", completely expurgated.

A revealing French book was published now. Louis Ferdinand Céline's *Voyage au bout de la Nuit* howled absurdity at war, at politics, at existence, at the "crawling millions of suffering, diseased, sex-obsessed, maniacal human beings". It was a publishing sensation. Céline was footloose, filled with an angry numbness, splintered, savage, wracked by pain and prejudice, and by a sense of life's futility. He had been with a cavalry unit at the outbreak of the war. Two months later, he was acting as a runner near Ypres when he was badly wounded in the head and shell-shocked. He was awarded the *médaille militaire*, with a citation signed by Joffre. He suffered partial paralysis, tinnitus and trauma for the rest of his life. He was discharged, a hero, on medical grounds. He was a clerk in the French passport office in London, and then qualified in medicine. He worked in the Cameroon and Cuba, and as a staff surgeon at the Ford plant in Detroit. He ministered to the poor of Paris when he returned home.

Voyage had no hero, no comradeship, no saving emotion, cast in a pitiless and searing demotic. Its central character, Bardamu, followed his own life. He gets into the war accidentally. He tells his colonel the war must be stopped. The colonel is killed in front of him. Bardamu is used as a runner, decides to desert but is wounded and gets a medal before he can run away. He meets the world of the *derrière*, where "the women were in heat and the old men had greed written all over them". He runs a trading post in Africa. He walks through Manhattan, in "a sick sort of jungle light, so grey that the street seemed to be full of grimy cotton waste". He returns to Paris to work as a doctor; he lives in a muck of despair; he prays to an anarchist's God, a "deep sensual God who grunts like a pig". Bardamu has no will, no illusions. "We keep going, we fuel and refuel, we pass on our life to a biped of the next century, with frenzy, at any cost," he says bleakly, "as if it were the greatest of pleasures to perpetuate ourselves."

In Germany, they were beginning to celebrate the triumph of the will; in France, of hopelessness. The French had packed cinemas showing *All Quiet on the Western Front*, the anti-war film of the novel by the former German infantryman Erich Maria Remarque. In Germany, Hitler's thugs had disrupted screenings. The film was now banned by the Nazis, as "defeatist", and Remarque was living in exile in Switzerland.

The futility Céline found in war echoed in Roger Vercel's Goncourt-winning novel about a war hero, *Capitaine Conan*, who is drinking himself to a sottish death in the provinces. "If you should run across the men who won the war," the captain says, bloodshot, clothes stained, "look closely: they'll look like me." The novelist Roger Martin du Gard, a Nobel laureate, was an out-and-out pacifist. "Anything rather than war! Anything!" he wrote to a friend. "Nothing, no trial, no servitude can be compared to war." In Raymond Bernard's brooding film *Les croix de bois*, a squad of *poilus* – the stolid peasant, the wisecracking Parisian – was slowly reduced to a single survivor as the others slept beneath their wooden crosses. Fighting was celebrated only where it was remote, sanitised by the desert sun and sand. A spate of films were made on the Foreign Legion. The song "Mon Légionnaire" – "he was slender . . . he smelled like hot sand" – made a star of Édith Piaf, the "little sparrow", whose sad genius was matched by Jacques Prévert, her song-writer.

Foreboding of war hung in the air, a foggy, ever-present miasma. The crippled hero Colonel Jean Fabry told the Chamber that the dread of invasion "is in our blood. Time will not alter it." Strasbourg University was already planning to evacuate to Clermont-Ferrand when war came; in a bestseller, René Chambre wrote of attacks by a hundred aircraft carrying asphyxiating bombs, which would cover Paris in a sheet of gas 20 metres high, "all in an hour". André Maginot, to die of typhoid after eating oysters, told the American ambassador that there was "probably no other nation in Europe that is less warlike". Édouard Herriot, whilst prime minister, observed that France could not always be asked to stretch itself to the point where it might break. "It needs a rest," he said.

The pacifist streak in France was scarcely cowardly – René Gérin, a *lycée* professor and a leader of the International League of Fighters for Peace, was a former infantry captain, three times wounded, with a Légion d'Honneur and four citations – but it compromised. No politician, striving for balance in the topsy-turvy world of Third Republic coalitions, could ignore it. And other pressures were diluting the instinct to face down the *Boches*. Unemployment, 32,292 in February 1931, was up to 326,340 and rising two years later. Something had to give. The Paul-Boncour cabinet proposed an austerity budget with tax increases and a cut in government spending. The Socialists joined the conservatives in defeating the government. Paul-Boncour was gone. He had lasted forty days.

He was replaced on January 30, 1933 by the Radical Socialist Édouard Daladier. He was the thickset "bull of the Vaucluse" in body, the son of a baker from Carpentras, but weak, indecisive and slow in mind. He wore his socialist principles on his sleeve, and he was square-shouldered and Roman-nosed; but, despite this "appearance of rather brutal firmness", Paul-Boncour noted that he was "hesitant" and "highly sensitive to lobbies and rumours". When the bankers called on him to slash the budget, so Léon Blum complained, they left him "terrified, crushed" and unable to resist. He got an austerity package through the National

Assembly on March 1. The sharpest axe fell on the military. Five thousand officers went; so did a quarter of the regulars in the ranks. The regulars were the backbone of a conscript army. The journalist Pertinax was shocked at Daladier's "lack of intelligence" on defence; he held it "an indisputable truth that the last word of the art of war was to build entrenchments and hold them solidly". All the rest, he said, "is just words".

Colonel Charles de Gaulle released a preview of his book *Vers l'armée de métier* which argued the contrary, that only aggressive, mobile war gave any hope of success. France could not match Germany in numbers, he said; thus it must excel in quality and in offensive strategy. Instead of discontented, barrack-bound conscripts, de Gaulle wanted an all-professional force of 100,000 men, trained to strike hard with tanks. Unless France waged aggressive, mobile war against the Germans, it would be defeated. Leftists found his thinking to be "elitist", and despised it; the maverick conservative Paul Renaud apart, the right was happy to accept the assurances of officers like General Louis Maurin, that offensive doctrine had "cost us quite dear enough for us to avoid it henceforth. How can it be that we still think of offensives, when we have spent billions to set up a fortified barrier?"

Civil service salaries were also cut in the budget, and taxes raised. The policy of deflation worsened the depression. In an index of 100 in 1900, prices reached 129 in 1929. By 1933, the index had tumbled to 81, a fall of 40 per cent that threatened farms and factories alike with ruin. Civil servants went on strike. Coty's former secretary Marcel Bucard founded another extreme-right *ligue*, which Mussolini was pleased to subsidise. The new Francistes strutted their stuff in berets and uniform shirts, with pickaxe handles on their shoulders, and riding boots if they could afford them.

Daladier, pinned to the wavering centre, fell in October. His replacement, Albert Saurrat, lasted less than a month. On November 26, 1933, the Radical Socialist Camille Chautemps formed a cabinet. He had been premier before, for four days, a record of its sort. He was tall, elegant and eager to please. "Clever, too clever," a journalist wrote. "He makes appealing phrases, splits hairs, never answers any question precisely." The omens were not good.

Early in 1934, on the night of February 6, a full-scale riot in the place de la Concorde seemed a death-knell for democracy. "A lurid lithograph of burning bus barricades, hamstrung horses and men and women stoning and shouting," the *New Yorker* correspondent reported. "Both the populace and the police showed a dreadful courage . . . It is not unlikely that the Third Republic *will* fall." The police were overwhelmed as the hard men of the *ligues* battered at the cordon blocking the bridge over the Seine that led to their target, the Chamber of Deputies. The police opened fire, killing 15 demonstrators and wounding a thousand, in the worst scenes of violence since the Commune.

The man who caused this night of flame and bloody darkness was Alexandre Stavisky, a swindler of exquisite greed and imposing connections. Stavisky had been found dead in a ski chalet in Chamonix on January 8, with a bullet wound in his head. The police said it was self-inflicted. The rioters, and many others, believed it to be murder. He was shot, they said, lest he betray the officials and government ministers he had corrupted.

Stavisky, born in the shtetls of the Ukraine in 1886, promoted phoney companies, and sold counterfeit Treasury bonds and stock certificates. He was charged with multiple fraud in July 1926 and was arrested at a smart dinner party in Marly-le-Roi. His mistress was a Chanel model of classic beauty, Arlette Simon, and his lawyer, Joseph Paul-Boncour, was a future prime minister. Indictments dating back to 1909 began catching up with him as he languished in La Santé prison. He bribed a police officer to destroy many of the incriminating documents in the case, however, and the prosecutors were forced to postpone his trial. He was released from prison on medical grounds at the end of December 1927.

He now married the lovely Arlette, so elegant, so perfumed, who helped him burn with a brilliance that dazzled and sucked in the gullible. He liked to show off his "straight, sharp, even teeth by smiling with his thin lips . . . The top half of his face, which was energetic, firm, almost beautiful, was given the lie by the bottom half, which was weak and cunning."

A richer and more original scam began which involved pawning stolen jewels at *crédits municipaux*, the dozy city-owned pawnshops that enjoyed a monopoly of the trade. The supply of stolen jewels was inadequate to meet his voracious needs and he began pawning fakes. Among them were listed some of the German crown jewels, supposedly emeralds, in fact glass. By June 1929, the Orléans pawnshop, which usually turned over a few thousand francs a month in pawned household goods, had advanced Stavisky-Alexandre 30 million francs in supposedly secured loans.

The volume was large enough to trigger a visit by outside auditors from Paris. Those pledges that were not stolen were fakes. Stavisky had to redeem them. He did so by floating unsecured bonds in the name of the Orléans pawnshop, which, when endorsed by a friendly government minister, Albert Dalimier, appeared to be an official state offering. In 1931, a magistrate was appointed to find out why Stavisky was still at large. He recommended immediate arrest. Nothing happened. Powerful and corrupt men kept him safe. They probably included the brother-in-law of Camille Chautemps, who became prime minister in 1933.

Stavisky gambled, and lost millions at baccarat; he entertained show business stars, including Mistinguett, who was photographed with his intimidating bodyguard, Jo-Jo Le Terreur. He bought a large Paris theatre, l'Empire, and put on a lavish musical, the Russian-inspired *Katinka*, which ran at a staggering loss, apparent proof – like his gaming and his racehorses – that he could withstand any loss. He summered in Bayonne, where the deputy and mayor, Jean Garat, was deeply impressed, and he fell victim. Stavisky and his associates issued bonds supposedly worth hundreds of millions, backed by the Bayonne pawnshop, and turned them into cash by selling them to insurance companies and banks. He also persuaded workers' social insurance funds to invest in them, falsely claiming that the bonds were backed by the state.

The more Stavisky spent, on publicity, press, the theatre, on meals, on hotel suites, on furs and jewellery for his heavily-bedecked wife, on bribes and favours for politicians, the more pledges and bonds he had to issue. The interest on the bonds had to be met, or the whole edifice would collapse; but the only way to meet it was to sell more bonds, so that he was caught in an ever-accelerating spiral of fraud. His gambling was an attempt to recover, to set matters right with one long glorious winning streak. In August 1933, he had to defer payment on the bonds. He lacked the money to buy off criticism in the financial press. The pyramid began to collapse. The press scented a vintage scandal involving a Jew and Radical politicians, two pet hatreds of many readers. Inspectors of the Police Judiciaire were constantly frustrated by prosecutors and investigating magistrates.

On Christmas Eve 1933, when it was clear that the bonds were unredeemable, the director of the Bayonne pawnshop, Gustave Tissier, was arrested. On January 5, it was revealed that Tissier had accused mayor Garat, a Radical Socialist close to power, of complicity in the affair. There were violent scenes in the Chamber of Deputies, where the minister of commerce, Dalimier, was said to be a Stavisky accomplice. Chautemps was finally forced to instruct the police to bring in Stavisky for questioning. In a powerful car, through rain and driving snowstorms, Stavisky fled Paris for Chamonix, and death. On January 27, the speaker of the Chamber, Eugène Raynaldy, resigned after being caught up in a separate swindle by a disgraced banker named Sacazan. The same day the Chautemps government was forced to resign. It had been in power for two months and four days. Édouard Daladier returned in a new Radical Socialist cabinet with centrist backing. He promised to get to the bottom of the *affaire* in short order. His first embarrassment was Jean Chiappe, the Paris *préfet de police*. Like so many senior policemen down the decades, Chiappe was a Corsican, a short dapper figure in bowler hat, white silk scarf and overcoat, and a pair of immaculate white gloves, which he wore as a symbol of his "clean hands".

Chiappe was a stern law-and-order man, the darling of the conservative bourgeoisie, who broke up left-wing demonstrations with gusto, swept prostitutes off the main boulevards into the side streets and *maisons closes*, and had arrested Marlene Dietrich for wearing trousers in public. He was also popular within the force, caring for his agents and their wives, whom he often placed as concierges, thus ensuring a good supply of informers.

White gloves or not, alas, Chiappe had taken no action over Stavisky. An inspector named Cousin had submitted three criminal dossiers on the swindler since 1931. The *préfet* had ignored them, even though he was known to have received Stavisky at police headquarters. Madame Stavisky spoke of assurances of "support" that he had made to her late husband. Daladier fired Chiappe, reputedly too close to the far right, on February 3.

Into this seething pot, the Comédie Française tossed a new production of Shakespeare's *Coriolanus*. The choice of a play about a would-be dictator, in a Rome riddled with factions and "bald tribunes" and "reckless senators", seemed a calculated insult to parliament and democracy. The play sold out, mainly to trouble-makers from the extreme right and left, who cheered or jeered every line that could be twisted into a *double entendre* for Paris politics. Daladier now sacked Émile Fabre, the Comédie director. It was an impulsive act, out of character, a botched attempt to show determination, and it backfired. The prime minister replaced Fabre with M. Thomé, the head of the Sûreté, thus earning mocking headlines: "A police-man to run the House of Molière!"

On February 6, Daladier planned to ask the Chamber for a vote of confidence for his week-old government. In response, *l'Action française* ran a call to arms on its front page. "The thieves are barricading themselves in their cave!" it proclaimed. "Against this abject regime, all in front of the Chamber of Deputies this evening!"

By 6 p.m., the early arrivals were in the place de la Concorde, testing the cordon of mounted *gardes mobiles* and *gendarmes* that blocked access to the pont de la Concorde, which led across the Seine to the Palais Bourbon and the Chamber. Their courage grew as more paramilitaries from the *ligues* joined them. After half an hour, a full-scale battle was taking place. The mob attacked the police with paving stones, bricks and metal grilles ripped from round the trees in the Tuileries. Canes and sticks with razor blades were used to slash at the legs of the police horses, and marbles were flung under their hooves.

The mob forced the cordon back across the Concorde bridge, and the police, some colleagues crushed under their fallen horses, others thrown into the river, opened fire as a desperate last means of stopping them. Panic-stricken deputies tried to flee, only to find that the exits from the Chamber had been barricaded against the mob with gilt Louis XV furnishings. Then the moment passed, and the mob tide ebbed. The deputies discovered an unlocked exit at the back of the Chamber and fled. It was obvious who the "noble riot" had been against: "Communists," *l'Action française* explained, "Socialists, Radicals, Republicans, Jews and Freemasons." It was much less clear who or what the fifteen victims had died for. Colonel de La Rocque had not been with them. No man on horseback was ready to claim his prize. Pierre Taittinger felt it unnecessary to lead his Jeunesses Patriotes in person. His fellow millionaire, François Coty, remained safely tucked up in his château at Louveciennes, the arsenal of weapons he kept in his wine cellars unused. Charles Maurras, who had done most to rouse the rabble, spent the evening writing poems in Provençal dialect. If the right gained nothing in return for its broken heads, it succeeded in unifying the left against it.

L'Humanité used its front page on February 9 to call for a mass meeting in the place de la République. That evening, rival columns of Communists and Jeunesses Socialistes ran into one another. Insults and fisticuffs would normally be part of such an encounter. The times were abnormal. Cries went up for comradeship to save the Republic. The two sides embraced, and marched off arm in arm, chanting: "Unity of action!" The unofficial pact was sealed in blood when rioting broke out, and four were killed in clashes with the police.

The Socialists called for "all Republican forces" to join a general strike on February 12. The Communist CGTU union, which had defied the Socialist CGT since splitting from it 13 years before, now called on its members to participate. At least 150,000 demonstrators marched to the place de la Nation. Here, though *l'Humanité* was still describing the Socialists as "the last rampart of capitalist society", they fraternised. "Le Fascisme ne passera pas!" the leftist paper *Le Populaire* rejoiced.

The notion that the fascists had come within a whisker of toppling the Republic during the great Stavisky riot is tempting but fanciful. It is debatable whether, at this stage, the *ligues* were fascist at all – de La Rocque clearly was not – or merely neo-Bonapartist. They were paramilitary, certainly, authoritarian, socially conservative, union-busting and imperialist; their prime aim was to defeat the Marxist threat, and in doing so to be rid of the political liberalism and democracy that allowed Marxism to survive. But mainstream conservatives were adept at taking the wind out of their sails; they had no battle plan, and they were divided and fractious. The gulf between them and power was much wider than the pont de la Concorde. Fascism in France was a phantom pregnancy.

The breeding conditions were not right. France had nothing to match the galloping disintegration that had persuaded Victor Emmanuel to ask Mussolini to form a government in 1922. The franc crisis was a pale shadow of the hyperinflation that rotted the mark and drove the desperate German middle classes away from their natural conservatism towards reckless political experiment. France had no "lost" territories or peoples to regain, no Sudetenland, no Danzig; there was no military "stab in the back" to avenge, no lost honour, no humiliations. The *ligues* were full of sound and fury, and mistrust of parliamentarianism. But when their moment came, on February 6, 1934, they, like the Boulangists before them, turned out to signify little.

However, the Stavisky affair was still immensely damaging. It ushered in old and tired men. Daladier was replaced by 70-year-old Gaston Doumergue, the former president. The foreign minister, Louis Barthou, was a year older. Pétain was appointed defence minister to appease the veterans in the *ligues*. The marshal was 78. This government of geriatrics represented the only great and stable democracy on a continent where the grisly 55-year-old Joseph Stalin already had some ten million dead peasants to his name, where 51-year-old Benito Mussolini was preening himself and planning to invade Abyssinia, and, in his 45-year-old prime, Adolf Hitler was preparing to put his murderous ideas into action. It gave, above all, invidious substance to the political extremities, and fresh music for the old left-right hatreds to dance to. How they loved it! Rally and counter rally followed each other; the right gathered at the Arc de Triomphe or Notre-Dame, the left at the place de la République or the wall where the Communards had been executed in Père-Lachaise. Both sides played the numbers game, exaggerating the turnout to stab fear in their opponents. The left claimed up to 300,000 at the cemetery; the police estimated the crowd at 50,000.

On July 14, 1935, de La Rocque's Croix de Feu paraded with 150,000 other nationalists on the Champs-Élysées. Half a million gathered at the Bastille, however, under huge red banners proclaiming "Paix, Pain, Liberté". These were the old Bolshevik slogans of 1917 Russia. No-one was at hand to remind the masses that the Bolsheviks had in fact given Russia war, starvation and dictatorship. In a blaze of goodwill, and oblivious to the experiences of those for whom the red banner was the symbol of death and slavery, the Front Populaire was launched. The physicist Jean Perrin, a Nobel laureate, complained that the rightists had stolen powerful symbols. They had adopted Joan of Arc, though this "daughter of the people" was "abandoned by the king . . . and burned by the priests who have since canonised her"; they marched under the tricolour, though this was "the flag of 1789"; and they had purloined "this heroic Marseillaise, this ferocious and revolutionary song".

Each side, in the French way of things, produced its writers and intellectuals. The totalitarian right had Robert Brasillach, the young and fashionable author of *L'Enfant de la nuit*; until he finally succumbed to Hitler mania – "the man with the distant eyes who is a god," he wrote, "who descended from heaven, like an archangel of death .." – he displayed real talent. So, before falling prey to violent anti-Semitism, did Drieu La Rochelle. The eminent historian Pierre Gaxotte outlined the ultra-right viewpoint with elegant economy – the choice was "either Parliament, with its *incurable* defects, its *incorrigible* intrigues, its *necessary* waste, its *fundamental* anarchy – or a national dictatorship" – whilst the ever-energetic royalist Charles Maurras fretted that leftist plots were subverting the nation.

Andé Gide had come out as a homosexual – "I consider it much better to be hated for what one is than to be loved for what one isn't" – and then swerved to the totalitarian left. His *Voyage au Congo* gave colonialism a mauling. Next, he took up communism. He had a need to "unite with something larger than myself", he said, and he wished to stay close to the "progressive young". The French Communists naturally welcomed this high-profile convert. He delighted in attending party congresses, where he was treated with deep respect.

It is odd that this witty, independent and stylish man, who wrote so vividly of the conflict between the spirit and the body, should have embraced a philosophy as materialistic in principle as Marxism and as vicious in practice as Stalinism. He was driven by his desire to shock, to *épater la bourgeoisie*, of course, but he was also conforming to the facile and romantic view of the distant proletariat that embedded itself in many bourgeois intellectuals. Louis Aragon, toeing the Communist line as he continued to crank out novels in his *Le Monde réel* series, also fell into that category.

Most writers, like the great majority of voters, rejected dictatorship, be it of left or right. But the clash between the two, noisy, sometimes bloody, acted as an irritant. It caught the attention, it led to fevers and night sweats; the centre could not ignore it, and it dimmed its concentration. A price was paid, too, for the existence of so many factions; the right, in particular, was so divided that it was said to do little more than accommodate people who did not vote left. In the seven years before the next war, the country went through 19 governments. Nine different men got to be prime minister, and eight to be finance minister. It was not the time to lack continuity, or for cynicism to plumb new depths. The public despised politicians. The demoralised army did not trust them. And they hated each other. "Espèce de député!" became the insult of choice for angry car drivers.

The slump in France, when it came in 1932, was longer-lasting than elsewhere. The British were back to 1929 levels of industrial output by 1934 and the Germans a year later, but the French barely reached this level in 1939.

The rentier class, the half million or so people who had lived off investments before the war, was all but finished off. Landlords, caught by rent controls, often found that a property cost more to maintain than it brought in. The building industry contracted by 40 per cent as investment in rental property dried up. The Bolsheviks had defaulted on the most widely held foreign bond, the Russian 5 per cent. The return on French 6 per cent bonds, savaged by inflation in the 1920s, was slashed further when the government forcibly reconverted them to pay 4.5 per cent in 1932. Small savers may have fared better than their German equivalents, whose destruction had helped to destabilise society across the Rhine, but deep anger and mistrust was bred among them.

Money hoarding, more elegantly known as *thésauration*, prospered with the dislike of government, tax collectors and the banks. An issue of silver coins to replace paper notes in 1932 was scrapped for fear it would encourage the mattress-stuffers. The new five-franc piece that appeared the following year was made of nickel.

The British and the Americans quit the gold standard and let their currencies float. The French remained doggedly wedded to gold. It cost them dear. Prices that had been well below the competition in 1929 were soon a third or a half higher. Tourist revenue, which had reached 9.6 billion francs a year, plummeted by two-thirds. In Nice, 22 large hotels shut down, and the number of building permits issued in the Alpes-Maritimes fell 45 per cent.

Tax revenues were hit hard by the depression and tax evasion; the American ambassador thought there was "almost as much tax evasion, through graft and carelessness, as in Mexico". The old tax on doors and windows had been abolished at the end of the war, but tax inspectors still used it as a way of estimating wealth that could not be concealed. Ingenious new taxes were devised, on advertising hoardings and neon signs, on postage stamps, and the ancient octrois continued. These were duties levied on goods crossing municipal borders, mostly on bulk food, alcohol and fuel, and sometimes on the contents of parcels and bags carried by individuals. Octroi staff in Paris rode on trains and buses to collect dues, and lines of cars and trucks were inspected for fuel and cargo. Some left-wing municipalities used flat-rate taxes on cars, horses, pianos, billiard tables and other apparent signs of wealth; but over a thousand municipalities were still using the classic system at the end of the decade, and the last octroi collection posts, at Bar-sur-Aube in Champagne, were not dismantled until 1948. A taxpayers' federation had gathered half a million members by 1934. Public employees, whose numbers had ballooned to 858,000, attracted much anger. Their salaries, excluding pensions, soaked up a third of the national budget.

In October 1934 a new prime minister, Pierre-Étienne Flandin – cool, elegant, and, so Paul Reynaud said, "wrong on every major question" – gave the possibility of devaluing "the most cursory study", and in foreign policy "believed that appeasing the Hitlerian ogre would sate his appetite". Flandin feared and loathed Laval, but made him foreign minister, on the grounds that it was easier to co-opt than to confront. Laval, foxy, sly, intrigued pitilessly against him, using *fonds secrets* from his ministry to bribe the press. The new cabinet, faced by escalating unemployment, barred immigrants and put strict controls on existing foreign workers.

With almost three million foreigners, France had a higher proportion than in the United States. They were an often lawless tribe, accounting for a quarter of all arrests in Paris, and branded as *métèques* (dagoes) in papers like Coty's *L'Ami du Peuple*. Italians made up the biggest group. Fascist officials in Italy provided them with cheap fares home and holiday camps, and free hospital care for mothers who returned to Italy to have their babies. Groups of fascists held blackshirt meetings in the big French cities. They chanted ritual territorial claims – "Who does Savoy belong to? To us. Who does Nice . . ." – and engaged in murder and counter-murder with emigré Italian communists.

Both left and right encouraged repatriation. Half a million foreigners had left by 1936, but even more had got their naturalisation papers. Technically, the *macaronis, polaks, sidis* and *bicots* had become French. Whether they were accepted as such was another matter. A recently naturalised German girl, Mlle Pitz, won the Miss France title in 1935. The press was so hostile – "Miss France sera française!" – that she resigned in favour of the runner-up, the buxom and undeniably French Giselle Préville.

Professionals as well as workers felt threatened. Many students who came to France to read law and medicine stayed on to practise after graduation. Lawyers retaliated by restricting access to the bar. A foreigner had to wait ten years after he got his naturalisation papers before he could practise. The following year, Action Française called medical faculties out on strike to demand a similar ten-year ban for naturalised doctors, and to exclude foreign students from internships. *Je suis partout* whipped up demonstrations against "les métèques médecins". A chance press photograph showed a young law student called François Mitterrand to be among them. The pressure paid off. From 1935, only naturalised foreigners who had done military service in the French army were permitted to practise medicine and dentistry. Even so, as late as 1939 a third of Paris medical students, and 28 per cent of those in the faculty of letters, were foreigners.

Jews had been absorbed without difficulty before the war. Politically, the successful were mostly right wing; they included, indeed, a few extremists in the Groupe des Croix de Feu Israélites and the Union Patriotique des Français Israélites. More now came from North Africa and the Levant. The first of the 50,000 Germans to flee Hitler were arriving. Not all of them were Jews, of course, and many "German Jews" were not German at all. They came from further east, from Poland, Romania, the Baltic states, poor, Yiddish-speaking, as wary of Frenchified Jews as they were of the French bourgeoisie. The Yiddish Workers' Theatre staged plays thick with revolution. At Yiddish schools, the choirs sang of the police shooting down striking workers, promising that when they grew up, they would be "a hero, a soldier, a Communist." Militants demanded a boycott of German goods, and called for retaliation for the persecution of German Jews. This angered both French pacifists and right wingers, who did not want to be dragged into a "Jewish war" with the Germans.

Jewish immigrants were damned both ways. If they refused to assimilate, and stuck to their own in business, with their own schools and entertainments and restaurants, they were accused of disloyalty, and spurned for bringing a cultural ghetto with them. If they did mix with the French, they were accused of stealing jobs, of underselling honest Frenchmen, of worming their way into law and medicine, and then looking after their own, excluding the French whenever possible.

A wave of xenophobia splashed over the old self-confidence in the arts. Musicians picketed foreign orchestras. Marcel Pagnol's film *Le Schpountz* made gentle fun of a great French film director with a Russian name, a Turkish passport and an Italian accent. Not all were as good-tempered as he. Fernandel, the rising comedy star, called for foreigners to be purged from show business. *Le Journal* complained that "Hollywood-Vampire" was destroying the French identity.

Anti-Americanism united both sides of the political divide. To the novelist and doctor Georges Duhamel, America was not a society but a system, which pumped out Hollywood films as a diversion for the mindless "helots" who slaved on its assembly lines. His book *Scènes de la vie future*, translated into English as *America the Menace*, ran through dozens of printings. Its author, with his conviction that the "barbaric simplicity" of America was breeding a generation of morons, was elected to the Académie Française. Something fevered, neurotic, clung to such denunciations. Robert Aron and Arnaud Dandieu said only France could save the world, but she had failed. "Fascism, Bolshevism, Hitlerism, Americanism – dictatorial regimes all – are born of our absence," they said, "because France threw in its hand." To blame France for the rise of Stalin or Mussolini was ludicrously to overestimate her influence, of course; and to equate Americanism with Hitlerism or Bolshevism was simply puerile. But this anti-American streak has proved a constant. It has many strands; a sensitive revulsion at the grosser products of American culture, envy, a sense of fading French grandeur, a brave insistence that France represents eternal values that are worth preserving. Specific irritants – the American attitude on reparations, the flood of Hollywood imports – were added from time to time.

War was in the air. In January 1935, the Saarlanders voted to rejoin Germany. Hitler continued to rearm. In March, parliament approved extending military service to two years, in response to Hitler, and to a critical manpower shortage.

Hitler seized on this. On March 16, he repudiated the military clauses of Versailles, which forbade Germany to rearm, and re-established compulsory military service. Flandin sent Laval, his foreign minister, to Moscow to sign a mutual assistance pact with the Soviets, the groundwork for which had been done by Louis Barthou, a previous foreign minister. Stalin wanted to revive the old pre-1914 alliance, worried by the rise of Hitler and communist reverses in China, Spain, Britain and America. Laval then failed to present the draft treaty to parliament, for fear of upsetting Germany, showing weakness that Stalin would remember. At home, the government refused to devalue – Germain-Martin, the incompetent finance minister, claimed that "our finances and banks are perfectly healthy" – and the jobless rose. By June, Laval was prime minister: small, dark, "almost Armenian looking", a columnist described him now, "the eyes evasive and moving constantly, speaking in the purest slang." He was given powers to legislate by decree "in defence of the franc and to guard against speculation".

In the countryside, the agitator Henri Dorgères, master of the market day soapbox, formed the Chemises Vertes. This rural *ligue* – potentially a vast movement, for a third of the labour force still worked on the land – was fuelled by a brutal drop in the value of wheat, wine, milk, butter and cheese. Average farm prices were down 50 per cent. The peasants were traditionally conservative. They still cursed land taxes as the *taille*, the term for the old poll tax swept away in the Revolution; they counted in *pistoles* (of ten francs) and *ecus* (three francs) and set prices in markets in *sous*, the five-centime fraction of the 100-centime franc. Living was tough. Few villages had electricity, and few houses had running water. They mistrusted townspeople, loathed bureaucrats – "le fonctionnaire, voilà l'ennemi" – and liberals and Marxists.

Huge crowds heard Dorgères lash the politicians. In fact, the government, far from ignoring the countryside, spent more on supporting the wheat price in 1935 than on national defence. Dorgères nonetheless used action squads of Greenshirts as strike-breakers against farm labourers who came out against the big wheat and sugar growers of the Paris basin; he created a Comité d'Action Paysanne, and led a tax strike; his Jeunesses Paysannes battled hecklers and blocked bailiffs from seizing property for non-payment of taxes.

But the Greenshirts, too, were a noisy irrelevance. France had nothing remotely like the rural fascism of the Po Valley, where the Italian landowners had used *squadristi* against the *braccianti* (rebellious day labourers). Dorgères was good on the trappings – the green shirts, oaths, rallies, berets, the self-publicity – but he hedged his bets on ideas. "Neither fascism nor communism", he said. Beneath this froth, however, *la France profonde* remained constant and moderate. He claimed to have 150,000 members by the end of 1935; even if that were true, they were vastly outnumbered by the 1.2 million members of the deeply conservative Union Nationale des Syndicats Agricoles.

Laval chose this moment to use *décret-lois* to ram through deflation. He issued 29 of these decrees on a single day, July 16. They cut all treasury payments by 10 per cent. The salaries of all state employees, from schoolteachers to street cleaners and judges, and payments to all state pensioners and treasury bond holders, were cut by one-tenth, as were all state subsidies. The result – predictably, inevitably – was to reduce prices and incomes yet further. Tax revenues, 65 billion francs before the crisis, shrank to 39.4 billion in 1935. Unemployment shot from 800,000 through the million mark, and four million of those still in jobs were on the poverty level with earnings of less than 9,600 francs a year. Artists were paupered. A salon was set up where they could exchange their works for towels, silk stockings, eau de cologne, packaged nails and other goods they could hawk from door to door. The Association des Dames Françaises started an "Intellectual Social Centre" which gave food, clothes and medicine to needy thinkers.

Mass strikes and demonstrations against the pay cuts escalated into the winter. Three days of street fighting in Brest brought three dead and 200 injured. Two were killed in Toulouse. Striking tram workers brought Lille and Roubaix to a halt. Senior army officers and magistrates sometimes marched arm-in-arm with teachers and town hall *fonctionnaires*. Tax offices, cigarette and match factories, law courts and libraries closed down,

Curiously, Laval was brought down, not by this, but by Abyssinia. Mussolini invaded Haile Selassie's African empire on October 3. Laval responded to the invasion of one League of Nations member by another with a limp protest. The League voted for sanctions, with French support, but avoided a petrol embargo, the only effective weapon it had. Even this outraged the *ligues*: Charles Maurras urged his Action Française readers to "chop the heads off" those who supported sanctions, if not with a guillotine, then with "a gun, a revolver or even a kitchen knife".

The British – a constant through the Thirties – had as many appeasers as the French. So, indeed, did the Americans, who continued to trade oil with Italy. Since the British were the uncontested great power of north-east Africa, and their navy controlled the sea routes from Italy, they were in a better position to act than the French. The British foreign secretary, Sir Samuel Hoare, was quite as accommodating to Il Duce as Laval. The Hoare-Laval pact was cobbled together on December 7.

Italy was to get two-thirds of Abyssinian territory, and would be allowed to send colonisers into the remaining third. As some sort of fig leaf, Haile Selassie was to remain the ruler of the rump of his empire.

This proved too much for the British parliament to stomach. Hoare was forced to resign when the pact leaked out. George V, with rare humour, chuckled: "No more coals to Newcastle, no more Hoares to Paris!" Humiliated by the British and by the Socialists – Léon Blum spoke scathingly of his "petty huckstering and trafficking" with Italy – Laval was forced from office. His deflation had half-ruined the country, and he had greatly encouraged the dictators.

He was succeeded in January 1936 by Albert Sarraut, a 63-year-old Radical with the advantage of having no known ideas of his own. It took him 30 hours of tortuous negotiations to put a cabinet together. An aide watched a parade of "those who were begged to take a ministry and refused", followed by "those whom no one wanted but themselves". His cabinet was spilt between conservatives and liberals. The defence minister was not a politician at all, but an ageing and torpid nonentity called General Maurin.

A frisson of the street violence commonly used by Hitler's Brownshirts came to Paris on February 13. Léon Blum was being driven back from the Chamber to his apartment by friends. The car was blocked at the rue de l'Université by the funeral procession of Jacques Bainville, an ultra-right historian and anti-Semite, and *L'Action française* writer. Blum was dragged from the car by Camelots du Roi among the mourners, and badly beaten about the head; he would probably have been killed had some building workers not rescued him.

The same evening, Action Française and the *ligues* closest to it were declared illegal. Maurras responded fiercely to the firm treatment. "Our patience is at an end," he wrote in an editorial. "Down with the Jews! Those whom we make the mistake of treating as if they are our equals display a ridiculous ambition to dominate us. They shall be put in their place and it will be a pleasure to do so."

Blum was an ideal target, as the prime mover in building a Popular Front of his Socialists with the Radicals and Communists. "There would be no Popular Front without the Fascist menace," the Radical's general secretary said, and indeed its purpose was precisely to see off the *ligue* bully boys who almost murdered him. Blum was a Socialist of sincere conviction from a well-off Alsatian Jewish family, brilliant as a young man, a *normalien* from the École Normale Supérieure, and a lawyer. He remained a Socialist after the split with the Communists, but retained his belief in socialist revolution and refused to join any "bourgeois" government. The right thus loathed him with particular venom, as a class traitor and as a Jew, Jaurès and Dreyfus rolled into one odious personage.

It was gruelling work to fashion a Popular Front from un-comradely components. Blum himself had described the Radicals as "proto-fascists". Édouard Herriot responded that Blum-type Socialists, who simultaneously believed in parliamentary democracy and the dictatorship of the proletariat, were barking mad. The Communists liked him little better, for he was a jurist with a deep belief in the sanctity of the law, opposed to any leftist seizure of power that was not based on victory at the ballot box.

He was, or so it was said, "always given to gestures when there was little or no risk attached". This had much truth. Blum talked tough and acted soft; his ideals were as noticeable on his sleeve as in his deeds. He was indecisive, rendered powerless by conscience, a man who preferred to leave an option open rather than take it. It was Blum's misfortune to be a man of principle and moderation when neither of these virtues was much in fashion; his reserve was taken for coldness, his abhorrence of demagoguery for aloofness, and his honesty for prudery. His lack of pragmatic sense, however, his angst, the shortfall in his political nous, was all too evident. He would be tested soon enough.

On the afternoon of March 7, Hitler sent in his troops to occupy the demilitarised Rhineland, a move foreseen by French military intelligence and the ambassador in Berlin. This violated Versailles, which the Germans had been forced to sign; it also violated the Locarno Pact, which they had entered freely and gladly. France was legally and morally within her rights to expel them. Sarraut considered sending in the army, but was happy to be let off the hook by allies, experts and generals alike. General Maurin, the defence minister, said that nothing could be done without a general call-up. Sarraut asked General Gamelin, the head of the General Staff, for his views. Gamelin confirmed that there was not a single unit, in a French army totally geared to the defensive, which could move forward.

In fact, the Germans were lightly armed, and might have been expelled without the need for calling-up reservists. It was, however, an article of faith that – with the United States deep in isolationism – France could not contemplate a major war without firm British support. Profound misgivings about the Anglo-Saxon financial, commercial and cultural threat were set aside. France needed the British empire, for its men and raw materials; the British navy, to safeguard the movement of its own colonial troops and supplies; the British ties with Wall Street, to help finance a long struggle.

The Royal Navy might be majestic still, but the British army was small and run-down, the economy had not recovered from the depression, and the public was as ill-prepared to have another go at the Germans as the French. More, the British, with their traditional search for a balance of power on the continent, had thought France too strong vis-à-vis Germany throughout the Twenties, and had pressed for French disarmament. Largely disarmed themselves, the British still sought to restrain their ally. London made it clear that the French would be on their own if they intervened. So did the Belgians.

Other factors pressed on Sarraut. Elections were due in six weeks. The hard right accused the left – "German Jews, social democrats, Italian exiles" – of war-mongering; the Socialists said that any action would have to be within the – inactive – framework of the League of Nations; the Communists said very little. The centre was preoccupied with manoeuvre – the Soviet ambassador wrote of its "self-doubt, peril, distrust and hesitation" – and its fear of the home-grown extremists. "The Germans", they said, "are only invading Germany."

Nothing was done. Instead of facing down the men in field grey, Gamelin found himself inaugurating a monument to carrier pigeons in Lille. "France wants peace," William C. Bullitt, the American ambassador, noted, "fears war, does not conceal that fear, and will be forced to take the consequences." It was a cruel remark – it omitted to mention that the British, and the Americans themselves, were aboard the same boat – but it was true. In effect, French post-war policy had collapsed. The collective security of the League of Nations and the alliances with eastern Europe both proved chimeras. If the French would not fight when he moved his guns onto the Rhine within range of Strasbourg, Hitler knew they would not fight for the Czechs. He knew, too, that the British instinct was not to stiffen their ally's sinews, but to abandon them to appeasement.

Very soon the Rhineland was back on the inside pages. The Popular Front won the spring elections. The Socialists unseated the Radical Socialists as the largest party in the Chamber, and the Communists made large gains. Hitler had no reason to worry over the result. The French were busy antagonising one another across the left-right divide. The Popular Front held a great parade at the Mur des Fédérés on May 24 to rub salt in old wounds. "Vive le Front Populaire!" they cried, adding, to make sure that the inhabitants of the *beaux quartiers* shivered in their silken socks, "Vive la Commune!" A production at the Vieux Colombier theatre had Figaro in a red scarf threatening the *classes possédantes*. An aperitif for leftists, Le Popu, red in colour, was launched.

Nearly two million went on strike, demanding a 40-hour week, with wages for 48 and holidays with pay. The workers in the Nieuport aircraft works pioneered the *grève sur le tas*, the sit-in on the factory floor, playing cards and boules, and singing and dancing. Soon the Farman aircraft plant was out, as were the Citroën, Renault and Gnome et Rhône plants. It mattered not that these were arms plants, vital to the struggle against fascism. Sightseers went to watch the Renault strikers parading with red flags and playing football in the big Paris factory. Striking musicians gave the Galeries Lafayette strikers a concert in the glove department. A huge banner created by shop girls of the Trois Quartiers department store near the Madeleine proclaimed: "Our future is a sanatorium or prostitution."

Blum formed the Popular Front government on June 5. The Communists chose to support it rather than join it. Women were appointed cabinet undersecretaries for the first time – Irene Joliot-Curie was at Research – though they were no nearer to having the vote. Léo Lagrange was appointed undersecretary for leisure and sports. The right promptly dubbed him "Minister for Laziness". Free time, and the higher pay to enjoy it, were indeed the first fruits of victory. In the course of a weekend, meeting at the Matignon, the Blum cabinet, the trade unions and the employers' federation had signed up to collective bargaining, union recognition and wage increases of 7 to 15 per cent. Laws giving workers a forty-hour week and two weeks holidays with pay followed. The shorter week, so Blum mistakenly theorised, would boost employment. The strikes continued. On June 11, Thorez, exasperated, told the Communists: "You must know when to end a strike." The Renault workers abandoned their sit-in two days later. On June 18, the new interior minister, Roger Salengro, issued a decree forcibly dissolving the remaining *ligues*.

Thus, *en principe*, was France transformed. In practice, as Laval told the American ambassador, "even in politics two and two are not six". Blum could not restore pay and pension cuts, slash the working week, balance the budget and maintain the franc. Labour costs at the Renault plant in Paris were 35 million francs a month in April. They now shot up to 57 million francs, and productivity per worker fell by 12 per cent. Something would have to give.

Neither could Salengro wish away the *ligues*. De La Rocque was back in business without missing a beat; he simply transformed the Croix de Feu into a political party, the Parti Social Français (PSF). He was not alone. Jacques Doriot, the ex-Communist mayor of Saint Denis, came up with a new fascist party, the Parti Populaire Français. A grand parade of the left was held to mark July 14. Blum attended with the Communist Maurice Thorez. The right protested against the identification of the Republic with the Revolution. The ultras coined a menacing new slogan – "plutôt Hitler que Blum" – and gave notice that Salengro would be made to pay for outlawing the *ligues*. *L'Action française* ran a story on its front page, reviving an old story that the interior minister had been condemned to death in 1916 for deserting to the enemy.

As this squalid affair soured the country, the last hopes of averting war in Europe bled away in Spain as the extremes of left and right, whose games had so weakened France, went for each other's throats on the outskirts of Madrid. To the east, in Colonel de Gaulle's vivid phrase, German troops across the Rhine were "resting on the soft pillow of the Maginot Line". For France, the phoney peace had begun.

7

Phoney Peace,
Phoney War

"I had the feeling, in spite of everything, of having brought a little blue sky into their dark and difficult lives," Blum said of the poor. "We had given them hope." The roads were full of jalopies, motorcycles and tandems, with working-class couples in matching sweaters pedalling them. Boxer, footballer and cabinet minister Léo Lagrange was a success as the Popular Front's leisure supremo. He browbeat the railways into cutting fares, with special holiday "Lagrange trains" and family tickets. In August 1936 alone, 600,000 tickets were sold at discounts of up to 60 per cent, and the railways made their first profits since 1928. The Popular Front took the credit, but Lagrange himself was happy to say that his model was Hitler's Strength through Joy programme. The French also caught up with the German love of hiking and the open air. Some of the older peasant women were shocked by hikers' shorts, however, and refused to sell milk to girls with bare knees. Country folk came to Paris on three-day trips at 100 francs a head, with meals, lodging, a guided tour and a visit to the theatre thrown in.

As a great watershed between town and country was reached – for the first time, more than half the French were urban, with marginal land in the Vendée, the uplands of the Massif Central and the stony fields of Provence abandoned and dying – a new sentimentality was felt for rural life. *La France profonde*, old country France, the eternal and deep-rooted guardian of pride and tradition, was idolised as never before. The charms of the Midi were invoked in a stream of songs and films, the sun, the scents of lavender and roses and pastis, the ochre-washed *cabanons* with violet shutters, the games of *pétanque* in dusty squares, the *galéjades*, the tall stories told in southern accents, and Marseilles and the Canebière, the great avenue that rolls down through the dusty plane trees to the Old Port at the heart of the city. Maurice Pagnol built his studio in the city, and created films full of foibles and fun, shot beneath the shimmering white stone of Notre-Dame de la Garde. The mobile-faced actor Fernandel escaped from work in a Marseilles soap factory to carve an international career as the Provençal peasant who was not as dumb as he looked.

The number of bicycles rocketed to nine million. "Elle fait de la bi-bi, de la bicyclette," sang Fernandel, "et ça fait mon bonheur." Citroën were producing the Traction Avant, a car as radical as it was beautiful, designed by Flaminio Bertoni in a single night with sculpting tools. It had a chassis-less, monocoque construction, with front-wheel drive, a low centre of gravity, independent suspension and a gearbox over the front wheels. Bertoni achieved near perfection down to the elegant door handles. The car was a classic, but making it bankrupted Citroën. It was taken over by Michelin, the main creditor, who brought in American machinery and methods to halve the assembly time. Michelin noted that 90 per cent of first-time car buyers bought second-hand at under half price, so it commissioned Bertoni to design a highly practical little car for tradesmen and small farmers, selling at a third of the price of an ordinary saloon. Bertoni's brief was for a car that could carry four people and 50 kilos of potatoes at up to 60 kph across rough tracks. His Très Petite Voiture, known as the "Poubelle" (dustbin), or TPV, did so in style. It developed into the eccentric and much loved 2CV, powered by a flat two-cylinder air-cooled engine, and held together by 16 bolts. A Citroën director called it a "deckchair under an umbrella"; its cloth seats were hung beneath an opening fabric roof; it had a corrugated bonnet, and it was equipped with a single headlight, a wiper, a stick fuel gauge and a speedometer. It was just emerging from the prototype stage when production was stopped by the war.

The roads were increasingly crowded, and the annual death toll passed the five thousand mark. The slaughter was fuelled by bad surfaces, the vulnerability of cyclists and the ease of passing the driving test. Jacques Le Roy Ladurie recollected that he hit a wall, killed a chicken and narrowly missed a pedestrian before being warmly congratulated by the examiner on passing his test. Skiing, once the preserve of the rich, opened up as new resorts were built and magazines like *Confidences* assured readers that, with cheap rail fares, boarding houses and thick home-knitted sweaters, it was affordable. The Channel resorts, once the preserve of the blazered and the boatered, filled with trippers. Over half the visitors interviewed on the Riviera had never seen the sea before. Not everyone approved. Chic shops in Nice put harsh notices in their windows – "Interdit aux congés payés", no entry to those on holidays-with-pay.

New products celebrated the cult of sport and the sea and sunbathing. Fizzy Orangina made its appearance in its stylish round bottle. L'Oréal brought out l'Ambre Solaire suntan oil. The tennis player René Lacoste, champion of Forest Hills, and husband of a textile tycoon's daughter, invented a light and airy shirt to survive the humid heat of American courts. A Boston newspaper nicknamed him "the Alligator" because he travelled with alligator skin suitcases. The French turned it into "crocodile", and the distinctive Lacoste logo was born.

The beauty industry underwent a revolution in service that opened it to ordinary people. Hairdressers, manicurists, seamstresses and the like had traditionally gone, at a price, to their customers' houses to attend to them. Now they set up their own salons and boutiques – the number of registered hairdressers soared from 61,000 in 1926 to 170,000 at the end of the Thirties – and their customers came to them at much lower cost. These modest new followers of fashion were greeted by *Marie Claire*, a magazine launched for them. It was soon selling a million copies, alongside a flourishing *presse du coeur* catering for working women eager to read with titles like *Confessions* and *Confidences*.

The number of radio sets mushroomed over the decade from 500,000 to 5.5 million. A vast audience was opened up for a dazzling generation of popular singers. Tino Rossi broke all records with "O Corse, île d'amour"; Edith Piaf sang of hot sand and passion and lost love in "Mon Légionnaire"; *le fou chantant*, Charles Trenet, reassured the world that "Y'a d'la joie", and Yves Montand began his career. Le Hot Club de France gave native blood to the lasting passion for jazz. The theatre, with its revivals of Dumas classics and the witty word plays of Jean Giradoux, was in light-weight mode. Most new films were foreign; imports, mostly American, accounted for 327 out of 430 releases in a typical year. Complaints remained loud and bitter, but the industry was partly to blame. It was difficult to raise money in France. The capital markets were undeveloped, and credit through investment banks and venture capitalists was in short supply. Pathé and Gaumont, the old titans, were in receivership. Most films were made by one-off companies financed at high rates by British banks and insurance companies. Even so, the French had huge natural talent that the Popular Front succoured with subsidies, and which gained from the arrival of refugees like Fritz Lang and Max Ophüls.

In fashion, the whacky Zazou look, with its too-short trousers and oversize jackets with too-loud stripes, added to the gaiety of the nation. So did the Surrealists. They mounted a major exhibition in 1936, which starred the mobiles of Alexander Calder and Meret Oppenheimer's memorable fur-covered spoons, cups and saucers. They also changed allegiance with panache. At the start of the decade, they had sent a telegram to the Kremlin assuring their "fellow revolutionaries" that they could count on Surrealist support "in case of imperialist aggression". They now published an open letter denouncing the "cretinising wind that blows from Soviet Russia".

There was nothing of the cretin about Blum, the only premier to take a real interest in science. He put Irène Joliot-Curie in charge of scientific research with a budget of 32.5 million francs. The Centre National de Recherche Scientifique (CNRS) became a great engine of new ideas and invention. An observatory for astrophysics was set up, together with a national chemical institute, laboratories for atomic transformation and low temperatures, and the Institut des Textes with a magnificent collection of texts. Irène Curie had joined her mother at the Institut du Radium in Paris, and worked on radioactivity with her husband Frédéric Joliot. They made the first artificial radio isotope, winning the Nobel Prize for Chemistry, and developing a range of radio isotopes that have had a tremendous impact on medicine and industry.

The government also backed the creation of the Musée de l'Homme, and popularised science by making technology and the Palais de la Découverte focal points of the great Paris exhibition of 1937. The Joliot-Curie cyclotron was the showpiece of the pavilion. Other contributions to science were made by minds of the quality of Louis de Broglie, pioneer of wave-particle duality, the physicist Jean-Baptiste Perrin, the mathematicians Émile Picard, theorist of complex surfaces and integrals, and Émile Borel, politician, journalist and expert in complex analysis. Their work was of fundamental importance.

For all this, the Popular Front did not usher in an age of bonhomie. Paid holidays and cheap facilities were not the bolt from the blue of Popular Front mythology. Blum appointed three women as junior ministers, but he stopped well short of giving women the vote, since they were likely to vote conservative. A little paper progress was made; a wife no longer needed her husband's consent to go out to work, and she had more control over her property and earnings. But the depression turned women into unwanted rivals to men. The national congress of mayors urged them to return to the home, where they could "do most good". The motion was carried unanimously, Communists and Socialists included, and the general attitude remained, as Clemenceau had famously said: "We already have universal suffrage for men. No need to aggravate a futility."

Philosophy was stubbornly pessimistic. Jean-Paul Sartre had recently returned from Berlin, where he had been deeply influenced by Martin Heidegger, the eccentric, city-hating, knickerbocker-wearing, wilfully obscure author of *Being and Time*. He held that man's existence is the central fact, and that reason and intellect are "hopelessly inadequate guides to the secret of being". Death is the second great factor; it is fear of it that gives meaning to our being, as we spend our existence on earth creating ourselves, "moving into an open, uncertain, as yet uncreated future". Sartre, a sophisticated *normalien*, turned to philosophy, developing his own concepts of existentialism when back in Paris. He found man alone in a world being drowned by materialism, standardisation and Americanisation. Life in this dimming world was "absurd"; freedom existed only for those who broke away from the norms of existence. Other philosophers, like the young Communists Georges Politzer and Paul Nizan, savaged the academic tradition. So did the historians Marc Bloch and Lucien Febvre. Their review, *Annales d'histoire économique et sociale*, was unrestrained in its onslaught on established ideas.

The Popular Front defined itself as anti-fascist, proving its credentials by suppressing the *ligues*; in this it was at one with churchmen like Léonart and the pope, who had condemned Action Française. But, beneath its anti-fascism, the old anticlericalism lived on. Catholicism continued strong. *The Life of Jesus* by the left-leaning Catholic liberal François Mauriac was a 1936 bestseller. A third of the world's missionaries were French. Many among the 130,000 nuns and novices had lives of medieval piety and discomfort. They dressed in stiff brown linen with whalebone collars, and slept on straw palliasses on wooden planks in windowless cells, washing themselves with used rags. Novice nuns were expected to apply hot poultices of grease to their breasts each evening, so that after a month they became "flaccid pockets".

More men were going into the priesthood than for over half a century. They went into factories and ran soup kitchens and preached of *Christ ouvrier*. Armand Vallée, the "Red priest of Saint-Brieuc", lived with the unemployed and organised Christian trade unions in the Côtes-du-Nord. The church ran flourishing youth groups for students, workers, shop assistants and peasants. *Coeur Vaillant*, the Catholic children's magazine, with its cartoons of Tintin and his dog Milou, sold 200,000 copies a week. No self-respecting group was without a uniform shirt in the Thirties; the young readers had beige ones with scout-type scarves in green and orange. The CFTC, the big Catholic union, had 150,000 members by 1936.

The left could not let such *lese-majesté* pass. Members of the new Comités de Defense Anti-Fasciste held provocative feast-days during Lent, and denounced church groups as "unbearable, insolent and violently anti-Soviet". Particular wrath was heaped on the Davidées, Catholic laywomen who taught in elementary schools. They were, the militant leftist Marceau Pivert declared, "innocent dreamers enrolled in an army of murderers and fanatics".

Reactionary churchmen gave as good as they got. The bishop of Quimper warned against marrying the unbaptised and Bolsheviks. "We have enough animals in our stables," he said. "We do not need any in our homes." For good measure, he forbade the faithful of Finistère from dancing after dark. Abbé Bethléem, a mentor of Catholic reading habits, advised against reading anything by Jews, Protestants and leftists, who "abuse all decent Frenchmen".

Blum was a gentle spirit for this time of hatreds. He was tall and slender with slim sensitive hands, his long face parted by a drooping pale moustache. He was elegant, a fine dancer, and a little foppish, apt to receive workers' delegations in his library at midday in mauve pyjamas and dressing gown. His high-pitched voice, his love of spats and buttonholes and scented handkerchiefs, gave him an air of camp, though he was happily married; Ambassador Bullitt noted the "quicksilver intelligence and the little fluttery gestures of the hyper-intellectual queer ones", and Léon Daudet amused *L'Action française* readers by calling him "the circumcised hermaphrodite".

His socialism was bedded deep in compassion, and he was honest, honourable and brave; but he was not quite the finished article as a politician. André Delmas, a teacher's union leader, was struck by his guilt at being a bourgeois and an intellectual. Blum lacked, too, the stomach for power and the will to hold on to it. He had heard of his election victory whilst in a restaurant; he was so astonished that he poured salt over his strawberries. He was an idealist with an unnerving habit of claiming the opposite. "I am not describing a Utopia, a visionary paradise," he had said during the campaign. "I am describing a society all of whose elements exist, ready to be fused into life by your will."

He found it painful to come to a decision. "I have often thought", he said in a telling remark, "that morality may perhaps consist solely in the courage of making a choice." He disliked confrontation, and his instincts were for compromise. "Blum valued conciliation", André Malraux was to observe, "as de Gaulle valued inflexibility."

He was thus vulnerable to the great issue of Spain. He had strong reasons to steer clear of involvement: fear of civil war spreading to France, pressure from the British and from Radicals within his cabinet, and the conduct of the Spanish Republicans themselves, for whom so tender and misplaced a regard is often expressed. His policy was at the very least understandable; but the vacillations and breast-beating that went with it caused him to be reviled.

His first reaction, when asked for aid by José Giral, the Spanish premier, was to send aircraft and artillery. The British at once indicated their extreme concern. The

Communists and left-wingers in the cabinet such as Lagrange supported Blum; but a raft of others, even excluding the pro-Franco extremists, were deeply opposed, many appalled at the prospect of a Red neighbour. Blum soon feared that aiding Spain could set off a general war, in which the British would be neutral and "half of France would not follow me". He was, he admitted, tied to the Spanish socialists by "personal friendship". He recognised that it was in France's direct interest to have "a friendly government on Spanish soil", and that the "success of Republican legality" was essential to "international freedom". His sympathy for the cause made the bald rejection of help that followed the more damning.

It cost him dear. Germany and Italy seized the initiative, sending weapons and men to Spain, tightening the Rome–Berlin Axis, and showing off the power of fascism. The Belgians were rattled by French non-intervention, and Brussels withdrew from the Franco-Belgian Pact, looking to neutrality for salvation, and leaving an unfortified border north of the Maginot Line. An undying myth was born, too, of the betrayal of Spanish democracy, in which Blum was aided and abetted by the supine British.

This ignores the unpleasant realities of the time. Spanish Republicans had developed dark traits – strikes, assassinations, bombings, peasant invasions of estates – since forcing the king into exile in 1931. The Popular Front that won the elections of February 1936 was an uneasy coalition of Socialists, Republicans, Communists and Catalans. Manuel Anzana, who became president in May, was a devout anticlerical who set about proving his boast that Spain had "ceased to be Catholic" by closing Church schools and announcing that "all the convents in Spain are not worth a single Republican life". In the weeks before Franco landed his troops in Spain, there were 160 church-burnings and 269 political killings. "Do not tell me that this is contrary to freedom," Anzana snarled at liberals. "It is a matter of public health." Communists and anarchists had a particular hatred of the Church – and their victims were to include 12 bishops, 249 novices, 283 nuns, 2,494 monks and 5,255 priests. How could France and Britain, decent Christian democracies, condone such atrocities, let alone arm those who were committing them? Even their instant intervention would not have prompted the Republicans to temper their behaviour. Indiscriminate priest-killings had broken out immediately; when the left-wing parties took control of Madrid on the night of July 19, 1936, they at once set 50 churches on fire.

It is true, of course, that the Spanish nationalists committed atrocities enough of their own. So did their German and Italian allies. Picasso created a giant mural for the Paris exhibition of 1937 to record the destruction of the Basque city of Guernica by German bomber crews one market-day afternoon. But it was Stalin who controlled the Communist effort in Spain, the flow of arms and advisers, and the Comintern and International Brigades. This was the man whose assault on the kulak peasants, and the terror-famine that accompanied collectivisation in the Ukraine, had killed perhaps 14 million people in the previous six years. When André Gide went to Russia in 1936 he was greeted by "spontaneous" crowds at every railway stop, and winsome young Red Army soldiers were thoughtfully provided in a swimming pool he visited. But Gide was not fooled. When he got back, he published *Retour de l'URSS* in November 1936, lashing the attempt to enforce "total unanimity of thought" through terror. Louis-Ferdinand Céline visited in 1936 to spend the rubles owed him in book royalties. He wrote *Mea Culpa* on his return, a forty-page pamphlet that burned up Bolshevism with the incandescent rage he was soon to turn on the Jews. He found the Soviets foul and venomous. Prolovitch, as he called his proto-proletarian, had been promised paradise; instead, he was trapped behind "a hundred thousand barbed wires" by "the most suspicious, most vindictive, most sadistic police on this earth!" Only three things, Céline wrote, were doing well among the Soviets: "Army, police, propaganda." They had "dressed up a turd as a caramel". It was with Stalin that Blum would have associated himself if he had joined Russia in sending arms.

The British, whose fleet could have imposed an arms embargo, were indifferent or hostile to the Republicans. Stanley Baldwin's conservatives did not want a Red victory; in this war of "rebels against rabble" they leant towards Franco. So did Franklin Roosevelt. But it was Blum, not Baldwin or Roosevelt, who drew most blame for inaction. It was part of a general appeasement. Blum refused to appoint a new ambassador to Rome, on the grounds that the letters of accreditation would have to be addressed to Victor Emmanuel's illegal new title, the king of Italy and emperor of Ethiopia. But he agreed to lift the League of Nations sanctions against Italy. Nothing was done to warn the Germans against sending arms to Franco. French athletes went to the Berlin Olympics, which opened on August 1. Blum welcomed the German economics minister, Hjalmar Schacht, to Paris.

Dolores Ibarruri, La Pasionaria, the great orator of the war, spoke at a huge rally in the Vélodrome d'Hiver, pleading, whispering, demanding the arms that Blum would not give, to a backdrop of yellow and red streamers; she spoke in Spanish, but she held a crowd of 30,000 hushed and hanging on every inflexion, each word splitting the Popular Front more cruelly between interventionists and neutrals. "It may be your turn tomorrow," she said, and it was not only extremists who felt that the fevered abnormalities of Soviet Russia and Germany were about to become a norm, and that sides must be taken. "Fascism has spread its great black wings over Europe," André Malraux said, joining the Republicans. "Soon there will be action, blood for blood." The writer of *La Condition humaine*, the Goncourt winner of 1933, Malraux was a man of ideals and loose living, an explorer and revolutionary, a looter of antiquities, an egotist and self-promoter, and a writer of brilliance.

He was obsessed by the legend of Lawrence of Arabia, and he saw in Spain the chance to fashion himself into the great fascist-slayer. It did not concern him that the left was also soiled; he wrote of Russia as the land of the free, though he knew full well, from the crude ideological meddlings that appeared without his agreement in the Russian edition of *La Condition humaine*, that it was not. He revelled in doing publicly what Blum dare not. Malraux obtained some French aircraft, Dewoitine fighters and Potez 540 bombers, with the clandestine connivance of Blum and Pierre Cot, the air minister; he added an assortment of other aircraft, recruited some mercenary pilots, and flew this strange airborne caravan over the Pyrenees from Toulouse shortly before Blum's arms embargo began.

His pilots were described as "a bunch of racketeers"; the aircraft were so slow and vulnerable that a mission was counted a triumph if they returned, and bombs were dropped out of windows and through latrine vents. But his book on the civil war, *L'Espoir*, gave graphic accounts of Franco's Moors fleeing in terror as Malraux's bombs sped down on them "with the free movement of torpedoes", hurling their trucks into somersaults, and breaking up their assault. Malraux romanticised, but he had a dash and swashbuckling brilliance that burned off the grey and ill-tempered mist of the times. The French could still be French, and he heartened them.

Spain was not Blum's only blight. The Popular Front's economic record was dismal. Industrial production climbed by 8 per cent in the 12 months before it came to power. It fell by 5 per cent over the next two years. Worse, German production rose 17 per cent over the same period. The attempt to boost demand by cutting working hours and increasing wages failed miserably. In May 1936, labour costs at Billancourt were 35 million francs. By that December, they were at 57 million francs and climbing, and productivity per worker had tumbled by 12 per cent. The Renault workers there thought of themselves as the spearhead of the Popular Front – they had celebrated its victory with a vast parade, with a tableau vivant of workers in Phrygian caps and a truck-borne orchestra that played the "Marseillaise" and the "Internationale" alternatively as a symbol of unity – and labour relations were sour. "Continual stoppages, repeated indiscipline, a systematic slowdown in production", Louis Renault complained, "rendered the atmosphere of our factory more and more poisonous." He reacted by bringing in cheap Arab labour and employing more women. Industry did not modernise: investment was a dirty word for employers, as was automation for their workers.

Something had to give, and in September the government allowed business to recoup wage rises through price hikes. The higher salaries were swiftly soaked up by inflation, and fear of a devaluing franc led to a stampede to transfer capital abroad. Eighteen billion francs flowed out in September alone. The gold reserves of the Banque de France, over 80 billion francs in 1935, had fallen to 54 billion francs by September 4. Another 1.5 billion francs leaked out over the following fortnight. Panic-stricken, Blum devalued the franc by 30 per cent against the dollar on September 26. It was done hastily, fearfully, belatedly. The exercise was bungled. One rushed devaluation was followed by another, and within two years the franc was worth half its 1928 Poincaré value. "Prices are falling at last!" the wags said. "You can pick up a franc for ten centimes."

Investors were leery of lending to a Socialist-led government, and the swelling deficit was financed by inflation. The balance of trade deteriorated further. Unemployment hardly budged. Reforms had varied success. The Banque de France was made more accountable. A modest programme of nationalisation was begun. Overall, though, the record was poor. The left blamed the flight of capital. Some of this money might have gone into modernising industry, it is true; but the main constraint on production was the continuing shortage of skilled technicians, and businessmen's lack of confidence in the government.

It did not help that Blum treated finance with almost aristocratic disdain. It was, he assured Pierre-Mendès France, a future prime minister, of no importance: "Mon petit Mendès, un gouvernement ne tombe pas sur des problèmes financiers" ("My dear Mendès, a government does not fall because of financial problems"). When Mendès retorted that every government for 15 years past had fallen for financial reasons, Blum protested: "Mais non, mais non!"

Blum appealed plaintively to patriotism, but it was simple economics to export capital when government policies were eroding its value at home. A renewed flight of capital early in 1937 forced his hand. On February 13, he announced that "a pause is necessary". The reforms were over, and monetary orthodoxy returned. It was made illegal to strike without first going to arbitration. Restrictions on the circulation of gold were lifted. Treasured programmes – workers' pension schemes, an unemployment fund, a sliding scale of wages – were abandoned. "Its more than a pause," *Le Temps* noted acidly on March 8, "it's a conversion." The Popular Front, launched with such recent rapture, had failed.

A rally was held by La Rocque's Parti Social Français, his revamped Croix de Feu, in a cinema in Clichy on March 16, a provocative choice of venue. Its Socialist mayor and Communist deputy drummed up a counter-demonstration. Amid violent clashes, police fired into the crowd, killing five and injuring Blum's cousin. Blum himself had been at the opera and rushed to the scene in evening dress and top hat. The Communists used the "fusillade de Clichy" to accuse Blum of being soft on fascists and hard on the left, baying for his blood and making much of his "bourgeois" attire. Right-wing cartoons showed the Jewish premier steeped in the carnage and asked invidiously: "Who says this man has no French blood?"

A final gesture was left to him. He opened the 1937 Paris Exposition, which he thought of as a battleground where "democracy would deal fascism in all its forms its death blow". It was intended to promote international amity: a speaking clock in the Pavilion of Peace reminded the spectators that four soldiers had been killed every minute in the Great War. His hopes were soon dashed.

The Exposition had a Pavilion of Labour, but the 20,000 workers building it were out of sorts. The site was a closed union shop. Firms were forbidden to use their own labour or to employ members of Catholic unions. The full range of sit-ins, slowdowns, work-to-rules, meetings and delegations put work hopelessly behind schedule and the official opening had to be postponed from May Day to May 25. The grounds, running down and across the Seine from Trocadéro, were still a huge building site. Plywood screens, some bravely decorated with tricolours, blocked off much of it, including the Labour Pavilion. Only five of the scores of buildings were completed, including the glowering pavilions of the totalitarians that mocked Blum's noble thoughts of friendship. The Italians had a vast equestrian statue of the "Genius of Fascism", and displayed large pictures of the conquest of Ethiopia. An eagle clutched a swastika in its talons on the German pavilion, its eyes fixed on the Soviet display opposite. Here, their bronze scarves fluttering as they strode forward, a giant proletarian and a women from a collective farm carried a hammer and sickle. Parisians, waking each morning to headlines on the grotesque show trials in Moscow, in which Stalin's Old Bolshevik ex-colleagues parroted bogus confessions, christened the display "Hurrying to the Lubianka". Some of these victims appeared in a frieze in the pavilion; an artist had to disguise them, adding a hasty beard to Marshal Tukhachevsky, sideburns to Radek, hair to Zinoviev.

And the British, with their hosts the only weighty democrats left in Europe, possessors of the largest empire ever known, an elephant to Mussolini's swaggering little mouse, what of them? Their pavilion was described as a cross between a suburban cinema and a sweet stall, with displays of golf balls, tennis rackets, the coronation robes, and a cardboard model of Neville Chamberlain fishing in long rubber boots. It is easy to mock such humdrum symbols in the face of the bully boys, yet there is surely something splendid to this non-grandeur, and to what the French chose for their displays. Technical progress was celebrated with a 600-square-metre cinema screen, the world's largest, a title also held by the electric sparks generated in the Palace of Discovery; but most affection was lavished on *la France profonde* and its folklore, food, dress and crafts. The Pavilion of Cinema showed finely shot films on Burgundy, the Jura, Savoie and the Pyrenees. The Rural Centre had an idealised country village, stripped of clericalism, war memorials and the grinding poverty that still drove peasants off marginal land; it was a place of conciliation, where the right, with its sentiment for the values of rural life, was joined to the left, with its new passion for vacations and country rambles.

Seven hundred searchlights transformed the Eiffel Tower into a "cathedral of light", threaded with a lacework of fluorescent tubes, and then cascaded with fireworks. Fred Astaire and Ginger Rogers danced. The La Scala opera company came. The architect Le Corbusier, having no official commissions, boldly set up his own Pavilion of the New Era, using a steel framework and waterproof cloth instead of masonry walls to save money. The Palace of Elegance gave Schiaparelli a chance to show off her brilliant – and sometimes anti-fascist – concoctions; she designed an evening outfit of Abyssinian warrior's tunic worn with imperial purple trousers to honour the emperor Haile Selassie. She drew immense crowds with a washing line, from which were suspended a fashionable lady's ensemble, complete with shoes, stockings and underwear.

The Exposition's public lavatories were ready in July, a long wait indeed. Hotels refused to charge lower rates; instead, they increased them. The cost escalated from a planned 300 million francs to 1.5 billion francs. Taxi drivers and café and restaurant staff came out on strike. Some pavilions were still being opened in August. By then, after 382 uneasy days in office, Blum had been voted out. On June 14, Vincent Auriol, his finance minister, had asked for plenary financial powers to govern by *décrets-lois*. The Senate refused. The franc had fallen from 15 to the dollar in January 1936 to 21 francs a year later. It now fell to 26 francs. Blum again asked for plenary powers to deal with speculation against the franc. The Senate blamed him for corrupting workers by assuring them that "freshly roasted larks" and other delicacies awaited them. Blum resigned on June 21.

He was replaced as premier by Camille Chautemps, who had survived the Stavisky affair to manoeuvre himself back as a leading Radical. He was known, so William Bullitt reported, as a "jellyfish with lots of common sense", and indeed he drifted easily and invisibly, was difficult to hold, but had little sting. Blum continued as vice-premier, to give an appearance of Popular Front continuity, but the game was up.

The Senate gave Chautemps the powers it denied to Blum. He and his finance minister, Georges Bonnet, raised taxes, slashed social expenditure and chipped away at the 40-hour week. The franc sank further. Power workers, steelmen, merchant seamen, car assembly workers and hotel staff came out on strike. Truck drivers walked out, and army lorries had to ferry in food to the vast wholesale market at Les Halles in Paris. Terrorists blew up the headquarters of the employers' federation and the metal industries in September. Police said it was the work of the CSAR, the secret committee of revolutionary action, ultra-rightists whom the press dubbed the "cagoulards" (hooded men). The leaders of the *cagoule* hoped the Communists would be blamed and that this would incite army officers to turn the army against the Republic.

Abroad, as at home, the government was fatalistic and inactive. "The Quai sees no possibility of preserving the peace and nothing to do but wait," Ambassador Bullitt reported. "Helpless in the face of events, all they can do is bury the dead." Fitzroy Maclean, a young diplomat at the British embassy, caught the feeling of drift and helplessness. "Occasional telephone calls," he wrote. "Occasional visits to the Quai d'Orsay: the smell of bees wax in the passages; the rather fusty smell of the cluttered, steam-heated offices; comment allez-vous, cher collègue? Luncheon . . . more dispatches, more telephone calls till dinner time. A bath. A drink. And then all the different lights and colours and smells and noises of Paris at night."

On the left, Malraux published *L'Espoir* in December. He sketched idealised volunteers from the International Brigades, who "knew poverty well enough to die fighting with it . . . and came to lie, one after another, on the Spanish earth." A howl of fury came the same month from the extreme right, if a tag can be given to the anarchic and now sadly hate-filled Louis-Ferdinand Céline. In his *Bagatelles pour un massacre*, he poured verbal filth over "those Yids who run the world . . . They're all vampires! Rotten . . . send them back to Hitler." They were forcing decadent France into a fight with Hitler that would be lost in a fortnight, he prophesied. "Fighting a war for the bourgeoisie, it was already shitty enough, but now . . . I can't imagine a worse humiliation than to get yourself killed for the Yids." For so fine a writer to drop into the sewer was tragic; it was sad, too, that *Bagatelles* sold 86,000 copies.

There were more strikes around Paris in December. When the *gardes mobiles* were sent in to eject the strikers, the movement spread across the country, with particular strength in the north and Lyon. A general strike of the public services brought Paris to a halt at the end of the year. By March, the financial position was grievous. The franc had fallen to a record low of 153 against the pound sterling, and the treasury was almost bare; the Chamber of Deputies chose this moment to vote themselves 30 per cent salary increases. Chautemps asked for plenary powers to impose austerity and deflation. The Socialists said they would abstain. Chautemps resigned on March 10. Hitler scented the power vacuum; the next day the Germans began to occupy Austria.

The times were desperate. Blum tried to form a ministry of national union, but the right did not wish to share power with the left when it might be able to rule alone. He then tried to avoid war by agreements with the Germans and Italians. The reworked Popular Front that Blum was obliged to construct was a fragile thing. The Chamber voted him plenary powers, but the deputies knew full well that his ministry would collapse at the first puff of protest from the Senate. His economic policy was more realistic, if more antagonistic to the rich and their "wall of gold", than before. He proposed to get the economy moving with massive deficit spending on arms. His rather addled justification for this, however, showed the pacifism at his core. Far from praising arms-making at a time of acute military menace, he damned it as a "painful task". His spirit was at odds with the times.

Strikes and sit-ins continued. Arms plants were badly affected. As Jewish refugees began arriving from Austria, tempers rose in the Chamber. "Jews to the scaffold!" some deputies chanted. *Je suis partout* gloated over the pogroms in the Vienna ghettoes as "a splendid example of distributive justice". By March 22, Bullitt reported, people had "forgotten about Austria". Fear now switched to getting caught up in a war on behalf of the Czechs.

Morale had a fillip when Édouard Tenet defeated the German boxer Jupp Besselmann for the world middleweight title on April 7. Léon Blum was flattened by the Senate the next day. It voted by a huge margin, 214 to 47, to reject his economic programme. The Socialists called for a mass demonstration to protest outside the Palais de Luxembourg that evening. It was a dismal failure. No longer could the left call out its supporters in the scores of thousands; the working class had lost the stomach for it.

Daladier took office on April 12. The British were glad to see Blum go, and delighted by the arrival of Georges Bonnet at the Quai d'Orsay. He was clever, charming and polished, the son of a well-off Dordogne magistrate, whose attractive wife Odette was known as *soutien-Georges*. He was said, however, to be "congenitally uncandid" and an acquaintance said that, when he walked, he moved sideways, so that all that was seen was "a long and powerful nose that seems to scent every danger and every prey". When danger threatened, Georges Mandel said, Bonnet "will hide under any stone to avoid it." His blue eyes were hooded, he was bald and spindle-shanked, and he used his inside knowledge to speculate on the Bourse. Winston Churchill found him "the quintessence of defeatism". That, of course, was why more powerful Englishmen – notably the prime minister, Neville Chamberlain – so approved of Bonnet, and why he was a man of his hour.

Daladier was a solid and popular figure, the thick-set veteran of 15 cabinets. His quick intelligence was matched by a sense of irony, and he had the virtues of the "République des professeurs", with a firm grasp of realities and a patriotic if rather authoritarian respect for democracy. He was, too, an honest man. His mistress, the marquise de Crussol, was the heiress to a canned fish fortune – "a sardine", the wags said cruelly, "who thinks of herself as a sole". She maintained a salon to promote his ambitions, and he had little need to compromise himself.

He had a flaw, however, and the times made it worse. His bark was much worse than his bite – he was said to be "a reed posing as a lance" – and beneath his apparent bluff resolve lay a pliant eagerness to accommodate. He complained that the British had no need for an embassy in Paris, since the Quai d'Orsay did their every bidding; yet he made little effort to deny them influence, tamely appointing Bonnet as foreign minister after it was clear that London opposed Joseph Paul-Boncour, an anti-appeaser who had memorably described Mussolini as a "fairground Caesar".

International tensions played into his hands. The Communists and Socialists agreed to support his government in the Chamber; they kept out of the cabinet, but the no-nonsense conservatives Georges Mandel and Paul Reynaud joined it. In a rare display of togetherness, an overwhelming majority of deputies granted him decree powers. The vote in the Senate was unanimous.

He used his powers to devalue the franc by 10 per cent in May 1938. Sound money, hard work and the scrapping of the Popular Front's over-generous perks were needed, Daladier said, to boost production. He called the economy the "fourth arm of defence", and the threat of war dominated the summer. Hitler had incorporated the Austrians in the Reich, but other ethnic Germans remained outside it, notably the 3.5 million of them in Czechoslovakia's Sudetenland. The French were pinioned by the alliance signed with the Czechs in the 1920s. If Hitler reclaimed the Sudeten Germans by force, and he was already massing troops along the border, this unwanted legacy of the Petite Entente could force France into war.

Fear of cataclysm hung heavy over Europe. The young prepared to die. A character in Jean-Paul Sartre's novel *The Reprieve* bought a photograph of a *gueule cassée*, a maimed and broken face, its nose gone, a bandage slapped on its eye, because "I want to know what I shall look like next year". General Édouard Requin, commander of French forces opposite the German Siegfried Line, warned that attacking the Germans on behalf of the Czechs would mean "the death of the race".

The press drummed up fears. It was "notoriously venal", the American embassy complained; speeches by distinguished men were "overlooked unless the required sum is forthcoming", and foreign powers joined with banks, ministries, government contractors and tycoons in providing it with brown envelopes stuffed with secret funds to do their bidding. It fed the fevered political temperature with predictions of war and inflammatory headlines. "Should the French get themselves killed for Benes?" *Je suis partout* asked of the Czech president, adding nastily, "the Freemason."

The airman Charles Lindbergh, settling on the isolated island of Illiec off the Brittany coast to escape the American press, found France much changed since his transatlantic triumph. It had "an air of discouragement and neglect . . . such fear of military invasion, such depression and such instability." Édith Piaf and Charles Trenet offered some relief, topping the music-hall bill; Piaf boldly ridiculed Hitler in her song "Il n'est pas distingué". The biggest box office success was Walt Disney's *Blanche-neige* (*Snow White*), entertainment that was pure escapism. The other hit, though, was *Le Quai des brumes*, a film of *ratés* (losers), in which Jean Gabin, playing a colonial army deserter, snatches an evening with Michèle Morgan at a funfair, and a single night of love in a cheap hotel, before, a hunted man, he is shot down by a young hoodlum. "Never perhaps have we seen a darker, more bitter, more atrociously despairing film," a reviewer wrote, "one with more ugliness, more discouragement, more sadness."

In Spain, on the river Ebro, republicans poured the last of their reserves into a final counterattack. The men wore twigs and packets of camphor about their necks, the first to bite on during the nationalist artillery barrages, and the camphor to hide the reek of death. It was the last hurrah of the International Brigades who, torn by Franco's guns and aircraft, then paraded through the battered streets of Barcelona and went home.

Daladier had been a history teacher of distinction. He saw the looming Czech crisis clearly, and if he had a haunted look at times, a cigarette nervously on the go, it was because he knew the weaknesses of the Third Republic, and the ignorance and disdain of his principal allies. Austen Chamberlain, the foreign secretary, had resisted British "entanglement" in Briand's alliances with Czechoslovakia and Poland in the 1920s; his half-brother Neville, now prime minister, was equally reluctant to become involved, and wanted the Czechs to fob Hitler off with the Sudetenland. Far from improving, France's demographic sickness was getting worse. In 1913, 660,000 young men had celebrated their twentieth birthday by preparing for military service.

The annual crop of 20-year-olds in 1938 was reduced to 400,000. And, for the past three years, deaths had outnumbered births. Why, was no mystery. Almost a quarter of couples, 23 per cent, were childless, and a third had only one child. The number of Germans grew by 36 per cent between 1900 and 1938, of Italians by one third, of British by 23 per cent. The population of France crept up by 3 per cent, a figure attained only with large-scale immigration.

This dearth was something tangible, visible, clear. France was a country of widows and single women, a land of mourning, of the veils of *grand deuil* and the crêpes of *demi-deuil*, of the still ruined landscapes of Verdun, where Simone de Lattre de Tassigny saw nothing but craters of turbid water and shattered tree stumps as she drove her husband to take command of an infantry regiment. Health was poor, too, worryingly so in those of military age. The British outlived the French by three years, and the Dutch by seven. Bad living conditions bred typhoid and diphtheria. Almost half the Parisian poor lived in a single room, without running water or mains sewers. Slop buckets and chamber pots were the norm. Much of rural France had no electricity. In the towns, a mass of inefficient private companies supplied it at such a price that living rooms were often dimly lit by 40 watt bulbs. The Germans and British used four or five times as much electricity per head, and the Americans ten times more.

Syphilis and other venereal diseases were rife. A report blamed this "public calamity" for 80,000 adult deaths and 60,000 stillbirths and miscarriages a year. If its claim of eight million syphilitics was an exaggeration, the ravages of alcoholism were all too real. Wine consumption, almost 250 litres per adult per year, was the highest ever recorded. The government bought votes by easing the regulations for home distilling – in fruit-growing regions, up to half the electorate busily concocted their own *eaux de vie*. Tuberculosis was often transmitted in a bar – "la tuberculose se prend sur le zinc" – and accounted for a third of all deaths in middle-aged men. Eager scouts sold anti-TB stamps, but the Office of Social Hygiene, which had campaigned against TB, venereal disease and diphtheria, was closed in 1935, a victim of budget cuts. Family allowances, soft loans, cash subsidies and lower inheritance taxes were dangled in front of married couples. It was not enough. A crackdown was made on illegal abortions, estimated to be running at over half a million a year. Before 1914, the accused were acquitted in almost three-quarters of abortion cases. Four in five were now found guilty, and the penalties were harsher. The feminist Madeleine Pelletier, herself a doctor who held that contraception and abortion were rights, was charged as an abortionist in 1939 and was sent to a mental clinic, where she died.

The lack of young men fed through into a defensive military strategy, in which the nation's scarce lifeblood was to be sheltered deep beneath a carapace of stone, earth and concrete. The Maginot Line seemed as impregnable as its namesake – "I'm like my leg," old André Maginot said of the wound that had crippled him at Verdun, "I won't bend" – with the wire, minefields, dragon's teeth and ditches that screened its mighty forts, with their turrets, bunkers, barracks, generators, cinemas and hospitals, each able to fire four tons of shells a minute. But the Line stopped abruptly short of the Belgian frontier. It soaked up money, too, so that most *poilus* still had 1886 Lebel rifles; and worse, it sapped adventurous thought, so that tanks were seen, not as a new cavalry, but as walking-pace bolt-ons to the infantry. Heinz Guderian's *Achtung, Panzer!*, the classic textbook of mobile tank warfare, was translated into French and distributed to garrisons across the country. The French general staff – and, it might be added, the British – ignored it.

The B1 heavy tank was made partly by hand in three separate factories, a process that took up to two years per machine. The problems of under-investment and a plethora of small companies in the aircraft industry were made worse when it was moved from the supposedly vulnerable Paris to Bordeaux, Toulouse and Marseille. French newsreel footage showed soldiers drinking wine, cavalry charging as it had a hundred years ago, and "not one tank, not one motorised unit". General Gamelin, the chief of staff, issued standing orders that he was not to be disturbed between 8 p.m. and 8 a.m. The nickname his subordinates gave him was not reassuring: "Gagamelin".

As proof that the two great democracies and their Entente Cordiale were still alive and kicking, George VI and Queen Elizabeth came on a state visit to Paris in July. The king wore the uniform of a Royal Navy admiral and, shy and nervous though he was, cut a more resplendent and comforting figure than the parvenu dictators with their contrived uniforms and fasces and swastikas.

It was a solemn visit – the guests broke precedent by not going to the races – and the emphasis was on sacrifice and the dead. The king laid a wreath on the Tomb of the Unknown Soldier, visited the Military Hospital in Paris, and unveiled a memorial to the Australians killed in the war. The visit was also fraught with an undertone of appeasement, and a wispy hope that the alliance might stave off a future slaughter merely by existing. If not, "Everything depends on the English," Daladier admitted. Without them, France could not contain Germany. The defensive "long war" strategy envisaged the slow strangulation of Germany through naval blockade, the steady build-up of allied stockpiles and weapons, the transfer of huge numbers of colonial troops to metropolitan France; it drew heavily on imperial Britain's ships, factories, mines, oilfields and plantations, on British capital, and on London's links to Wall Street.

Off-stage, relations between the allies were as prickly as ever. Madame Lebrun, the president's wife, was so overawed that she broke protocol and curtsied to her royal guests. It was, outraged Republicans hissed, a "génuflexion catastrophique". In private, Daladier told US ambassador Bullitt that the king was a "moron", and that Queen Elizabeth was so obsessed with ambition that she would gladly "sacrifice every other country on earth" as long as she remained on the throne. He added that

Chamberlain was a "desiccated stick". For their part, the British privately described Daladier as looking like "an Iberian merchant", and referred to the return state visit of President Lebrun to London with distaste as "Frog week". This was nothing new, of course – where Daladier said he had yet to meet an Englishman whose "intellectual equipment and character" he could respect, Balfour, then British prime minister, had dismissed the French a few years earlier as "intolerably foolish" – but these were dangerous times to indulge in sour asides and mutual mistrust. Daladier, it was observed, was never closer to conceding than "when he was thumping the table", and his outburst was triggered by impotent fury at British pressure for France to betray its Czech allies. He claimed that the French commitment to Czechoslovakia was "sacred and immutable". He allowed Bonnet to act otherwise. Crucially, Bonnet concealed an offer to hold military staff talks made by Maksim Litvinov, the Soviet commissar for foreign affairs.

In Paris, Georges Mandel, the colonial minister, tough-minded like his mentor Clemenceau, argued that, if Cardinal Richelieu could ally with the Turkish sultan in the seventeenth century, then France could do so with Stalin, the Red tsar. But Mandel, as the appeasers hastened to point out, was a Jew, like Litvinov. How the Soviets would have supported the French over the Czech crisis is far from clear. The Poles, also tied to France by treaty, would not have given the Red Army free passage through their territory; indeed, it was feared that they might be driven into the hands of the Germans.

Daladier continued to claim that France was steadfast, but the game up was up. The Sudeten German leader, the gym teacher Konrad Henlein, provoked incidents which the German press blew up into violent outrages. Goering described the Czechs as a "vile race of dwarfs without any culture". Neville Chamberlain, taking the fate of the world on his black-coated shoulders, flew to see Hitler, once, twice, three times. "I am very much afraid that the senile ambition of Chamberlain to be the peacemaker of Europe will drive him to success at any price," said Jan Masaryk, the Czech ambassador, adding bitterly "and that will be only at our expense." He was right.

In Paris, public and politicians panicked. Meetings on international affairs were banned – for fear of offending the Nazis – but strident voices on the right led the race to abandon the unloved Czechs, whose nation was described as a *macedoine*, a vegetable concoction not worth fighting for. The left, the Communists apart, generally agreed. "It is better to live as a German," the secretary-general of the teachers' union declared, "than to die as a Frenchman." The roads to the south and west clogged with traffic as more than half a million decanted themselves into the countryside. Shops were deserted, except those selling luggage. The Louvre was shut, and its treasures were crated up. Street lamps were painted blue. Families fought each other for seats on trains at the railway stations. Supplies of gas masks ran out. Little piles of sand appeared in lieu of fire extinguishers. Corrupt doctors did a thriving trade in military exemption certificates. In Strasbourg and Dijon, Jews were attacked.

Sartre predicted a war so violent that it would turn the earth liquid and leave it a storm-lashed sea; war would be "the hecatomb of righteous men, the massacre of the innocents". The air minister, Guy La Chambre, told Ambassador Bullitt that he had no aircraft to defend Paris. He had sent his wife and child to Brittany, and said everyone else should so the same. The diplomat said that it was "difficult to exaggerate the degree to which the leaders of French political life did not – repeat not – rise to the demands of a tragic occasion."

Mussolini acted as peacemaker at a four-power conference held in Munich at the end of September. The Czechs were absent as Daladier and Chamberlain agreed to the cession to the Reich of important rail junctions and industrial zones, as well as the Sudetenland. Daladier knew it was a desperate humiliation. He was astonished that he was cheered by the crowds who mobbed his aircraft on his return to Le Bourget. He had half-feared they would tear him limb from limb. "Ah, les cons!" he sighed – did they not realise what he had done? They knew very well, and they loved him for it.

Only the Communists and a handful of others opposed Daladier in parliament. Politicians evolved the most ingenious reasons for supporting him. Paul Faure, the Socialist Party general secretary, claimed that fascism would now "die of its own success to be replaced by socialism". More remarkably still, he said that, by abolishing borders, Hitler was turning out to be "a true internationalist". Nonetheless, an opinion poll showed that 37 per cent were in fact hostile, but they tended to keep their doubts to themselves. Many recognised Munich as a "Te Deum of cowards", in Georges Bernanos's vivid phrase. De Gaulle warned that it would bring no more than a "brief respite", and compared it to Madame du Barry's pathetic plea to her executioner for a few seconds more of life, as she lay beneath the guillotine in 1793. The American journalist William Shirer visited Paris in October. Even the once-sound waiters and taxi drivers, he found, "are gushing about how wonderful it is that war has been avoided, that it would have been a crime, that they fought in one war and that was enough". All this would be fine, Shirer thought brutally, only "if the Germans, who also fought in one war, felt the same way. But they don't."

That, of course, is the rub. Hindsight has attributed the Third Republic with all manner of vices – defeatism, cowardice, blind folly, decadence – but the fundamental French flaw, from which all else flowed, was not to be German. The French, having won one war at horrendous cost, were sensibly determined to avoid another at almost any cost. The Germans, having lost it, had given themselves up to a man who was hell-bent on having another. Indeed, Hitler, his appetite sharpened by the Sudetenland, was already slavering at the prospect of future feasts. He ordered a massive expansion in arms making and was prepared to devote up to 80 per cent of the budget to it. Prospects for the French were forbidding. Roosevelt had snubbed them, and the Tommies, the sixty sturdy divisions who had fought in France in 1918, were ghosts. The British had reverted to their old habits: a powerful navy – and, providentially if belatedly, a rapidly strengthening air force – but a home army that was little more than a parade-ground force. Two divisions, with a further two to follow, were earmarked for France. No staff talks had been held with the French. The British still had no conscription. Robert Vansittart, the great anti-appeaser at the British foreign office, had warned time and again of the folly of obliging the French to take upon themselves almost the whole weight and fury of a German ground war. No notice was taken. In military terms, France was all but alone with the psychopath. Who was to say she should not try to negotiate with him?

There was a last dose of humiliation to come. Bonnet continued to negotiate a non-aggression pact with Germany, which was completed on November 22. Joachim von Ribbentrop, the Nazi foreign minister, was invited to Paris a fortnight later. He gave a sumptuous reception at the German embassy for cabinet members and other senior figures, Jews included. Bonnet was fearful of upsetting his visitor. The Jewish ministers Georges Mandel and Jean Zay were not invited to the return reception at the Quai d'Orsay.

This was the low point. From now, the Third Republic begun to enjoy a final Indian summer. A poll showed that a solid 70 per cent were in favour of resistance to any further German demands. Daladier had appointed Paul Reynaud as finance minister on November 1, and gave him plenary powers to drive through a series of harsh decree laws. Reynaud was sixty-two, and short, but he dyed his hair, had lifts in his shoes and stood almost on tiptoe to look taller, his thumbs hooked into his waistcoat. He kept a mistress, Hélène de Portes, daughter of a shipping magnate and a society adventuress, like the premier's mistress, Jeanne de Crussol. Both women had married aristocrats as part of their ferocious social climbing and were part of a milieu of power that had changed little since Proust had described a "middle-class circle cross-bred with minor nobility", in which the very rich were connected by marriage to "an aristocracy the higher aristocracy does not know".

Reynaud was experienced, a barrister and a good orator, and the veteran of many cabinets, at colonies, finance and justice. He had opposed Munich, and wanted a stronger line taken with Hitler. "We are going blindfold towards an abyss," he said in a radio broadcast after his appointment. His prescription was brutal. He increased arms spending from 29 billion francs to 93 billion, slashed public works and scrapped price controls and the 40-hour week. He fired thousands of the newly nationalised railway workers, and cut overtime rates.

The "Saigneur" of Billancourt, the bloody nickname given to Louis Renault by his workers, took special delight in reversing the concessions given to the unions. The car men began another sit-in. Police were sent in to evict them. They were met with a furious rainstorm of engine parts, pistons, crankshafts and gearsticks hurled from behind makeshift barricades of oil drums. The police responded with tear gas and trucks converted into battering rams. Defeated at length, the men made the fascist salute to police as they marched out of the factory. Reynaud thought the union rank and file had lost the stomach for a fight. He was right.

The economic recovery gathered pace in 1939. There were few strikes. Decrees were pushed through covering increased armaments, additional manpower for the armed forces and a reduction in the civil administration. Family allowances were raised to try to boost the birth rate. Self-confidence grew. A record 1,059 tanks were produced during the year. The French Somua S35 was the best medium tank in western Europe, fast, well-armoured, with greater firepower than its German equivalent, the Panzer III. The French heavy B1 tank, too, was better than the German Panzer IV.

Belatedly, the British stirred. For the first time, they worried that they were failing to give the French adequate support. If this was not corrected, a memorandum by the chiefs of staff warned in January 1939, the French might tire of the "unequal task" of containing further German expansion. Two sets of high-level Anglo-French staff talks were held in February.

It was becoming obvious that the alliance was soon to be tested. Hitler marched into Prague on March 15, gorging himself on the rump of Czechoslovakia. The French were already committed to the Poles, who were likely to be Hitler's next meal. The British joined them, guaranteeing Polish security on March 30. On April 13, the French and British extended the guarantees of assistance offered to Poland to Romania and Greece as well. The same month, the British introduced conscription.

Hitler declared his next objective to be Danzig. The grimy Baltic port was no treasure in itself, unlike Prague, but it was the stopping point. Hitler thought, understandably enough, that the new British resolve was a bluff. As Bonnet found, it was not; imbued with "pactomanie", looking for ways to evade the old 1921 alliance with Poland, he found himself boxed in by London. All knew that the clock was running.

"Underlying everything," Simone de Beauvoir wrote of the last days of peace, "a feeling of unfathomable horror." Fire destroyed the liner *Paris* in harbour at Le Havre. An ensign convicted of passing information on the Mediterranean fleet to the German Abwehr was shot by firing squad for treason in Toulon. The mass murderer Eugen Weidmann, a German who had killed tourists at the 1937 Exposition, was guillotined at Versailles on June 16. An immense crowd climbed trees and roofs, and chanted and catcalled, amid the smell of chip fat and the cries of *merguez* sausage sellers. Weidmann was the last to die amid a throng. The next day, President Lebrun banned public executions, citing the "hysteria" of the spectators.

Marcel Carné completed *Le Jour se lève*, his bleakest film: "Tout le monde vivait dans la désespérance." Jean Gabin played a sandblaster who falls in love with a poor orphan girl. She has a seducer, a smart-talking, nattily dressed showman. Enraged,

Gabin kills him, and then, as the police prepare to storm his room high above the crowds in a cordoned-off street, he waits for dawn and the long jump to the cobbles.

Opinion hardened. Marcel Déat tried to stir the appeasement appetite on July 10, with an editorial in *l'Œuvre* whose headline asked: "Why die for Danzig?" An opinion poll found that 76 per cent were willing to fight for it. The Third Republic was not as defeatist as it was painted. No German or Italian riders took part in the 1939 Tour de France.

The stock market boomed, and there were bumper harvests. The Polish ambassador led dancers across the lawns at the embassy ball in the early hours of a warm July night. "It is scarcely enough to say that they are dancing on a volcano," Reynaud remarked as he watched a mazurka. "For what is the eruption of Vesuvius compared to the cataclysm which is forming under our feet?" Renoir's *La Règle du jeu* opened, a cruel and finely observed study of a collapsing society. "We live at a time when everyone lies," a character said; at cinemas in the *beaux quartiers*, angry at the portrayal of the venality and falseness of the rich, well-heeled audiences howled and booed at the screen. Albert Camus, writer-philosopher, a poor white from Algeria, echoed Renoir's message in his diary. "Never had the individual been more alone in the face of the lie-making machine," he wrote.

The 1937 budget had allocated 30 million francs for fuel for military transport, and 128 million for fodder; the position had improved since then, but a newly mobilised infantryman found his divisional transport was all horse-drawn General Louis Chauvineau, the director of the military engineering school, had just published a book with a glowing preface by Marshal Pétain. He argued that concrete would always withstand a motorised assault, and that manoeuvre was swifter in defence than attack.

A half-hearted attempt at a Soviet alliance came to naught. An Anglo-French mission had been sent to Moscow at the end of July. The British delegation was led by Admiral Sir Reginald Plunkett-Ernle-Erle-Drax. He was ordered to proceed with caution. An aircraft was ruled out as too speedy. Instead, he and the French general Doumenc sailed aboard a slow steamer from the British-India run, *The City of Exeter*, playing deck tennis and eating curries served to them by turbaned waiters. They took the Red Arrow express from Leningrad to Moscow, where the Soviet marshal Voroshilov treated them with near contempt.

The holidays were brought to a grisly end by news of the German-Soviet Nonagression Pact on August 22. Hitler invaded Poland. A general mobilisation was ordered. On September 3, France declared war on Germany at 5 p.m., several hours later than Britain, Bonnet delaying to the last. A few Communists at railway stations shouted "Don't go!" at troop trains, but there was little emotion. The mood, so the prefect of the Rhône reported, was "something between resolution and resignation". The men were as indifferent to the Poles as they had been to the Czechs, another observed. "All obeyed," he added, "but did no more than obey." An attitude of wait and see was already implanted. The tune of the moment was "J'attendrai", soft, mournful, sung or hummed in the streets and the barracks for the first weeks of the war with an obsessive melancholy. *Je t'attendrai, le jour et la nuit, j'attendrai toujours, j'attendrai ton retour* . . .

The main characteristic of the new war was its absence. "Il faut en finir" was the watchword, "let's finish it", but it seemed not to begin. The guns at the front fired a few symbolic barrages. The troops were tucked out of sight in villages along the border and in the subterranean fortresses of the Maginot Line. An occasional lone Luftwaffe reconnaissance aircraft flew across Paris in place of the expected bomber fleets. The only casualties were caused by an anti-aircraft shell with a faulty fuse that landed on the rue de Mirbel. In a speech to deputies on December 22, Daladier remarked on how few lives had been lost – just 2,000, when 450,000 had already been killed by this stage in the first war. The army toyed with the idea of replacing infantry puttees with leather leggings. The general staff, not happy with its cuisine, hired a leading chef to prepare its meals.

Paris was in fine fettle. Military fashions were in vogue. Lanvin designed a "Spahi" suit, and Schiaparelli's imagination ran riot, with "air raid" outfits, a "camouflage" coat, dresses with built-in muffs for queuing, and fabric prints based on ration cards. A visiting diner was astonished to find that, though the restaurant's maître d' apologised for the absence of butcher's meat and pastries, the menu ran to seven kinds of oyster, rabbit, caviar, anchovies, six or seven kinds of fish, fruit salad, and pineapple with kirsch.

The new revue at the Casino de Paris, *Paris-London*, was dedicated to the Entente Cordiale, but relations with the British were their normal frosty selves, and the conviction, spread by German radio, was that the British were ready to "fight to the last Frenchman". Claude Jamet noted that "Anglophobia appears practically endemic in the French army". All soldiers moan, of course, but the *poilus* had less reason than most. Lessons had been learned from the first war. Leave was prompt and generous. The wine ration was raised from half a litre to three-quarters, a bottle a day. Charities and the government provided extra mulled wine over the winter, *le vin chaud du soldat.* Boredom was the main enemy. The men played cards, *belote*, and in the spring Daladier sent them 40,000 footballs.

Jean-Paul Sartre had changed his mind on war. He no longer foresaw annihilation, he told Simone de Beauvoir when she visited; it would be "a modern war, without massacres as modern painting is without subject, music without melody, physics with no matter".

Politics continued its danse macabre. The Communists were split asunder by the Nazi-Soviet Pact. A third of the deputies quit the party; a score of them went off to join their combat units, Maurice Thorez included, and those left in the Chamber voted for war credits in the first week of the war. Orders came from Moscow later in the month ordering them to denounce what the Comintern described as an "imperialist" war, fought on behalf of financiers. Thorez deserted from the army, re-emerging in Moscow. Daladier banned the party and arrested forty of its deputies in October. "We'll disappear body and soul from this place like the Gauls," Céline prophesied from the far right. "They left us hardly twenty words of their language. We'll be lucky if anything more than 'merde' survives us." Like the Communists, though, those on the right fought too.

Having overrun half Poland, as allowed for under a secret protocol agreed by Ribbentrop and Molotov, the Soviets invaded Finland at the end of November. Finnish courage caught the French imagination. Daladier and Gamelin planned a campaign to relieve them, and to deny the Germans Swedish iron ore. It was too late. The Finns capitulated in March 1940. The disaster brought down Daladier on March 21, and Reynaud became prime minister. He suffered the usual Third Republic afflictions. His political weakness was reflected in the huge size of his cabinet, with 21 ministers and 14 secretaries of state; he loathed Daladier, but had to keep him as defence minister as the price of Radical support.

Allied indolence was encouraged by the strategy of the long war. It was taken as gospel that the resources of France and the British empire were greater than those of Germany. Time, it seemed, was on the Allies' side. A new armaments ministry was entrusted to Raoul Dautry, one of the brilliant technician-administrators France has excelled in producing. Production soared. More than a thousand tanks were produced in 1939, and 854 in the first six months of 1940. Albert Caquot, equally gifted, got to grips with the shortfall in aircraft. The workforce increased from 48,000 to 250,000. Emphasis was switched from multi-role aircraft, poor as fighters and bombers and little better for reconnaissance, to fighters and bombers.

The front was quiet. Even the simple step of advancing into the intended defensive positions in Belgium was ruled out by the Belgian declaration of neutrality. Brussels feared that Flemish separatists would not stand for a war fought supposedly in French interests against the Germans.

Pockets of doubt persisted. Jean Giraudoux, a delicate spirit who had been miscast as Goebbels's opposite number directing the French Information Service, said gloomily: "One prepares for war as one prepares for an exam. We shall not pass this one." In the army itself, Second Lieutenant Jacques Delmas, fresh from officer school at St Cyr, noticed that officers would cross the street to avoid groups of soldiers whom they knew would not salute them. Sartre noted that the men were sullen and ill-tempered, and that they looted the deserted villages near the front.

Deeply alarming thoughts plagued General Sir Edmund Ironside, the British chief of staff, after he visited France at the beginning of 1940. "I say to myself that we must have confidence in the French army," he wrote. "It is the only thing in which we can have confidence. Our own army is just a little one and we are dependent on the French. We haven't even the same fine army we had in 1914. All depends on the French army and we can do nothing about it."

Was too much being asked of the *poilus*? The answer came soon. On the evening of May 9, troops facing the German lines heard a "vast murmuring". Before dawn, at 4.35 a.m. on May 10, German paratroops began landing in Holland, and the first ground units crossed the borders of Luxembourg and Belgium. At 6.30 a.m., despite his orders, General Gamelin was woken. The *drôle de guerre* was over.

The Fall

The battle was lost in five days. "The front is broken near Sedan," Reynaud told Winston Churchill by telephone on May 15. "They are pouring through in great numbers with tanks and armoured cars." Churchill, now prime minister, made the dangerous flight from London the next day to meet Reynaud, Gamelin and Daladier at the Quai d'Orsay. A map was propped up on a classroom easel, with a black line showing the Allied front. In this was drawn a "small but sinister bulge" at Sedan, whose significance was shown by the utter dejection on every face. Churchill asked Gamelin: "Where is the strategic reserve?" He repeated it in French: "Où est la masse de manoeuvre?" Gamelin turned, shook his head and said: "Aucune." He had not a single corps at his disposal between Laon and the capital. Churchill looked out of the window. Clouds of smoke were rising from large bonfires in the ministry courtyard. He watched elderly officials pushing wheelbarrows full of archives to feed to the flames. Parisians could see the smoke, too, and they realised what it meant. A tragedy of overwhelming scale was taking place.

The two sides started roughly equal in men and materiel. Hitler had 135 divisions, the French had 92 and the British had 10 in the field. The Allied deficit was not crucial in itself, the more so since the Germans had drawn 22 Belgian and 12 Dutch divisions against themselves by violating their neutrality. All Hitler's divisions were German, though, which gave them coherence of command. The French had a slight edge in tank numbers. The French Somua S35 remained the best medium tank of 1940. The French heavy tanks, too, the B1 and B1bis, were better than the Panzer IV. Their armour was twice as thick, and they had turret and hull-mounted guns. They had their shortcomings: the whole tank had to be aimed to fire the hull-mounted gun; the turret gun was served by one man, who had to load, aim and fire. It was slower than the panzer, at 25 kph to 40 kph. It soaked up fuel, and its endurance at speed was less than three hours.

Well handled and well used, though, French tanks were more than a match for the Germans; and it was here that the seeds of defeat were sown. The panzers operated together, swarming across country like fleets of landships or heavy cavalry. They used their momentum and firepower to drive clean through defence systems, destroying the enemy's communications in the rear, and then wheeling to cut off his armies. Squads of assault engineers bridged rivers under fire. Above them, squadrons of Stuka divebombers acted as mobile artillery, blasting enemy strongpoints and breaking enemy morale with the shrill raptor-like whistle that accompanied their swoops. "Klotzen", said Heinz Guderian, the brilliant panzer general, "nicht kleckern." Make waves, not ripples.

A French general, Jean-Baptiste Estienne, had created the world's first armoured division, the DLM, the "light mechanised division", two years before the Germans. Three DLMs were available in 1940, with four DCRs, reserve armoured divisions

Jean Cocteau, seen here in front of a characteristic sketch, was a human kaleidoscope – actor, film and opera director, poet, novelist and writer of scenarios, and percussionist. He was also a promoter of talents such as Picasso, Stravinsky, Giorgio de Chirico, Les Six and Coco Chanel.

The princesse de Polignac, (below, at the races), had perhaps the most glittering salon in Paris. Born Winnaretta Singer, into the fabulously wealthy sewing machine family, she was a lover of men and women. Manuel de Falla, Stravinsky and Les Six all performed in her music room, and it was there that Satie's Socrates *was first heard.*

Parisiennes (right) had a style and dash that could even carry off the beret, for which the French developed an extraordinary passion that kept thousands of beret-makers in business.

WORKERS VICTORY

Workers celebrated the victory of the socialist and communist Popular Front in the spring of 1936 by going on strike (below). It was a reminder that they believed they were the masters now. Two million came out, demanding a 40-hour week with wages for 48, and holidays with pay. They pioneered the grève sur le tas, *the sit-in (right), settling down on the factory floor, playing cards and* boules, *and singing and dancing. Sightseers came to watch them. A new proletarian aperitif was launched, Le Popu.*

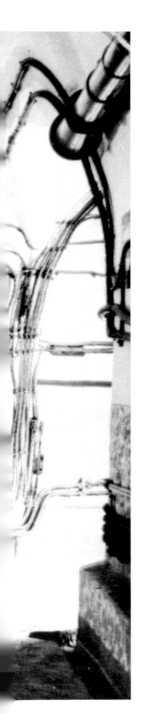

The Maginot Line took all the lessons of the Great War to heart bar one: that the then experimental but mobile tank had proved able to overwhelm static defence lines. The Line enshrined the doctrine of defence with deep underground fortresses (left), whose railway lines, barracks, sports halls, clinics and cinemas were tucked away beneath the earth. Édouard Daladier, succumbing in part to British pressure, helped sign away Czechoslovakia's Sudetenland to Hitler at Munich in September 1938. Shortly after he landed in Paris (below) he was mobbed. He half-feared the crowds would tear him limb from limb. "Ah, les cons!" he sighed as they cheered him – did they not realise what he had done?

A grande peur, *a flight of refugees so immense it seemed a "geological cataclysm",*
seized the country after the Germans broke the front in May 1940 (below). Looking
down from his aircraft, northern France reminded the pilot-writer Antoine de Saint-
Exupéry of an anthill scattered by a gigantic boot. Below him, the "ants were on the
march. Without panic. Without hope. Without despair. On the march as if duty bound."
Between six and ten million fled their homes, leaving them like Rouen (right) to
the flames and the invaders.

The Germans entered Paris on June 14, 1940. Life in the capital rapidly
returned to a surface normality. The invaders soon felt themselves
at home, reading the newspapers in the cafés on the grands boulevards
(right). Marshal Pétain, hero of Verdun, feeling collaboration to be
the least bad path, met Hitler (below) at the railway station in the little
Loire town of Montoire on October 24, 1940. But resistance still flickered,
in London, where a little-known general, Charles de Gaulle (bottom),
was rallying the Free French.

The battleship Bretagne *is hit by the Royal Navy at Mers-el-Kebir in Algeria on July 3, 1940. The British were still fighting, if alone. If Hitler was given any chance of dominating the Channel invasion routes – by, for example, German seizure of French warships – they were done for. Mers-el-Kebir was proof of their earnest.*

A British fleet sailed from Gibraltar and gave the French commander an ultimatum: join the British, take refuge in neutral American waters, scuttle his ships, or sail to a distant colonial port. He refused. The British opened fire. It was a massacre. Only four destroyers and the battlecruiser Strasbourg, *escaped from harbour. The rest were destroyed, with the deaths of 1,147 French sailors. The shock and disgust was useful to Vichy. It helped to salve the humiliations of the armistice, and to grant the new regime respectability. By re-establishing the British as the real and ancient foe, it made it more wholesome to collaborate with the Germans.*

FRENCH WOMEN, FRENCH JEWS

June 1942. Jews in the occupied zone were ordered to wear yellow stars (far right) made from special gold-coloured cloth. They were charged two clothing tickets apiece for thus branding themselves. French police, carefully checking identity papers (right), were used to round up Jews when deportations began. By June 1944, as this most stylish cyclist made her way up the Champs-Élysées (below), hope was in the air: one of the signs for German troops points to the newly opened Anglo-American front in Normandy.

VICHY DEALS

Right: A figure to become familiar stands leaning against the wall in the Vichy department dealing with the 1.8 million prisoners who remained as hostages in Germany. François Mitterrand, himself an escapee from a German camp, helped with repatriations. Laval tried to cut a deal, the relève, *or relief shift, where one French prisoner would be released in return for three volunteer workers going to Germany. These ex-prisoners happily praised Laval and Pétain (below) for a propaganda picture as their train reached France. But too few volunteers came forward, and most prisoners remained in the Reich.*

THE FACES OF VICHY

Marshal Pétain (far right, with hat) ran his regime from this commandeered hotel in the genteel spa town of Vichy. Some young Frenchmen (right) volunteered to fight with the Germans on the Russian front. Many more joined the Resistance. Vichy militia guard suspected resistants (below) as maquis *and* milice *became entwined in a civil war within the war.*

243

*A great exodus – "la grande fuite des Fritz" –
began from Paris on August 19, 1944. But
the German commander still had 17,000 men,
100 heavy tanks, and enough explosives to
destroy much of the city. "Fifis", the Interior
French Forces, seized and held the Hôtel de
Ville the next day. They captured this German
officer (left) in fighting round the Hôtel
Majestic, the German high command
headquarters, a few hours before General
Leclerc's tanks entered the city on August 24.
Help was too late for this* fifi *(below),
one of the 901 killed liberating their city.*

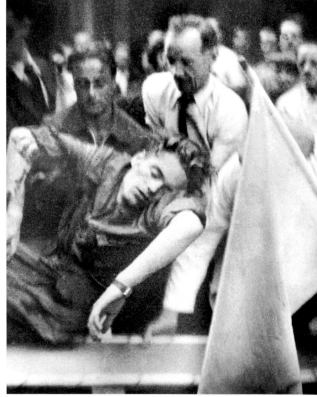

The trial of Pierre Laval, pre-war prime minister and head of the Vichy government, so Pastor Boegner wrote, was "a scandal beyond description". The outcome would no doubt have been the same even had the highest standards been applied. Yet he was denied access to witnesses. He had had five sessions of questioning instead of the 25 the case called for. His lawyers refused to attend the opening of his trial in protest at the lack of time and facilities to prepare the case. When Laval spoke, still wearing his trademark white tie (left), the jurors goaded him like "Andalusian urchins who leap into the bullring". It was a reminder of the strange absence of strict legality at the highest levels in France. His execution was set for October 15, 1945. He swallowed cyanide and went into convulsions early on that morning. It took two hours to stomach-pump him into some consciousness, before he was carried, strapped shoeless to a chair, and shot, whilst other prisoners shouted: "Salauds! Assassins!"

The Vél' d'hiv', the Paris bicycle racing stadium notoriously used as a corral for the detention of French Jews before they were entrained for the extermination camps, was employed in 1944 as a centre in which those accused of collaboration with the Germans could be sorted and screened (below). A woman accused of collaboration has just been slapped at Brignoles in the Var in August 1944 (left). The épuration sauvage, the "wild purge" of "popular" or mob justice, was at its crudest in humiliating women said to have slept with Germans. They often had their heads shaved in public, and swastikas drawn on their cheeks, before being herded through the streets half-naked.

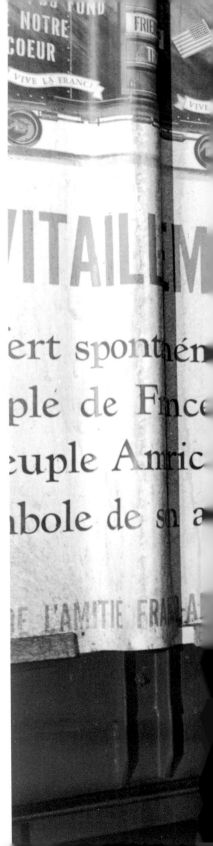

VIVE L'AMERIQUE

Dockers carry crates of aid (below) sent from the US. The severe winter of 1946 showed that Europe would not lift itself out of its hunger and despair without the massive American help to be made available through the Marshall Plan. Food as well as financial aid was sent. Here, a young girl (right) chalks her thanks on a railway wagon alongside a poster confirming the gift from the American people to the French as a "symbol of their affection". The sentiment was not always reciprocated. Communists derided it as American "imperialism". Le Monde railed against Coca-Cola. The French had already accepted chewing gum, Cecil B. de Mille and bebop. "After Coca-Cola," it thundered, "enough!"

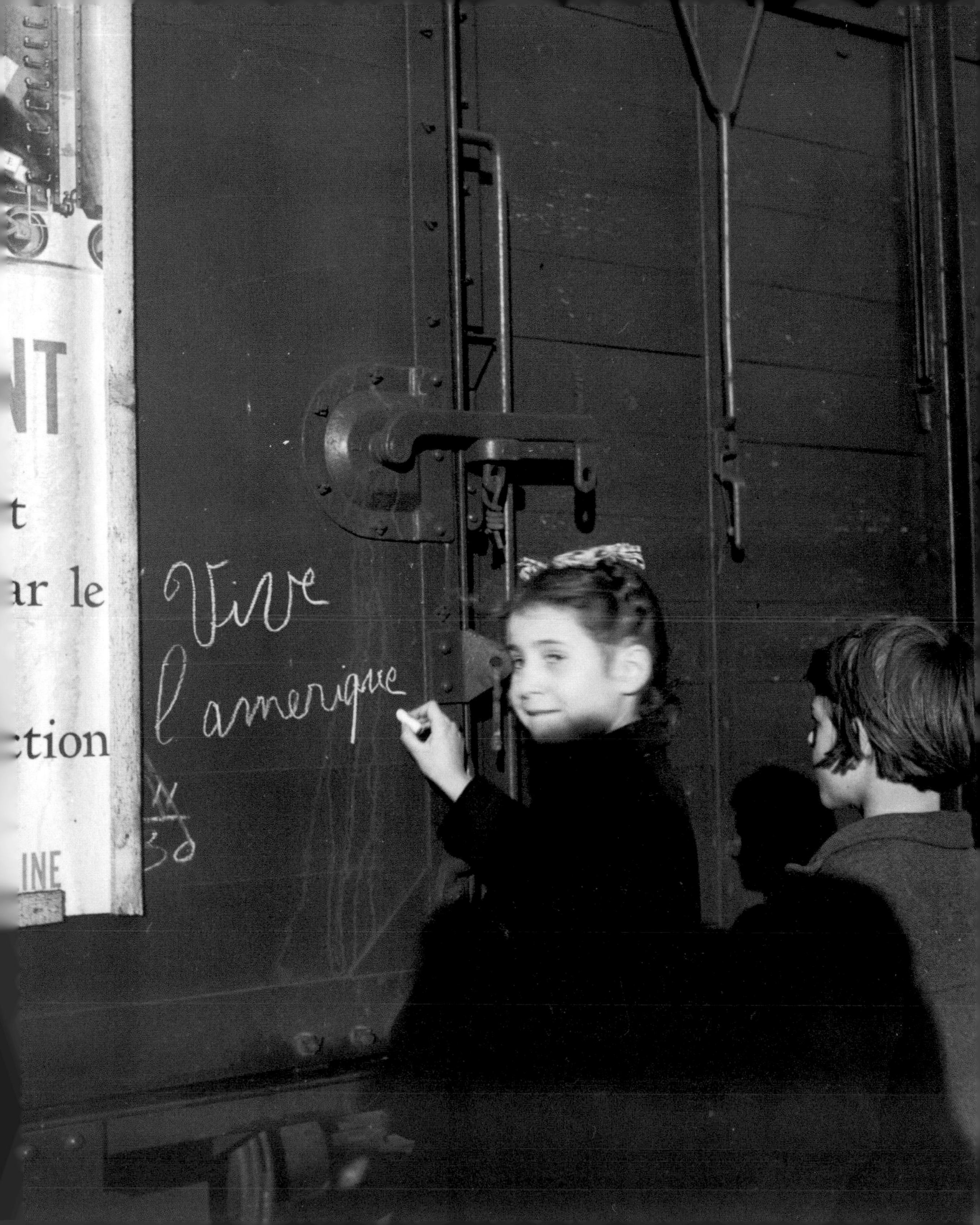
Vive
l amerique

NEW LOOK, OLD STYLE

The "New Look" presented by Christian Dior in 1947 (below) was a post-war sensation. An American buyer in Paris found "more ideas in a thimble here than in all America". Dior was as brilliant a salesman as a designer. The first couturier to develop boutiques for ready-to-wear (prêt-à-porter) clothes, he created the "designer label" industry by branding spin-off scarves, sunglasses, jewellery and perfumes. Society (right) had not lost its pre-war style.

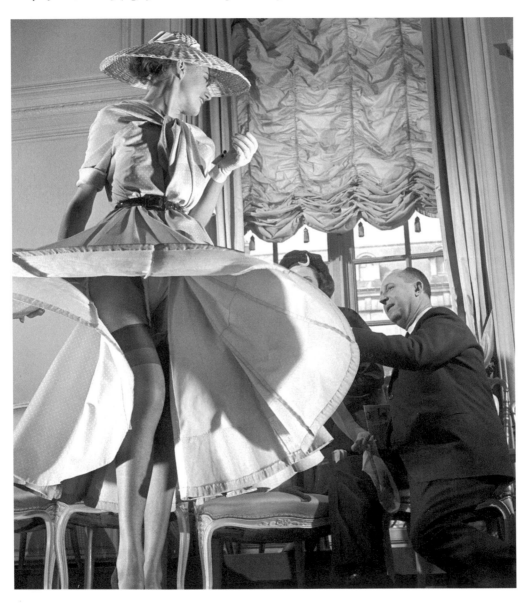

DECISION BY BALLOT

*Women got the vote – belatedly – in October 1944. Only the legs of
these children's mother are visible (below) as she gets her first chance to use
it, in the municipal elections of April 1945. A reluctant majority followed
the advice to vote "Oui" (right) in the constitutional referendum in October
1946, so that the Fourth Republic replaced the unfairly unlamented Third.*

France was the most hard-thinking country of the post-war world in the philosophical sense. The polymath Jean-Paul Sartre (right), philosopher, dramatist and novelist, and the Catholic novelist François Mauriac discuss the escalating Algerian crisis at the Palais-Royal in 1957. The battle of Algiers, a bloody affair of terror and counter-terror, was under way. Albert Camus, Algerian-born and bred, author of the masterpieces The Outsider (L'Étranger) *and* The Plague (La Peste) *struggled to elucidate values from the absurdity of being. All three were Nobel laureates: Sartre declined to accept his prize.*

Sartre, and *"la grande Sartreuse"*, *as his companion and soulmate Simone de Beauvoir (right) was known, also signed the manifesto. De Beauvoir's* The Second Sex (La Deuxième Sexe), *a study of the predicament of women, was a ground-breaking feminist work of profound importance. The jury of the Prix Tabou, an existentialist literary prize, meet in Saint-Germain-des-Prés in 1946 (below).*

*"A charming little monster",
Mauriac said of Françoise Sagan
(above), 19-year-old writer of the
precocious and million-selling novel*
Bonjour Tristesse. *She combined
life as a wild child – turning her
Aston-Martin upside down, and
taking drugs – with political
conscience. She signed the
"Manifesto of the 121" inciting
conscripts in Algeria to desert.*

SPORTING TRAGEDIES

*The Fourth Republic cut a sporting dash, but it came at
a price. The boxer Marcel Cerdan (below) won the world
middleweight title and eight million francs in 1949, before
losing to the American La Motta. He was killed when
the aircraft flying him from Paris to New York for
the rematch crashed. This was no crude bruiser: Édith Piaf
was waiting for him in New York. In the Le Mans 24-hour
race of 1955 (right), 82 were killed when Pierre Levegh's
Mercedes was catapulted into the crowd.*

*The black-haired, black-dressed
singer Juliette Gréco (below), once
a striking street vendor of the
communist daily* l'Humanité, *showed Marlon Brando the sights
of Paris from the pillion of her
motor scooter. Heart throb of
the western woman's world,
as Brigitte Bardot was for men,
Alain Delon (far right) usually
packed the cinemas where his
films were playing. Other stars in
France's firmament (from the
top): film director Jean Renoir,
playwright Jean Anouilh, actress
Simone Signoret and singers Yves
Montand and Édith Piaf.*

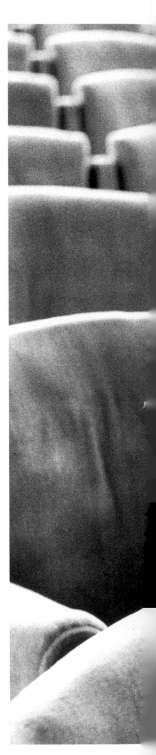

The career of the director-actor Jacques Tati stumbled, as wildly as his character M. Hulot, between fame and bankruptcy.

(Divisions Cuirassées de Réserve). But these accounted for only 960 tanks, and the DCRs remained under corps or army command, locked into larger infantry units. They had no air cover – no joint armour–air force manoeuvres were held – and they played little part in the battle. A further two thousand other French tanks were tied to infantry units in penny packets. The *bataille conduite*, the closely controlled and systematic engagement, was at the heart of French philosophy. The weight of modern firepower, the strategists thought, had doomed the *attaque à outrance*, the old all-out attack where local commanders seized the initiative. Defence was all. If the enemy did break through, the response was *colmatage*, plugging the gap with reserves as the road-mender fills a pothole with fresh gravel.

German thinking was the reverse. All their tanks were concentrated in ten panzer divisions, which were grouped into panzer corps, and backed by truck-born infantry and divebombers. The DLM and DCR had 160 tanks apiece. The panzer division had 270, and it was the spearpoint of German strategy. The most junior commander was encouraged to use his initiative, and to fight fluid and improvised battles with *élan* and *cran*, those old abandoned hallmarks of the French, dash and guts.

The French edge in artillery – they outgunned the Germans by 11,200 pieces to 7,710 – was more than offset by German air power. The Luftwaffe had 3,530 aircraft against 1,286. Their Stuka pilots were highly trained in giving close air support to the marauding panzer divisions; although the Dewoitine D520 fighter was as good as the Messerschmitt 109, only 80 were available in May 1940, and the RAF aircraft in France provided most of the opposition to the tactical air strikes that swept the front through the long daylight hours.

One other aspect was decisive. The Germans relied on radio even at the lowest, tank-to-tank level. Gamelin's command post had no radio whatever, nor indeed any carrier pigeons. Communications were by telephone or messenger. The fact is extraordinary, the result predictable. The French command was very slow to react, where German commanders, sometimes riding with the armoured spearheads, made instantaneous decisions.

A January fog had brought a strange trespasser to a Belgian field in 1940, a lost and burning German aircraft amid whose debris were found top-secret documents on the planned German invasion. Hitler's generals, fearing that they had fallen into Allied hands, persuaded him to make a momentous change. Instead of the main German attack being made across the Belgian plain, it was shifted further south, through the forests of the Ardennes.

"If any enemy attacked here," Marshal Pétain had declared of this hilly country, "he would be pincered as he left the forest. This is not a dangerous sector." The French nonetheless did not ignore it. They held a map exercise early in the spring of 1938, which assumed that the Germans would be able to move armoured forces through the Ardennes in 40 hours, near enough what it was to take them two years later. That still left them the Meuse to cross, however, and the French were sure they would have time enough to reinforce the sector before they could do so.

The Germans' plan rested on three army groups. The central group was to burst through the front in the Ardennes. It would then wheel northwest – in a *Sichelschnitt*, a slash of the sickle – to cut off the allied forces in Belgium. These were to be lured into the trap by the northern army group, advancing into northern Belgium. The southern German army group was to maintain pressure on the Maginot Line to confuse the French over the main thrust of the attack, and to prevent reinforcements being sent north. It was, in effect, the Schlieffen Plan in reverse. In 1914, the Germans had swung south-east after crossing the frontier; this time, they would turn clockwise, for the Channel ports.

A colossal weight, of 130,000 men and 1,222 tanks supported by a thousand aircraft, was about to fall upon the junction of André Corap's 9th Army and Charles Huntziger's 2nd Army. The two generals were responsible for holding the Ardennes sector. Their divisions included light cavalry, fortress troops and units made up of B-Series reservists, men of 35 and more, some of whom had done their military service two decades before. Peacetime anti-militarism in politics, books, films and theatre had done its bit to rot the reserves. Corap was unhappy about his men and their equipment. He worried about a "slackening of discipline in certain billets . . . soldiers insulting and sometimes attacking locals . . . not saluting". He wanted more regular troops to stiffen the reservists. His misgivings were shared by a British general, Alan Brooke, who found unshaven men and ungroomed horses at a 9th Army parade. What shook him most were the looks in the men's faces, "disgruntled and insubordinate".

It was known that the Germans were assembling bridging equipment on the Luxembourg border. There was also a large build-up of tanks and trucks. But Belgium was still thought to be the critical front. The Germans had trained hard through the dull days of the phoney war. The "impregnable" fortress of Eben-Emael was a key to the first Belgian defence line. The paratroops who landed their gliders on top of it on May 11 had practised with mock-ups for six months. They took it swiftly, whilst others seized bridges on the Albert Canal. The RAF attacked the bridges with slow-flying, vulnerable light bombers the next day; every aircraft was lost, and the Germans continued to pour forward.

The Belgians immediately fell back to the river Dyle. This created an immediate crisis, for French plans required the Belgians to hold the Germans long enough for the French to deploy. French regulars nonetheless fought with skill and courage. At Gembloux, two divisions held a panzer attack in a rare example of infantry stopping armour in open country without air support. Two DLMs under General René Prioux held two panzer divisions near Hannut for two days from May 12. This was the first tank battle in history, and the French won it in style, destroying 165 panzers for the loss of 105, in the face of total German air superiority.

A sharp-minded aide at Gamelin's headquarters noted that the Luftwaffe was allowing French columns to advance into northern Belgium almost unmolested. He suggested that this might mean they were concentrating elsewhere. He was ignored. Allied aircraft were not sent to attack the long and vulnerable columns of tanks and trucks that were beginning to move up into the wooded lanes of the Ardennes. This was the crucial moment. Gamelin continued to send his best troops and the whole British contingent into Belgium, whilst Giraud took the most valuable reserves up to Holland. These were fool's errands. The real blow was about to fall elsewhere

On the morning of May 13, a thousand aircraft attacked a narrow front on the Meuse near Sedan. The Stukas, with their screaming sirens and 500-pound bombs, were overhead for eight hours. The German assault engineers sustained heavy casualties at the river, but by dusk they had three bridgeheads across the Meuse near Sedan. Further north, at Monthermé, a half brigade of Tirailleurs Coloniaux blocked a panzer division for two days, withdrawing only when their flanks were exposed. The French defenders were all regulars. General Erwin Rommel's panzers were stopped in their tracks by other regular troops at Dinant. He feared his own men might lose their nerve. It took him all night to get a toehold on the west bank of the river, and he was hard-pressed to hold it.

The crossings at Sedan, though, were a gaping wound. It was small wonder that the 55DI, the B-Series division holding the sector, had cracked. It had almost no anti-aircraft guns. Only one officer in 25 was a regular. The standard allocation of anti-tank guns was ten per kilometre. The division had fewer than four. In the event, it mattered little. The brunt of the Stuka attack fell on the 147th fortress infantry regiment. A third of its reservists had been conscripted between 1918 and 1925; the average age of the ordinary soldiers was 31, and of captains 42. The 147th snapped before the first German tank had crossed the river. That night, some 20,000 soldiers fled, telling each other ever more fantastical and terrifying stories, as if they "wanted to forbid themselves any hope of return".

The RAF sent 71 bombers to attack the bridgeheads after dawn on May 14. Only 41 returned. Obsolete French Amiot bombers were also mauled by German flak. Guderian made a risky but inspired decision after crossing the Meuse. Instead of stopping to regroup, he sent his spearheads crashing on, pulling the rest of his corps behind him. Another French reservist division, 71DI, cracked in the now familiar pattern. The 1st DCR was sent in and destroyed some 100 panzers before it was itself obliterated, many of its tanks running out of fuel. Arthur Koestler, with the finely tuned antenna of an émigré, noticed a paragraph in a newspaper that referred to the "glorious recapture" of a fort at Sedan. He sped off to tell his friend Frédéric Joliot-Curie that the Germans were at Sedan. The scientist told him not to be a *paniquard*.

By the morning of May 15, when General Corap was relieved of his command, the situation of 9th Army was catastrophic. The German bridgehead was 95 kilometres across at its widest point, and the panzers were pouring through it, and wheeling for the Channel coast deep in the French rear. The Allied armies in Belgium now began to fall back, to try and save themselves from this encirclement. On May 17, Reynaud took over the defence ministry from Daladier. He was not strong enough to be entirely rid of his rival, who stayed in the cabinet as foreign minister. Another, fateful decision was made. Marshal Pétain, ancient and defeatist, became vice-premier.

Near Montcornet, north of Reims, Colonel Charles de Gaulle attacked with the hastily thrown together 4th armoured division. Some of his 179 tanks were in poor repair, he lacked radios and air support, and he made little impression. Each evening, the air force commander, General d'Astier de la Vigerie, telephoned the army commanders to say that he had spare aircraft the following day. Did they have missions for them? The reply was always the same: they had no use for them. Exhausted RAF pilots were flying up to five sorties a day, losing 208 fighters between May 10 and 21, but shooting down at least 299 German aircraft.

As de Gaulle made another quickly blunted attack at Laon on May 19, losing 73 of his 179 tanks in four days, Gamelin had his last lunch as commander-in-chief. He was, General Georges said, "still calm and apparently indifferent" as the headquarters cook put all his pain and frustration into a meal as lavish as a wedding breakfast, with a gigantic confection covered in spun sugar as the dessert. Georges found the scene "grotesque and pathetic", but Gamelin ate heartily, drank his coffee and left, as imperturbable as ever. "The guard turned out on the steps of the château and regimental trumpets sounded. Georges never saw Gamelin again. He was replaced at 9 p.m.

The new commander-in-chief, Maurice Weygand, who had been brought out of retirement in 1939 to lead troops in the Middle East, was stunned to find that "the transmission centre of the general staff has no radio sender or receiver", and that commanders in the field were reduced to sending "colombograms" by carrier pigeon. Weygand was a blustering and ill-tempered pessimist, and an arch-conservative with little affection for the Republic. At 73, he was older than the man he replaced. Behind him, Pétain was 84. When Roosevelt asked Bullitt what was happening to the French army, the ambassador told him that it had died 20 years ago. "All this generation of France's field officers were lost in the first war," he said. "Every time I should be talking to a 40-year-old French major, I'm talking to a 70-year-old officer called up from the reserves to take the place of his son, a lieutenant killed 25 years ago."

During the day, Reynaud attended public prayers at Notre-Dame. The panzers reached the channel coast at Noyelle on the mouth of the Somme in the evening. The French armies who had marched into Belgium, the cream of the regulars, and the British Expeditionary Force, were cut off. A miracle was indeed needed.

An Allied coordinator, General Billotte, had been appointed, but he lacked the staff for the tricky task of liaising between five armies. The British sent the lofty General "Tiny" Ironside to see General Billotte at the liaison headquarters in Douai on May 20. He found Billotte "in a state of complete depression . . . no plan, no thought of a plan…très fatigué and nothing doing". Far from liaising with his ally, Ironside lost his temper and began shaking him by the button on his tunic.

An assault on the vulnerable "turtle's neck", the zone immediately behind the German spearhead, offered some prospect of success. A limited attack towards Arras was made by two British battalions on May 21, covered by a handful of squadrons of light French armour. It shook Rommel and cost him dear in tanks. But coordination was poor. The expected pincer movement from the south failed to materialise. Weygand could not contact General Gort, the British commander, who feared he would be cut off from the Channel and began falling back on Dunkirk. The Germans were in Calais and Boulogne.

In a graceless château south of Lille, on May 24, in a dining room full of mortuary wreaths and bogus medieval furniture, the historian Marc Bloch saw a dolt-eyed and gloomy figure, with no rank badges on his sleeve, moodily chewing a cigarette. It was a general of division who had been relieved of his command a few hours before. Bloch was a captain on the staff of the 1st Army. It was retreating steadily, at 20 to 30 kilometres a day, billeting itself in a series of girls' schools. It never withdrew far enough to be able to organise strong positions before being overrun; instead reinforcements were "continually dribbled into every breach as it occurred" with the "inevitable result" that they were cut to pieces. The fuel dumps Bloch had carefully built up, concealed in public parks and abandoned brickfields, were left for the enemy.

King Léopold ordered the Belgian army to surrender early on May 28. "Ce roi!" Weygand exclaimed. "Quel cochon! Quel abominable cochon!" Reynaud turned white with anger. He told his radio audience that evening that "there has never been such a betrayal in history". For once there was heartfelt agreement from the British. When Gort's chief of staff was asked if some Belgians might be evacuated with the BEF, Reynaud said: "We don't care a bugger about the Belgians." The Belgian army had in fact fought valiantly, though outnumbered and without either tanks or planes.

That evening, Bloch wrote that the 1st Army had "ceased as such to exist". It died hard, however. More than 30,000 of its troops, though completely surrounded by stronger German forces and subject to incessant shelling, fought on street by street at Lille. They ran out of ammunition on May 31, having greatly aided the British and other French units to reach Dunkirk. Even then, Lieutenant Colonel Dutrey, one of their officers, committed suicide rather than surrender.

The evacuation of British troops began on May 26. Weygand did not authorise French troops to leave until May 29. By then, Churchill had already confirmed to Reynaud that he had ordered French troops to be included among those being plucked from the beaches by the armada of naval ships, pleasure steamers, and yachts and motor boats as small as 10 metres that criss-crossed the Channel. Gort was told, however, that the safety of British troops should be his prime consideration. He interpreted this to mean, he said, that "every Frenchman embarked is at a cost of one Englishman".

The bridgehead was defended from May 29 to June 4 by some 8,000 men of 12 DIM (Division d'Infantrie Motorisée), who had fought at Gembloux. Their commanding officer, General Janssen, was killed on June 2. British naval and air support continued after Gort left the bridgehead on May 31, and British destroyers and cross-Channel ferries were sent over one more time on the night of June 3–4 specifically to pick up over 26,000 French rearguard troops. Churchill warned that Dunkirk was not a victory – "wars are not won by evacuations" – but he added that there "was a victory inside this deliverance, which should be noted. It was won by the RAF." Most of the 2,739 sorties it flew were unseen, high above the smoke over the beaches or inland. The pilots flew to the edge of exhaustion and beyond. One logged 56 hours combat flying in a week, with up to six sorties a day. They shot down 390 German aircraft for 160 losses of their own. The last patrol over Dunkirk was flown on June 4. The French and British troops who had missed the last boats waved to the pilots as they waited for the Germans, but in all, 338,266 men escaped to England, and 129,000 of them were French.

Among them, Marc Bloch had a strange English interlude. He was taken to Dover aboard the *Royal Daffodil*, whose pretty name he noted. He felt it his duty to return to France and went by train to Plymouth to pick up a ship. Groups of cheering children waved at him from level crossings, and girls and clergymen passed ham and cheese sandwiches through the windows, and sweet-smelling tea with too much milk in it. Bloch was struck by the contrast when he got to Cherbourg. The boat had to wait out in the harbour for a long time. The dock officials did not get to their offices until 9 a.m., war or no war. In place of cheering children, the welcome was "formal, dry, rather suspicious".

To many, Dunkirk was no "miracle". It was evidence of British cowardice. Bloch thought the evacuation was "the only wise decision" that could have been taken. It would have achieved nothing for the BEF to have been pounded into pieces. It was "harsh", he admitted, and it was asking a great deal of the French soldier to see things "from so lofty a standpoint"; but it was "despicable" to exploit the Anglophobia of ordinary Frenchmen. Weygand was among those doing so on June 3. "Every people has its virtues and defects," he said. "The Englishman is motivated by almost instinctive selfishness." They could not, he added savagely, "resist the appeal of the ports . . . Even in March 1918, they wished to embark."

He set up a defence line on the Somme and the Aisne, badly outnumbered in infantry and armour. The Germans attacked with ten panzer divisions and fifty divisions of infantry on June 5. Reynaud had his final cabinet reshuffle that day. Charles de Gaulle, given the rank of brigadier-general, was appointed undersecretary of state for defence. The French were becoming inured to the shrieking Stukas, and tactics had improved. A "chessboard" defence replaced the continuous front, with "hedgehogs" or strong points sited on natural obstacles and protected by artillery. It was a last-ditch effort, however. The Germans breached the Somme line west of Amiens on

June 6. The Aisne line held a little longer. On June 8, distant gunfire was heard in Paris for the first time, with a "faint sweet smell" of resin and burning trees.

A *grande peur*, a flight of refugees so immense that it resembled a "geological cataclysm", had seized the country. It seemed to Antoine de Saint-Exupéry, as he looked down from his aircraft, that a gigantic boot had scattered an anthill somewhere in northern France. Between six and ten million fled their homes, using anything with wheels. Arthur Koestler, himself making for Limoges from Paris, was astonished to see a Paris By Night tourist bus, a fire engine from Maubeuge, an ice cream van from Évreux, a milk van from Rouen, a street sweeper with revolving brushes from Tours, and hearses and butchers' carts. German aircraft sometimes strafed the columns. The roadsides were littered with abandoned cars and dead horses.

Jacques Le Roy Ladurie met the villagers of Damblainville in Normandy in a procession of handcarts, bicycles and horses, with their cats and dogs. At their head was the sexton, carrying a cross, and their priest, reading his breviary. The abbé explained that they were simply going – "we don't want to be Boches" – though he knew not where. They refused pleas to turn back and went on their way singing canticles.

On June 6, three days after the capital had been bombed for the first time, the fear reached Paris. The embassies were full of people trying to get visas to flee. Vladimir Nabokov was rescued by Rachmaninoff, who loaned him 2,500 francs so that he could buy tickets for his family to get to New York aboard the liner *Champlain*. Dalí left for America with his fellow Surrealist Man Ray, a *baguette* of French bread strapped to his head with a belt, and his moustache waxed into acrobatic twists. James Joyce abandoned Paris for Saint-Gérand-le-Puy near Vichy, where he went for long walks, his pockets weighted down with stones to hurl at stray dogs. He feared dogs more than Germans. He eventually got to Switzerland.

Peggy Guggenheim bought up the works of fleeing painters at knockdown prices. She bought Georges Braque's *La Valse* for $1,500 before he left for Varengeville in the Midi; Picabia sold her his *Very Rare Picture Upon This Earth* for $300, but Picasso turned her down flat and, as if she had mistaken his studio for a department store, told her: "Lingerie is on the next floor."

A flood of refugees came in from the east. Some herded cattle with them, and grazed them in the Luxembourg Gardens. Elderly patients from mental clinics in Vincennes passed through in a convoy of hearses, sitting bolt upright. Cars had mattresses on the roofs, as scant protection against strafing attacks by German aircraft. One had a canoe on the roof, for emergency river crossings. A busload of choristers from Saint-Eustache cathedral sang as they travelled. The rich still travelled in some style. The aperitif heiress Ann Dubonnet left in the family Hispano-Suiza with banknotes rolled up in her doll and the hollow shafts of her father's golf clubs. Peggy Guggenheim drove off in her Talbot with her maid and Persian cats for Megève.

The crowds outside the Gare Montparnasse stretched for a kilometre by June 10. It took fourteen hours to get to Versailles by road. Most newspapers were closed. The government declared Paris to be an open city, saving it from the ravages of street fighting. Then it went too. "The prime minister is on his way to the armies," the radio announced in a rare burst of candour. Reynaud headed for Tours and the Loire châteaux. Mussolini, hyena-like, chose this moment to declare war on France.

Reynaud ended in the Château de Chissay, high above the river Cher. It was reached by a narrow road awash with refugee traffic, directed at one stage by his mistress Madame de Portes, clad in red pyjamas and dressing gown. A cabinet meeting was held on the evening of June 12. There were two broad options. The government could pursue the war from abroad, by taking itself to French North Africa with whatever troops could follow, leaving the mass of the army to surrender in the field and sign a ceasefire. Or the government could remain in France and negotiate an armistice.

Weygand said that the war was lost. France must sue for an armistice, so that the army remained intact and anarchy was avoided. "You are taking Hitler for Wilhelm, the old gent who took Alsace-Lorraine from us, and that was that," Reynaud warned him. "But Hitler is Genghis Khan." He added that the British would have to agree to any armistice, since the Allies had a formal agreement that neither would sue for peace without the agreement of the other. Churchill was invited to come to Tours for discussions and flew to its badly bombed airfield the next morning. There was no-one to greet him. He eventually found Reynaud, who told him that much of the government inclined to an armistice. Churchill said that, though he understood and would not indulge in recriminations the British were not prepared to release France from its pledge. He flew back to London.

Marshal Pétain was not being swept along by events. He read out a carefully prepared statement, formal and lethal. It was, he said, the government's duty to stay in France, "whatever happens"; to do otherwise would be to "deliver her to the enemy". He said that he would accept the hardships that awaited the country. He added a note of optimism – "the French Renaissance will be the fruit of this suffering" – and repeated that "I will refuse to leave Metropolitan soil." That ruled out bolting to North Africa. "The armistice", he concluded, "is in my eyes the necessary condition of the durability of eternal France." Pétain's statement was concealed by the fog of war, but it was a sensational event, an absolute and direct challenge to the government. Its most senior military figure had spelled out, with brutal clarity, that he would refuse to carry on the fight from outside France even if ordered to do so. Reynaud's authority was utterly undermined.

The following day, June 14, as the government moved on to Bordeaux, the *Blutfahne*, the "blood banner" with the swastika on a red background, was flying from the Hôtel de Ville and the Eiffel Tower. Near Verdun, a sergeant in the 23rd Colonial Infantry Regiment, François Mitterrand, was wounded by a shell. He was spared death – "What would really annoy me", he had written a few months before, "is dying for values in which I do not believe" – but was taken prisoner when he arrived at a military hospital.

The air was thick with Anglophobia, the natural partner of defeatism. For a settlement with the Germans to be seen as an honourable and inevitable act, it was necessary to believe that the British, having abandoned France at Dunkirk, would themselves be defeated. Pétain had told Bullitt that the British, having "fought to the last Frenchman", would soon sue for peace. In April 1918, they had insisted that Foch become the Allied generalissimo, finding Pétain too cautious and pessimistic; he had not forgotten it. Reynaud sent de Gaulle to London on June 15 to sound out the possibilities of fighting on. The same day, he asked Admiral Darlan how many troops could be evacuated to North Africa. Darlan, another Anglophobe, told him that he would need at least 200 ships, of which only ten were ready at Bordeaux. Weygand was adamant that he would rather be put in chains than leave France.

On June 16, Pétain threatened to resign unless an armistice was sought immediately. Churchill, ever a Francophile, desperate to avoid an armistice and all it implied, made an extraordinary offer of complete political union and joint citizenship between Britain and France. General Spears, liaising in Bordeaux, took a copy of the Declaration of Union to Reynaud's cabinet. "There stood the inevitable Mme de Portes," the Englishman recalled. "As I handed a secretary the pages she stepped behind him and read over his shoulder, holding his arm to prevent his turning the page too fast for her to read them. It was difficult to tell from her expression whether rage or amazement prevailed." She at once went to work to undermine the offer. Weygand dismissed it as a "blague", a joke, and Pétain demanded why France would wish to "fuse with a corpse"?

Reynaud, outmanoeuvred by Pétain, outnumbered in his cabinet, badgered mercilessly by Mme de Portes, gave way. He resigned that evening, to be replaced by Pétain. De Gaulle heard the news when he returned from London in the evening, and went straight back to England the next morning, "alone", he wrote, "and stripped of everything, like a man on the beach proposing to swim across the ocean". Pétain made his first broadcast to the French people later that day, June 17. "It is with a heavy heart," he said, "that I tell you today that we must cease hostilities."

The war, he calculated, was lost. An armistice would save the army from humiliation, and enable him to build a new society untainted by the decadence of the Third Republic. The British, selfish as ever, would settle with Hitler, or go under. This was an entirely realistic view, shared by neutrals, notably in Washington. Pétain, and most others, erred in assessing the future too rationally. They thus failed to predict that Churchill's arrival in Downing Street would mean that the British would continue their forlorn and now friendless struggle, and that Hitler would prove to be a lunatic, who would invade the Soviet Union and declare war on the United States, and pile upon the Germans a weight of enemies that no people could resist.

Nonetheless, French troops were still fighting hard as he spoke. On the Loire, near Châteauneuf, a battalion of the 109RI was holding off most of a German division. The cavalry cadets at Saumur were fighting with light weapons against German armour to hold the Loire bridges. They did so until their ammunition ran out two days later. Fifty were killed. The Germans, impressed by their courage, freed them after they surrendered, though Simone de Beauvoir said that such "delaying actions" in which men "got killed for mere shows of resistance" were a "terrible absurdity". German casualties were running at 2,500 a day during the breakthrough period from May 10 to June 3. They then doubled, to over 5,000 a day, from June 4 to June 18. German losses were light indeed for so vast a victory, with 45,000 killed and missing. French casualties topped 100,000, evidence that many units put up a stiff fight.

Pétain's broadcast put an end to that. At least half of the 1.5 million or so French prisoners of war surrendered between the broadcast and the signing of the armistice five days later. "A whole country seems suddenly to have given up," wrote the philosopher Georges Friedmann, serving as a lieutenant in Niort. "I have only observed a sort of complacent relief, sometimes even exalted relief, a kind of base atavistic satisfaction at the knowledge that for us it's over."

That same day, June 17, saw one of the earliest of those many moments that were to turn men into *résistants*. The high-flying young prefect of the Eure-et-Loire, Jean Moulin, was one of only 800 people left in Chartres when the Germans took the city. A number of local villagers had been killed by German artillery. The Germans asked Moulin to confirm that they had been raped and massacred by retreating Senegalese troops. Moulin was arrested and beaten when he refused to sign a statement dishonouring the Senegalese. He cut his throat that night, but found he was still alive the next morning, with his mind set on resistance. That afternoon, Bloch also met his first German troops, at Rennes. He went back to the hotel where he was billeted, took off his tunic, borrowed a jacket and tie, and signed into another hotel under his peacetime occupation: "historian". He, too, was to join the resistance, and, like Moulin, would die for it.

The armistice was signed on June 22, in the same railway carriage at Rethondes outside Compiègne used in 1918. France was divided into a German-occupied zone, in the north and along the Atlantic seaboard, and a southern zone to be administered by Pétain's government. A small slice of the Côte d'Azur, from Menton to the border, was designated an Italian zone of occupation two days later. The army was to be demobilised apart from 100,000 troops to maintain internal order. French POWs were to remain in captivity until the war was over, an event expected in months if not weeks. The French were to pay the costs of the German occupation.

Paris and Bordeaux were in the occupied zone. The ministers went first to Clermont-Ferrand. Bullitt caught up with many of them there. He found them physically and morally wrecked by defeat. "That they may have as many companions in misery as possible," he observed, "they hope that England will be rapidly and completely defeated." They had one other wish, "that France may become Germany's favourite province". In as far as he had any plans for France, indeed, this was what Hitler vaguely wanted, talking of France becoming a sort of Switzerland, a "place for tourism and fashion".

Workers in the local Michelin plant had proved troublesome in the past. New quarters were found in impeccably bourgeois Vichy, an elegant spa and casino town in central France conveniently blessed by large numbers of empty hotels. President Lebrun disliked it – "Everyone will say we are a casino government," he said, "that we're only here for the season" – but it suited Pierre Laval. He was born in Châteldon, a few miles away and, in classic local-boy-made-good style, he had bought a château nearby. Laval had a new and overriding ambition. He wished to persuade the Third Republic to finish itself off. "A great disaster like this," he said, "cannot leave intact the institutions which brought it about."

Some French officers and administrators in Syria, and North and Equatorial Africa, had urged the government to fight on from the empire. The British sent envoys to North Africa to contact the group of 27 anti-Pétain, anti-armistice parliamentarians who had sailed from Bordeaux for Casablanca. Obedience died hard with generals and governors alike. This group, Daladier and Mandel among them, found themselves rounded up and referred to by the press as "deserters": General Noguès, the key commander in North Africa, was alarmed at British meddling and sent away the envoys. He stayed loyal to Pétain.

The British were deeply concerned by the French fleet moored near Oran at Mers-el-Kébir. In principle, it was neutralised. Under the terms of the armistice, however, French warships had to return to their home ports; four of these were in German-occupied France, with only one, Toulon, in the unoccupied zone. No seapower, struggling for life, could ignore the fleet. Hitler was hardly to be trusted; neither, it must be said, was Vichy France. For the British, she was an ex-ally that had betrayed the terms of that alliance by unilaterally signing the armistice. The war had not been switched off at Compiègne like some light bulb. The British were still fighting, if alone; give Hitler any chance of dominating the Channel invasion routes, and they were done for.

A Royal Navy task force was sent from Gibraltar to Algerian waters. The French commander, Admiral Marcel Gensoul, was given an ultimatum on July 3. He could join the British, take refuge in neutral American waters, scuttle his fleet, or sail his ships to distant French colonial ports. The last option was perhaps the least bad. It is not clear that it was received in time; even if it was, however, Vichy could not have accepted it without breaking its brand-new armistice. Gensoul rejected the ultimatum. Churchill said he was faced with "a hateful decision, the most unnatural and painful in which I have ever been concerned". The British opened fire. It was a massacre: only the battlecruiser *Strasbourg* and four destroyers escaped from harbour. The rest were destroyed, with the deaths of 1,147 French sailors.

As a myth, Mers-el-Kébir was potent and corrosive. By re-establishing *perfide Albion* as the real and ancient foe, it made it more wholesome to collaborate with the Germans. Laval was, of course, well pleased that a parliamentary democracy had carried out the "infamy" on the Algerian coast. It helped his plans for the suicide of the Third Republic. Pétain's popularity remained a phenomenon, based on real affection and intense relief. Laval needed him as a figurehead, while he would provide the political skills. He underestimated the marshal's ambition, but not his appeal.

Meeting in the Vichy casino, parliament agreed on July 9 by 624 votes to four that the constitution be revised. The following day, by 569 votes to eighty, it slit its throat. It agreed to suspend the constitutional laws, and to grant plenary powers to Pétain to revise them. Léon Blum's sadness was icy: "Je considère la France comme déshonorée." Pétain was given a new title, "head of the French state". A second act gave him full powers to appoint and dismiss ministers; a third adjourned parliament until further notice; a fourth allowed him to designate his successor, and he chose Laval. The seventh act, allowing him to sanction all civil servants, completed a full hand. He had, an adviser noted, more power than anyone since Louis XIV, and Laval was his dauphin.

The Third Republic deserved better than its squalid end in a provincial casino. It was the longest surviving regime since 1789. It had calmed the psychoses of the Commune. It was sturdy enough to withstand the extraordinary strains of the First World War, and the toil of rebuilding the ruined towns of the north. It was decent and honourable enough to have seen off the extremisms of right and left in the Thirties. Under its benign tolerance, France had been an unrivalled creative and artistic hub; it had accepted refugees on an unmatched scale; its appeasement of Hitler was no deeper than that of the British, who in part dictated it. It recovered strongly, in its morale and economy, after Munich. Defeatism had passed; only 1.5 per cent refused the call-up in 1939, an identical figure to 1914. It was not responsible for the debacle of May and June: France fell because it was beaten on the battlefield. The war was lost, not by its politicians or popular mood, but by its military leaders; or, put more fairly, it was won by brilliant use of new tactics by an enemy leadership of the highest quality. "We didn't lose the war because of a lack of materiel," Daladier said when he was tried for his part in the debacle. "We lost it because of the mind-boggling incompetence of military leaders mired in the past."

The purpose of the armistice was clear. It shifted the onus of defeat away from the army. That was why Pétain and Weygand strove for it. It opened the myth of betrayal. "The word *trahi* began as a whisper," the journalist Clare Booth Luce wrote, "and then the whisper became a great wail that swept through France, a great wail of the damned: *trahi . . . trahi . . .*" The British and the Belgians were scapegoats for some. Most settled for decadence and the Third Republic. The captured sergeant François Mitterrand was typical in holding the system responsible. "I was a defeated soldier in a dishonoured army, and I felt bitter towards those who had made that possible," he wrote, "the politicians of the Third Republic."

This, of course, was exactly what Laval and Pétain wished him to think. By blaming politicians for the catastrophe, it justified their construction of a new France, one based, not on the Liberty, Equality and Fraternity of the disgraced Republic, but on the new Vichy trinity of Work, Family and Fatherland.

For Weygand, "The old order of things, a political regime made up of masonic, capitalist and international ideas" – a convenient expression that covered both Jews and communists – "has brought us where we stand." But there was one officer, now in London, who accepted that it was a military catastrophe. Charles de Gaulle was the antithesis of Pétain, under whom he had served in an infantry regiment in 1912. He had written a history of the French army on Pétain's behalf. The marshal wanted other officers to contribute to it. De Gaulle, though a mere colonel, had loftily refused to allow this, eventually bringing the book out under his own name. A brief exchange in the margin pointed up the difference between them. De Gaulle had written that the Revolution had stripped some generals of "prestige, often of life, sometimes of honour." Pétain said that "life" should be at the end of the sentence. De Gaulle noted: "It is an ascending gradation: prestige, life, honour." He underlined "honour" three times.

It was this that estranged them. Life was the essence to Pétain. He believed that he was breathing it back into France. That, he said in his first broadcast, was why he was seeking an armistice. De Gaulle made his own first broadcast, from studio 4B of the BBC, the following day. Honour required France to keep fighting, and to be frank about what had happened. "We have been, we are," he said, "submerged by the enemy's mechanised forces, both on land and in the air." The Germans were winning, he said, because they were the better side. It was not to do with numbers. "It is the tanks, the aircraft, the tactics of the Germans". he said, "which have made us fall back . . . and taken our leaders by surprise."

No cowardice attached to the armies that blitzkrieg overwhelmed. The Soviets had the prodigious advantage of hindsight when their turn came, a year later. They knew the nature of blitzkrieg; they had observers in France, and military attachés in Berlin, and they had many more men and tanks than the Germans. No-one questioned the courage of their troops. Yet the panzers and the Stukas won the frontier battles in a week, taking more than a million prisoners; within three months, the Red Army had lost three million men, and the Germans were lapping towards Moscow. Size and distance, assets unavailable to the French, saved Russia from the reeling impact of the first German blows.

Field Marshal Ironside, the British commander whom Weygand so despised, made clear that no shame should attach to French troops. A politician angered him by referring sarcastically to "these bloody gallant allies". "I told him that we had depended on the French army," he said. "That we had made no army and that therefore it was not right to say 'these bloody allies'. It was for them to say that of us."

Marc Bloch thought that French officers were outfought "principally because their minds were far too sluggish". The Germans relied on action and improvisation, he noted during the campaign. "They took no account of roads," he wrote. "They were everywhere. We, on the other hand, believed in doing nothing and in behaving as we always had."

Because these weaknesses lay within the métier, the military itself could correct them. It could learn from German superiority. And therein, de Gaulle realised, lay hope. "Struck down today by mechanised force," he concluded, "we shall be able in the future to conquer by means of a superior mechanised force."

"We have lost a battle," he said. "we have not lost the war." He was right, though hardly anyone in France heard his broadcast, and in his use of pronoun he was already creating a myth. "Tell the truth, general," Saint-Exupéry pointed out tartly. "We have lost the war. Our allies will win it."

9

Zones O and Nono

Hitler met Pétain at the railway station in the little Loire town of Montoire on October 24, 1940, on his return from talks with Franco. In his thin, reedy voice – he sounded like "a skeleton with a chill", Arthur Koestler thought – Pétain described his meeting on the radio. He had gone to Montoire voluntarily. He had been under "no diktat, no pressure . . . A collaboration was envisaged between our two countries", he said, to preserve the honour and unity of the nation, and in the context of building a new European order. He stressed that collaboration must be "sincere" and free of "every thought of aggression". Only thus, he said, could French suffering be assuaged, the plight of the prisoners of war improved, the cost of the occupation lightened, food supplies increased. He stressed that the decisions were his alone. "C'est moi seul", he said, "que l'Histoire jugera." For all the obligations that France had towards the victor, he added, "du moins reste-t-elle souveraine." At least she remained sovereign.

That was the rub. Vichy was not some grotesque throwback to the riots of February 1934, run by fanatics and ex-*ligueurs*. It was the legal government of France, led by a marshal of France, helped by respectable men: Laval, a former Socialist and prime minister, François Darlan, an admiral of the fleet. It was based on the loyal service of magistrates, police, prefects, and civil servants of every description. It was this swollen army of state employees – 650,000-strong in 1939, 900,000 by 1944 – whom it corrupted. It was they who, under the terms of the armistice and the head of state's unequivocal command, were to "collaborate" with the Germans. All the occupied countries threw up collaborators; but they were quislings, renegades, whom the nation could disown. In France, it was the nation itself.

The armistice, Pétain claimed, had been reached "between soldiers . . . in the spirit of honour". It was no such thing. It was an absolute bargain for the Germans. France had been cheap enough to conquer; it was cheaper still to rule. With Vichy help, the Germans could control the entire country with 30,000 men; they supervised the policing of Greater Paris with just two high-ranking German specialists and six inspectors.

All German prisoners of war were released, but French POWs remained in their camps, cold, hungry, and dispirited, some put to work on farms and in factories, a reservoir of 1.8 million hostages. They were to be released only when a permanent peace treaty was agreed; it never was, of course. French citizens who continued to fight were to be treated as *francs-tireurs*, guerrillas, denied the protection of the Geneva Convention. Alsace and Lorraine were reincorporated into the Reich, and in the most spiteful manner. Beret-wearing was banned there; so was speaking French, in shops, schools and churches. Family names were Germanified – Dupont became Brückner – while Strasbourg was changed to Strassburg, and in a rare moment of amusement, the rue du Sauvage became the Adolf-Hitler-Straße. Those who had fled in May and June were allowed back only if they had been resident in 1918, before the provinces had been returned to France.

Three *départements* not mentioned in the armistice – Bas-Rhin, Haut-Rhin and Moselle – were effectively annexed in September 1940. Gauleiters were appointed to run them. Vichy complained, with no result. The Nord and Pas-de-Calais were dismembered and governed by the German command in Brussels. The *départements* along the new German border were a "reserved" or forbidden zone. The rest was split into the Occupied Zone, universally known as "Zone O", and the *Zone Libre*, hastily renamed the Non-Occupied Zone, or "Zone Nono", as soon as the propaganda dangers of using "Free" were realised.

Zone O was formally subservient to the "rights of the occupying power". It embraced the northern half of the country and a thick belt of the Atlantic seaboard. It held two-thirds of the population, and of cultivated land; it produced an even higher proportion of potatoes, milk, butter and wheat, and it was home to more than 75 per cent of industry. It paid the bulk of the prodigious tribute demanded by the Germans. This was set at an arbitrary 20 million Reich marks, which, at the inflated exchange rate of 20 francs to the mark, came to 400 million francs a day. It was reduced to a marginally less lethal 300 million francs a day in May 1941, before soaring to 500 million francs the following November. In theory, this was to pay the costs of occupation. In fact, it was enough to maintain an army of several million a sum so vast, indeed, that it enabled the Germans to use it to "pay" for what they plundered. Eventually, some 60 per cent of total national income was going to the Reich. France was the star asset in the profit-and-loss account of German war-making.

Vichy was an admirable, quiet, respectable little town, tucked away, free from bustle, a place of tearooms and afternoon band concerts, famous for its thermal waters and the cool, creamy soup that bore its name. The population was only 25,000, but it had enough beds, maids, chefs, doctors, receptionists and telephone operators for a government. Here, people took the waters for liver and digestive complaints, making it also a suitably symbolic seat of government, given the marshal's desire to regenerate the nation after its bout of loose living. He lived in a modest suite at the Hôtel du Parc, while his lantern-jawed wife, who resembled "a nineteenth-century armoire", was housed in a different hotel, the Majestic. He took a brisk pre-lunch walk through the plane trees in the park each day. On Sundays, he went to mass, more ostentatiously and more often than he had in private life, greeted at the church door by clergy and schoolchildren.

Pétain, de Gaulle once wrote, was "a great man who died in 1925". But he kept himself fit, and his pulse rate and blood pressure were normal. His masseur reported that his body was "like marble", and that he "pisses like a fountain". He had been born on a rough peasant farm near the slag heaps of Bethune; he passed out 406rd in a class of 412 from Saint Cyr, and a confidential note on him as a junior officer noted that: "If this officer rises above the rank of major, it will be a disaster for France." He was 60 when he put all this behind him at Verdun and 78 when he entered politics.

"Poor Marshal!" de Gaulle wrote then. "He is so far gone in senile ambition that he will accept anything." But de Gaulle was now a fugitive in London, under sentence of death by a French court martial for desertion and entering the service of a foreign power. No government recognised him as leader of the "Free French", except the British. No senior figure, no minister, prefect, ambassador, judge or top civil servant had rallied to him, no general other than the governor of Indochina, no colonies other than obscurities in Equatorial Africa. Fewer than 3,000 of the French troops evacuated by the British from Narvik and Dunkirk declared for him. Of the 18,500 naval personnel who landed in Britain over the summer of 1940, all but 250 chose to return to defeated France when given the chance.

His rival was so grand that his head replaced Marianne's on postage stamps. He promulgated all laws, which bore his name in the regal plural: "Nous, Philippe Pétain, maréchal de France, chef de l'État français." He named all state servants, civil and military; he controlled the armed forces, and could declare war without reference to the legislature; he had the right of grace and amnesty; he could declare martial law. The Senate and Chamber of Deputies were adjourned *sine die*, replaced by a national council of no consequence. They could reassemble only with his permission.

De Gaulle claimed that Vichy had forfeited its legitimacy. Pétain had failed in his overriding duty to defend the nation, he argued, and had abdicated his authority in allowing his government to become the tributary of Germany. In his place, de Gaulle and the Free French described themselves as the provisional guardians of the nation. This assertion was legally and constitutionally baseless. The last parliament of the Third Republic had unquestionably delegated its authority to Pétain, by an overwhelming majority of both chambers. The État Français was a properly constituted state, and recognised as such by most of the world's countries, including, at least at first, the Soviet Union and the United States.

It all started so well. Pétain was enormously, genuinely, popular. "I make the gift of my person to France to ease her suffering," he had said in his broadcast of June 17, almost in imitation of Christ. Adoration of Pétain had a religious fervour to it. The Vichy hymn, "Maréchal, nous voilà", called him "the saviour" and built to a final mystic line: "For Pétain is France, France is Pétain." At New Year, children were asked by their teachers to send him greetings, and 1.5 million did so.

He sacked Laval before Christmas, a move that won him great acclaim, though it reflected the spiteful jealousies and intrigues of his regime. Laval spent much time in Paris, where he mixed with the hard-line collaborators of the capital, Nazi idolaters who despised Vichy as weak and liberal. The Auvergnat would return, more powerful than ever. For the moment, he was replaced by François Darlan, known as "l'amiral au mouillage", the moored admiral, since it was not known if he had ever been to sea. Once a leftist sympathiser, clever, a lover of luxury with a penchant for military bands, he was an opportunist consistent only in his Anglophobia: "I worked with the British for 15 years and they always lied to me," he said. "I have worked with the Germans for three months, and they have never lied to me."

No German soldiers in *feldgrau* disturbed Zone Nono, though it seemed to visitors that everyone was wearing some sort of uniform, adorned with the *françisque*, the Vichy symbol of the ancient double-bladed battleaxe of the Franks. Teenagers joined the scout-like Compagnons de France, and served five months of *formation virile* in the Chantiers de Jeunesse, whose tree-felling, road-building and charcoal-making replaced military service, whilst the older men were members of the Légion Française des Combattants, the umbrella veterans' association.

Sport, the open air and country pursuits basked in official favour. Regional theatre, folklore, local festivals and music were encouraged. The Church was back in favour, and the strange phenomenon of the *grand retour* swept the country. Thousands of young Catholics made the pilgrimage to pray before the Black Virgin in the basilica of Le Puy-en-Velay on Assumption Day in 1942. The venerated statue of Notre-Dame de Boulogne was smuggled over the demarcation line from Zone O in a vegetable truck. Huge crowds greeted it as it was carried on to Lourdes, and it was decided to take it round the country on its way back to Boulogne as a symbol of the return of the French to God.

With its cardboard virtues of *travail, famille* and *patrie*, Vichy's vision for France was antiquated and musty. It stood for traditional influences, the Church, the *patronat*, the moneyed and veterans; for the conservative values of the old Vendée, whose villages at last had their vengeance on the Revolution, putting up statues of their anti-Republican hero Jacques Cathelineau.

Vichy knew what people were thinking. An average of 300,000 letters a week were opened; in one month, December 1943, 1.5 million letters, 1.8 million telegrams and 21,000 phone calls were intercepted. They mirrored the prefects' reports of opinion: "A sort of indifference . . . They are retreating into their shells . . . Each person limits themselves to their own life and the egotistical pursuit of their own interests." But Vichy, like the old marshal himself, had its familiar and comforting side. Chevalier mirrored it in his hit song "Ça sent si bon la France". It celebrated the long-loved little things that made France "feel so good": the corner bar that gave credit, the brunette with the paradise eyes, the steeple in the evening sun. The war would surely soon be over, the prisoners would come home, a definitive peace treaty would be signed; in the meantime, Vichy suited well enough.

A surface normality was rapidly restored in the occupied zone. Restaurants reopened. The Casino de Paris was soon back in business; Charles Trenet and Marguerite Gilbert were singing, Serge Lifar staged *Coppélia* at the Opéra, music halls and cinemas were full. Entertainment was entering a golden age, at least in terms of audiences. Box office receipts surged to record levels by 1943.

Even the Germans played their part. They were young, fit and suntanned, carried a camera as often as a weapon, and paid for their purchases, politely and in cash. "Ils sont corrects" was the relieved phrase on every lip, "They behave themselves." André Gide's early reaction was typical. "To treat with yesterday's enemy is not cowardice," he consoled himself. "It is wisdom: the acceptance of the inevitable . . . What is the point of battering oneself against the bars of one's cage?" He, at that time in Cabris on the Côte d'Azure, felt himself to have "unlimited possibilities of acceptance". The Communists professed themselves to be delighted to see their German friends in France. *L'Humanité* said on Bastille Day 1940 that it was "particularly comforting" in these times of misfortune to see many Paris workers "striking up friendliness" with German soldiers. "Bravo, Comrades," it declared. "Continuez."

The victors had their perks, of course, but these were not yet intolerable. The grand hotels were parcelled out between them. They travelled free and in first class on the Métro. First-class compartments in trains were reserved for them. Some restaurants and cinemas were requisitioned for their use. They were great *balletomanes*, and a third of seats were put by for them. The Wehrmacht tried to live up to its slogan, *Jeder einmal in Paris*, by sending every soldier to Paris on leave at least once. The military supremo in Paris, General Otto von Stülpnagel, was an officer of the old school, puritanical, with a bloodless face and tight-boned skull, ramrod straight and lean, and a disciplinarian. Other ranks had to be in barracks by 11 p.m., and NCOs by midnight. They were forbidden to walk arm-in-arm or to travel in *vélos-taxis* with Frenchwomen. They were ordered to show proper reverence at the tomb of the unknown soldier, something they were specifically forbidden to do in Poland. Musicians from the Reich came to give concerts and recitals; Elisabeth Schwarzkopf sang, Herbert von Karajan conducted a special performance of *Tristan und Isolde* by the Berliner Staatsoper to mark the anniversary of Wagner's birth.

But the warmth passed. Some called the Germans *les haricots verts* (green beans) after their field-grey uniforms – a "pale, dull green, unobtrusive stain" Sartre observed – or *la race verte*, to which the *Rauchen Verboten* (no smoking) signs in trains and the Métro could amusingly be defaced. By the end, the word most often used was simple and chilling in its alienation: *ils* (them). Conscious of averted gazes, Germans began to call Paris the *Stadt ohne Blick*, the city where no one looks. German bossiness was resented in Zone O. People were forbidden to take photographs outdoors or to fly flags, and fined for not using pedestrian crossings, and for riding bicycles three abreast. Symbols that might breed defiance – the statue of Rouget de Lisle, composer of the "Marseillaise", and those of anti-Prussian writers like Victor Hugo and Zola, the English bookshop W. H. Smith – disappeared. More than five hundred works of art deemed "unfit" by the Nazi censors were burnt in the courtyard of the Louvre. Miró's pre-war nightmares were justified. He was branded a "decadent" and his canvases consigned to the flames.

Publishers signed an agreement of self-censorship with the ambassador Otto Abetz. They agreed not to print works by Jews or subversives. The so-called "Liste Otto" was prefaced by a toadying statement of compliance by the publishers, in which they said they were eager to withdraw from all sale books that "have systematically poisoned our public opinion", particularly those by "political refugees and Jewish authors". Shakespeare, Virginia Woolf, Erich Maria Remarque, Brecht, Thomas Mann, Aragon, Mauriac, Maurois . . . the list was long and bizarre. The Sarah Bernhardt theatre became the "de-Jewed" Théâtre de la Cité. The publishing house of Calmann-Lévy called itself Éditions Balzac.

The first collective act of defiance took place at the Arc de Triomphe on Armistice Day 1940. Micheline Bood, a 14-year-old schoolgirl, went to the Arc on November 11 with others from her *lycée*. There was an air raid warning in the morning – "everyone says these alerts are done to annoy us and get us to detest the English, mais vive les Anglais quand même!" – but a good crowd assembled. Someone had laid a tricolour and a British flag on the tomb, and many of the students were carrying little French flags and Union Jacks crayoned onto bits of paper. They met up again in a *brasserie* on the Champs-Élysees. Plainclothesmen and police started dragging people out of the crowds and flinging them into German trucks that had pulled up. Those arrested were beaten up in the trucks, while German troops and women auxiliaries looked on and laughed. It turned young Micheline against them. They were "*cochons, vaches, salauds* and all the animals in the Ark", and she went home well pleased. "Je n'ai pas vaincu," she wrote proudly, "mais j'ai manifesté." Another reason for satisfaction was eternally French. She professed herself *enchantée* because she caught "the boche women looking jealously at my legs."

In December came the first execution of a Parisian, Jacques Bonsergent, accused of insulting a German soldier. The first *résistants* – and, alas, the first of another breed, the *délateurs* who denounced them – formed a little network among the ethnologists at the Museum of Mankind at the Trocadéro. They included the anthropologist Jacques Soustelle, who was to become the chief aide and then the most savage critic of de Gaulle; they produced an underground news-sheet, *Résistance,* until they were betrayed. Seven of them were later executed.

The hostility spread from Paris. The prefect of the Hérault reported in late 1940 that the "feeling of revolt against the aggressors only continues to grow"; his colleague in the Ariège described his *département* as "almost unanimously favourable" to the British. More and more people listened to the BBC. It was made an offence to listen to it in a public place in October 1940, with a 100 franc fine or six days in prison. That was extended to listening in private in 1941, and the punishment increased to 10,000 francs or two years prison. From the end of 1942, the death penalty was invoked.

Food was short almost everywhere. Bread, sugar and pasta had been rationed in August. Meat, cheese, butter and eggs joined them in October. Calorie intake plunged. People reared rabbits on balconies and in bathrooms, foraging the public parks for dandelions and plants to feed them. The Germans were blamed. "Ils nous prennent tout" (they take everything from us) was the universal cry.

A basic problem of collaboration was that Hitler never knew what to do with France. He admitted as much to Admiral Raeder, describing its future in the New Europe in only the vaguest terms as a place of leisure, "a greater Switzerland", as German propaganda put it, "a country of tourism . . . and fashion". He sometimes rambled in private about annexing Burgundy and Flanders to the Reich. Goebbels was equally hazy. "One must put the French on ice," he wrote in his diary. "The longer one leaves them hanging in the air, the readier they will be to submit." But submit to what? Not to any master plan, for there was none; only short-term stratagems, based on the lust for labour, food and materials, and for loot.

Three dates are key to Vichy. The first, almost coincident with its birth, is September 17, 1940. That day, the Germans indefinitely postponed Operation Sealion, the plan to invade Britain. They did not announce it, of course, and they continued to mount bombing raids across the Channel, but the expectation of a short war was wrecked, and with it Vichy's *raison d'être* as a prelude to peace. Next is June 22, 1941, when Hitler attacked his former Soviet friends with a force of 3,200,000 men. The demands of that campaign led directly to February 16, 1943, when Pierre Laval, back in the Vichy saddle, was obliged to introduce STO, the *Service du travail obligatoire*, under which young Frenchmen were conscripted for forced labour in Germany. The serf-like condition to which Vichy had reduced the nation was made clear, as layer after layer of its authority was stripped away. Tens of thousands of young men, *réfractaires*, avoided the labour draft. They took to the hills and joined the Resistance; they were given medical certificates listing fictitious ailments by willing doctors, or they simply declined to present themselves, confident that the local police were sympathetic.

The fabulous sums extorted from the French as occupation costs financed the purchasing offices opened by the German military and SS. The most important was the "Otto bureau", started by Hermann Brandl, alias Otto, an Abwehr military intelligence officer. He was employing a staff of 400 by the spring of 1941, with offices on the avenue Foch, and railyards where he assembled the train-loads of goods he sent to the Reich. Fortunes were made by the middlemen. Mendel Szkolnikoff was the chief buyer for the SS, ironically so, for he was a Russian Jew who had worked in the Paris garment trade, narrowly escaping pre-war deportation for writing dud cheques. He kept an open house with ten servants on the rue de Presbourg. Joseph Joinvici, another Jewish immigrant, and a pre-war scrap metal merchant, also grew fat dealing in food and metals for the military. He worked closely with Henri Chamberlin, alias Lafont, a thief who had teamed up with Pierre Bonny, a corrupt ex-police inspector.

Admiral Darlan prided himself on running the economy with tough-minded men; his first production minister, Pierre Pucheu, was a pre-war steel magnate and financier of the *ligues*, and the new planning agency was headed by a former Renault director. Darlan mocked the "soft-cheeked altar boys" on Pétain's staff; he surrounded himself, he said, with "sharp young fellows who will come to terms with Fritz and cook up a good soup for us". Fritz gorged himself. The Germans were soon taking 55 per cent of French aluminium, half its wool, almost two-thirds of its champagne, 85 per cent of vehicles, and nine-tenths of cement. By 1943, 40 per cent of total industrial output was going to Germany, and more than a third of the labour force was directly supplying German needs. Pierre Pucheu complained that his efforts to monitor and limit German contracts were overwhelmed by the eagerness of French business to sign them. Several thousand companies put in bids after the Germans held an industrial fair in the Petit Palais to exhibit the products they needed. Many French industrialists visited Germany to look at production techniques, six delegations travelling in November 1941 alone; they had round-table lunches at the Paris Ritz with their German counterparts, and the two national chambers of commerce held joint congresses.

National trade unions were banned, as were strikes, sit-ins and lock-outs; the acceptance of arbitration was made mandatory. The working week soon averaged 46 hours, but was higher in key industries. The Germans insisted that wages remain below German levels to encourage volunteers to work in the Reich. In real terms, they fell by at least a quarter, and by more when soaring black market prices are factored in.

A few *patrons* were ultra-right wing. The eccentric Georges Claude was besotted by Hitler; Eugène Schueller, the founder of the L'Oréal cosmetics giant, continued to finance violent quasi-fascist groups, as he had before the war. Some were as non-cooperative as circumstances permitted. The Peugeot family helped workers evade forced labour in Germany. The Michelins turned down German offers of synthetic rubber supplies to avoid being compromised. More typical, though, was Louis Verdier of Gnôme et Rhône. He greeted the Anglo-Americans with champagne in 1944, as he had a German purchasing team in 1941. Business was business. In general, the principle of "lack of intimacy" was applied. It was acceptable for an employer to have contracts with the Wehrmacht, provided he did not expect his employees to work with zeal, and protected them from having to work in Germany.

Industries in the Zone O had little room for manoeuvre, and the iron founders in annexed Lorraine none at all. Lyon, the business heart of Zone Nono, was thought *deutschfreundlich*, in trade terms, at least, for it also had an active resistance. The silk industry adapted itself to making parachutes; chemicals, Rhône wines, canned meat and precision instruments were shipped east, and Marius Berliet made his celebrated trucks for the Wehrmacht. He guarded his best workers from labour service by claiming that they had TB or syphilis – the Germans were terrified of disease – but he did so only because he needed them. He was happy enough to let slackers and malcontents be taken away, and even sent two of his own sons to work in Germany as volunteers to set a good example. He was typically forthright in defending himself against charges of collaboration. He saw no reason why German orders should not be treated like any other. "We were not at war," he said. "There was an armistice. I saw matters only as an individual *patron*."

This was, of course, precisely the dilemma that the armistice created. An industrialist in the Zone O could plead force majeure when fulfilling the orders of the occupiers. But for an industrialist in Lyon, the Germans were neither friends nor enemies in the legal sense. They were, too, the only major customers; manufacturing for them was the only way of recycling the daily tribute, so that some of the 400 million francs stayed in France in terms of jobs and pay for French workers.

Berliet's trucks were soon in service on the eastern front. So were French-built aircraft. Vichy had scruples about providing fighter aircraft, which could have been used offensively against Britain. Transport aircraft were another matter. By 1942, French factories were supplying just over a quarter of Germany's transport planes; by 1944, this had risen to 49 per cent. The industry was employing 100,000 men; had it refused to supply the Germans, the aircraft and engine plants would doubtless have been dismantled and taken to Germany, where the workers would have included French forced labourers. Marcel Bloch, the aviation pioneer later known by his brother's resistance code name as Marcel Dassault, showed the price paid for non-cooperation. He was sent to Buchenwald.

Hunger, a dull and constant ache, settled over the country. It brought listlessness, skin irritations, short-term memory loss, bad teeth, bleeding gums, boils and chilblains. Mortality in Paris had increased 40 per cent by 1942, and the number of tuberculosis deaths doubled. There were some improvements, though. Wine rationing led to a sharp decline in alcoholism, and the death rates in the *départements* of the north-west, notorious for heavy drinking, actually fell by 17.5 per cent during the Occupation.

The queues – it could take two hours to get one's single monthly egg – were hotbeds of anti-regime rumour. The shortages led to an attitude of *sauve qui peut*, of self-survival at any price, and to a corrosive black market. Prices were between two and eight times the official rate – ten times in the Haute-Savoie – and farmers held back produce if they could. Huge profits were made by those who bribed Germans to get passes for trucks to carry goods to Paris. Traffickers who bought wine in Chinon at 80 francs the litre in the winter of 1941–42 sold it for 450 or 500 francs in the capital. Stockings bought for 25 francs in Marseille were worth five times that in Angers. Relations between town and country soured. Vichy farm legislation was in fact commendable – subsidies for modernising farm cottages, inheritance law eased to allow a farmer to pass on his land intact to one child, encouragement to consolidate scattered holdings – but long-term. In the short term, unable to point at German greed, it railed at *la cupidité paysanne*, but the public held the regime responsible, powerless to feed its people or prevent the German plunder.

As well as feeding the occupiers in France, almost a fifth of farm produce was going directly to Germany by 1943. Even without that, farming was in distress. Wheat production fell by a fifth, and potatoes by more than 40 per cent. Many of the prisoners rotting in German camps were peasants, adding a chronic labour shortage to the near-disappearance of fertiliser and fuel. The separation of the grain-growing north from the wine-producing south compounded the problem. It was made worse by the highly centralised food distribution system, based on the vast wholesale markets of Les Halles in Paris. Zone O had produced all French sugar, 87 per cent of its butter and three-quarters of its wheat. Places with mixed farming, like the Loiret and the Seine-et-Marne, did best. The south as a whole was poorly fed. Regions of monoculture, like the wine-growing Var and Hérault, almost starved. No outside vegetables reached the Hérault from 1942 onwards, and people lived on chestnuts and potatoes. Cities suffered worst of all. Montpellier was said to be the hungriest place in France. Bread was coarse and a dirty-brown colour; white bread was a delicacy eaten "like *gâteau*" on birthdays and anniversaries. Factory records at the end of the war recorded an average weight loss of 8 kilos among workers. Girls growing up in the poorer Paris *quartiers* were 11 centimetres shorter than their pre-war peers, and boys 7 centimetres shorter.

Café national was a disgusting brew made from chickpeas and roasted acorns; *tabac national* used Jerusalem artichokes, dried nettles, corn silk, and oak leaves with camomile and peppermint. The big cities had soup kitchens that gave cheap, scanty meals to the poorest. People were encouraged to forage for acorns and chestnuts, and to keep *jardins ouvriers* (allotments). Carrots and swede were ever more important, and ever more loathed. Restaurant menus in 1944 consisted of little else. The *potage paysan* was carrots and water; the *filet de bœuf garni* was a scrap of gristle with carrots, and the *macedoine* was a mash of carrots and swede.

Improvisation, *le système D*, helped. Hunting was banned in Zone O, but fishing was allowed; fishing tackle suppliers boomed – it was said to be patriotic to have two rods, for these were "deux gaules" in French, an irresistible Resistance pun – and the banks of the Seine in Paris were lined all day with fishermen. Guinea pigs were advertised for sale as "the flat-dweller's rabbit", perfect for the smallest homes. Coffee-grinders were used to make flour outside the official system. Tomatoes were grown on south-facing balconies. Pigeons were tempted with crumbs and netted in the Luxembourg Gardens. Dogs gradually disappeared, seldom eaten, but not replaced when they died.

Staples were rationed, but caviar, foie gras, oysters and game were available at a price. The rich still dined sumptuously. Fifty or so restaurants in Paris were licensed for menus without tickets. Chantaco in the rue de la Pompe presented its clients with a *millefeuille* at the end of their meal, elegantly bringing their attention to a bill of 1000 francs a head. That would buy a hundred meals in a rationed category D restaurant; it was almost three months' pay for a Métro ticket inspector. A special thrill, so the German aesthete and writer Ernst Jünger found, was to be had in eating well and plentifully in such times. As he languidly ate sole and pressed duck in the Tour d'Argent, he looked down, with devilish satisfaction, like the nearby gargoyles of Notre-Dame, on the grey ocean of roofs that concealed the hungry.

Joy for most people was to have country cousins who sent regular food parcels. Those who lacked them scoured the countryside anyway, pouring out of the towns by train and bicycle in droves. The wife of a prisoner of war, Clémentine Allosio, cycled the back roads for hours to scrounge anything she could parcel up to send him. She was kept going by the "true comradeship" of other POW wives, who supported each other, passing on tips on how to resole shoes with old car tyres, skin a rabbit to make fur gloves, and make soap. "We had a sole idea in our head," she said. "Tenir le coup [stick it out]. Cela va finir [it'll end sometime] . . . tenir le coup."

Paris had 350,000 private cars before the war. Almost all rusted slowly, jacked up on blocks of wood. Permits were given out for just 7,000 during the Occupation. They went to German favourites, notoriously to Sacha Distel's Hispano-Suiza, and to a few midwives, doctors and the like. The lack of traffic brought a medieval stillness to the cities. A Parisian on the place de la Bourse, at the end of 1943, noted three cars, a motorbike and a horse-drawn cab in ten minutes. "As silent as the country," he wrote. After the midnight curfew, the only sounds came from the conquerors, the occasional roar of a car engine, and the familiar crunch of the hobnail boots of the five-man German patrols. Darkness and silence were the twins of the Occupation; the satirist and engraver Vercors (Jean Bruller) called his famous underground press Éditions de Minuit, and when the Gaullists in London reprinted his titles, they called them Cahiers du Silence. Silence was for the Germans, too. "They are surrounded by it," wrote the economist Charles Rist. "Silence in trains, in the Métro, in the street. Each keeps his thoughts to himself. And yet one *senses* the hostility." The darkness was violet blue, the colour of the blackout paint on street lamps and Métro stations; some called these years *les années bleues*.

Electricity supplies became more and more irregular. Hairdressers used pedal-powered generators to run hairdryers. As perms became more difficult, women wore turbans and wondrously exaggerated floral hats, brilliant plumage stitched up from pieces of spare material. Designers were limited to 40 models in each collection, and cloth was short. The Germans had planned to make Berlin and Vienna the style centres of the New Europe, by moving the great designers and their skilled workers there; it came to nothing, but the Germans forbade French fashion exports in a spiteful effort to break the Paris industry. Some were bankrupted. Long sleeves and linings were de rigueur among the survivors, to ward off the cold. Some families wore ski outfits through the winter. As leather disappeared, clogs and shoes with soles of compressed paper appeared. The clogs had hinged soles to make them more comfortable. Pebbles and dust jammed the hinges, so pedestrians frequently kicked them together to free them, like clay-court tennis players. Chevalier sang of their familiar click-clack in the hit song "La Symphonie de semelles de bois"; the most fashionable were extra-thick, anticipating the platform sole.

In small communities, individual Germans became so familiar that they were taken for granted, without anger or surprise, but this did not prevent displays of defiance. Two thousand came spontaneously to the funerals of three RAF aircrew at Lanester in Brittany in December 1941; earlier, 5,000 had mourned dead British pilots at Rennes. It became so common for audiences to boo German troops in newsreels that the government had to order cinemas to show them with the lights on.

Some were over-friendly with the conquerors. It was inevitable, if shaming, that numerous women became *collabos horizontales*. The better part of two million of the fittest young Frenchmen languished in German camps. Without breadwinners, their wives were needy and vulnerable; in some places, girls had no realistic chance of finding a French boyfriend. The number of women claiming child benefit from the German military authorities reached 85,000 in early 1944. Estimates of the number of children fathered by the Germans run up to 200,000. Marriages between French and German, though, were *rarissimo*: 25 were recorded in Paris in 1941, dwindling to nine in 1944.

Not all were simple girls. Coco Chanel lived in the Ritz with her Luftwaffe lover. Salons continued. The butler at the residence of baron Robert de Rothschild, now occupied by a General Hanesse, told Cocteau: "I'm not unhappy working for the general, since he receives the same people as the baron used to." Ernst Jünger, on the German embassy staff, mingled with the artistic elite, with the actress Arletty, the publisher Gaston Gallimard, Cocteau, the marquise de Polignac, Jean Marais. He ate at Prunier, Maxim's, La Pérouse and the Ritz. He visited Picasso's studio, and Braque's.

The high point of artistic collaboration was the exhibition of male nudes at the Orangerie by Arno Breker, Hitler's favourite sculptor. Aristide Maillol, famous for the grace and serenity of his own female nudes, expressed his admiration; Laval invited Breker to lunch, and Cocteau, a former lover, wrote him a "Salute". Yet, as so often, matters were less black and white than hindsight allows. Breker had lived in Paris in the 1920s. He had many French friends; he helped them, and he saved Maillol's young Jewish model Dina Vierny from being deported.

Colette and Cocteau had apartments in the Palais-Royal that "teemed" with Germans. Cocteau admired Hitler's artistic sensitivity, but Colette had special reason for care, since her husband was Jewish and her daughter was in the Resistance. Actor Sacha Guitry was pilloried during the *épuration* (purges) that followed the liberation; but he had made no political statements, and had gone on doing what he always did, "seeking to be the centre of attention." Maurice Chevalier ensured that he would have purge problems by being photographed with a bottle of Vichy water, and declaring that he "blindly followed the Marshal". He compounded this by singing on German-controlled Radio Paris, and visiting Germany. Édith Piaf and Charles Trenet went, too, but they did so to sing to French PoWs and workers. The choreographer Serge Lifar was frequently in Berlin; the Opéra director Jacques Rouché and the pianist Alfred Cortot went, too. Thirteen leading sculptors and artists, Derain, Vlaminck and van Dongen among them, made a well-publicised trip to the Reich in October 1941. Promise was made that some PoWs would be released as a reward for the trip, however.

The Paris ultras – the *ubiquistes*, the "everywheres" who wrote for *Je suis partout*, the leading *collabo* paper – were easy enough to condemn. They boasted of their respect for the Nazis. "Nous ne sommes pas des convertis," Robert Brasillach said proudly. They were not wartime converts to the Reich, but originals.

If there were few outright villains in the arts, there were fewer outright heroes than myth allows, too. Picasso was a case in point. He received Germans politely enough, but he could have gone to America. Though he denied it – "Staying on is not courage," he told his mistress Françoise Gilot, "it is a form of inertia" – it was brave for him to be in Paris at all. He was not allowed to exhibit, and the Germans raided his studio looking for incriminating evidence. "There was nothing to do but work and struggle for food," he said modestly, "see one's friends quietly, and look forward to the day of freedom."

German censorship was liberal enough in France for a great boom in reading to take place. French publishers led the world in 1943, with 9,348 titles against 8,320 in America. As to cinema, 225 full-length films were shot. They included masterpieces such as *Les Visiteurs du soir* and *Les Enfants du paradis*. The theatre flourished. More than 400 first performances were staged in Paris. The arts focus in the city migrated from Montparnasse to the cafés of Saint-Germain-des-Prés. There was good dry warmth from stoves, as well as companionship; a writer from a damp and freezing home could sit working all day in comfort for the price of the drink in front of him.

Simone de Beauvoir complained that she and Sartre were "reduced to political impotence", but they fared well enough, rambling down country lanes on bicycles, swapping gossip in the Café de Flore, and writing at length. The German *Paris Zeitung* was lavish in its praise of *Les Mouches*, Sartre's first play. He later claimed it was about resistance, but the Germans liked it well enough to have their own reading of it, with Orestes as a superhero pitted against a tyrannical rabbi clothed as Jupiter. His best-known play, *Huis Clos*, opened as the Allied landings in Normandy got under way. The supposed irony to its most famous line – "hell is other people" – escaped the censor. "Les autres" was a pseudonym the French used for the Germans, and Sartre claimed he used it in the line on purpose.

Sartre joined the Comité Nationale des Écrivains, a body of Communists and fellow travellers less defiant than they seemed, "less interested in the Resistance", a modern historian found, "than in drawing up lists of other writers and journalists they wanted proscribed and silenced after the war". Albert Camus parted company with Sartre to join the Resistance and form the underground newspaper *Combat*. Camus was unquestionably a courageous *résistant*. But it was in the nature of the Occupation that he, too, could be tarred by those who so chose, by them pointing out that he removed the references to Kafka, a Jew, in his *Myth of Sisyphus* in order to get it published in 1943.

The question of *collabos* remains a minefield; time has not healed the wounds, but reinfected them. "Voir n'est pas savoir," the philosopher Alain Finkielkraut has said. "To see", with the benefit of hindsight, a clear conscience and the absence of the occupier, "is not to understand."

There were the active collaborators, the *indicateurs* or *mouches* who passed information on to the Gestapo and the Abwehr. Captured German files showed them to range at haphazard across the social spectrum. In Paris, they included a viscountess paid to "frequent salons", hairdressers, butchers, the dance hostess codenamed "Jeannette", the cinema actor "Raymond C", the private detective "Serge", a magician, a parfumier, journalists, senior officials, the *concierge* of a block of flats in the rue de Grenelle. Industrialists were recruited by a Major Becker from his luxury billet in room 229 of the Hôtel Claridge.

There was, too, an epidemic of *délateurs* – more often *délatrices*, in fact, for women practised this least attractive of national pastimes with vigour – who denounced neighbours, husbands, friends and strangers to the Vichy authorities and the Germans. Publications like *Gringoire* spurred them on with a special slogan: *Répétez-le* (Pass it on). Poison pen writers, *corbeaux*, were sending 1,500 letters a day to the Paris Kommandatur in 1942. Prefects also reported a "veritable deluge of letters", so much so that they were told eventually to discourage them, and to pursue those supplying false information.

But mostly it is a grey area. It is made so because the État Français commanded its officials to collaborate. With very few exceptions, they did so. The classic apologia was made by Marcel Peyrouton, an official who also served as interior minister, at his post-war trial. "I did not ask questions," he said. "I repeat: I am not a Republican, I am not anti-Republican. I am an agent, a functionary." The government included few politicians, Laval apart. Its stock-in-trade were university men, senior civil servants, treasury inspectors, judges and councillors of state, grey men with forgettable names, with a leavening of writers and intellectuals.

It was not itself fascist. It kept the demagogues at a distance – Eugène Delouche, the ex-*cagoulard*, was shot by the Gestapo, Pierre Constantin died insane, Marcel Déat lost his mind – and did not found its own political party. For the first time since the Second Empire, high public servants were obliged to swear a personal oath of loyalty to the chief of state. All the country's prefects did so at a special ceremony in Vichy in February 1942. The corps of prefects had represented state authority in the *départements* since Napoleon. Pétain issued them with new gold-braided uniforms, and acknowledged their importance in a circular shortly after he came to power. They were to be "propagandists of truth" and "defenders" of the nation. Those hostile to the regime, like Jean Moulin, were removed. The Marseille regional prefect, Joseph Rivalland, bravely refused to provide the Germans with a list of hostages, giving only his own name. He found himself transferred to bean-counting in the Cour des Comptes. Of the others, few had much time for the Germans but, until the regime began to collapse in late 1943, they did their work conscientiously enough.

Of the judges and magistrates, only one, Paul Didier, refused to swear loyalty. He was dismissed immediately. There was no difficulty finding judges to sit on the state tribunal, the special court that judged cases endangering the "unity and security" of the state, even though it had the power to impose the death penalty, without right of appeal. Those who were pliable – or, as the justice minister Joseph Barthélemy preferred to put it, showed "firmness of character and devotion to the state" – were rewarded with fast-track promotion. They congratulated themselves on helping to safeguard French justice from German interference.

The police underwent a major reorganisation in 1941, when a national force was created for the first time. They complained of overwork and undermanning – many police were still in German prison camps – but they worked hard and loyally well into 1943. They mounted the largest operation in French police history in Marseille in January 1943, when the Germans first cleared and then destroyed the Vieux Port.

The Church, too, rallied to Vichy at first. In July 1941, the Assembly of Cardinals and Archbishops formally declared that: "We venerate the head of state." It called for "complete and sincere loyalty, without enthralment, to the established order". The German invasion of the godless Soviet Union had a special resonance. Cardinal Baudrillart, rector of the Catholic Institute of Paris, declared the young Frenchmen who volunteered to fight Bolsheviks with the Germans to be "the crusaders of the twentieth century. May their arms be blessed! The tomb of Christ shall be delivered!"

It was the treatment of Jews that caused some senior churchmen to round publicly on the regime. Here, too, it was a functionary and not an ideologue or scoundrel who rounded up Jews for the slaughter, skilfully and without fuss. René Bousquet was a devoted public servant from the same background as the greatest hero of the Resistance. Both Bousquet and Jean Moulin were rising young stars of the corps of prefects at the start of the war. Bousquet had been a national hero at 21, rescuing people during flash floods in the Tarn. He was prefect of the Marne in 1940, whilst Moulin was refusing to do German bidding in Chartres, and as hostile to the Germans. When two Communists were executed, he wore his prefect's uniform to place tricolour sashes on their graves. The Germans wanted him court-martialled.

Yet it was Bousquet who, over the summer of 1942, ensured as a matter of professional pride and principle that Vichy would bear direct responsibility for the arrests of Jews. He negotiated an agreement with Carl Oberg, the SS officer responsible for the police, by which the Germans recognised the independence of the French police. They also agreed that French courts should try all cases except those of a specific anti-German nature. For their part, the French were to struggle against "terrorism, anarchism and communism". A bargain wholly agreeable to the Germans was struck. In return for a nod to French "sovereignty" over the police, Vichy committed itself to maintaining order on the Nazis' behalf.

Vichy anticipated the conqueror's treatment of Jews. France became the only country, apart from the Reich itself, to enshrine official state-sponsored anti-Semitism. Within a fortnight of Vichy's creation, a commission was set up to investigate foreign Jews who had gained French nationality. A month later, laws prohibiting the publication of anti-Semitic diatribes were revoked. Jew-haters could write at will.

A Jewish statute was drawn up by Raphael Alibert, the justice minister, a lawyer and pre-war Action Française sympathiser. A German ordinance of September 27, 1940 defined as a Jew anyone who practised the religion or who had three Jewish grandparents. Alibert, a week later, went further. His statute embraced those of the Jewish "race", a wider term than religion, and included those with two grandparents if they were married to a Jew. To ensure the purity of the regime, Jews were forbidden to enter Vichy's *département*, the Allier, at all.

The persecution was entirely French. It was legalistic, embracing 26 laws and 24 decrees, precise and enforced by state functionaries. Prefects were able to intern foreign Jews at will from October 4, 1940. By early 1941, about 40,000 were being held in camps. The conditions were so appalling at Drancy, a bleak unfinished housing project on the outskirts of Paris, that the Germans ordered 600 sick detainees to be released.

Jews were banned or made subject to quotas as public servants, teachers, journalists, film-makers, elected officials, doctors, dentists, pharmacists, lawyers. First their radios were confiscated, and then their telephones and bicycles. They were banished from all public places and entertainments, from swimming pools, restaurants, cafés, cinemas, music halls, markets, libraries and circuses. They had to travel in the last carriage on the Métro; they were allowed to shop only in the afternoon, when supplies had often run out.

This, as much else in Vichy, was justified by the theory of the lesser evil. Paul Baudouin, the foreign minister, put it succinctly in his journal: "It is now clear that the only way to prevent the application by Germans of harsh anti-Jewish measures is to draw up more moderate measures for all of France." If Vichy did not persecute a little, then the Germans would a lot. Baudouin was an inspector of finances, from the cream of the administration, a Catholic and a pre-war admirer of the public-spirited ideals of Marshal Lyautey. He was a moderate, who was to resign in protest over Pétain's meeting with Hitler at Montoire. He felt Alibert's statute "severe, much too severe. My point of view is that the Jewish problem should be treated as a problem of foreigners . . ." This was the "moderate" position, that "moderate measures" could be taken against foreign Jews.

Such was the moral cancer of Vichy, infecting decent men with whom it had dealings. By March 1942, some 3,400 Jewish public servants had been dismissed in France, and 2,500 in Algeria, almost without a murmur. Paris doctors defied the quotas by allowing 203 Jews to continue to practise instead of the 108 allowed for. But lawyers applied the quotas with notable smoothness, including the Conseil d'État, which purged itself of its Jewish members. The only academic who refused to apply the quotas, Gustav Monod, a senior professor at the University of Paris, was sacked and went back to teaching at a *lycée*.

Zone Nono was in general more scrupulously anti-Semitic than the north. Parisians made a point of booing vendors of racist sheets like *Au pilori*. When Jews in the Occupied Zone were ordered to wear yellow stars in June 1942 – 5,000 metres of gold-coloured cloth were ordered from the textile makers Barbet-Massin, and Jews were charged two clothing tickets apiece for thus branding themselves – the *collabo* press tried to whip up feeling against them. A reporter from *Cri du Peuple* said he had counted 268 stars on a ten-minute walk from the Porte Saint-Denis. Even the "dumbest Gaullist", he said, would have to admit that this proved the reality of "the Jewish peril". In fact, there was public outrage. On his first day out with his yellow star, Jacques Biélinsky found no hostile looks; indeed, the reverse, for a shopkeeper gave a friend's wife two cheeses, "to show her sympathy", and a Jewish girl who was frightened she would lose all her Christian friends found they all came round to her house, and wanted to go out with her "wearing her decoration".

Vichy was too nervous to impose the stars in Zone Nono, but the fear may have been misplaced. "Here we can still move around freely and we don't fear arrest…" a Jew commented in the south. "But as for the attitude of the French, one feels more at home in the Occupied Zone." This was partly because it had more non-local Jews, who had fled there from Zone O; but it may also have been because the measures were seen as French, made respectable by bearing the marshal's approval. The Marseille police intendant, Maurice Roidellec de Porzi, despised the Germans, but he supported the Vichy ideal of a nation sanitised from foreign influence, and he rounded up Jews with a will. Informers, head-hunters and criminal gangs kept up a flow of information. They were paid 1,000 francs per arrest, and what they could steal or extort from their victims; keeping the spoils of Aryanisation was an area where French sovereignty was closely guarded.

The arrests of 1941 gave way to the deportations of 1942; the Germans described them as *Abwanderung* (migration), in the same way that the hostages they shot were sanitised as *Sühnepersonen* (expiators). The first train was loaded at Drancy on March 27, 1942 by *gendarmes*, who accompanied it to Novéant on the Moselle, the new border town with the enlarged Reich; of the 1,112 people aboard, one escaped on the journey, and twenty returned alive after the war. The turning point came with the great *rafle*, or round-up of Jews, that began at dawn on 16 July, 1942. Opération Vent printanier (spring wind) had been delayed until the summer by its sheer scale. It involved 9,000 French police, under René Bousquet. They worked their way methodically through the streets, schools, apartments blocks and Métro stations of the capital. Over two days, 12,762 were arrested including almost 6,000 women and 4,115 children under 16. They were penned in filth and hunger in the Vél' d'Hiv', the city's covered bicycle-racing track. Scenes of horror were imprinted on the public mind: a hundred or more suicides; a policeman carrying a suitcase in each hand, followed by a little group of children and old people, tears pouring down his face; and "the sort of screams you hear in hospital delivery rooms". It was followed by a further round-up in the Gironde, where the Vichy official responsible was Maurice Papon, a post-war police prefect and Gaullist minister.

All the prefects' reports mentioned public reaction, almost invariably of outrage. The long Catholic silence was broken on August 23. Cardinal Saliège, the partially paralysed archbishop of Toulouse, spoke in his pastoral letter of the outrage that "women, men, fathers and mothers, should be treated like a vile herd". He told of families being separated and sent to unknown destinations. "You cannot do whatever you like to these men, these women," he said. "They are part of humanity. They are our brothers." The prefect of the Haute-Garonne banned the letter, but most parish priests flouted him and read it to their congregations.

The horrors that awaited those arrested are beyond imagining. The majority were taken to Drancy, and from there they were put into locked wagons on freight trains that steamed for three days eastwards, across Germany and two-thirds of southern Poland to Auschwitz. George Weller, who was deported from Drancy in 1944, could not grasp its evil even when he arrived there. A spur track ran into the camp. At the ramp, an instant selection was made between the fit, who were worked to death, and the unfit, who were at once gassed. "One had to be mad to believe it," Weller said.

The children in Drancy invented a make-believe name for their unknown destination. They called it Pitchipoi. That so many children were consigned there was in part the personal handiwork of Pierre Laval, who had returned as "head of government" in April 1942.

No one liked Laval. Hitler loathed him. Laval was scruffy and chain-smoked, both pet hates of the Führer. Laval did not mind that he was despised. "I am like a duvet," he said of himself. "I can take blows." Perhaps he enjoyed it, so long as he was noticed, a power in the land, indispensable. He had a slick lawyer's tongue, and a market trader's ability to close a deal; he prided himself on knowing his *métier*, and being able to work in the tightest corner. His apologia, as he awaited trial in 1945, was brief and to the point. He was accused, he said, of "lacking idealism". This was because he believed – "and I still do" – that politics must be based on realities, above all in the foreign field. "Regimes follow one another and revolutions take place," he said, "but geography remains unchanged. We will be neighbours of Germany for ever." A simple realist, then, in difficult times.

He prided himself on his ability to do the dirty work, to cut any deal in the interests of the people. "It is always I who must repair the damage," he sighed. "I must remain so that France is not handed to a Gauleiter." But he was nastier than he thought, or perhaps intended to be. He misjudged himself. He looked at his lack of scruples as freedom from illusion, his cynicism as ultra-realism, the absence of compassion as unsentimentality. He thought he could outfox the Germans, but he could not; and in his cunning, he found himself doing terrible things. It was he, not the Germans, who proposed that the deportations should include children under 16; to keep families together, it was claimed, but in reality to get parentless children off the regime's hands. He traded German and foreign Jews to save French Jews; he allowed French police to make arrests to keep the Germans out.

A much higher proportion of Jews did survive in France than in the neighbouring Low Countries. Of a total of some 320,000 Jews, about half of them foreign-born, rather less than a quarter perished in the death camps. A further 4,000 died in the squalor of French camps or were executed in France. Two-thirds of those who were foreign-born died. In Holland, under a German military government, 110,000 or almost four-fifths of Jews were deported and died. In Belgium, also German-governed, the dead were 40 per cent of the total.

The French survival rate seems to support the Vichy plea of the *double jeu*. It was kind to be cruel: for every Jew arrested by French authorities, the Germans would have seized two or three. This glosses over the moral issue, of course; and the insistent question of why Vichy felt itself compelled to do the Nazis' murderous work for them is thrown into the sharpest focus by the experience in the south-east. French Jews made their way here in such numbers that Cannes became known as Kahn; and in this Italian-occupied zone, they were safe. Only after the Italians had gone did black Citroëns begin cruising the streets, looking for victims to send to Drancy; and, though the Germans hoped for a haul of 25,000, they found only 1,800. In Italy itself, the Germans were unable to deport more than 16 per cent of Jews, due to Italian non-cooperation. Admiral Horthy's Hungary, despite anti-Jewish legislation going back to the 1920s, refused to hand over Jews until the Germans occupied the country in March 1944.

The Germans did not have enough personnel – the Gestapo had four men and one officer in Saint-Étienne in mid-1942 – or local knowledge to have arrested the numbers involved. They were dependent on French police, camp guards, administrators, informers. Berlin turned down constant appeals to send more French-speaking Gestapo men. Had the French not collaborated, the Germans might have deployed their own people in sufficient strength to attain a similar or worse result. As it was, thanks to the armistice, they found Vichy eager and willing.

Individuals across France helped Jews, however, often at the risk of their lives. A camp guard at Drancy, Camille Matthieu, helped a Jewish tailor to escape, and hid him and his family at his mother's house in the Aude; André Trocmé, the pastor of the isolated Protestant village of Le Chambon-sur-Lignon in the Haute-Loire, hid hundreds of Jews among his flock, some for days, some for months; nuns hid women and children in their convents; policemen warned when arrests were imminent. In the Marseilles region itself, Antoine Zattara at the prefecture helped many escape before being deported himself, and Madame Rodrigues, an official in the Cassis town hall, helped Jews get false papers and refuge.

Marcel Ophüls' film *Le Chagrin et la Pitié*, screened for the first time in 1972, began a vogue for the bleakest and most strident accusations of guilt to be raised against French society as a whole. Stanley Hoffman, who was a 15-year-old when German troops occupied Nice in 1943, found the film too severe: for him, one man had wiped out "all the bad moments, and the humiliations, and the terrors". His history teacher, he said, had given him hope in the worst days, dried his tears when his best friend was deported, and provided forged papers so that he and his mother could flee the city and survive the rest of the Occupation in a tiny spa in Languedoc. The teacher was not a Resistance hero but, Hoffman wrote, "if there is an average Frenchman, it was this man".

By November 1943, Laval knew the game was up: the Germans would lose, and de Gaulle would return. "He is supported – and I have no illusions about this – by 80 or 90 per cent of the French people," he said. "And I shall be hung." The first unmistakable warning had come on November 8, 1942, when the Allies landed in Algeria and Morocco. President Roosevelt sent Pétain a message breaking off diplomatic relations with the United States. The Germans flew men and equipment into Tunisia the following day. Coats now began turning in earnest. Admiral Darlan was in Algeria – by chance, visiting his son in hospital – when the invasion began. He quickly realised which way the wind was blowing, and ordered French troops in Algiers to observe a ceasefire. Laval drove through sleet and snow to Munich to see Hitler on November 10. The Führer kept him waiting for several hours, and dismissed him once it was clear that Vichy had lost control in North Africa. At 7 a.m. the next morning, 24 years to the day since the end of the First World War, German troops crossed the demarcation line. The whole of France was occupied. A fortnight later, Hitler ordered the Armistice Army, the 100,000-man figleaf, to be disbanded. There was no resistance from Vichy, but from now on it grew rapidly in the country at large.

The trigger was often a personal "resistance moment". For Edmond Michelet, a teacher in Brive-la-Gaillarde, it came with reading a line of Charles Péguy: "In wartime whoever does not surrender is my man, whoever he is, wherever he comes from, and whatever his party." For André Maurice, a poacher and smuggler in the Jura who helped get Jews to Switzerland, it was an instinct. "The urge was stronger than I was," he said. "It gripped me like the wish to catch a pike or trap a hare. Time and again, just to irritate the Germans." Yves Farge was on a tram in Lyon, which stopped to let a German column pass, and a fellow-passenger chilled him by accepting it: "At last the French have to learn what order really is."

Communists had double reason to resist. The party was eager for martyrs to expiate the Nazi-Soviet Nonagression Pact – "26,000 resistants were killed by the Germans," Jean Galtier-Boissière said when it was over, "of whom 75,000 were Communists" – and its members were convinced that action in France relieved the pressure on the distant Red Army. Some groups supported de Gaulle; others, like the young Vichy official François Mitterrand, initially backed Henri Giraud, the rival general whom de Gaulle outmanoueuvred as leader of French overseas forces.

One of the earliest groups was founded in Lyon by a liberal Catholic, the law professor François de Menthon, and joined by Communists, left-wing Catholics, Christian Democrat university dons and former Action Française men. De Menthon edited the first edition of the underground newspaper *Liberté* at his family château near Annecy. Emmanuel d'Astier de la Vigerie was a jobbing journalist and opium addict before the war, the despair of his aristocratic family, before ruthlessly devoting himself to his Libération-Sud movement. Libération-Nord was based on Socialist and Catholic trade unions. The risks were always great, but much of the work was humdrum. The first resisters had no weapons or explosives, no training in sabotage, and, since they as yet had no contacts with London, no prospects of any parachute drops. They had to fashion a concept of resistance itself, and here the printed word was master. Killing Germans was, at first, a Communist speciality that many thought a repellent and belated apology for the Nazi-Soviet Pact. A young naval lieutenant, Alphonse Moser, an unarmed pen-pusher, was shot dead on August 21, 1941 as he boarded a Métro train in Montmartre. His killer was a young Communist, as were those sent from Paris to kill the Feldkommandant in Nantes and another officer in Bordeaux. Ninety-seven hostages were executed in reprisal.

De Gaulle appealed for the killings to stop, but the Communists continued, and paid the price; most of the 88 hostages shot after a grenade attack on Luftwaffe airmen in a Paris sports stadium were Communist. The party sensed the psychological gains to be made from its martyrs, and the pathos of their last letters. Louis Aragon fashioned an intense poem from the exquisite phrase of hope in the future used by the former Communist deputy Gabriel Péri as he awaited the firing squad: "les lendemains qui chantent . . ."

De Gaulle wanted gradually to build up the armed strength of a united resistance. By playing an active military role when the time for the invasion came, it would prevent the general's greatest nightmare: France liberated from top to bottom by the Anglo-Saxons. A second horror lurked behind that: AMGOT, an Allied Military Government of the type installed by the Americans and British in other liberated territories. To the prevention of this, and to the preservation of the grandeur of France, he devoted himself body and soul. He took the least slights as an attack upon the nation. Some were real, if understandable. The British kept sensitive information from him; they believed his entourage had leaked plans for the disastrous attempt to win Dakar for the Free French in November 1940, and German documents later confirmed leaks among his staff in Algiers. Many were imagined. As General Spears's shrewd and sympathetic wife observed, he was like "a man who has been skinned alive", and the slightest contact with friendly and well-meaning people "got him on the raw to such an extent that he wanted to bite".

It was vital, of course, that he be seen to bite the British hand that fed him. Vichy propaganda painted him as a stooge, as London's traitor-vassal. He needed to make his independence clear. But his loftiness was within a whisker of arrogance – a superior officer had warned of "his contempt for other people's point of view and his attitude of a king in exile" back in 1924 – and his mistrust and loathing of the English-speaking world approached the pathological. He manufactured a new monster-myth, the "Anglo-Saxon domination of Europe". In June 1943, he told Jean Monnet that it was already a "growing threat", and that if it continued after the war, France "will have to turn to Germany or Russia". Within Gaullist hagiography, this is proof of his remarkable prescience; certainly, almost the whole of French foreign policy in the 1960s is contained in that sentence, but his Anglophobia drove his staff to distraction. "The General must constantly be reminded that our number one enemy is Germany," Pierre Brossolette complained. "If he followed his natural inclination, it would rather be the British."

It was fortunate indeed that Churchill was a Francophile who, though he complained that "the greatest cross I have to bear is the cross of Lorraine", responded to de Gaulle's sense of history and forgave his surly outbursts on the grounds that he had to be rude to prove "to French eyes he was not a puppet". Not everyone forgave him, though, and his irritation of Roosevelt was grotesque. It gained him nothing, for no one in France was aware of it, and it jeopardised much.

De Gaulle made Jean Moulin, who had slipped out of France to join the Free French, in effect his ambassador to the Resistance. In two long and dangerous missions, Moulin succeeded in linking resistance groups, to one another, and to London. He first had the three main groups in the south, Combat, Libération and the Communist FTP (Francs-Tireurs et Partisans) work together under the aegis of de Gaulle as the Mouvement Uni de la Résistance (MUR). Its military wing was the Armée Secrète. At the end of May 1943, Moulin presided over the first meeting in Paris of the new umbrella organisation in the north, the Conseil National de la Résistance (CNR). It included political parties, unions and local groups. It, too, acknowledged de Gaulle. Moulin was captured by the Lyon Gestapo chief, Klaus Barbie, at a villa in Caluire on June 21. He died after prolonged torture. It has never been proved who betrayed him.

Unification continued after Moulin's death. In February 1944, the Forces Françaises de l'Intérieur, the FFI or *fifis*, embraced both the *résistants* in France and the Free French units fighting with the Allies outside it. Numbers multiplied as the *attentistes* who had waited to see who would win came off the fence. Changing sides could be dangerous. Darlan was assassinated after throwing his lot in with the Allies in North Africa. Pierre Pucheu, the ex-industrialist and Vichy interior minister, decided he had backed the wrong horse after the Allied landings in North Africa. He slipped over the border to Spain and arrived in Casablanca in May 1943 after being promised safe conduct. He volunteered to enlist in the Chasseurs d'Afrique, but was arrested for treason, tried and sentenced to death. De Gaulle, under Resistance pressure, did not commute the sentence.

The best recruiting sergeant for the young was forced labour. Fritz Sauckel, the man appointed by Hitler to exploit foreign labour for the factories of the Reich, knew French labour was the most highly skilled in all the occupied territories and wanted as much of it as he could get. Laval thought he could cut a deal with him: the *relève*, or relief shift, where French POWs would be liberated in return for workers. But he achieved a rate of only one POW for every three workers, and Resistance newspapers warned of 12-hour days, Allied bombings and foul conditions.

A few came forward – immigrants, labourers from the jobless Var and the Aude – but not enough. Sauckel was insatiable. On February 16, 1943, Laval was forced to bring in the Service du Travail Obligatoire, drafting 20- to 22-year-olds to the Reich for two years. Miners and farm workers were exempt. The age range was soon 18 to 60; farm workers lost their exemption, and childless women from 18 to 45 were also drafted. Women and men over 45 could do their labour in France, building the Atlantic Wall defences against Allied landings.

Draft-dodging was immediate and on a massive scale. Sauckel's men resorted to *shanghaillage*, pouncing on villages, cinemas and railway stations to seize people. Thousands joined the deserters, escaped PoWs, refugees and others living with false papers. Vichy called them *réfractaires*. They called themselves *maquisards*, from the Corsican word for thickets and scrubland, for many of them took to the hills and joined Resistance groups. A recruiting pamphlet urged them to bring camping equipment – canteen, knife and fork, torch, compass, sleeping bag, extra blanket, spare buttons, needles, thread – and warned them that they would live badly and dangerously, cut off from their families, and be liable to torture if captured. They named themselves after animals or the leaders of their bands – Maquis Puma, Maquis le Doc – and they lived off their wits. They robbed banks, post offices, factories and railway stations, and town halls for papers and ration cards.

Vichy hunted them down with the *milice*, led by a war hero. Three Frenchmen had been hailed as "artisans of final victory" in 1918: Clemenceau, Marshal Foch, and a 22-year-old sergeant called Joseph Darnand. He had penetrated behind German lines, bringing back 27 prisoners who alerted the French to the offensive that Ludendorff was about to unleash. It was said to be the turning point of the war, but it was not enough to earn him a commission.

Embittered, he ran a garage in Nice and dabbled in far-right politics before rejoining the army and fighting bravely in 1940. After the defeat, he ran the Nice office of the veterans' Legion, and fretted. Many of his sort joined the *maquis*, but he felt bound to Pétain. "What is this Resistance shit?" he asked. "Shepherds to whom the archangel appeared?" Darnand set up the *milice*, with Pétain's blessing. It had its own uniform of khaki shirt, blue trousers, black tie and black beret, and recruits swore a 21-point oath, vowing to defend Christian civilisation against, inter alia, democracy, individualism, international capitalism, Bolsheviks, masons and "Jewish leprosy". It had a membership of some 30,000, with anti-Communists and fanatic Catholics bolstered by large numbers of thugs, petty criminals and youths avoiding forced labour.

Suspicious of French paramilitaries, the Germans denied them arms, and the *milice* stuffed their holsters with paper. Darnand was frustrated enough to put out feelers to the Free French, but in August 1943 he swore a personal oath of loyalty to Hitler. He was rewarded with the rank of *Sturmbannführer* in the Waffen-SS, and with money and arms for his men.

The Germans also used the gangs from the purchasing offices to hunt *résistants* in the cities. Henri Lafont's was the most notorious, drawn from Fresnes prison. Lafont was a former pimp, his good looks spoiled by a falsetto voice. To interrogate women, he recruited a pair of lesbians, Sonia Boukassi, a drug addict, and the one-time French weightlifting champion, Violette Morris. The SS chief Oberg despised Lafont as a common criminal, but made him a *Hauptsturmführer* in the SS, and allowed him to go about in SS uniform. The Berger group, a similar gang, trapped 35 young *résistants* by pretending to supply them with arms. It then shot them all by the fountains in the Bois de Boulogne.

Maquis and *milice* became entwined in a civil war within the war. This greatly reduced the impact of the Resistance, as much of its energy was dissipated in fighting fellow Frenchmen. It was a nasty conflict. The *milice* who did not desert became ever more desperate, as their families received drawings of coffins in the post, to remind them of what awaited them when the Germans lost. In military terms, though, the Resistance was a fleabite to the Germans. The number of active *maquisards* in the spring of 1944 was perhaps no more than 30,000. Their achievements seemed impressive, with large areas of the south in their hands. It was a measure of their courage, however, that the Germans could crush them more or less at will. In the Haute-Savoie, a famous centre of resistance, 153 Germans and Italians were killed during the Occupation. Elsewhere the figure was no more than a few hundred. When *résistants* fought the Germans in large units, they were routed. An armed force of 500 men, mixing Gaullists, Communists and Spanish republicans, dug in on the Plateau de Glières near Annecy in March 1944. There was propaganda to be made from their stand – the BBC said that three countries in Europe were resisting, "Greece, Yugoslavia and the Haute-Savoie" – and a sense of national honour restored. Militarily, however, they were a minor irritant for the German 157th Alpine Division, which swept through them in two days. Some 150 *maquisards* were lost in the retreat, and the *milice* killed a further 200, with civilians, over the next few weeks.

In the cities, Gestapo men in black Citroëns and green fedoras cruised the streets with coerced *résistants* who pointed out familiar faces. People vanished. Under the *Nacht und Nebel* (night and fog) decrees, Hitler ordered sabotage suspects to be taken to the Reich, there to disappear into the concentration camps. A friend would phone, but it rang in an empty flat; the concierge would force the door, and there would be the butts of German cigarettes on the floor; if anyone had seen what happened, Sartre wrote, they would say the person had been taken away by "very polite Germans".

None of the 58 German divisions awaiting the Allied landings was diverted to deal with the *maquis* before D-Day. But this proves only that lightly armed guerrillas pose little threat to experienced troops with heavy weapons, armour and air support. The half million Soviet partisans fighting behind German lines had little effect on the outcome. In Italy, a force of 6,000 partisans who set up a "free republic" north of Lake Maggiore in October 1944 were defeated by half that number of Germans in two days. The British parachute drops of arms were important to de Gaulle, since they tied the *résistants* to him, but they were meagre nonetheless. The Allies dropped 16,470 tons to the Yugoslav partisans. France got 2,878 tons. The 4,000 *résistants* in Lyon had 150 weapons. Worse, they had almost no anti-tank weapons to cope with armour, and no mortars to answer artillery fire.

The *résistants* did, however, put what explosives they had to good account. Allied bombing raids were often ineffectual and caused heavy casualties. Ground-level sabotage was much more accurate. Elaborate preparations – Plan Vert for the railways, Bleu for electricity, Violet for telephones and telegrams – were made for large-scale sabotage. Shortage of explosives meant that the full potential was not exploited. Intelligence, on the defences of the Atlantic Wall, on rocket sites in the Pas-de-Calais, on troop deployments, was another matter. Transmitted over parachuted radio sets, it was of real value to the Allies. So was sabotage once the landings were under way.

But the Resistance was about more than killing Germans. Being killed was vital, too. Those hard deaths, alone in a torture chamber, in a group in front of a firing squad, restored national honour. "We never quite knew if we were doing right or doing wrong," Sartre said of Vichy. "A subtle poison corrupted even our best actions." But even in these deeply equivocal circumstances, the spirit of France could still be regenerated.

10

Liberation
and Beyond

French troops had a limited effect. Many of the forces outside France were scattered on garrison duties across the empire. The 120,000 Frenchmen fighting in Italy in the early summer of 1944 became a vital component of Operation Anvil, the landings in southern France that followed D-Day. But the hard slog of the Liberation took place in the north. Only one of the 39 divisions assigned to Normandy, General Leclerc's renowned 2nd Armoured Division, was French. It did not land until August 1, after the break-out from the bridgehead, and eight weeks after D-Day.

These realities, however, de Gaulle was at pains to conceal. He wished it to seem that the nation had liberated itself. He was driven, in his own words, by "a certain idea of France". France alone warmed and animated this cold and awkward man, so tall and oddly shaped, with "a pineapple head and a woman's hips" a British observer thought.

His constant and overriding concern was to preserve French grandeur and status as a first-rate power. This was threatened, in his eyes, not by the Germans, but by the Anglo-Saxons who were beating them. He feared that they would impose a military government during the Liberation. Special currency had been printed. For months, Americans had been on training courses preparing to administer France. De Gaulle warned of the "disaster" that would follow the imposition of military government, AMGOT, against the will of the people.

To pre-empt it, the National Liberation Council over which he presided in Algiers proclaimed itself formally as the provisional government of the French Republic. The general and his staff then flew to England. They arrived on June 4, to discover that the Allies were in Rome and the invasion of France was at hand. He flew into a towering rage when he discovered that General Eisenhower's D-Day proclamation made no mention of himself or the provisional government, but asked the French to execute Eisenhower's own orders, as supreme Allied commander. He thought of himself as France – when Churchill told him "you are not France" during one famous row, he retorted "why are you discussing this with me if I am not France . . ." – and he was sensitive to any slight. A sympathetic official in London, Alexander Cadogan, wearily observed that, though the Allies might cause the initial offence, "then de Gaulle puts himself *more* in the wrong". This time, he so excelled himself that Cadogan felt that "he deserves to lose". The general refused to broadcast on the BBC, or to provide Free French liaison officers to go with the first waves of Allied troops.

This he did on the eve of the greatest seaborne invasion in history, whose perils were made more desperate by poor weather, and whose purpose was the liberation of his country. Churchill found it treason to the cause, and threatened to have de Gaulle sent back to Algiers "in chains". The general's admirers, himself prominent among them, justified it as raison d'état. The humiliations of Vichy could only be soothed by the balm of perceived self-liberation. France must be seen to restore herself.

These were the aims. The method was brute argument. He thought it the only way to win. "With the English", he observed, "one must bang on the table and they will submit." In his memoirs, he recalled his response when Anthony Eden told him he had caused more difficulties than all Britain's other allies combined. "I don't doubt it," he replied. "France is a great power." It was a dangerous game, but he played it with brilliance, and he won. There was to be no AMGOT. Liberated France ruled herself from the outset, seamlessly, with no American interregnum. She emerged, too, as one of the "Big Four" powers, sitting with the British and the new Soviet and American superpowers.

After hours of "pandemonium", aides managed to calm Churchill and persuaded de Gaulle to send a token 20 liaison officers. He made a broadcast, too, though at 5.30 p.m. on June 6, eight hours after Eisenhower. "The supreme battle is engaged," he said. "It is France's battle and it is the battle for France ... It is a battle the French will fight with fury." He ordered the people to obey the orders of the "French government". He knew that no French units had taken part in the landings. But he made no mention of the young Americans, British and Canadians, nine thousand of them, who already lay dead or wounded on the beaches as he spoke. His silence diminished him, and in as far as he was France, it diminished France, too.

The general did not set foot in Normandy until July 14. He was allowed ashore in the British sector for only a few hours. Once ashore, he told two confused *gendarmes* on bicycles who he was, and asked them to precede him into Bayeux and announce his arrival. They pedalled off into the town. He claimed that a "sort of stupor" seized the inhabitants when they saw him. He produced tears, cheers and "extraordinary emotion", as, for the first time in four years, "the crowd heard a French leader [*un chef français*] say in front of them that the enemy is the enemy." There were plenty of people on the place du Château in Bayeux, because the Allies were distributing food. None of them recognised him, for no photographs of him had appeared in the Vichy press. The first civilians muddled him up with General Béthouart, who was with him, and who had five stars on his *képi* to de Gaulle's two. But, however brief, the visit was a model. It placed de Gaulle in Normandy, the main theatre of the Liberation. And he took with him in his little party a *commissaire-général*, to install as administrator in Bayeux. Already, he was forestalling AMGOT.

This was a most dangerous time. Jean Zay, freemason, Jew and former Popular Front cabinet minister, an amalgam of Vichy hatreds, was taken from his prison cell by members of the *milice* masquerading as *résistants* on June 10. They told him they were rescuing him before shooting him in a spot so lonely that it was two years before his body was found. In a reverse bluff, on June 28, *résistants* posing as members of the *milice* tricked their way into the apartment of Philippe Henriot, the most brilliant of Vichy broadcasters. They shot him in front of his wife. His funeral in Notre-Dame was the last great ceremony of Vichy. It was said that 400,000 filed past his coffin in the Hôtel de Ville as he lay in state. He was given a state funeral in

Notre-Dame, conducted by Monsignor Suchard, the cardinal-archbishop of Paris. To avenge him, a band of *milice* took Georges Mandel from the Santé prison in Paris to the forest of Fontainebleau and shot him. The streets named in honour of Henriot reverted to their old titles soon enough. The avenue Georges Mandel remains an elegant reminder in the heart of Paris of the man whose courage Churchill so much admired.

The *maquis* could be as brutal as the *milice*. They were not content to murder the *milice* chief at Voiron, near Grenoble. They killed his wife, too, and his ten-year-old son, infant daughter and elderly mother. A communal grave was found in May in the hills above Saint-Laurent in the Haute-Savoie. It held the bodies of eight police officials the *maquis* had kidnapped from Bonneville. Henriot, with typical exaggeration, had called it the "French Katyn" in his radio broadcasts and blamed it on the Communists.

Resistance came into its own with railway sabotage. A German infantry division, ordered to move from Redon in Brittany to the front on June 6, a 320-kilometre rail journey that should have taken a day or so, arrived on foot on June 11. Another division took 22 days to move to Normandy from Bayonne. It was expected that it would take 90 days to get as far north as Grenoble after the southern landings near Cannes and Saint-Tropez. A French armoured car regiment, supplied with intelligence and open roads by *résistants*, roared along the old Route Napoléon through Grasse, Digne and Gap to reach the outskirts of Grenoble in less than a week. The Durance valley was effectively liberated by the Resistance; so were towns like Quimper, Nantes and Saint-Brieuc.

The Gaullists, leery of a national uprising that might be crushed or used as a launching pad for a Communist takeover, warned against mass uprisings and attempts to create large-scale *maquis* fortresses. The Isère *maquis* ignored this, and a grisly repetition of the slaughter on the Glières plateau unfolded. Eugène Chavant, the local FFI leader, summoned his men to the plateau of Vercors southwest of Grenoble as soon as he heard of the Normandy landings. Three thousand had assembled by June 9. A huge air-drop by 360 American Flying Fortresses was made on Bastille Day. No heavy weapons were among them, however, and no French troops were dropped. The Allied landings in the south were postponed until August 15. The Germans were free to attack. They did so with the same Alpine division as at Glières, supported by SS glider troops and Panzers from Lyon, and the result was the same: 650 *maquisards* were killed, some as they lay in a field hospital, together with 200 local villagers and doctors tending the wounded.

Where *résistants* prematurely took a town they were not strong enough to hold, or harassed retreating Germans, a terrible price might also be exacted. After a *maquis* band shot at a German column at Maillé in the Loire on an August evening, the German rearguard massacred everyone they found in the village, set it alight, and shelled it as they withdrew. Among the ruined fragments of the houses, 126 bodies were found, including mothers and nursing babies. One man lost his wife and all seven children.

Communists with the FTP temporarily expelled the German garrison at Tulle in the Corrèze on June 7 and 8. They killed more than 40, and executed ten prisoners. The town was retaken by men from Das Reich, who hanged 99 men from trees, balconies and telegraph poles. A further 150 were deported to German concentration camps. A 120-man company from Das Reich arrived in Oradour-sur-Glane, a quiet village near Limoges, in the early afternoon of June 10. By midnight, they had killed every living soul they found. The men were herded into barns and shot, and the women and children were collected into the church, which was then burnt to the ground.

It was the end of July before the Allies broke out of Normandy to the west, and mid-August before the Germans were trapped when the Falaise gap in the east was closed. It was one of the greatest battles of history. The British and Americans destroyed 27 out of 48 German infantry divisions, and 11 out of 12 Panzer divisions, together with 2,200 German tanks. A quarter of a million Germans were killed or wounded in Normandy, and a further 200,000 were taken prisoner. Allied casualties were 210,000, with 40,000 dead. Many towns, such as Lisieux, Coutances, Saint-Lô, Falaise, Caen and Le Havre were 90 per cent destroyed. In their ruins, and in other Allied bombardments, 50,000 civilians died or were wounded.

On August 13, Parisians heard the sound of shellfire coming from the west. A spontaneous, rolling uprising began, slowly gathering pace. It was led by "Colonel Rol", Henri Tanguy, a Communist veteran of the Spanish Civil War. Alarmingly, he said that "Paris is worth 200,000 dead." Hitler was equally keen to see the city destroyed. From his Wolf's Lair in East Prussia, he asked General Dietrich von Choltitz, the German commander in the city: "Is Paris burning?" Trucks with powerful naval torpedoes crossed the city as demolition charges were prepared for major monuments and landmarks. A Luftwaffe general offered to shuttle bomb the city at night with aircraft based at Le Bourget. Hitler spoke of switching V1 rockets from their targets in London to deluge Paris with warheads. A giant 600 mm mortar, "Karl", was despatched from the Reich.

Paris had at most 15,000 *résistants* in mid-August, Chaban-Delmas thought, but the number began to swell mightily. Those who jumped aboard the bandwagon and put on FFI armbands were known as RMAs in Paris, *résistants du mois d'août,* and as *Septembristes* in places where liberation was delayed; officers and men who reappeared in their old 1940 uniforms were called *naphtalinards*, for the smell of mothballs that clung to them.

The Paris police came out on strike on August 19. They were still armed, and they took over the Préfecture de Police on the Île de la Cité. Here they hoisted the *tricolore*. A great exodus – "la grande fuite des Fritz" – now began. *Miliciens* in Paris massed at the Lycée Saint-Louis and drove off to the east in a convoy of trucks. The "grey mice", the German women auxiliaries, were followed by the security forces, and all but the bare bones of the garrison.

De Gaulle returned to France on August 20, the day that the resistance took the Hôtel de Ville in Paris and arrested the Vichy prefect. The general landed at Cherbourg, and made his way through Rennes to Rambouillet, the country seat of French presidents. The stakes were unbearably high – Paris might be destroyed, like Warsaw; France might be plunged into leftist revolution and civil war, a reprise of 1871; such chaos might be let loose that the Americans would impose AMGOT – and he calmed his nerves in the library of the château with a copy of Molière's *Le Bourgeois Gentilhomme.*

The 2nd Armoured Division was at hand. It had 15,000 men, equipped with American uniforms, tanks and half tracks. It was commanded by General Leclerc, the *nom de guerre* of Jacques-Philippe Hautecloque. He was a viscount, born into the northern aristocracy. His father, a landowner and a regular officer, had sent him to the school where de Gaulle's humbler parent had been headmaster. He took the name Leclerc to protect his wife and six children when, after escaping in 1940, he rallied to de Gaulle in London. He was sent to Fort Lamy in Chad, where the garrison came out for de Gaulle. Its troops were mainly Senegalese, formidable fighters, with tough and adventurous officers. In 1941, after a desert trek, he fell upon the Italian garrison at the Kufra oasis in Libya. Leclerc then joined the Anglo-American armies in Tunisia.

The 2nd Armoured Division was raised to fulfil the promise de Gaulle had extracted from General Eisenhower, made in 1943, that a French unit would liberate Paris. It had a core of men who had been with Leclerc since Chad. To these he added an astonishing mix of shipless sailors, converted into an anti-tank regiment, Senegalese, and *pied noir* settlers from Algeria. Christian Arabs from Lebanon served as engineers, and the 9th infantry company was known as "la nueve" in honour of the Spanish Republicans who filled its ranks. It was under General Patton's overall command. The division was a rich brew of Gaullists, communists, monarchists, Socialists, Giraudists and even anarchists. Leclerc himself was a soldier of the highest quality, brave, selfless, compassionate and strong, and his "Deuxième DB" reflected his own virtues.

The Allies now half-encircled Paris from the west, with Patton's army up to the Seine both upstream and downstream, and only 40 miles distant. Eisenhower had planned to bypass the city, and leave the German garrison to wither on the vine. The uprising meant it could no longer be ignored. A stroke of fortune now rewarded de Gaulle's persistence. Roger Gallois, the FFI chief of staff in Paris, slipped out of the city on August 22 and made his way to General Patton's headquarters. He convinced Patton's intelligence staff that a truce, which had been briefly brokered by the Swedish consul between Choltitz and the *résistants*, was still in force, but would end the next day. Choltitz then planned to crush the uprising, but would withdraw if the Allied armies approached. It was thus vital to have regular troops in the city as early as possible.

In fact, the truce had already broken down. Choltitz had 17,000 men, 100 Tiger and Panther tanks, and large stocks of explosives. Had he wished to destroy the city, as he had before retreating from Sebastapol on the Soviet front, he could have done so. But Gallois's misinformation was passed on to Eisenhower, and the FFI appeal bore fruit. Eisenhower, reluctantly, but with great diplomacy, ordered General Bradley, the US commander, to authorise the 2nd Armoured to advance. On the afternoon of August 22, Leclerc rushed from a meeting with Bradley, the US commander, and shouted to his operations officer: "Mouvement immédiat sur Paris!" As the division rolled past Rambouillet the next day, de Gaulle urged Leclerc to be fast: "We cannot have another Commune."

It took 40 hours. On the evening of Thursday, August 24, three tanks of the 1st Chad Infantry Regiment nosed into the city and made for the Hôtel de Ville. The bulk of the division arrived the next morning. It was met in the still dangerous streets with an explosion of joy, kisses, flowers and wine. By the grim standards of the time, Paris escaped almost unharmed. Choltitz made a show of resistance. Fighting was heavy in the Luxembourg Gardens and round Les Invalides. German snipers in the Tuileries Gardens had many victims. The 901 *fifis* who were killed, and the 582 dead civilians, were evidence enough that Parisians sacrificed themselves to free their city. But Choltitz's heart was not in it. He ate lunch at the Meurice on August 25, told his orderly to pack a case for a stay in a PoW camp, and prepared to surrender. He then went to the Préfecture de Police to sign the surrender document that Leclerc gave him. Leclerc signed it as the representative of de Gaulle's provisional government of France. No mention was made of the Americans or the British; there would have been none of the Paris FFI, and the Communist leadership of the uprising, had Colonel Rol not arrived uninvited at the meeting, and insisted on adding his signature.

De Gaulle arrived in Paris on August 25. He walked to the Hôtel de Ville, clearly the man in charge, his speed outwitting the Anglo-Americans, and indeed Colonel Rol's Communists. "War, unity, grandeur," he told his entourage. "That is my programme." Then he stepped onto a balcony, and made a speech to the crowds below. It was brief, brilliant and intense. "Paris violated!" he cried. "Paris broken! Paris martyred! But Paris liberated! Liberated by its own efforts, liberated by its people with the help of the armies of France, with the help of the whole of France, of fighting France, of the one and true France, of eternal France!" Carefully tucked away, he made a single reference to the "help of our dear and admirable Allies".

This was myth-making on a heroic scale. He repeated it the next day. He placed a wreath of gladioli at the Tomb of the Unknown Soldier at the Étoile. He then walked down the Champs-Élysées. The Americans of the US 4th Division in the city were not to be seen; the streets were lined by Leclerc's men alone, although the Allied high command had ordered them to rejoin the advance on Germany. De Gaulle dismissed their protests. "I loaned you Leclerc," he declared. "I can perfectly well borrow him back for a few moments."

His progress towards the place de la Concorde was grand and risky. At Concorde, shots rang out. The crowd went to ground. The general walked on. The entourage reached Notre-Dame for a Te Deum in the late afternoon. Shots were fired again. The huge congregation suddenly fell flat on their faces. A young British intelligence officer, the writer Malcolm Muggeridge, observed an exception.

"One solitary figure, like a lonely giant," Muggeridge wrote. "It was, of course, de Gaulle. Thenceforth, that was how I always saw him – towering, and alone, and the rest prostrate." By his political insight, the charisma of his "mysterious and angular character", his sureness of himself and his destiny, "he was the government and was accepted as that". During these days, he saved France from carnage between rival factions, perhaps from civil war.

Paris enjoyed its moment. Ernest Hemingway came back to liberate the Ritz, ordering 50 martini cocktails for his entourage, sparking off a brief period of *Ritzkrieg*. His fellow war correspondents made their headquarters at the Hôtel Scribe by the Opéra. "An American enclave in the heart of Paris," Simone de Beauvoir wrote peevishly, "white bread, fresh eggs, jam, sugar and spam." The Jockey Club offered membership to senior American and British officers. Coco Chanel presented them with bottles of her No 5 perfume, though, as we shall see, she had an ulterior motive; the Tour d'Argent gave them pressed duck. The restaurant Lucas Carton unblocked the cellars where it had hidden its wines, and fine vintages flowed.

In the New Year the Americans and French lost their mutual novelty. GIs, tiring of the children who swarmed round them begging for candy, took to chalking "NO GUM CHUM" on their tailboards. The French resented their wealth, their chocolate bars, coffee, peanut butter, tobacco, their fountains of whiskey and petrol, their officers' clubs and bars, the way their films, music, dances and clothes fascinated the young. It was a time of disillusion, too, for the Resistance. It was among the first victims of the liberation, treated by de Gaulle with cool disdain. His priority was to reassert the authority of the state, stressing that it was "above all the manifestations" of the Resistance – and he pursued it with ferocious single-mindedness.

On August 27, he told the National Council of the Resistance, assembled with such care and courage by Jean Moulin, that it was now surplus to requirements. Its members were to pass into the government, or the Consultative Assembly, which was shipped from Algiers to Paris. Next day, he ordered the FFI to be dissolved: those who wanted to go on fighting must do so in the army. When he met *fifi* leaders, he commented icily on the numbers of self-styled colonels among them, and asked them pointedly what jobs they had in civilian life. "I have already witnessed human ingratitude in my life," one of them said, "but never on this scale."

He moved on to disband the patriotic militias at the end of October. These were largely Communist creations, with the potential to develop into a people's army. The Communists were furious, and paraded their militia through Paris on Armistice Day, claiming a turnout of 100,000. The two Communist ministers in the government, however, at air and health, did not resign. De Gaulle sweetened the pill by saying that he was prepared to amnesty Maurice Thorez, the Communist leader who had deserted from the army in 1939 and fled to Moscow, where he still languished. Thorez duly returned, after Stalin had made it clear to him that the party was to behave itself in France until the Reich was definitively beaten.

The time of the amateur guerrilla was over. De Gaulle needed regular troops, to fight their way into Germany with the Allied armies and thus justify France's seat among the Big Four. By November, 75,000 ex-*résistants* had joined up. Resistance groups in areas still occupied were beyond de Gaulle's writ, of course; German garrisons in pockets on the Atlantic coast were to hold out until the fall of Berlin.

Eighteen *commissaires* were to replace Vichy's regional "super-prefects", keeping law and order until central authority was restored. They were hand-picked moderates, drawn from lawyers, academics, civil servants and former parliamentarians. The administrative changeover was smoothest when it was simultaneous with liberation. Michel Debré, the new *commissaire* for Angers, arrived in the town on August 10, within hours of the arrival of the Americans and the German withdrawal. He was himself an example of how seamlessly a Pétainist could become a Gaullist. He was the able product of a *grande école* and the Saumur cavalry school, who had been a member of Vichy's Conseil d'État. When he entered the Resistance, Jean Moulin had chosen him to join the clandestine Comité Générale d'Études, which helped plan the post-Liberation political future. In Angers, he went straight to the office of Charles Donati, the Vichy regional prefect, who was fresh from bidding farewell to the German military commander. Debré told him that he was replacing him, at the behest of de Gaulle and the provisional government. The two men shook hands, and Debré settled himself behind Donati's imposing desk. "I had become the state," he said.

It was different in Toulouse. The city was a "souk for adventurers". It teemed with exotics, Russian deserters from units that had fought for the Nazis, Spanish Republicans, who mounted a futile raid on the Val d'Aran in Franco Spain, and anti-Communists of the *maquis blanc* who were loyal to the French royalist pretender. The new *commissaire*, Pierre Bertaux, a professor at Toulouse University, sat in a near empty prefecture whilst all but a few *naphtalinards* avoided him. Real power resided with two Resistance barons. Colonel Serge Ravenel, a *polytechnicien*, mountain climber and Communist, was a regional hero at 25. The senior officer in the south-west for SOE, the British special operations executive that supported and armed the Resistance, was Colonel George Starr, a tough British mining engineer.

Bertaux told de Gaulle when he arrived in the city how Starr would come to his office and offer to sort out any problems with his 700 armed men. The general, furious at the slur to French authority, asked why the Englishman had not been arrested. Bertaux admitted that, far from that, he had invited Starr to lunch. De Gaulle told him to cancel the invitation, then gave Ravenel such a dressing down – as a professional soldier, and a real general, addressing an amateur masquerading as a colonel – that the young man remembered it as one of the saddest moments of his life. "I discovered an immense abyss between this man who had lived all of the war outside France", he said, "and the metropolitan Resistance which had such a difficult time."

When he bumped into Starr later in the day, de Gaulle ordered him to leave Toulouse immediately. Starr, wearing his British uniform, refused. He was under the orders of Allied headquarters, he said, not of the provisional government. De Gaulle sensed a crisis point, shook Starr's hand, and backed down, later honouring the Englishman with a Croix de Guerre.

Resistance expectations were in part fuelled by de Gaulle himself – "France liberated by her own people, with the help of the armies of France" – in insisting that the nation was freeing itself. In reality, the military significance of the *résistants* was in inverse proportion to their moral impact. They made a minor contribution to an outcome decided in the meat grinder-battles of Normandy: the Allies would have won without them, if at greater cost. But that is why, in terms of pride and conscience, they were the salvation of the nation. All of them, including the much-mocked "RMAs" and *attentistes* who swelled the *fifi* ranks from 50,000 in January 1944 to ten times that number by August, were volunteers. They had no need to risk themselves in a war the Germans were clearly losing; but they did so, and some 24,000 paid with their lives. De Gaulle had good reason, nonetheless, to tackle them. The provisional government had to be master in its own house. Where its hold was tenuous, revenge could run amok.

The *épuration sauvage*, the "wild purge" of alleged collaborators, was at its crudest in the humiliation of women accused of sleeping with Germans. In the common punishment for this *collaboration horizontale,* the women were put on public display, on a platform or a balcony on the town square, and their heads were shaved. Swastikas were often drawn on their cheeks or heads; they were tarred and feathered, too, forced to give Nazi salutes, and driven naked through the streets, sometimes with their German-fathered babies in their arms. In Toulouse, a woman who had done no more than speak to a German soldier through her window as he patrolled her street was stripped naked, shaved and dragged round the streets with her 14-year-old daughter behind her. At the least estimate, 10,000 women were treated in this way, and probably many more. Many of the shavings were not spontaneous, but organised and even advertised on posters by the local Resistance.

No one kept a tally, either, of the number of killings that took place. The Historical Committee of the war found that some 9,000 were killed before, during and in the immediate aftermath of the Liberation. Most were shot without trial. The fate of a *milicien* captured in the Haute-Savoie was recorded in a *maquisard*'s diary: "Aged 29, married three months ago. Made to saw wood in the hot sun wearing pullover and jacket. Made to drink warm salted water. Ears cut off. Covered with blows from fists and bayonets. Stoned. Made to dig his grave. Made to lie in it. Finished off with a blow in the stomach from a spade. Two days to die."

The Resistance might set up "courts", but in practice these were tribunals which meted out summary justice. The fiercest bore some comparison to the Terror. At Pamiers in the Ariège, the guilty were made to dig their own graves, whilst the townsfolk looked on and shrieked at them; the last four of some 50 executions took place 15 minutes before the time fixed by the prefect for prisoners to be brought under his authority. The Resistance court in Périgueux sentenced 33 people to death, one for no more than being defeatist and "threatening patriots". Old scores were settled. At Issigeac in the Dordogne, the town worthies – the mayor, priest, doctor and dentist – were killed because they had objected to the local Resistance chief opening a brothel.

From September onwards, special courts were set up so that the state could conduct an official *épuration*. With them, an old French weakness resurfaced. Demagogic notions of "justice" were placed above the duller but infinitely sturdier rule of law. Due process was ignored. Defendants were booed and barracked in court. Jurors were largely *résistants*, many of them *attentistes* eager to prove themselves; some were relatives of those executed or held in camps in Germany. They had every reason for bias. Most magistrates had served under Vichy. They were predictably anxious to make amends at the expense of the accused. The *cours de justice* of the Liberation were quite as partial as the Vichy's own *cours spéciales*.

One of the purposes of AMGOT was precisely to prevent kangaroo courts and vengeance killings in the occupied territories. Having fought so hard to avoid an Allied administration, de Gaulle had a particular responsibility to ensure that high legal standards were upheld. It cannot be said that he made much effort.

The legitimacy or otherwise of the Vichy regime was basic to the prosecution of offenders. Collaboration had been its stated policy. If it was the properly constituted government, how could collaborators be punished? Were they not simply following official policy? And was not this policy eminently sensible, and endorsed by the great majority of the people, at least until German vulnerability was exposed by the surrender at Stalingrad in February 1943? The provisional government tried to sidestep the issue by charging most collaborators with treason under article 75 of the penal code, covering "intelligence with the enemy". But who, after the armistice was signed, was the enemy? Not the Germans, with whom hostilities had formally ceased. The British, perhaps? It was, after all, on the grounds of his treasonable dealings with the British that de Gaulle himself had been sentenced to death in absentia by a French court in 1940.

De Gaulle insisted that Pétain, in accepting the armistice, had forfeited his regime's legitimacy by failing in his supreme duty to protect the nation. This was dubious – no one held that legitimate government in Germany had ceased with the armistice in 1918, only to be restored in 1935 when Hitler broke with the armistice by rearming – and was never properly debated.

Communist enthusiasm was another factor. The party saw great profit in the purges. They were a smokescreen for what it had been up to before June 1941. Every policeman and administrator who was dismissed, too, created a vacancy that a Communist could fill. A wholesale clearout of senior figures would have destabilised the administration and increased its vulnerability to the Communists. It was avoided.

At the *cours de justice* level, nonetheless, 6,760 death sentences were pronounced in person and in absentia. Of the 2,853 passed in the presence of the accused, 767 were carried out. De Gaulle commuted the rest. The great mass of collaborators – those sentenced to less than 15 years or to *dégradation nationale* – were amnestied at the start of 1951. Fourteen Alsatians who had taken part in the Oradour massacre, after being forced into the Wehrmacht, were tried by a military tribunal in Bordeaux in January 1953. One of them, who admitted to volunteering for the Waffen-SS, was condemned to death. Public opinion in Alsace-Lorraine would not stand for death sentences for the other conscripts so they were given sentences of five to 12 years. War memorials in Strasbourg and other Alsatian towns were still draped in black in protest. The National Assembly voted by 319 votes to 211 to amnesty the men. The outraged relatives of the dead returned the Légion d'Honneur that had been awarded to the *village martyrisé*. In August 1953, a second general amnesty effectively ended the *épuration*.

Or so it seemed. Thirty years later, it was resurrected in the guise of *devoir de mémoire*, the duty to remember Vichy. Unfinished business was found – cases against René Bousquet, the Vichy police chief, and Maurice Papon, the secretary-general for the Gironde, the two areas that had been most sensitive to Communist pressure – and early careers, ranging from François Mitterrand's to Jacques Cousteau's, were exhumed. The motives of the grave diggers, however, as we shall see, were often dictated as much by their current interests as by the past.

Getting past the purge committees was a tricky business. Everyone had perforce cohabited with the Germans, in the sense of being occupied. The point at which this became collaboration was imprecise. The Oxford philosopher Isaiah Berlin came up with a rough and ready benchmark. Survival made it acceptable for a waiter, or an actor or writer or shoemaker, to do business with the Germans; but "you should not be cosy with them". A family could talk to a soldier who was billeted with them, for example, but he should not dine at the family table.

Thousands of suspects were arrested. In Fresnes prison the actress Arletty and Sacha Guitry represented the arts, though Arletty was allowed out of the prison under escort to shoot the final scenes of *Les Enfants du Paradis*; the singer Tino

Rossi and the publisher Bernard Grasset rubbed shoulders with Albert Blaser, the head waiter from Maxim's. Sacha Guitry was arrested early one morning, and led off in yellow-flowered pyjamas, green crocodile shoes and a Panama hat. It was, however, difficult to paint him as a hardline *collabo*. Asked by the examining magistrate why he had met Hermann Goering, he replied: "Par curiosité." Coco Chanel had a German lover at the Ritz, too, a possible Abwehr spy, known as Spatz: hence her largesse with Chanel No 5. She was arrested and then released, and left Paris for Switzerland, to be reunited with Spatz.

Colette had written for a *collabo* paper, *Le Petit Parisien*, but under the most extenuating circumstances: her husband, Maurice Goudeket, whom she hid in her apartment in the Palais-Royal, was Jewish. Charles Trenet found himself blacklisted for his Radio Paris appearances. Chevalier made amends for his with his ingratiating hit, "Fleur de Paris". The German-controlled studio Continental had filmed books by Georges Simenon, creator of Inspector Maigret; Simenon was under house arrest for a few months, but was then released.

Some writers paid a heavier price. The process against them was speedy, it was said, because "these 'intellectuals'" had provided the prosecution case during the Occupation: "It was only necessary to reread their articles and other published work to establish, without any argument, the indictment they deserved before sending them in front of the court." This explanation, with its assumption that press cuttings are an adequate basis on which to try a man for his life, was made by Pierre-Henri Teitgen, de Gaulle's justice minister.

At the end of December, Henri Béraud, the editor of *Gringoire*, was sentenced to death. Béraud was unquestionably right-wing and an Anglophobe, qualities it might be said he shared with de Gaulle; he was anti-Semitic, too, but he was not over-fond of the Germans, either. He had some most unpleasant ideas; but, as François Mauriac wrote in *Le Figaro*, there were no grounds for condemning him for "intelligence with the enemy". It was a courageous stand by Mauriac and it helped save Béraud's life. De Gaulle commuted the sentence.

No such grace awaited Robert Brasillach, the editor of *Je suis partout*. He was 34, a *normalien* and classicist, a precocious novelist and essayist, a Maurrasite and a former literary editor of *Action française*. Though not impressed by Hitler – a "sad vegetarian functionary" – he was a dreamy and homo-erotic admirer of Nazis. His wartime writing was unquestionably venomous. He described the republic as "a syphilitic old whore stinking of patchouli"; he called the Jews "monkeys" and said that the French must separate from them "en bloc" and "not keep any little ones".

His trial, in January 1945, lasted a day. The magistrate had served under Vichy; the four jurors had Resistance credentials. They took 20 minutes to find him guilty. Mauriac got up a petition for a reprieve. Brasillach himself wrote to de Gaulle asking to be pardoned. The general would have none of it. "In literature, as in everything, talent confers responsibility," de Gaulle wrote in his memoirs. It was a haunting remark from a man with the gift of clemency: would Brasillach have lived if he had been a poorer writer? He was executed in February.

The winter was bitterly cold. A foot of ice blocked the canals from the northern coalfields, trapping barges with 70,000 tons of fuel aboard. Over 20,000 kilometres of railway track had been destroyed, and snow blocked others. Freight marshalling yards were damaged by bombing, and the Germans had taken locomotives and rolling stock as they withdrew. The equipment in the mines was so dilapidated that fatal accidents were running at twice the pre-war level. The major Channel and Atlantic ports were choked with bomb rubble.

Many factories had been bombed, or stripped of machinery by the Germans. The Communists insisted that managers who had fulfilled lucrative contracts with the Wehrmacht should be punished. The furore helped dim memories of how the Soviets had supplied the Nazis with oil and raw materials at the start of the war. After a campaign in *l'Humanité*, Louis Renault was sentenced in September for having sold over 6 billion francs' worth of material to the Germans. He was 67, and within a month he was found dead in his cell in Fresnes prison. Marius Berliet and his son were imprisoned without trial in Lyon; they had sold 2,239 trucks to the Wehrmacht, against 93,000 vehicles provided by Renault, Citroën and Peugeot.

Food deliveries depended on rickety charcoal-burning *gazogène* trucks. Peasants resented *la collecte*, the compulsory purchase of food at fixed prices. In places, prefects threatened to treat the *affameurs des villes* as collaborators if they continued to starve the towns. Black marketeers came down to Touraine in droves before Christmas to buy up geese and turkeys at prices only the richest could afford. Road checkpoints were set up to catch them. The big Paris restaurants responded by using army lorries, which the *gendarmes* did not dare stop. The police caused near riots at the Gare Montparnasse when they began opening the suitcases of passengers returning from the rich north-western farmlands.

There was a moment of warmth in relations with the Allies when Churchill laid a wreath at the Arc de Triomphe with the general on Armistice Day. Spitfires circled overhead to guard against German fighters, the crowds cheered, and the two men made a curious pair, so Malcolm Muggeridge thought, "the one so robust and merry, the other so tall and grave, like Mr Pickwick and Don Quixote." Iciness resumed, to reach new lows in February when de Gaulle was not invited to join Roosevelt and Churchill at the major conference hosted by Stalin at Yalta.

The remnants of Vichy were meanwhile concentrated in Siegmaringen, a small town not far from Lake Constance. Laval was working feverishly on his defence for the trial he knew would await him when Germany collapsed. Marshal Pétain was awarded 16 ration cards, in deference to his rank, but the *milice* families were half-starved, and 60 children died of cold and malnutrition. Two thousand five hundred of the *milice* were enlisted with other French volunteers in the Waffen-SS Charlemagne division. This numbered 7,340 men when it was sent to a railhead in the snows and slush of Pomerania in February 1945.

Russian armour appeared as the division was at its most vulnerable, disembarking from its trains. It was routed and broken up into three wandering battle groups. One of these disappeared into the Red Army's maw. A second tried to fight its way westward but perished in early March. The third group escaped across the Baltic to Denmark and refitted in Mecklenberg, where 700 men volunteered to stay loyal when the rest were released from their vows. They were ordered to Berlin on April 24. Thirty surviving Frenchmen are thought to have been taken prisoner by the Russians when the surrender came on May 2.

A fresh outburst of anger was triggered by the return of the first group of women deportees in April. Well-wishers had set out to welcome them at the Gare de Lyon with gifts of lilac blossom and lipstick. But they were in need of more than a wash and brush-up; they were waxen and greenish, with sunken eyes that "seemed to see but not to take in". A quarter of the 820,000 deportees were thought to have died in captivity; 6,000 were so weak that they died after their return. Newsreels revealed the grisly secrets of the concentration camps. Returning PoWs added to the tales of horror from the Reich. These included accounts of rape and murder by Red Army troops, and of how Soviet PoWs were simply transferred from Nazi to Soviet servitude. Party leaders in Paris fumed against these "calumnies"; "No word against the Red Army must be permitted," they ordered.

When Pétain heard that he was to be charged with treason on the radio in Sigmaringen, he wrote to Ribbentrop demanding to return to France to face his detractors. There was no reply. Instead, as French troops under General de Lattre de Tassigny closed on the Black Forest, he was escorted to the Swiss frontier by his German minders. The Swiss offered him asylum, but he refused it. On April 26, a Swiss guard of honour accompanied him to the French border. The condition of the returnees hardened opinion against Pétain. Only a third had wanted him punished in an opinion poll in September 1944, and three per cent favoured a death sentence. Those demanding punishment had risen to 76 per cent in the summer of 1945, and 37 per cent wanted him executed.

The trial opened in the Palais de Justice on July 23, 1945. "The work of justice was carried out as impartially as humanly possible", de Gaulle was to write; but he added a shameful caveat, "in the midst of the passions aroused." This was the most important trial since Louis XVI's in 1793, and once more the Revolution's failure to embrace legality was evident.

A guilty verdict was a formality. The jury was made up of 12 members of the Resistance and 12 parliamentarians: 569 parliamentarians had voted to grant Pétain full powers in 1940, but the 12 were chosen exclusively from the among the 80 who had not. The prosecutor and the court president were both working their passage away from their Vichy past. The defence pointed out that High Court judges had sworn an oath to Pétain. The prosecutor, André Mornet, a brutal incompetent who had obtained the death penalty for Mata Hari, snapped that "an oath made to a government under enemy control is an oath without value". The president of the court, Mongibeaux, himself had taken that oath.

As the head of the Paris bar, Jacques Charpentier, observed, the armistice itself was put on trial: "The prosecution seem to think that the Marshal lost the war in order to overthrow the Republic." Pétain said that he had "inherited a catastrophe" not of his making; that the armistice was "an act both necessary and a salvation", agreed with the military leaders; and that the government then entrusted to him was "recognised by all countries, from the Holy See to the Soviet Union".

But he was on weaker ground with what Charpentier called Vichy's real crime: the "appalling ambiguity" which was "cloaked in the unequalled prestige of the head of state", and which had "led so many into treason". The marshal claimed that every day, with a dagger to his throat, he struggled against the enemy's demands. The Occupation, he said, "forced me to treat the enemy with tact . . . and to make, against my will and desire, certain remarks and to carry out certain acts".

It was, ironically, Joseph Darnand who caught his slyness and deceit. The marshal had written to the *milice* leader on August 6, 1944, expressing his "horror" at hearing "for several months" of rape, murder and theft by the *milice*, and of their cooperation with the Gestapo. For four years, Darnand replied, "I received your compliments and congratulations . . . And today, because the Americans are at the gates of Paris, you start to say that I am going to be a blot on the history of France." He might, Darnand said, have "made up his mind a little earlier". The same point was made in court by a Protestant pastor, Marc Boegner. He testified that he had told Pétain of the deportation of Jewish children from a railway station near Lyon in 1942. Pétain declared himself horrified and indignant, Boegner said, and did nothing to stop it. But, as Charpentier said, these things were "never tackled head-on". The major figures of the Third Republic appeared, like an ancient and flickering newsreel, to give evidence about 1940. Much of it was pure hearsay or opinion. Daladier said that Pétain had "betrayed his duty to the French"; that was his opinion, he said, though on the crucial point of "intelligences avec Hitler", he agreed that "je n'en sais rien." He knew nothing. Georges Coustaunau-Lacau, a former Pétain aide and a *résistant* who had survived Mauthausen, said he was "sickened" by the parade of all those "who try to pass all their errors onto an old man".

The marshal was duly sentenced to death, but the jury asked for the sentence to be commuted to life imprisonment. Pétain's lawyer said they did so to prevent de Gaulle having the credit for sparing a 90-year-old. Pétain was to be a prisoner on the Île de Yeu until his death in 1951. Darnand followed. The brutalities of the *milice* ruled out clemency, and the death penalty given to this much decorated hero was carried out.

Laval himself was the last of the majors to be tried in 1945. His trial, Pastor Boegner wrote, was "a scandal beyond description". Laval was denied access to witnesses; he had five sessions of questioning by his lawyers instead of the 25 the case called for. They refused to attend the opening of his trial, in protest at the lack of time and facilities to prepare the case. Mornet began by saying the examination was not hurried, for he claimed it had "started five years ago on the day that Pierre Laval, with Pétain, seized power". This was, of course, grotesque, and Laval realised he was finished. "You were all under government orders, even you, Monsieur le Procureur-Général!" he said. "Condemn me straight away. That will make things clear." Jurors goaded Laval; they spoke of giving him "a dozen bullets" in his hide. Laval's defence relied on the *double jeu*. What he had done, on deportations, forced labour, would have been worse without him; and what he had said, most notoriously that he hoped for a German victory, was aimed at winning concessions. After three days, on October 6, he refused to appear at all, gambling that the irregularities and his absence would force the government to order a new trial.

He was sentenced to death on October 9. There was to be no retrial, and no reprieve. And so this figure, the darkness of his face and soul lit by the whiteness of his trademark tie, a man "universally hated", Charpentier said, whose conviction after a proper trial would have raised not a murmur, was "turned into a victim". Boegner saw de Gaulle personally to tell him that the trial was "a travesty", and to ask him to commute the sentence. Not a flicker of emotion disturbed the general's face; it was as if Laval was already dead, the pastor said. Laval swallowed cyanide and went into convulsions early on October 15, the day set for his execution. It took two hours to stomach-pump him into some consciousness, before he was carried, strapped shoeless to a chair, and shot, whilst other prisoners shouted: "Salauds! Assassins!"

Capitalism – fleshed out as the *trusts* and the *deux cent familles* – was also to be punished. Léon Blum, in his first speech on his return from the German camps, said that socialism was "the meeting point of all the great currents" now sweeping across the globe. "Economic liberalism", he pronounced, "is dead." It was nonsense, of course. Economic liberalism in the United States was creating the most prosperous society in history, and was strong enough to save half Europe from the Soviet socialism that blighted the remainder.

But *progressisme* was king for the moment. The old right was almost shamed out of public existence, its supporters clinging quietly to the MRP or Gaullism, and even the bourgeoisie, François Mauriac wrote, "is resigned to the inevitable". Simone de Beauvoir declared Paris to be "in the year zero". *Vogue* published a poem by Paul Éluard and a portrait of Marcel Cachin, Communists both.

The party won the largest slice of the vote, 26.1 per cent, in the elections to the Constituent Assembly a few days after Laval's execution. But no party was close to winning a majority. The Communists had 160 seats, the Mouvement Républicain

Populaire had 152 seats, and the Socialists 142. The MRP – the Communists called it the "Machine for Reassembling Pétainists" – was a centre party in the Christian Democrat mould. It attracted much of the old conservative and Catholic vote, too, from Brittany, Normandy, Alsace and the *beaux quartiers* of Paris. The Communists wanted to draw the Socialists into a coalition of the left, the better to devour them in due time; the Socialists wisely avoided a new Popular Front, and refused to govern without the MRP, diehards of *laïcité* thus associating with clericals.

Maurice Thorez demanded nationalisations, and, here at least, de Gaulle went along with him. The general was notoriously uninterested in economic affairs, but he welcomed *dirigisme* – and had an austere mistrust of financiers and entrepreneurs.

The northern coalmines were nationalised in September 1944. The Renault and Berliet factories were confiscated without compensation, as a punishment for industrial collaboration. Much of transport, the aviation industry, merchant shipping and the Paris transport network was requisitioned. The state became the sole shareholder in the Bank of France and the four major clearing banks. Gas and electricity, and some of the insurance industry, followed.

The Communists used the changes to gain influence and patronage. Personnel were sacked and replaced by inflated numbers of Communists and fellow travellers recruited through advertisements in *l'Humanité*. The workers were pressured to join the Communist-dominated CGT, where their union dues, supposedly destined for welfare schemes, were spent on party propaganda.

Great corporations were created. EDF and GDF, with near monopolies in electricity and gas, proved able to meet the growing demand for energy. SNECMA was to build jet engines for aircraft operated by Air France, another product of nationalisation. The new Régie Renault was run by Pierre Lefaucheux, a believer in dynamic capitalism, who ignored state instructions to concentrate on heavy lorries, and instead launched the hugely successful Renault 4CV car. The creation of a new managerial elite, in place of amateurs appointed for their Resistance or trade union credentials, was to owe much to two new institutions. The École National d'Administration (ENA) was a super-elite school for training high-flying administrators in the civil service and nationalised industries. Jean Monnet's Commissariat Général au Plan gave central impetus to the modernisation and re-equipping of industry and transport.

The tensions between de Gaulle and the Assembly were political, more than economic, and they were palpable. Thorez demanded a top ministry – interior, foreign affairs or defence – for the Communists. De Gaulle refused. Troops and police checkpoints surrounded the Assembly anticipating trouble, but Thorez accepted four other ministries for the party. The general found horse-trading of this sort highly distasteful. His ministers complained at his heavy hand. They could not take notes at meetings, or smoke before he lit his first cigarette; and Bidault still smarted from the general's rebuke when he had walked abreast of him to the Te Deum at Notre-Dame in August 1944: "Monsieur, un peu en arrière, s'il vous plaît."

When the Socialists wanted 20 per cent cut from military spending, de Gaulle summoned his ministers to the rue Saint-Dominique on a Sunday morning, January 20, 1946, in uniform, tired and grey, and told them he was resigning. The regime of the parties had returned, he said: "I condemn it." But unless he used force to set up a dictatorship – "which I do not desire, and which would doubtless come to a bad end" – he had no means of preventing it. "So I must retire."

It was his escape from the politics of *dosage*, the sharing of the cake between Communists, Socialists and the MRP, without which no government could survive. He had yet to realise that a little flattery goes further than a lot of scorn, and was "too much of a soldier", Jacques Dumaine realised, to accept the "perpetual life of compromise" that goes with public life.

If he disliked parties, however, he despised the Anglo-Saxons even more; and in view of this, it was as well he went when he did. France was too weak to go its own way: it had to make up its mind which side it was on, and de Gaulle's phobias ill-equipped him to throw in his lot with the West. At a huge parade on June 18, 1945, to commemorate his own first broadcast from London, not a reference was made to the British or Americans, though they had supplied every tank and aircraft on display. "There was no evidence of an ounce of gratitude," Duff Cooper, the Francophile British ambassador, observed, "and one felt throughout that France was boasting very loud, having very little to boast about."

His immodesty was untempered by his resignation. The mass of the people "retreated into sadness", he said. An opinion poll showed that 60 per cent were, in fact, glad that he had gone, or were indifferent; but there was truth in his claim that many people felt that "the general" – he referred to himself in the third person – had taken away "something primordial, permanent, necessary", and that "he incarnated history in a way that the party regime could not do." He was to be away very much longer than he expected.

11

The Reupholstered Republic

The Fourth Republic was itself the sixteenth regime since 1789. A people less obsessed by the Revolution and the search for political perfection might have been happy to improve the Third, but the desire to strart from scratch was irresistible. In elections for a second Constituent Assembly, the MRP shaded the Communists to become the largest single party. The draft constitution they produced with the Radicals retained an upper house, with a stronger executive. This scraped home in a referendum in October. Nine million voted for, ignoring de Gaulle's thunderous warning that government would remain a creature of parliamentary whim, and eight million against. As a sign of apathy and voter fatigue, eight million did not vote at all. "So many years lost," Mauriac wrote, "simply to arrive at this patching together, this reupholstering."

Paul Ramadier was first premier of the new regime, a moderate Socialist like the new president, Auriol, whose buttoned boots and white goatee gave him an old-fashioned air. His coalition was tripartisan, a fractious mix of Communists and Socialists on the left and centre-left with the MRP, radicals and independents on the right. Their simultaneous presence in government, Blum warned, was "both indispensable and impossible".

Severe strains arose over Indochina, where French forces were fighting a Communist insurgency. When members of the Assembly rose to their feet to show solidarity with the troops, François Billoux, the Communist defence minister, remained seated with his party colleagues. He commanded the loyalty of the soldiers as minister; on party orders, he insulted them.

A pay strike at Renault, led by Trotskyites, finished matters. Thorez came out against the government line of wage restraint and price controls after a time. He was confident that Ramadier would not dare try to punish him. Auriol proved impervious to the leftist mantra of "pas d'ennemi à gauche". The early stirrings of the Cold War were in his favour. Communists had quit the government in Belgium, and were about to be driven from it in Italy. The president was determined to keep the premier in office. Ramadier won a vote of confidence in the Assembly by the impressive margin of 360 votes to 186. On the back of that, he summoned a cabinet meeting and insisted on a collective stand on wage restraint. He reminded his ministers that the constitution permitted him to withdraw their portfolios. Thorez and his four colleagues walked out of the room. The Communists thereby resigned from the government. Like de Gaulle, they gravely miscalculated; what they thought would be a brief absence from office lasted 34 years.

A surface prosperity returned. The ban on casinos was lifted, and they boomed as a perfect means for black marketeers to launder their profits. Five thousand real taxis replaced the old *vélos-taxis* bicycle rickshaws and it no longer needed a government pass or a medical certificate to take one. The only rehabilitation needed in the arts was of the *collabos*. Arletty was soon starring again. Serge Lifar served only a year of a lifetime ban; Sacha Guitry was quickly back, too.

Foreign writers again fluttered to Paris like moths. The black American James Baldwin revelled in the lack of prejudice, writing *Go Tell it on the Mountain*; a very different type of New Yorker, Norman Mailer, pinned down his experiences in the Pacific war in *The Naked and the Dead* from a scruffy apartment in Montparnasse.

The genius for fashion was stronger than ever. The industry relaunched itself in brilliant style, using dolls as mannequins, just like those that had promoted Paris fashions on tours of the courts of Europe a century before. The couturiers were a mixed bunch. Cristóbal Balenciaga was the son of a Basque sea captain, and Hubert Taffin de Givenchy was a marquis. Most interest centred on the battle between the fresh talent of Christian Dior and Jacques Fath, in New York as well as Paris.

Dior's new house in the avenue Montaigne got off to a flying start with his first collection in February 1947. Each model was greeted with wild applause, and a remark by the *Harper's Bazaar* fashion writer – "your dresses have such a New Look!" – gave his designs their name. The most renowned outfit was a white silk jacket, nipped at the waist to show the hips, and a wide pleated black skirt. Dior worked frenetically, designing 500 costumes a year, a bachelor employing 785 women, 732 in his workshops, and the others as *vendeuses* and mannequins. He soon accounted for three-quarters of French fashion exports, a major hard currency earner with his establishment on Fifth Avenue. He did not please all. Women stall-holders, outraged at such luxury in austere times, tried to rip the clothes off his models during a photo shoot in Montmartre. The same fury overcame Yves Montand as he sang in a nightclub and watched a diner at the table below the stage pick at a lobster and then grind his cigar into it. He was so angry that he punched him.

A harshness, eagerly exploited by the Communists, hung between the classes. Society was said to have three strands: the poor, the rich, and the Anglo-Saxons. The normal fare of a GI – processed vegetables, chocolate bars, fruit juice, coffee, bacon, powdered egg and milk, canned meat – was sold at luxury prices on the black market. Trawler skippers stayed in port, and made fortunes by selling on their fuel ration. Cigarettes butts were sold in tens. Wits brought the perfect knight of ancient chivalry, *sans peur et sans reproche*, up to date as *sans beurre et sans brioches*. Cattle had to be imported, largely from Ireland, to restock French farms. A wine scandal – the ration was 2 litres a month, but millions of litres of Algerian wine were said to have been diverted to Belgium and Switzerland – produced a 1,779-page parliamentary enquiry.

The bread ration was already miserable – 250 grams a day of yellowy maize bread – and a millers' strike made matters worse. A rumour that wheat was being exported by profiteers led a mob in Nevers to sack the *préfecture*. By the end of May 1947, stocks were down to ten days and the ration was cut further.

Auriol complained in September that "everyone is discontented . . . the madness is not far from panic, a sort of psychosis at rising prices". The price index had roared up from 856 to 1336 since the start of the year, with food prices outstripping that. The Republic was not yet established, he confided to his diary, and "it wouldn't take much to sweep it away"; the hostility of both the right and left wing was leading to "a real crisis of regime".

He had good reason to worry. A secret meeting of Communist parties was held in a Polish hunting lodge at Sklarska Poreba. At it, Andrei Zhdanov laid down Moscow's new line. Cooperation with the democratic left was to end. The Comintern was to be resurrected as Cominform, whose purpose was to defend the Soviet Union against American imperialism and a revived West Germany. On his return from Poland, Jacques Duclos declared that the "only objective" was now to "destroy the capitalist economy" and to "destabilise the government". He added that Moscow was now in "complete control". The French party had, in effect, become a Soviet recruit in the Cold War.

The new hostility was soon evident. Thorez told a rally in October that the party task was now "to rally all the forces in France against the American imperialists and their agents", among whom he classified everyone from Gaullists to Socialists. Orders went out to prepare for clandestine activity. Lock-up garages were hired, and cars and vans bought that could not be traced to Party members; printing presses and radio transmitters were made ready, false identity papers and ration books printed, and the weapons hidden since de Gaulle's disarming of the *maquis* were retrieved and oiled ready for use.

Two American initiatives, which the Communists ran together as the "Plan Truman-Marshall", were the cause of this anger. The president had outlined his Truman Doctrine in Washington on March 12, 1947. He said that the West must "assist free peoples to work out their own destiny" and help them to resist "attempted subjugation by armed minorities or by outside pressure".

The Marshall Plan, named for the US secretary of state, was the economic arm of this effort. The bad winter of 1946 had shown that Europe could not lift itself unaided out of its hunger and despair. The US offered aid in unprecedented amounts, and with few controls. George Marshall said that it would be wrong for Washington to impose a programme on those it helped; the implementation "must come from Europe".

A conference was held to discuss Marshall Aid in Paris in July 1947. All war-torn Europe was invited, including the eastern half to whose subjugation Truman had referred. Only the west Europeans attended, approaching the Americans, so Isaiah Berlin observed, with the attitude of "lofty and demanding beggars approaching an apprehensive millionaire". As well as underpinning European prosperity by denying the Communists a breeding ground made fertile by poverty, it also became clear that the Americans wished to rebuild West Germany, in industrial and eventually military terms, as a counterweight to the Soviet bloc.

These plans frightened the French – "French mothers must start trembling again!" *l'Humanité* led its front page – but a colossal sweetener accompanied them. Between April 1948 and January 1952, France received American aid equivalent to 48 per cent of the total amount spent by the Fonds de Modernisation et d'Équipement. Having enabled the Liberation, the Americans now restored France to prosperity with their money: gifts made the more generous by the predictable lack of gratitude.

Self-interest played some part in the handouts, of course. Free trade was a condition of aid, and it suited American business for French consumers to prosper. Some misgivings were justified. When Blum had gone to Washington cap in hand for a loan a little earlier, Hollywood used French vulnerability to grab 50 per cent of the French market, half-crucifying the brilliant native film industry in the process. It was accepted, if not formally spelled out, that aid was conditional on keeping Communist influence in check.

Spite and protectionism, nonetheless, were the core components of a new wave of anti-American ill-feeling. It broke with particular ferocity on any product – children's comics like *Tarzan* and *Zorro*, magazines like the *Reader's Digest*-controlled *Sélection*, bebop music, ketchup, denims and blue jeans. Communists and *intellos* naturally led the assault. Coca-Cola was the main target. "The Yank substitutes the machine for the poet, Coca-Cola for poetry," Louis Aragon wrote. "It is not the drink," *Le Monde* said, "it is the civilisation, the lifestyle that goes with it – gigantic red trucks, garish neon signs, vulgar advertisements. The very soul of our culture is at stake."

The Coke crisis was settled by French courts, which ruled that an import ban by the health minister was illegal since the drink was not a health hazard. Pernod and Les Glacières de Paris, Coke's bottling plant partners, were soon reaping rich profits, and *l'Humanité* accepted Coke ads. The furore was not a one-day wonder, however. It went on for three years, and the anti-American streak proved to be lasting. It often reflected a healthy pride in French culture; it also served to shelter inefficient industries against competition, and it sometimes lurched into meanness of spirit.

American money – 20 per cent of Marshall Aid, against 11 per cent for Italy and 10 per cent for West Germany, and the lion's share of free grants – came at a time of critical vulnerability. The country had a gaping balance of payments deficit, and no currency reserves. It had already had billions in American credits, grants and loans, for the coal, food and raw materials required by industries to survive. The fresh money, invested in key sectors by a generation of brilliant young planners, enabled it to thrive.

What de Gaulle would have made of Marshall Aid is academic, of course; he was in self-exile in his homely manor house amid the woods of Colombey-les-Deux-Eglises, and, given his American phobias, it is probably as well for France that he remained there. Auriol fretted nonetheless that he wanted to return, and was about to "do everything to get the top job back". He visited the general at Colombey to warn him that he would not be accorded the honours of First Resistant if he opposed the government. His reception was frosty – a servant introduced him as someone "who says he is head of government", and he was offered not so much as a glass of water – but de Gaulle assured him that he remained averse to Boulanger-style adventures and to political parties.

The general was less than frank. His prediction in the spring that France would soon recall him to power was more than his habitual "egocentrisme vertigineux", as Mauriac's son Claude put it. He began a mass movement, the Rassemblement du Peuple Français. He was nettled when people called it the RPF, as though it was the common or garden political party it appeared to be. He insisted that it was a *rassemblement*, a "gathering", and thus quite different: it was an "elemental force" which "corresponds exactly to the French people's promptings and instincts".

At an RPF rally on Vincennes racecourse, de Gaulle mocked political parties as a whole, "boiling up their little soup, over their little fire, in their little corner". He nursed a particular dislike of Paul Ramadier, jealous perhaps of the premier's effective purge of Communist influence. He showed himself as testy, or plain rude, as ever, by refusing to attend the dinner at the Elysée after Ramadier, who had himself won the Médaille Militaire at Verdun, conferred the country's highest military decoration on Winston Churchill.

The RPF had a huge initial impact. It won almost 40 per cent of the vote in the municipal elections in October 1947, taking control of more than half the major cities, including Paris and Marseille, and, treated as an integral part of France, Algiers. The Communists were second with 29 per cent. This was a point of maximum danger: the centre – the MRP, savaged by the Gaullists, with the Socialists, radicals and moderates – alone supplied the government, and it had barely 30 per cent of the vote.

In one respect, though, the RPF did differ from the normal party. Though he had created it, de Gaulle did nothing with it. "He marched us at full speed to the Rubicon," André Malraux put it, "and then told us to get out our fishing rods." He did not deign to play party politics, remaining aloof, spurning government, and calling for fresh parliamentary elections. This stiffened MRP and Socialist resolve to remain in power.

Their nerve was to be tested. In Marseille, the Communists exploited a rise in tram fares to stir up violent protests. A mob forced judges in the law courts to suspend sentences passed on rioters, and then moved on to sack the town hall and beat up the newly installed Gaullist mayor. The outgoing Communist mayor hailed them from a balcony for their "reconquest of the People's House". The police stood by then and later in the evening when the demonstrators pillaged nightclubs and bars said to be used by black marketeers. The mood in the city was so black that Gaston Defferre, the local Socialist baron, drove with a gun on his lap.

The miners came out. The Communist administrator of the coal board was dismissed, and fomented trouble. Exhausted, hurt by the election result, Ramadier resigned on November 19, 1947. He was replaced by the finance minister, Robert Schuman, despite opposition from both Communists and Gaullists. Schuman was a Lorrainer, who had thus been drafted into the German army in the First World War; he had been a Pétainist minister, too, if briefly, before being arrested by the Germans. He was a solid and austere Catholic bachelor, slow-speaking, calm, big-eared and bald. The interior minister, Jules Moch, was the other key figure, old-fashioned, with round tortoiseshell glasses and a toothbrush moustache.

Much of the rail network was shut down. The metalworkers came out, and the sewage workers and Paris undertakers. Low gas pressure made it difficult to cook. Water pressure was so poor that the top floors of many buildings were without it. There were frequent power cuts.

Moch was short of police, and some of the CRS units were manned by unreliable Communist ex-FTP *résistants*. He called up 100,000 reservists in mid-November. Colonial Spahi troops were ordered to protect the northern pits against sabotage. The men stacked their rifles on the station platform at Lens, and refused to take them up. Moch sent a trusted CRS force to seize the weapons and escort the *spahis* back to their barracks.

Postmen walked out. A mob of 300 young Communists smashed all the police telephones in the XVIIIe arrondissement in Paris, and tried to take over the telephone exchange. The chief of police had just 150 men in reserve in the whole city. Suburban commuter trains were stopped by the wives and children of strikers lying across the tracks. A further 80,000 reservists were called up.

Troops and police cordoned off the Palais Bourbon on November 29. The government had decided on a parliamentary fight to establish the right to work. Three million were on strike, but many were intimidated by militants who beat up blacklegs or *jaunes*. Anti-Communists demanded that secret ballots should be held on strike action, rather than a show of hands, which left individuals at the mercy of Communist thugs. Schuman introduced an emergency bill laying down prison sentences and fines for industrial sabotage, intimidation and interference with the right to work.

The debate within the National Assembly seethed with hatreds. Schuman and Moch were calm, though public order seemed on the verge of collapse, and it took them five days and nights to get the bill through. "Voilà le boche!" Duclos screamed at Schuman. "Where were you a soldier in 1914, Prime Minister?" asked Charles Tillon, himself a Black Sea mutineer in 1920. Others shouted "Hitler" and "Nazi" at Jules Moch, a Jew who had fought in both wars, and whose son had been murdered by the Gestapo.

On the third day, the Communist deputy Raoul Calas appealed to the army not to obey the "murderers of the people". This was incitement to mutiny. A resolution excluding Calas from the Assembly was passed, to redoubled Communist fury. Calas refused to leave the tribune throughout the night. When a colonel of the Garde Républicaine arrived at dawn with orders to expel Calas, the Communists burst into the "Marseillaise" each time he moved forward, obliging him to stand to attention and salute. At length he reached the tribune, and took Calas by the arm, who shrieked: "Je cède à la force." The government finally won its emergency powers.

In the event, it hardly needed them. The night express from Paris to Turcoing was derailed, killing 16, with 30 badly injured. Twenty-five metres of track had been sabotaged. The news reached Paris in the early morning. By mid-afternoon, there was almost no traffic; the city appeared in a state of siege, with armed police at every intersection. Communist deputies expressed no sympathy for the victims, accusing the "fascist" government of staging it to put the blame on the Communists. They staged crude provocations to hide behind; when Thorez was safely absent, a "fascist" handgrenade exploded in his garden.

It did them little good. Newsreels showed wrecked carriages, and sad scraps of clothing and shoes, and it needed little to persuade the public that the "anonymous criminals" who had carried out the "abominable attack" were hardline Communist miners, who thought the train was full of riot police. Opinion turned against the strike, and for the government. Moch's cool nerve was rewarded. Non-Communist unions voted to accept a cost-of-living bonus and call off the strike. The socialist Force Ouvrière, helped by money from the American Federation of Labor, left the CGT and set up on its own. Wives pressured their men to go back to work. Postmen did so under police escort, a daily spectacle that helped convince people that the Communists were hell-bent on ruining the economy.

Then the CGT threatened to flood the mines by withdrawing maintenance teams, and the strikers barricaded themselves at the pit heads. Moch was again interior minister, and as feisty as ever. He brought 40,000 troops back from the French zone in Germany to tear down the barricades. Two were killed and many wounded. But the situation did not have the same menace as before. The world was to change in 1948; the Communist coup in Prague, and its murders, and the Berlin airlift, made many leery of anything that smacked of Communism.

The collapse of the strikes in December 1947 was the real start of *les trentes glorieuses*, so dubbed by Jean Fourastié, one of the planners who made possible the coming thirty years of peerless growth and prosperity. In this period, life expectancy itself went up from 62 to 69 for men, and from 67 to 77 for women; farm workers fell from a third to a tenth of the workforce, whilst those in the new services mushroomed to 51 per cent; the number of cars was up from 1 to 15 million. Income per head, with a base of 100 in 1939, was up from 125 to 320. No precedent existed for the boom years that arrived with the new republic. Even the demographic storm clouds lifted. The population went up from 40 million to 52 million, equalling, in 30 years, its growth over the previous 150 years.

These defeats did not finish off the Communists. The party was the largest in the free world, with 400,000 members even after its post-war peak, and it accounted for around a quarter of the electorate. Its intellectuals were Moscow's most influential apologists. A reason the party remained so stable was the way that it enveloped its grass-roots supporters, at home and at work. It was, as *Le Monde* admitted, the "most competent machine in the country". It supplied houses, loans and insurance, and jobs, through its control of municipalities, banks and agencies, and the CGT union. It entertained, with women's circles, jamborees, cinema clubs, evening classes, theatre companies, folk music festivals and summer camps. It published cookery books for mothers and comics for children, with a comic strip starring Pif le Chien, the anti-fascist underdog. It was a militant's heaven. It gave him – or her – posters to paste up, papers and badges to sell, demonstrations to organise. The *fête des remises de cartes*, the day when the cell secretary gave out party membership cards, was a family gala with cakes, wine and dancing. Pilgrimages were made on May Day to revere the 1871 martyrs at the Mur des Fédérés. In September, the faithful washed down *merguez* sausages to the sound of accordions at the Fête de l'Humanité, a gigantic open-air picnic at Vincennes.

In domestic terms, though, the party was isolated in parliamentary opposition, a baleful presence that weakened governments without having much impact on policy. It was its artists and thinkers who gave it international renown. It is curious – disturbing – that writers like Louis Aragon, having so recently cried out for vengeance against those who had served Vichy, and by extension the Nazis, should abandon themselves to another totalitarian ideology directed from abroad. No other country produced a fraction of the French crop of Communist and fellow travelling intellectuals; least of all, of course, the Soviet Union itself, where the usual reward for a creative mind was a berth in the Gulag or a psychiatric ward.

And these were people of distinction. Picasso drew the famous dove and olive branch symbol of the Peace Movement, a Communist front; its card-carrying president was Frédéric Joliot-Curie, the Nobel prize-winning physicist, whose wife and fellow Nobel laureate, Irène, was a president of another front, the Congress of Intellectuals for World Peace. Picasso's membership of the party was announced across five columns on the front page of *l'Humanité*. "Joining the party is the logical progression of my whole life, of my whole work," he gushed. "How could I have hesitated? . . . I feel much more free, much more fulfilled."

Marguerite Duras, whose flat on the rue Saint-Benoît was the salon of the Communist literati, was a writer whose rare gifts were displayed in novels like *The Sea Wall* and the film script of *Hiroshima mon amour*. Paul Éluard and André Breton had written poetry of distinction before becoming militants. *Les Temps modernes*, the intellectuals' journal, was founded after the war by a trio of equal brilliance: Jean-Paul Sartre, Maurice Merleau-Ponty, a distinguished professor of philosophy whose insights into the nature of consciousness illuminated his *Phénoménologie de la perception*, and Simone de Beauvoir. One day, she said, she had wanted to explain herself to herself. "I began to reflect all about myself," she wrote, "and it struck me with a sort of surprise that the first thing I had to say was: 'I am a woman.'" From this came her book *Le Deuxième Sexe*, subtitled "La Femme, cette inconnue". It established with great force that others who were oppressed had a before – the blacks before slavery, the Jews before the diaspora – but as to half the inhabitants of the world, "women have always been subordinate, to men throughout all of their history". This was a work of profound significance, dealing in every taboo: prostitution, abortion, sexual equality, divorce. Modern feminism is not the product of bra-burning Anglo-Saxon campuses. Its origins are French.

No tight-lipped bigots, these: they had friends and lovers, and charm and warmth, they chatted easily to students, they enjoyed a drink and a night out together at the Bal Nègre. Yet they paid obeisance to Stalinism. Merleau-Ponty wrote a piece in *Les Temps modernes* vilifying the ex-Communist Arthur Koestler for denouncing the 1936 Moscow show trials and executions. These were justified, Merleau-Ponty wrote, because they defended the revolution, and for Koestler to deny this was treason. Simone de Beauvoir thought this wonderful. "Merleau subordinated morality to history, much more resolutely than any existentialist yet," she wrote. "We took this leap with him – without yet letting go – conscious that moralising was the last defence of bourgeois idealism." Sartre, though called by Thorez, an "expression of a rotting bourgeoisie", also announced his submission to the party in *Les Temps modernes*. "To oppose Communism is to oppose the proletariat," he said; Marxism was "l'Horizon indépassable", and the root of all culture.

I Chose Freedom, the memoirs of the Soviet defector Viktor Kravchenko, appeared in French in 1947. It laid bare Stalin's terror: the famine in the Ukraine, the liquidation of the kulaks, the labour camps of the Gulag. No major publisher dared touch it, for fear of offending the party, but it sold 400,000 copies. *Les Lettres françaises*, a hard-left journal, ran a counter-attack, an article by "Sim Thomas", who claimed that the book was in fact written by his former colleagues in American intelligence, and that Kravchenko was a lying alcoholic. Kravchenko sued for libel. The case opened in January 1949. It was a sensation. Communism itself was effectively put on trial. The intelligentsia lined up to deny the existence of the Gulag, and to show their solidarity with French Stalinists. The NKVD flew in witnesses to blacken Kravchenko's character, including his first wife.

She sat in court with a NKVD minder, almost dumb with fear, her family left in Russia as hostages. Her voice, as her ex-husband said, was as flat and monotonous as a looped tape recording as she went through her litany: he had beaten her, he drank, he lied. At the moment of insight, Kravchenko said gently that she had not come to France voluntarily, and then demanded: "But she must say why she came here!" She collapsed, and was hurried from court by her minder, and taken to Orly, where a Soviet military aircraft flew her back to Russia. Kravchenko's witnesses, survivors of the Soviet camps, described their ordeals with plain horror. They, and the non-appearance of "Sim Thomas", won the day. Thomas was not in Paris for the trial for the excellent reason that he did not exist. *The Lettres françaises* piece was found to be the work of André Ulmann, editor of the Soviet-funded *Tribune des nations*.

Sartre and his circle were less slavish than some. Merleau-Ponty came to blame Stalin for the Korean War. At various times, notably with the Soviet invasion of Hungary in 1956, Sartre was critical. Yet he made the grotesque claim on his return from a visit to Russia in 1954 that "la liberté du critique est totale en URSS". And he condemned the publication of Khrushchev's "secret speech" detailing Stalin's crimes in 1956. It was "madness" to reveal the crimes of this "sacred personage", Sartre said, because it revealed the truth to "the masses who were not ready to receive it". "Il ne fallait pas désespérer Billancourt", he added; he feared that the fragile psyches of the Renault workers at Billancourt would also be reduced to despair by the revelations. Had he said the same of Hitler and the Nazi camps, the outer darkness would instantly have swallowed him; his voice silenced, his person boycotted, eventually perhaps to be charged with denying the Holocaust. The "progressive" mind drew – still draws – an absolute distinction between Communist "errors" and fascist "crimes".

Sartre emphasised the need for the intellectual to be *engagé*, to be committed, and to "embrace the epoch". "I hold Flaubert and Goncourt responsible for the repression that followed the Commune," he wrote, "because they did not write a line to stop it." Revolution was good, be it in eighteenth-century France, in 1930s Russia or, as the elderly Sartre was soon to say, in 1960s Maoist China; revolutionary violence was "honest", Merleau-Ponty said, and had "a humanistic future".

If the Paris-based apologists had a worldwide presence, it must be said, so did the city's anti-communists, François Mauriac, Albert Camus, Koestler and Raymond Aron prominent among them. Aron dismissed Marxism as a mindless religion in *The Opium of the Intellectuals*, and its Parisian supporters as "intellectually backward" hypocrites. Falling out of friendship with Sartre, Camus castigated those who saw "nothing but doves in the East and vultures in the West"; it was "blindness, the frenzy of the slave, a nihilistic admiration of force". The right was "not brilliant", he said, but the left was "in complete decadence", at a loss when faced with the truth, "caught in its own vocabulary", where a grey sky became blue.

The world noticed because post-war Paris was again at the heart of the intellectual universe. A few streets round the old abbey of Saint-German-des-Près were the creative cockpit of the city. It was a tight-knit place of cafés, bars, bistros and coldwater hotels. A cheap room at the Louisiane, the Montana or the Pont Royal, with a bed and basin and a peeling wardrobe, served as a base. It was forbidden to cook in hotel rooms, and cheap cafés and bistros provided a coffee, a meal, warmth and a table.

It had other essentials for the creative life. Experimental drama sprang from a string of small theatres such as the Théâtre de la Poche and the Théâtre de La Huchette, theatres of the *absurde*, the *révolutionnaire*, *des idées*, where the cast manned the box office, shifted the scenery, and made the costumes. Jean Anouilh's *Antigone* had premiered in 1946. Eugène Ionesco was writing his short, Surrealist plays, *The Bald Prima Donna*, *The Lesson*, *The Chairs*. All the ingredients, too, for a new magazine – writers of all sorts, illustrators, editors, designers – were at hand.

The Café de Flore was "like a classroom" in its heyday. Sartre sat writing at one paper-strewn table, with de Beauvoir grappling with a manuscript at another, and Arthur Adamov writing a theatre piece in a corner. Alberto Giacometti, the sculptor of "thin man" bronzes, long and spidery, might be spotted with Picasso at Le Catalan. Raymond Aron drank at the Deux Magots, Camus at the Café de la Mairie. Samuel Beckett, now writing *Molloy* and *En attendant Godot* in French, supped beer at the Montana hotel bar. The waiters at Merleau-Ponty's favourite haunt, the Rhumerie Martiniquaise, would confiscate his silver cigarette lighter until he settled his bill.

Jazz had a special niche. The French had an affinity for it, and for jazzmen; Sidney Bechet made his home in Paris, and the great players – Louis Armstrong, Miles Davis,

Duke Ellington – passed through. Local bands, like Claude Luter's, played well, too. The best-known jazz trumpeter was Boris Vian, who, in classic Saint-Germain style, was also a singer, bar-cabaret promoter, poet, columnist for *Les Temps modernes* and cuckold (by Sartre), as well as supposedly being the translator of American pulp fiction. A reader copied one of these "translations" when he murdered his mistress, leaving an open copy of the book at the scene. It was eventually found that Vian had written the now bestselling book himself; it was banned, and he was fined.

A photograph of a tousled-headed young man, holding a candle in one hand and, in the other, a girl in trousers with cobwebs in her hair, assured the fame of the *quartier*. It was splashed across *Samedi soir* under the headline: "This is how the troglodytes of Saint-Germain live." The story described them as "two poor existentialists . . . drinking and loving their lives away in cellars . . . until the atom bomb – that they all perversely long for – falls on Paris". The girl was Juliette Gréco, the daughter of a police commissaire from Montpellier. Her husky voice, and jet black hair and chalk white and ebony-eyed face, made her a dramatic *diseuse*, at the mid-point between song and recital. The young lapped her up, across the West, as a sort of prototype Dylan. They idolised Sartre, too, and existentialism, because it preached the importance of action and choice, and it rebelled against analytic reason, which Sartre dismissed as "the official doctrine of bourgeois democracy". To be "authentic" was to be *against* things, a philosophy with a natural appeal to the young. They began to appear in Saint-Germain in numbers. The strong dollar helped transform it, an American journalist observed, into a "drugstore for pretty upstate girls in unbecoming blue denim pants", with Midwest boyfriends, in sandals and Beaux-Arts beards. A recognised sub-species of tourist, the intello-spotter, flooded the place, chasing Sartre for his autograph, and attracting souvenir sellers and con men. The Americans spent more, though, than the local existentialists, and the patron of the Flore was delighted to welcome them. "Sartre?" he said. "My worst client. Hours scribbling on a bit of paper, in front of a single drink, from morning to night."

A quieter revolution than that close to Sartre's heart was taking place in politics. A handful of politicians of the derided Fourth Republic, and Jean Monnet, the commissioner of the Plan, were, without anyone much noticing, redrawing postwar Europe.

Monnet was the son of a brandy maker from Cognac. He was bustling, lively and courteous, with a dapper moustache, a far-seeing and exceptional man who was obliged to no one and to no party, and hostile to all pretensions. It was pointless, he told de Gaulle, to "talk about grandeur" when the French were "the size of pygmies". Only industrial recovery could fatten them up, he said, and that required a medicine that the general found deeply distasteful. "For an unlimited period, we are going to cooperate with the Anglo-Saxons," Monnet said.

Politics had little say in the Commissariat Général du Plan, which was the central body that determined priorities and investment across industry and economy. Monnet's genius prevented it from becoming overmanned and flatulent. He ran it, from a former private house, with a total staff of under 100, secretaries included, and an inner core of four or five. The INSEE, the national statistical service, helped to keep track of economic trends. The CNRS, the scientific research council, was reorganised and improved. The technocratic edge was honed by the École Nationale d'Administration, the super-elite finishing school of the public service. *Énarques* – there were only 140 or so graduates each year – were the Jesuits of state-led revival, switching from ministries to industry and back, a technical lobby of immense influence.

The early focus of the first Plan was on production and infrastructure. "Modernisation commissions" in each sector met regularly with employers, experts and trade unionists to discuss aims and how to attain them. The consumer was last in line, and the achievements were not instantly recognised. But they included the great Rhône dams, the electrification of the railways, and the use of natural gas; in the farm machinery sector, the number of tractors quintupled, and, in coal and steel, one of the most important political concepts of the century was spawned.

Under the London Agreements of June 1948, the French, British and American zones of Germany were to be fully integrated into the European economy. It was a courageous move. De Gaulle, who talked of the Rhine as the natural frontier of France, was utterly scornful; the Communists spoke of the rebirth of the Reich. The able, highly strung and hard-drinking foreign minister, Georges Bidault, was soberly realistic. "If we go it alone, we lose everything," he said. "In the unfortunate situation we find ourselves, we must follow the logic of national interest . . . To get US help, we have to approve the London Agreements."

No new Germany, no Marshall Aid: and American money was breathing health into France by the day. Three mini-miracles took place in January 1949; a state loan was floated and fully taken up, bread-rationing ended, and prices stabilised. By the spring, milk, chocolate, fats and textiles were no longer rationed, and black marketeers were beginning to feel the pinch. On April 4, 1949, the North Atlantic Treaty establishing NATO was signed in Washington. French security was assured.

Rambling through the Swiss Alps on a walking tour in the early spring of 1950, Jean Monnet had an idea that was to be "the very yeast" of European unity. Back in Paris, he had his little team at the Commissariat Général du Plan devise a scheme in which all French and German coal and steel production, and that of any others who cared to join, would be placed under a High Authority whose decisions would be binding on all. The project seemed too modest to live up to Monnet's claim that it would provide "the first solid base for the European federation essential for the preservation of peace". In that lay its strength. Attempts to promote European unity at the highest political level produced little but verbiage. Monnet saw that the economy could foster a less showy but deeper integration from below.

His plan was highly practical. It tackled French fear of renascent German industry, particularly the mines and steel mills of the Ruhr, head on. Steel was facing a crisis of over-production, and the independent Authority would aid modernisation and the closure of ageing and loss-making mills. It defused American concerns, too. They wanted Europe to be defended as far to the east as possible. West German reconstruction – and eventual rearmament – was vital to this. Monnet's plan gave them the evidence they wanted that France was prepared to take a fresh approach and to cooperate with its traditional enemy.

Monnet kept his plan secret, wisely, for the establishment leaked at every seam. A member of Schuman's personal staff went to Bonn to secure the swift approval of Konrad Adenauer, the chancellor. The British were not told until a few hours before the official announcement; the National Assembly, and the French steel masters and coal board, were not consulted at all.

France had seized, and was to retain, the initiative in European diplomacy. Many, of course, felt Schuman was merely boasting. De Gaulle denounced the Plan as supranational, and the Communists as anti-Soviet. The British failed to recognise that the French had outflanked them. They dismissed the Plan as ill thought out and flimsy, and stayed out. The three Benelux countries and Italy joined the French and Germans in creating the European Coal and Steel Community in 1951. This was simply a first stage. A project for a European Defence Community followed, the basis for a European army and a political Europe. The Gaullists and Communists were hostile to German remilitarisation. In August 1954, the Assembly rejected the project. On an economic basis, the same six nations signed the Treaty of Rome in March 1957, establishing the European Economic Community.

The country cut a dash at almost every level right through the Fourth Republic. The boxer Marcel Cedran won the world middleweight crown, and the heart of Édith Piaf, before being killed in a plane crash. The Fifties saw the French win rugby's Five Nations Tournament for the first time. A talent for exploring the remotest parts of the earth began to develop. Maurice Herzog and Louis Lachenal went higher than men had ever been in 1950. The conquest of Annapurna, the first 8,000-metre peak ever climbed, cost them severe frostbite and snow blindness. Haroun Tazieff began his dangerous and ultimately fatal quest into the secret life of volcanoes. Jacques Cousteau, inventor of the aqualung and an underwater television system, became the commander of the oceanographic research ship *Calypso* in 1950. His films on the mysteries of the deep pioneered a new genre of television. Two years later, the marine biologist Alain Bombard floated across the Atlantic in a rubber dinghy, thus proving his claim that a castaway could survive on nothing more than fish and plankton.

In the theatre, Jean Genet's *Les Bonnes*, a Gothic tale of two maids who plan to murder their mistress, showed that the old ability to outrage an audience was in fine fettle. It shocked – Genet punched the critic of *Le Figaro* for his damning review – but Cocteau thought it "a treasure", and Sartre and friends lobbied the jury to award it the Pléiade prize. Genet, a former reform school boy, male prostitute and prison inmate, crop-headed and broken nosed, was hailed as the "Proust of marginal Paris". Cocteau himself was thriving: in 1951, he staged *Les enfants terribles*. Alain Robbe-Grillet, whose first novel *Les Gommes* was published in 1953, established the *nouveau roman*. He wrote film scripts, too, of the quality of *Last Year in Marienbad*. The organist and composer Olivier Messiaen was bringing a new religious spirit to music, in works like his Livre d'Orgue. His interest in birdsong produced the Catalogue d'oiseaux in 1956. His pupil Pierre Boulez was musical director of Jean-Louis Barrault's Théâtre Marigny. Céline broke his silence in 1957 with his novel *D'un château l'autre*. He had escaped from Sigmaringen to Denmark in 1945, thus avoiding the death sentence passed on him in absentia. He returned to France after this was reversed. He suffered tinnitus, and partial paralysis, and bouts of near insanity, but he wrote as well as ever. The same year, Camus, who had just finished *La Chute*, won the Nobel prize.

Jean Dubuffet, once a rich wine merchant, earned colossal sums for Art Brut. He fashioned his pictures from cement, tar, gravel, silver paper, scraps of newspapers, broken glass, and plaster scratched and dirtied to look like an old wall. His style was midway between the primitive and the disturbed art of psychotics, half-graffiti, half-tribal; it was later said to be a precursor of Pop Art. Bernard Buffet reached his high-earning peak in 1956. The very least of his canvases fetched 500,000 francs. He emerged from a miserable adolescence, spending much of the winter in the centrally heated warmth of the Louvre, to paint stylised and sentimental portraits of clowns, still lifes of teapots, and Manhattan skyscrapers. His poster sales were phenomenal, enabling him to set himself up as "un gentleman-farmer". Every Western student seemed to have one in his room.

If Buffet prices soon collapsed, older talents helped maintain French importance. The venerable Matisse worked on his *Blue Nude* series almost to his death in 1954; Braque was still active, and Chagall returned from America in 1947. Jacques Tati's wonderfully deadpan comedies advanced from the delightful *Jour de Fête* in 1949 to *Mon Oncle* in gadget-ridden 1958.

In 1952, Brigitte Bardot, a ravishing young actress from Louveciennes, married Roger Vadim, the young man photographed with Juliette Gréco in Saint-Germain. She was a well-bred girl, with her own cocker spaniel, the stamp of respectability; he was a *Paris Match* reporter, of Russian blood, whose real name was Plémiannikov. "BB" showed how facile it was to fear Coca-Cola. France could produce her own worldwide symbols and brands. Raymond Cartier also analysed her as a new phenomenon in a de-Christianised world, with elegant insight. He wrote in *Paris Match* of a "degenerate spiritualism" that transfixed crowds in front of "les stars". It made Bardot the "ersatz madonna . . . of an eternal cult", with the pretty fishing port of Saint-Tropez as its cathedral. Old stars had dripped diamonds and haute couture; BB was in tune with "an epoch that rejects ties, make-up and corsets", and, in her case, often as not clothes as well. She "eclipses the greatest names of the era"; she earned millions, "domesticating money like an animal". She was, in short, the first of the modern superstars.

Another well-bred young girl, Françoise Sagan, was also a pioneer of morals. "A charming little monster", Mauriac called her. Her novel *Bonjour Tristesse* was published in 1954 when she was 19. It was an astoundingly precocious account of the end of an adolescent girl's innocence, anticipating the social and sexual adventures and pre-occupations of the 1960s, and her life itself was to have the sadness and emptiness that she wrote of so well. A wilful failure at school, she ploughed her second-year exams at the Sorbonne, and dashed off the novel in two months. The book sold a million copies. "So much money for so young a girl!" her rich industrialist father exclaimed. "Blow it!" She did so, setting a style for the modern "celebrity" and darling of the media. She turned her Aston-Martin upside down at high speed in 1957; she took drugs, and a coterie of soft-minded *intellos* demanded "Charge us too!" after she was convicted for cocaine possession. Radical-chic, she wrote naïve and politically correct pieces on Algeria and Cuba, finally driving student rioters to the 1968 barricades in her Maserati.

For years, she said, her image had been that of a "dissolute life". It wasn't exactly what she wanted, "but it's more fun than the alternatives. In the end, whisky, Ferrari and gambling is a more entertaining image than knitting, housework and saving."

Life, if improving for most, was still bitterly hard for some. Their cause was taken up by Abbé Pierre, a small, unkempt man in a stained and threadbare soutane with a ragged blouson against the cold, and a beret and sandals, bearded, walking with a cane, blazing with guile and energy. His real name was Henri Grouès. He was the Jesuit-educated child of a rich Lyon silk manufacturer, who had entered a Capuchin monastery as a young man. The war changed him. He joined the *maquis*, fought, was captured and escaped to Spain and on to Algiers. He entered the National Assembly as an MRP deputy after the war. He resigned in 1950, to start his own more left-wing party; he failed to win a seat, and became a near down and out himself in Paris. Here, amongst his fellow poor, he found his vocation. He got some seed money by appearing on a radio quiz show, winning 300,000 francs for answering questions on international affairs. At the start of 1954 there were 100 deaths among the old, homeless and infants of Paris caused by freezing weather, which caused in him a moral outrage that, for a few months, struck a deep chord with the nation. Speaking in theatre intervals, and on radio, within two weeks he had raised a billion francs. The Métro turned three unused stations into shelters for the homeless. Volunteers served meals and collected clothing. The *abbé* dared the housing minister, Maurice Lemaire, to attend the funeral of a slum child. Lemaire had little choice – Pierre had leaked the challenge to the press. The minister promised to introduce measures to spend 10 billion francs on public housing over the next year. Then the weather warmed; the public forgot its outrage, and, inevitably, the government fell before Lemaire could get his housing bill through.

Another traditional phenomenon – the arrival of a new political adventurer – kept the old cabinet instabilities company. Pierre Poujade, "le p'tit Pierre", who peeled off his coat and tie, and sometimes his shirt, as he got to work on an audience in his Auvergnat accent, emerged from the small-town southwest in 1953. In 1956, his brand new anti-tax party won nearly 2.5 million votes and 52 seats in the National

Assembly elections. By 1957, he was finished. The life-cycle of the mayfly comes to mind, but Poujade had more to him than that.

The seventh child of an impoverished builder in the Lot, he fled to Spain when the Germans moved into the unoccupied zone. From there he made his way to Morocco, and joined the Free French air force. He returned to his home town of Saint-Céré, and set up as a stationer and travelling book salesman. The town was in decline. Its population, 5,000 under Napoleon, Poujade's boyhood hero, had fallen to 3,000 with the drift of the young to the big cities. The number of small shopkeepers remained the same. Times were hard, and a government drive to enforce tax payments threatened to make them worse. Two tax collectors arrived in Saint-Céré in July 1953. A mob drove them away. Poujade watched, pondered and exploited. He had a mass of potential support to work on. Half the French were self-employed, compared with 5 per cent in Britain, tradesmen and shopkeepers frightened by the rise of chain stores and supermarkets. Tax evasion was a norm. "Of course I cheat on my taxes," Poujade admitted. "I always have. I couldn't survive otherwise."

He had a coarse country wit; his warmth and regard for the small man was real, and his nostalgia and affection for *la France profonde*, and contempt for bureaucrats, were unforced. By 1955, his party had 400,000 members. Their subscriptions financed two newspapers, and were used at public auctions to buy up property confiscated from tax evaders and return it to them. A crowd of 100,000 turned up at a Paris rally to hear him threaten a general tax strike. He said he could raise half a million people for a march on the capital.

It was no idle boast. After his success in the 1956 elections, he became more popular still when technicalities were used to invalidate the wins of 11 Poujadistes. He peaked when Pius XII granted him an audience in July 1956. It became clear that his deputies – small men like himself, plumbers, electricians, students, and, generally more able, disillusioned veterans of the Indochina war, like the Breton paratroop officer Jean-Marie Le Pen – were bruisers with few political skills. Poujade kept an eye on them from the gallery and the corridors of the Assembly, but his book *J'ai choisi le combat* revealed that he had few policies. Soon enough, in January 1957, Poujade tired of watching debates as an outsider. He made the fatal error of standing for the Assembly in a Paris by-election. The capital was not a small-time place. It humiliated him, giving him 19,906 of the 324,000-odd votes cast. He was finished.

Despite these alarms, the economy was growing strongly. Industrial production, measured at 100 in 1938, climbed from 50 in 1945 to 159 in 1954. By the Fourth Republic's last year, 1958, it was up to 213. If the German *Wirtschaftswunder* was stronger still, that was partly because it had started almost at zero in 1945. The French performance was much better than the British; it was better still than the heady days of the *belle époque*. The black market and ration books were gone. "Bof" – *beurre, œufs, fromages* – was no longer a mark of the rich or corrupt. The reason for the much-ridiculed campaign by Mendès-France to substitute milk-drinking for wine-bibbing was clear. The two adults in an average family were drinking 300 litres of wine, 168 litres of beer, 58 litres of cider and 3.7 litres of aperitif a year. Air travel doubled in the 1950s. Retails sales climbed by 40 per cent. Dior proved as shrewd a salesman as a designer. He was the first couturier to develop boutiques for ready-to-wear clothes, and he exploited his logo to sell branded spin-off scarves, sunglasses, jewellery and perfumes, exploiting the new "designer label" industry. It took time to get to grips with housing through HLMs (*habitation à loyer modéré*), low-cost state housing. Only 74,000 units were built in 1952. That had increased to 270,000 by 1957, however. These now included *grands ensembles*, high-rise estates with populations of 30,000–40,000. The first of these was built north of Paris at Sarcelles in 1954.

Then, at least, the drift to the cities made the estates welcome. In two decades from 1946, in the process that had hit Poujade's shopkeepers, the numbers living in rural France fell from just under half to a third of the population. A third of the houses in many southern villages were empty, the only market for them now was as holiday homes. Over the same period, however, the number of tractors on France went up from 20,000 to more than a million. Those who stayed on the land did well; when the EEC's agricultural policy kicked in, paying them to overproduce, they did very well.

The *cadres*, professional managers, emerged as a new component of the elite. The *ingénieur* produced by the *grandes écoles* served as a template for a rapidly growing caste that, from 1953, had its own magazine in *L'Express*. Managers of talent were found in the public sector: Pierre Massé at Électricité de France and Pierre Lefaucheux at Renault were outstanding men, and Louis Armand at SNCF railways saw a Paris-Lyon train claim the world record at 243 kph.

Women were emerging as more than factory fodder. They appeared in numbers in the professions, as doctors, lawyers, scientists, magistrates and bankers. They sat at the peak of public service on the Conseil d'État and the Cour des Comptes; from 1954, women stockbrokers were allowed to trade on the Bourse, and journalists like Françoise Giroud of *L'Express* had much influence. They were honoured, too. When Colette died – "What a beautiful life I've had," she said. "It's a pity I didn't notice it more" – she was the first woman to be given a public funeral in the Cour d'Honneur of the Palais-Royal.

Jacqueline Auriol, the president's daughter-in-law, became the first woman to fly at more than 1,000 kph in 1955, at the controls of a Mystère fighter, an aircraft that consolidated French airframe and engine manufacturers at the forefront of military aviation. The Caravelle airliner had its first test flight the same year. This highly successful aircraft put France into the passenger jet market, a factor of great future importance, for it was ultimately the French aircraft industry at Toulouse that enabled Europe to survive in the wide-body commercial sector. French engineering genius was running strong.

The "hexagon", mainland France, did not cause the fall of the Fourth Republic. Far from it. Its successive governments, obliged by coalition to be moderate, did the country proud. They saw off the threat of civil war; Socialists like Jules Moch showed real courage in facing down striking miners. Growth rates were spectacular, and proved sustainable. State-owned industries, sluggish in most countries, were dynamic. Even the highly sensitive nuclear programme survived the political uncertainties: the development programme for nuclear power stations and weapons was well advanced by 1958. In foreign policy, too, the results were happy. Bidault allied the country decisively with the West; Schuman and Monnet brought reconciliation with Germany, and leadership in a unifying Europe. De Gaulle's anti-Americanism, and his nationalist "Europe des patries", might have done for both.

The general himself had written his memoirs. It seemed unlikely, at the beginning of 1958, that any call would arise for another volume. He was photographed in his bosky manor house, sitting with a book in a corner of his study, whilst Madame de Gaulle knitted. Here, it seemed, was a man deep in retirement.

His startling comeback was entirely due to events outside metropolitan France. They brought down the Fourth Republic, but they pre-dated it. The first stirrings of distant trouble took place before its birth. Control of French Indochina had passed to a Vichy-appointed governor after the fall of France. He retained nominal power after Japanese troops burst violently into northern Vietnam in September 1940. After French border forts were overrun, the Vichy government signed an agreement permitting the Japanese to station troops in Indochina. The overthrow of Vichy in 1944 had no immediate impact, since liberated France had no means of dealing with its distant Asian empire. By early 1945, however, the Japanese feared that the French in Indochina would switch loyalties. In March, at Lang Son in the north, the French commanding officer and the civilian governor were decapitated under the eyes of the garrison when they refused to order it to surrender. Some French troops fought their way over the Chinese border, where the Nationalists interned them. The Japanese forced the emperor of Annam to proclaim Vietnamese independence under Japanese "protection". The continuity of French rule in Indochina was broken.

Two months later, trouble broke out in Algeria. Muslims streamed into Sétif, a market town on the dusty and treeless plain west of Constantine. Graffiti had been scrawled on walls – "Muslims awake!" – and a demonstration turned into a massacre of 103 Europeans, including women and children.

Government reports put the number killed in the pitiless repression ordered by de Gaulle at between 1,020 and 1,300. It was, however, Cairo Radio's inflated claim of 45,000 that persisted; and a sergeant Ben Bella of the Algerian Tirailleurs, who returned from fighting in Europe, said that "the horrors succeeded in persuading me of the only path: Algeria for Algerians".

"I have given you peace for ten years," General Duval, the French divisional commander who put down the rising, reported to Paris with great prescience. "But don't deceive yourselves".

De Gaulle gave the incident a single line in his memoirs. He sold it short. These two incidents presaged the wars that returned him to power.

12

Adieu to Empire

Indochina had a moist beauty, but it was a terrible place to fight, half as large again as France, much of it thick and steeply sloping jungle, which robbed the French of mobility. Bad precedents were set from the start. Soldiers and officials in the field took unauthorised actions that weak cabinets in Paris glossed over for fear of precipitating a government crisis. The politicians had no clear-cut policy on empire, other than not to negotiate with independence movements whilst violence continued, thus ensuring, of course, that it did. The mutual mistrust between the army and politicians bred a loathing that, transferred from Indochina to Algeria, was to bring down the Republic itself.

The Japanese surrender in August 1945 created a vacuum. British troops landed in Saigon to maintain order in the south whilst a small expeditionary force under General Leclerc sailed out from France. In Hanoi in the northern province of Tonkin, Ho Chi Minh, the leader of the Vietminh nationalist guerrillas, took advantage of the French absence to proclaim the independence of the Republic of Vietnam on September 2, 1945. Ho was in his mid-fifties, a mandarin's son who had sailed to Marseille as a cook aboard a French ship in 1911. He became a founder member of the French Communist party, present at its birth at Tours in 1920. His military commander was Vo Nguyen Giap, a French-trained lawyer who was to prove himself a brilliant strategist of revolutionary war.

The Vietminh's status as a pro-Allied force had earlier earned them American arms drops and support. Initial relations with Jean Sainteny, the colonial commissioner for Tonkin, were also good. An outline agreement was reached in Hanoi in March 1946. Ho agreed that French troops would enter the north, with Leclerc's troops replacing the ill-disciplined Chinese. Referendums on the reunification of Vietnam would be held. French troops would be withdrawn after five years. In return, the French would recognise the Republic of Vietnam, within the framework of the French Union, a commonwealth of associated states, territories and overseas *départements*. This smacked of a sell-out to Admiral Thierry d'Argenlieu, the hardline High Commissioner sent out by de Gaulle. He was a former Carmelite monk, thin-lipped and intense, said by one of his staff to have the "most brilliant mind of the twelfth century". He plotted to stymie Vietminh control of a unified Vietnam by creating a southern state run by a puppet government in Saigon. Ho was flying to Fontainebleau for talks in June 1946 when d'Argenlieu proclaimed the "autonomous Republic of Cochinchina". He did so without warning, but without rebuke. The military, too, were playing politics. Leclerc wrote to the MRP's Maurice Schumann, describing Ho as an enemy of France to whom no concessions should be made.

The new regime in Saigon soon unravelled, but it served d'Argenlieu's purpose in sowing mistrust. The Vietminh opened fire on a French naval crew who were boarding a suspect junk in Haiphong, the port of Hanoi, in November 1946. The French cruiser *Suffren* shelled the Vietnamese quarter of Haiphong in retaliation, and troops with tanks went in on the ground. The French estimated Vietnamese

And God Created Woman launched *Brigitte Bardot – "Initiales B.B.", as she called her controversial autobiography – as the global symbol of screen sensuality in 1956. Her presence also helped to transform Saint-Tropez into one of the world's most fashionable – and overcrowded – resorts.*

LA FRANCE PROFONDE

Traditional France survived in the 1950s, but it was coming under pressure. The first supermarkets would tempt these shoppers (below) in the Seine-Maritime. The Church still christened and buried most people, and married them, here (right) at Chinon in the Indre-et-Loire. But it saw them less and less in between.

An outline agreement between the Vietnamese leader Ho Chi Minh and Jean Sainteny, the colonial commissionaire for Tonkin (both seen left), in March 1946 soon broke down. After heavy fighting (right), the loss of the French position at Dien Bien Phu in May 1954 marked the end of French rule in Indochina. France did not remember heroes – Father Jeandel, a chaplain who parachuted into a doomed outpost, Lieutenant Grézy and his platoon of Chasseurs Laotiens, who held off a battalion for 58 days, and many more – and turned its back on the survivors. "They were not suffering sons who were returning home to have their wounds cleaned, but strangers," Jean Lartéguy wrote of the survivors of the Vietminh prison camps (below). "Bitterness mounted within them." They took those feelings with them to Algeria.

Algeria was the remaking of de Gaulle. An uprising by settlers in May 1958 – ominously for
the government – was backed by the army. De Gaulle alone had the moral authority to deal
with the crisis. On June 2, he was invested with full powers. Two days later, he flew to Algiers (below)
to stand in front of an enraptured crowd with his great arms stretched into a V. "Je vous ai compris,"
he said. Perhaps he had understood them, though not in the way they thought. Algerian women
got to vote (right) for the first time, in Oran in September, but no early settlement was in sight.

(Overleaf) The French were not only fighting Algerians. They were also scrapping among themselves.
As time drifted by, and settlers sniffed signs of a sell-out of their interests, they took to the streets
(here in Algiers on the rue Michelet in December 1960), and to the gun and plastic explosives.

END OF EMPIRE

Militarily, the war was won. The Algerian fighters were forced out of Algiers into the Atlas and the desert (right). Paratroops and legionnaires tracked down one group of fellagha through the sands for 35 days, killing 52 of them and liquidating them as a coherent force. But no end to the war was possible without a political settlement. The terms de Gaulle accepted meant the end of the French presence in Algeria, with crowds of settlers at the docks in Algiers (below) and harkis, Algerians loyal to the French, arriving at Marseille (left) in July 1962.

French cinema had a further golden age. Catherine Deneuve (right), overshadowed by her sister Françoise Dorléac before Dorléac's death in a road accident, became a star with the unexpected hit The Umbrellas of Cherbourg *in 1964, honing her image of exterior calm and inner passion as a psychopath in* Repulsion *and a bourgeois housewife turned prostitute in* Belle de Jour. *Intensity and sensuality were hallmarks of Jeanne Moreau, here (above) in the 1958 film* Lift to the Scaffold. *Jean-Paul Belmondo and Jean Seberg (below) charmed their way through* Breathless, *Jean-Luc Godard's racy 1960 take on American film noir.*

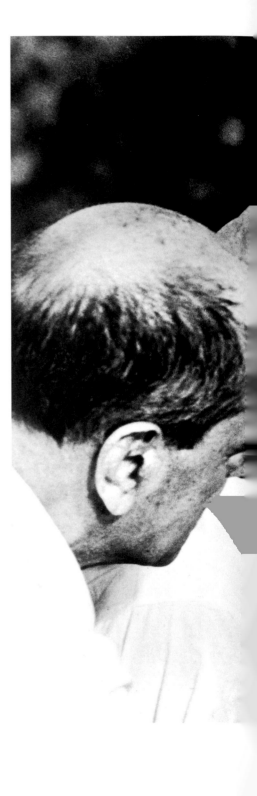

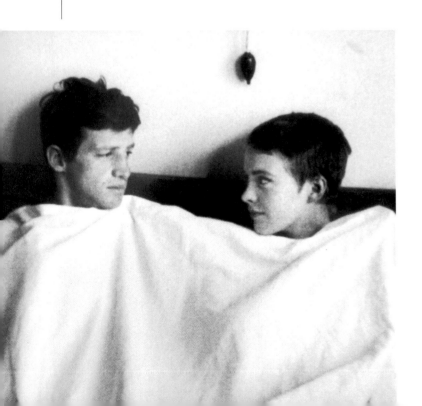

Only in France could intellect and cinema culture spark off massive rioting. The events of May 1968 began with the sacking by André Malraux of Henri Langlois (left, on the left), the crusty but well-loved creator of the Cinémathèque Française. Directors of the stature of Jean-Luc Godard (below left) marched in protest. Malraux, the culture minister (left, on right) had to give way and Langlois was reinstated. Gaullism's vulnerability to demonstrations was noted by university students in Paris. Twelve thousand of them were crammed into the muddy concrete campus at Nanterre. Trouble there spread to the Sorbonne in central Paris, with nightly battles (right) between riot police and students, and much tear gas.

(Overleaf) Cars were overturned on Left Bank streets (left) for use as barricades against the police as the clashes accelerated in May 1968. The most prominent leader of the student enragés was Daniel Cohn-Bendit (right), a 22-year-old sociology student, carrot-haired, gap-toothed, with "the heavenly blue eyes and suspect candour of a nursery favourite".

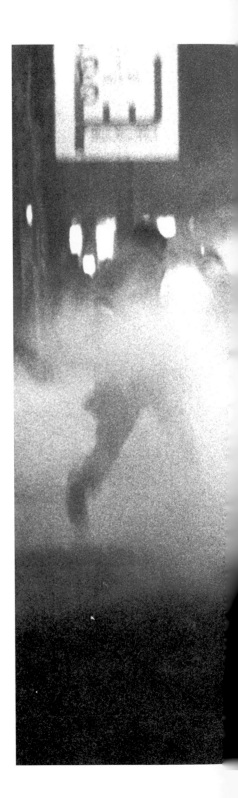

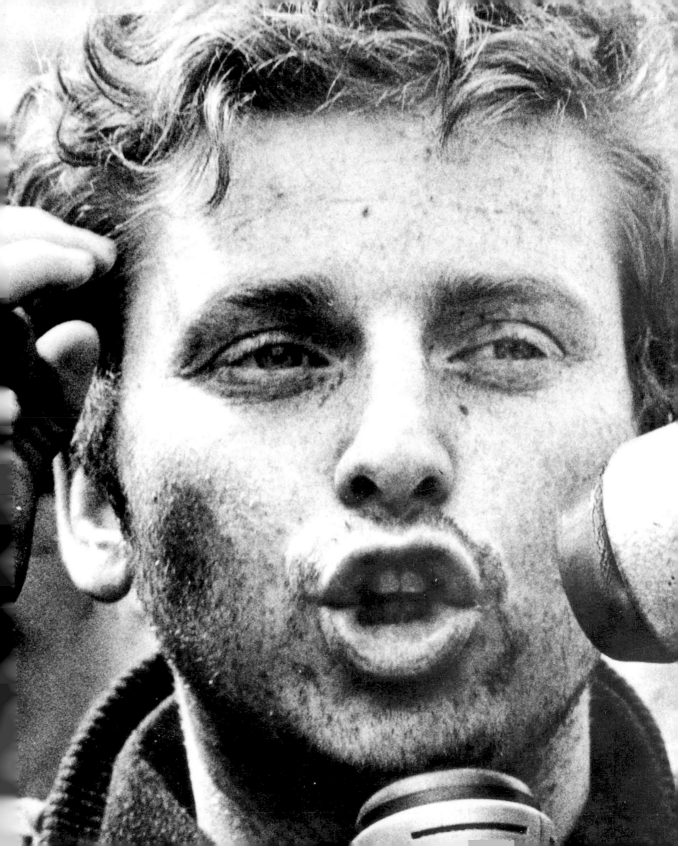

SPEED, SPACE, POWER

The oil shocks of the early 1970s and soaring fuel prices doomed commercial prospects for the Anglo-French Concorde (far right) from the outset. The Mach 2 aircraft was a technological triumph, setting still unbroken records for passenger aircraft, and a design of peerless if noisy beauty. The Ariane rocket programme (right) kept Europe in the space race and the satellite launching business. A massive and successful programme for nuclear power stations (below, at Marcoule on the Rhône) reduced French dependence on imported oil and gas, and was more environment friendly than its critics allowed.

POP AND PROSPERITY

Les trente glorieuses, *the 3o immediate post-war years, saw heady and unbroken expansion. Every indicator – life expectancy included – was sharply up. As the number of cars hurtled from 1 to 15 million, even some of the young were able to buy one (right). As incomes more than doubled, the young also had disposable money to spend on popular music by singers such as Serge Gainsbourg and Jane Birkin (bottom) or Johnny Hallyday (below).*

OFF THE LAND

*Farm workers fell from a third
of the workforce at the end of the
war to a tenth. People streamed
out of the countryside into the
towns, towing their possessions
behind them (bottom). But the
indomitable peasant woman
(below) clung on, and the lavender
fields of the Col des Tourettes in
the Drôme still flourished in
timeless tranquillity in 1969 (right).*

Informally clad hippies (left) attend a free radio "anti-jamming" festival at Yerres in the Essonne. Noise and cacophony were, of course, characteristics of the young generation all over the West. Environmental concerns were another. Tens of thousands went to the plateau of Larzac (below) to support Roquefort cheese-makers who had tried to block the expansion of a military base on land where their brebis *roamed, the sheep who gave milk for this queen of blue cheeses.*

SAVANTS

The philosopher Michel Foucault (facing page) succeeded Sartre as
the leading intellectual provocateur. His work **Les Mots et les choses**
had sold 100,000 copies by 1967. Foucault was stridently anti-Vietnam,
pro-gay liberation, pro-drugs, pro-counter culture, and studiously
outrageous. He argued that, but for rape and sex with children,
there should be no restraint on behaviour. Foucault was the star pupil
of Louis Althusser (middle right), the frail Communist philosopher,
who championed Marxism as an "unassailable and unavoidable"
science, before a tragic descent into madness and murder. The novelist
Claude Simon (top right), who was to win a Nobel prize in 1985,
wrote sensuous and complex novels, notably **The Wind** and
The Flanders Road, tinged with deep pessimism. Jacques Derrida,
seen at the Sorbonne (bottom left, on the left) with his fellow philosopher
Vladimir Jankelevitch, explored the use of language and the objectivity
of structures, and founded the school of "deconstruction".

TIME OFF

Holidays became ever longer and more complex. France offered great variety within itself. It had winter skiing (below, right), often as here in the Haute-Savoie with accommodation in high-rise apartments making no concession to the alpine architectural tradition of the wooden chalet. In summer, there was climbing in the Alps, with a rapid descent from the slopes of Mont Blanc by paraglider (right) for the bold. At Saint-Tropez (below, left) the sun worshippers were laid out like sardines on a grill, or ate on the beach (bottom right). The hexagon was stitched together by a rapidly improving road network (left).

ST-TROPEZ

HAUTE-SAVOIE

CÔTE D'AZUR

The eyes in Giscard's campaign posters were cruelly replaced by diamonds (left) in 1981. They referred to the precious stones given to the president by the Central African dictator Jean Bokassa. The affair was a factor in Giscard's loss of office to François Mitterrand. Mitterrand shares an aside with Édith Cresson (right), whose spectacular downfall as prime minister was followed by an equally unsuccessful stint as a commissioner in Brussels. Jacques Chirac adopted Nicolas Sarkozy (below) as a political protégé when the ambitious youngster was barely out of his teens. They fell out over Sarkozy's later support for Édouard Balladur. This lese-majesty was compounded by Sarkozy's popularity soaring past that of his old chief.

ONT MOIN
DE 25 ANS

VEC LE MOUVEMENT
HESSE SOCIALISTE

François Mitterrand holds hands with Helmut Kohl (right) in symbolic Franco-German reconciliation at Verdun. The gift of millions of francs to Chancellor Kohl's Christian Democrats was one of many scandals under Mitterrand. Another concerned gifts made to his foreign minister, Roland Dumas, by his mistress Christine Deviers-Joncour, who memorably described herself as the "Whore of the Republic". The pair are seen together (below) watching tennis at Roland-Garros in Paris in 1990. Alain Juppé, seen here (above) as prime minister in 1995, had to put his public life on hold after his conviction for misuse of public assets.

ARCHITECTURAL GEOMETRY

Mitterrand ensured that Paris would remember him by studding it with memorials to himself. They include the graceful Arche de La Défense (right), the troublesome Opéra Bastille, the equally fractious National Library, and the glass pyramid (below) forming the entrance to the Louvre designed by I.M. Pei and opened in 1989.

SPEED MERCHANTS

The French had a genius for the dangerous sport of sailing state-of-the-art boats at very high speeds over very long distances. Here Bruno Peyron and his boat Orange II *(right) approach Brest in March 2005 after sailing round the world in 50 days 16 hours 20 minutes and four seconds, clipping more than a week off the existing record. Other high-speed Frenchmen and women included the racing driver Alain Prost (left) and the athletes Christine Arron and Muriel Hurtis (above left) after the women's 4 × 100 m relay at the 2004 Olympics, where they won bronze.*

French goalkeeper Fabien Barthez jumps over the Brazilian Ronaldo as teammate Lilliam Thuram looks on during France's 3–0 victory in the 1998 World Cup Final.

casualties at 6,000. Sainteny used his links with the Vietminh to try to prevent a slide to war, but it was too late. Giap attacked French civilians and property in Hanoi on December 19. Forty people were killed, including women and children. French troops swiftly regained control of the city, and Ho and his staff fled to the country-side. Prime Minister Blum said that Vietnamese independence was the only way forward, and said that negotiations would resume, but only – and here he fell into the lethal trap – after order was restored.

It never was. The weak colonial minister, Marius Moutet, was sent out to Indochina. D'Argenlieu showed him photographs of women and children mutilated by the Vietminh. It was d'Argenlieu who again made the running, announcing in January 1947 that it was "from now on impossible for us to deal with Ho Chi Minh", and that the Vietminh had "disqualified themselves" from negotiations.

The French hoped to have done with the whole Vietminh force, by parachute drop and deep armoured encirclement, in the autumn of 1947. The Vietminh slipped through the *bouclage*, the French ring of armour and infantry, almost at will. In December, the French pulled back to the Tonkin lowlands, leaving a line of forts along the Chinese border.

The war settled into a bloody and dispiriting stalemate. At home, a series of scandals chipped away at morale, and there were leaks, dangerous to the men fighting in the field, who felt abandoned by France, even despised or betrayed. Equipment was sabotaged before it left France; sugar was found in fuel tanks, and emery oil in gearboxes. The barest minimum of operational detail was sent to Paris, for fear that it would be leaked to the Vietminh. Military salaries became linked to civil service pay scales in a way that rotted morale and status. Lieutenants with several years' service found themselves worse paid than third-level postal workers. A lieutenant-colonel with 24 years service was paid the same as a second-level customs official.

Mao Zedong's victory in the Chinese civil war was a strategic disaster. From the autumn of 1949 onwards, the Vietminh had friends across the Chinese border, where they could train, refit and rearm. Giap attacked the French border forts with overwhelming force in October 1950. Three paratroop battalions were dropped in as reinforcements, but by January 1951 the French had lost control of all northern Tonkin, and were digging in to hold the Red River delta. They had lost 6,000 men, and enough weapons to equip two Vietminh divisions. It was France's greatest colonial defeat since Montcalm at Quebec two hundred years before.

Giap now strove for the coup de grâce. "Ho Chi Minh in Hanoi for Tet" was the slogan of a massed offensive, aimed at breaking into Hanoi for the Chinese New Year, in mid-February. Human-wave attacks began on January 16 1951. Headlines in France announced the expected fall of the city. The new commander-in-chief, Marshal Jean de Lattre de Tassigny, sent ships that arrived to evacuate women and children back empty to France. "As long as they are here," he judged, "the men won't *dare* let go." Until the final months, the French never had more than 275 aircraft, with old British Spitfires and Junkers 52 trimotors taken as war booty from Germany, but they were decisive against enemy concentrations in open country. "Immense sheets of flame strike terror in the ranks," a Vietminh officer wrote of air attacks. "This is napalm, the fire which falls from the skies." Giap's offensive was broken. The war continued. De Lattre died of cancer. Political pressure from Paris for results to justify the Indochina budget led to forlorn offensives and heavy losses. In 1952, the paratroops surprised the Vietminh in a sweep to Tienyen – the operation was a success, *Paris Match* noted in a bitter aside, "because no one in Paris knew of it in advance" – but among the equipment they captured were Molotova trucks, evidence that the Soviets as well as the Chinese were arming the Vietminh. The ceasefire in Korea in 1953, though it led to an increase in already substantial military aid from Washington, equally allowed the whole Communist war effort in Asia to focus on Indochina. On moonless nights, in each *poste kilométrique* along the de Lattre line, a sergeant and nine men would listen in their hot and fetid concrete cube for the rattle of empty ration cans on the wire that presaged a Vietminh assault. Little epics of heroism passed unnoticed in France: the chaplain who parachuted into an outpost in the T'ai hills to be with the wounded when it was overrun, the Senegalese and Vietnamese dead at Bao-Chuc, Lieutenant Grézy of the Chasseurs Laotiens, who resisted for a month amid the ruins of his post at Muon-Khoa, fighting on from his bunker after the rest of the position was charred and lifeless, until a pilot at last saw the tricolour and the red flag with the three white elephants of Laos torn down from atop it, and knew that Grézy and his men were gone too . . .

The end was reached at Dien Bien Phu, a year later. The French commander, General Henri Navarre, was to claim to the commission that investigated the catastrophe that the government had made a political decision to defend Laos. He planned to achieve this by creating fortified camps with an elite garrison in a large bowl of land, 20 kilometres by 8, in rolling hills close to the Laotian border. Joseph Laniel, the prime minister, maintained that he had told Navarre that he was to ensure the safety of our expeditionary corps "above all else".

Reinforcement and resupply of Dien Bien Phu were possible only by air. It was thought impossible for Giap to bring up heavy weapons to this remote and roadless region. He did so, however, by bicycle and bicep, and dug his guns in on high ground. The muzzle flash when they fired was concealed from French artillery spotters by the thick foliage. When French aircraft braved Giap's Russian anti-aircraft guns and attacked with napalm, the leaves threw off a dense smoke that hid the guns. The aircraft on the landing strip were destroyed, and the 15,000-man garrison was effectively trapped. Ground attacks started. It became impossible to land aircraft by day, and increasingly perilous to do so by night. The last aircraft in landed at 3.45 a.m. on March 28. Aircraft had only one line of approach for supply drops, and the Vietminh concentrated their anti-aircraft guns along it. The lumbering C-47s had to make several runs to get their loads out of the side doors. Forty-eight aircraft were shot down over the valley, some of them flown by American civilian pilots. Volunteers continued to parachute in to replace dead or wounded specialists, 1,530 of them, and 94 jumped into the burning ruins the day before Dien Bien Phu was overrun on May 7. Eight hundred of these brave men were Vietnamese: Moroccan and Algerian *tirailleurs*, foreign legionnaires, and Laotians and Vietnamese fought side by side with the French.

At Sidi-bel-Abbès, the Foreign Legion headquarters far distant in Algeria, Colonel Gardy read the order of the day. "Let us present the honours to the flags of our units which have disappeared in the battle," he said. The rows of men in white kepis and crimson epaulettes were silent as the bugler played "Aux morts", the Last Post.

The war was quickly tidied away. The Laniel government collapsed. Pierre Mendès-France became prime minister with a huge majority. A Radical deputy before the war, he had escaped from Vichy imprisonment to navigate bombers in the Free French air force; he was a politician of the highest quality, and he had long warned of the "incoherence" of Indochina policy. The independence of Vietnam, Laos and Cambodia was recognised. Vietnam's partition at the 17th parallel proved a disaster for the region and the war between north and south, hugely expanded by the arrival of 500,000 American troops, was to suck all Indochina into fighting until 1975. But it was the best deal that Mendès-France could have got for France.

The army was less easily dealt with. Eight years after the bugle's sad notes at Sidi-bel-Abbès, Gardy, by now a general, was sentenced to death for rebellion against the state. The disillusion that brought him to that had festered since Indochina.

A good regular army has a family feeling. It underpins loyalty and esprit; but it also makes its collective soul vulnerable to the pain of individual casualties in a way that a conscript-fed machine is not. In all, 21 sons of French marshals and generals died in Indochina: Bernard de Lattre on a rocky crag above Ninh-Binh, Henri Leclerc de Hautecloque in the Vietminh camps, young Gambiez at Dien Bien Phu . . . Four generals were killed, too. This was not an army whose officers hid their own. More men died as prisoners than on the battlefield. After 57 days of continuous combat, the survivors of Dien Bien Phu were marched over bad terrain made worse by heavy rains to prison camps between 450 and 530 miles away, on a diet of cold rice. *Marche ou crève*, the men said, march or croak. In all, almost 95,000 troops were killed, and 1,200 of them were lieutenants. Professional armies do not forget such sacrifices. They are too intimate. As they themselves rose to major and colonel and beyond, the surviving officers mourned the lost lieutenants. They thought less fondly of the politicians who knew and cared so little for them, and who had reduced their status to a level unknown since the Bourbon Restoration. "They were not suffering sons who were returning home to have their wounds cleared, but strangers," Jean Lartéguy wrote of the officers coming out of the camps. "Bitterness mounted within them." They took those feelings with them to Algeria.

On November 1, 1954, a *Toussaint rouge* (bloody All Saints' Day) was unleashed by Muslim nationalists, with 30 explosions and eight murders south of Constantine. For all the defiance – "Algeria is France," the interior minister, François Mitterrand, retorted, "and France will recognise no authority in Algeria other than her own" – the peace in Algeria was over. General Duval had been prophetic indeed.

The Algeria of the French was in the coastal cities and the Mitidja, the rich, flat farmland they had created out of malarial swamps, with great vineyards and citrus and cereal farms centred on towns with shaded squares and plane trees and bandstands that were as French as their names, Rabelais, Orléansville, Victor-Hugo. It was not the *bled*, the vast outback formed by the Atlas Mountains and the Sahara.

Jacques Soustelle was appointed governor general by Mendès-France in January 1955. A former leader of the Gaullist RPF, his liberal reputation went down badly with the French Algerians, the *pieds noirs*. But on August 20, 1955, at the same time that Europeans were slaughtered in Morocco, the FLN (Front de Libération Nationale) carried out a massacre at Philippeville and the nearby mining village of El-Halia. The FLN commander, Zighoud Youssef, ordered that the killings be deliberately gruesome, with women disembowelled and decapitated, and children cut in pieces. The intention was to provoke Soustelle into massive French retaliation, which would stir up international opinion and bring Muslim moderates into the revolt. It succeeded. Many Algerians were indifferent or hostile to the *fellagha* of the FLN. Resentful of French repression and predominance, however, and intimidated by FLN terrorism, it was natural for them to ensure the safety of their families by clandestine support for their fellow Muslims. Apart from *harkis*, the often unreliable Algerians in French service, the French had little active support from the people.

Militarily, they achieved the 10 to 1 ratio that was the rule of thumb minimum needed to defeat guerrillas. After Mendès-France fell, brought down by the war and his unpopular efforts to promote milk in place of alcohol, Guy Mollet sent 500,000 conscripts to Algeria. This gave families in the *métropole* a new and personal interest in the fighting. Morocco and Tunisia won full independence in March 1956, but the army choked the supply routes to the FLN from them by building the Pedron and Morice lines along the borders. Infiltration was slashed to a trickle by electrified fences, floodlights, minefields and aggressive patrolling. In isolated and far-flung "forbidden zones", the population was forcibly moved out to create free-fire zones. Almost a quarter of the Muslim population, two million people, relocated from rural villages into camps where they were held for the duration of the war.

The most spectacular success came in the battle for Algiers, which lasted for most of 1957. General Jacques Massu, the army commander in the city, relied heavily on paratroops, among them Lieutenant Jean-Marie Le Pen, whose work in burying the remains of Egyptian soldiers during the Suez operation had earned him the nickname "Borniol", after the leading undertakers in France. Accurate intelligence on the

FLN network in the city, and the liquidation of its leadership, were the hallmarks of the operation. It was supplied by commando units led by Major Paul Aussaresses, an Indochina veteran. Torture was used "as a matter of course", Aussaresses admitted in a book he wrote as a retired general many years later. His men controlled the night – "At sunset we slipped into our leopard camouflage uniforms and the horse race would begin" – ranging through the city, arresting suspects, torturing and then killing them. The methods he used, he said, were always the same: "Beatings, electric shock and, in particular, water torture which was the most dangerous for the prisoner ... who would either talk quickly or never." The current used to inflict *gégène*, electric shocks, was supplied by the generators for field radios.

He had no qualms. People who opposed torture were "clearly FLN sympathisers", he said, or "bleeding heart idealists". The soldier had a simple choice: to torture a terrorist suspect, and thus avert an atrocity, or to allow the attack to take place because it was better for innocents to die than for "a single accomplice to suffer". Aussaresses had seen "civilians, men, women and children quartered, disembowelled and nailed to doors", and he had no pity for those who did it.

Neither, he said, had the government. The civil power had called on the military to re-establish law and order. Counter-terrorism and summary executions were a part of the process. Torture was "tolerated, if not actually recommended". Aussaresses noted that a judge, Jean Bérard, was the de facto representative to General Massu of François Mitterrand, the justice minister. The judge, he said, "covered our actions and knew exactly what was going on during the night".

Paul Teitgen, the secretary-general at the Algiers prefecture, and a survivor of Dachau, was one of a handful of officials who objected openly to torture. He calculated that the paratroops had executed 3,024 people. Jacques de Bollardière, a much-decorated general, was so upset at what he saw during the battle of Algiers – the abandonment "of the moral values which alone have hitherto created the grandeur of our civilisation and of our army" – that he asked to be posted back to France. He was sentenced to 60 days' fortress arrest when he made his views known in a letter to *L'Express*. Success ensured that most stayed silent. The campaign in Algiers was a model of ruthless brilliance. The FLN leadership, responsible for a campaign that bombed civilians at bus stops, restaurants, nightclubs and other soft targets, was eliminated. Aussaresses himself hanged Yacef Ben M'Hidi, the main organiser, at a farm outside the city. He passed it off as suicide, to the delight of Bérard, Mitterrand's man, who exclaimed: "Well ... it *does* make sense!" But it was impossible for the army totally to eradicate the *fellagha,* though it did all it could to win hearts and minds. The SAS, the *sections administratives spécialisées* or *képis bleus*, worked with great courage under Arab-speaking French officers to improve conditions in the villages, to bring water, medicine and schooling to the poor.

No end to the war was possible without a political settlement. The failure in Algeria was political, and demographic. Nine of the ten million people in Algeria were Muslims. Their number was growing exponentially, and they wanted – in part were terrorised by the FLN into wanting – their own state. The FLN, for its part, knew that its atrocities did not rule out independence, but simply put pressure on the French. Independence was gathering momentum in 1957, the year that Britain's great African empire began to dissolve, as the Gold Coast became Ghana.

But government was incapable of decision. It suffered a moral failure, too. Its authority was undermined by the lack of a stable majority, by the waltz of cabinets and the sniping from the margins, from Communists, Poujadists, Gaullists. The Fourth Republic suffered a slow collapse. It could not cope with Algeria; not with the army, the FLN or the *pieds noirs*, nor with torture and the other issues of terror and counter-terror.

Everyone knew this. It had been clear since February 6, 1956. Guy Mollet visited Algiers that day. The new prime minister, fresh from the electoral victory of his centre-left Front Républicain, had decided to replace Soustelle with Georges Catroux, whom the *pieds noirs* suspected of being soft on Arabs. They greeted Mollet with a hail of insults, tomatoes and rotten fruit, and rioting. "It is not Soustelle they wish to keep," Mouloud Feraoun, one of Algeria's finest writers, observed, "but their privileges, their wealth and their slaves." Mollet bowed to them, and Catroux was replaced. A month later, the National Assembly had formally granted the army police powers in Algeria. Mollet was no coward – he had a fine record as a *résistant.* He set up a Protection Commission for human rights. It found widespread evidence of brutality. The government suppressed its report, but details were leaked to *Le Monde*. A vivid, first-hand account of interrogation was written by Henri Alleg, the Communist editor of *Alger républicain* and an FLN sympathiser. In *La Question*, he described how he had been interrogated by paratroops during the battle of Algiers, and suffered half-drowning, electric shocks, burns and beatings. Sartre wrote a long review of the book in *L'Express*. He said that torture was corrupting young soldiers – "Hate is a magnetic field . . . it has crossed over to them, corroded them and enslaved them" – and France itself, for the country was "mute" to what it knew was happening. The whole edition of *L'Express* was confiscated on the orders of the interior ministry. Next, all copies of *La Question* were seized, the first such political suppression of a book for over a century.

"I was completely retired," de Gaulle claimed in his memoirs, living at Colombey, opening his door "only to my family and people from the village". It was nonsense. He went to Paris weekly, to his modest office in the rue de Solférino, seeing all manner of men, many officers among them. A Gaullist group in Algiers, known as the "Antenna", led by Léon Delbecque, worked to channel settler and army opinion into a movement for the general's return to power, and was backed by the Gaullist "barons" in France. Few *pieds noirs* or army officers were instinctively Gaullist.

Delbecque worked hard and subtly to convert their fears for *l'Algérie française*, and their vague plans for a military coup, into support for the general. He dealt with a strange swirl of people: politicians of distinction and experience, like Michel Debré and Jacques Soustelle, ex-Pétainists, Algerian Poujadists, Pierre Lagaillarde, the camouflage-clad demagogue and leader of young *pieds noirs*. He became close to politicised officers. Colonel Jean Thomazo, known as "Nez de cuir" for the leather strap that concealed a face wound, was typical of those who saw *l'Algérie française* as a bulwark against Communism. Its loss, he thought, would rot the *métropole*. Rather than that, the army should take power. Such views struck a chord with General Paul Cherrière, a former commander-in-chief and a Bonapartist whose great-grandfather had served in the imperial guard. Cherrière formed a loose group of Indochina veterans, called the "Grand O", and nurtured contacts with commanders in the fifth military region in southern France, where most of the paratroops were based. Delbecque shuttled between Algiers and France, making almost 30 trips in six months. He kept the "barons" informed, and they passed on news to de Gaulle. "We did not tell him everything," an aide, Olivier Guichard, said. "We told him all that was necessary."

The new year started angrily. Early in January 1958, 15 French soldiers were killed close to the Tunisian border by *fellagha*, who took four prisoners back to their Tunisian sanctuary. French bombers attacked a Tunisian border village and women and children were among the 69 dead. No advance warning was made by the military to Félix Gaillard, the prime minister, or to Robert Lacoste, the minister-resident in Algiers, who complained wearily: "They really are idiots." Surly police held a noisy demonstration outside the National Assembly on March 13. They shouted anti-Semitic slogans and demanded the payment of promised "danger money". A month later, the Gaillard government collapsed, and wild rumours swept Algiers. A "vigilance committee" was set up. Its members – Delbecque and his Gaullists, groups of ex-servicemen and *pieds noirs*, and ultras, Lagaillarde – had little in common beyond the desire to destroy the Fourth Republic and thus to preserve *l'Algérie française*. A mass demonstration on April 26 was followed by a call to President Coty for the formation of a government of public safety. No mention was yet made of de Gaulle.

On May 9, the FLN in Tunis announced the execution of three French soldiers, who had been held prisoner for over 18 months. There was still no government in Paris. That evening, the four senior generals in Algeria sent a telegram to General Paul Ely, the chief of the general staff. They said that the army, "to a man", would consider the surrender of Algeria "to be an outrage ... Its desperate reaction is unpredictable." The army's "anguish" would only be assuaged "by a government firmly resolved to keep the French flag flying in Algeria". The army had, nakedly, entered politics.

The Sunday stablemate of the *Echo d'Alger* on May 11 had a leading article, by the ex-Pétainist editor, Alain de Sérigny, that called on de Gaulle to act: "I implore you, speak, speak quickly, mon Général . . ." The general's name was out of the hat. A riotous mass of *pieds noirs* filled the streets round the war memorial on May 13, supposedly to pay respect to the executed soldiers. The slogan shouters grew harsher. "L'armée au pouvoir!" they cried. Lagaillarde, dancing in his camouflage at the head of a mob of students and teenagers, a wild Pied Piper, led them to sack the American Cultural Centre. He then moved on to the "GG" (Gouvernement Général), the main government building. Police fired tear gas, but Lagaillarde guessed correctly that the police and army sympathised with the crowd, and would not use live rounds.

The gates were battered open by a truck. Rioters ransacked offices, and threw files and papers out of the windows to the cheering crowd below. Paratroops replaced the police, and did nothing to restore order. General Salan was booed when he appeared on the GG balcony, but Massu, adored for his victory in the battle of Algiers, was cheered to the echo. At 8 p.m., the radio announced that Massu had agreed to lead a Committee of Public Safety. It was strange indeed for a general to go where Robespierre had trod in 1793; but revolution was in the air, and the radio spoke with awe of the "storming" of the GG, as if it were the Bastille or the Winter Palace.

Delbecque was caught unawares by the ransack of the GG, but he was on the committee, and his hard work now paid off. Salan sent an appeal to the Elysée. The military command, he said, thought it "an imperative necessity" for a "national arbiter" to set up a government of public safety. This could only mean de Gaulle. Parliament, however, was determined to thwart the Algiers plotters. In the early hours of May 14, it voted in a new government under Pierre Pflimlin, a reform-minded and moderate Strasbourgeois. In Paris, where he was paying his weekly visit, de Gaulle was asked how he saw events in Algiers. "What events?" he replied. This was, of course, pure theatre, for he was about to make his move. It reminded one admiring observer of Richelieu's dictum: "Savoir dissimuler, c'est le savoir des rois."

May 15 was decisive. Salan spoke to the crowd outside the GG in the morning. He finished with the ritual couplet: "Vive l'Al-gé-rie franç-aise. Vive la France." Then Delbecque prompted him to make it a trinity. Salan turned back to the crowd, and added: "Et vive de Gaulle." Salan was not a Gaullist. Neither, until then, was Algiers. But the name was received with rapture by *pieds noirs*, and with hope by Muslims.

At home in Colombey, de Gaulle was drafting a press statement. The "degradation of the state", he said, led inevitably to the "alienation of the associated peoples" and to "disquiet" in the army. The problems were "too harsh for the party system". In the past, France had trusted him, from "its heart of hearts", to lead it in unity. "Today, as it faces a grave new trial," he concluded, "may the country know that I hold myself ready to assume the powers of the Republic." It was masterfully nuanced. Who were those "associated peoples" to whom he offered comfort? Colons or Muslims? Did army "disquiet" embrace mutiny? And, if the "party system" had failed, with what did this unelected figure propose to replace it? But such subtleties passed unheeded when Delbecque read the statement that evening to the mass acclaim of the Algiers crowd.

Massu and Salan were conniving with generals in mainland France to plan "Operation Resurrection". Its aim was to use troops – paratroops from Algeria, units from the Toulouse command of General Roger Miquel, and tanks from Rambouillet – to pressure parliament into bringing de Gaulle to power. The general himself, not seen in public for almost three years, gave his first press conference since 1955 in the ballroom of the Palais d'Orsay on May 19, combining immodesty and indefinability – "I am the man who belongs to no one and who belongs to everyone" – to brilliant effect. He was masterful and decisive, or so it seemed, the ideal anti-toxin for the nation's poisonous politicking; but he was as careful as any party hack to leave no hostages to fortune. "Algeria must remain with us," he said. This had all the ring of *l'Algérie française*, and none of the content. By appealing to all men of goodwill – "to those French who want to recreate national unity, on one side of the Mediterranean or the other" – he avoided committing himself to any in particular.

Scorn was heaped, not on the rebels in Algeria, but on the party system. It had become "absolutely normal and natural" for the malcontents to "seek a remedy for their misfortunes outside parliamentary coalitions". He "understood full well" the attitude of the Algiers command. The army "is normally an instrument of the state," de Gaulle said, adding a scathing rider, "providing, of course, that there is a state." It was the disintegration of authority, he said, that made him willing to assume the powers that the Republic delegated to him. But he was as silent on his ideas for the future of government as he was on Algeria. He merely denied that he would harm public liberties. "Why should I, at the age of 67," he asked angrily, "begin a career as a dictator?" Pétain had been older still, of course, when he had set himself up with army backing in 1940. De Gaulle ignored the precedent. "Now I shall return to my village," he concluded, "and remain there at the disposal of the country."

On May 24, paratroops took over Corsica. This was treason, but the general remained silent. Towards midnight on May 26, he had a secret meeting with Pflimlin at the Château de Saint-Cloud. Pflimlin made it clear that he would not resign unless de Gaulle publicly condemned events in Algiers and Corsica. The general refused. As he was driven back to Colombey in the early hours of May 27, he prepared a communiqué. It was issued shortly after noon. He announced that he had begun the "regular process" of forming a "Republican government". This was a gigantic bluff, for Pflimlin remained prime minister, even if in desperate circumstances. This audacity was skilfully concealed beneath reassurances: to politicians, that he stood for a "Republican" regime; to the army, that he expected it to continue its "exemplary conduct" under officers "in whom I express my confidence"; to the nation that its "calm and dignity" would be rewarded.

Late that evening, the National Assembly gave Pflimlin a resounding vote of confidence. It was illusory. "Between the Seine and you," Georges Bidault told deputies after the vote, "there is only de Gaulle." A cabinet meeting was held at 2 a.m. on May 28. "We claim to exert power," René Pleven, the foreign minister, said, "but we do not have it." The army did not obey the defence minister. The interior ministry was losing control of the police. It was unsafe for the ministers of Algeria and the Sahara to visit the territories for which they were responsible.

In the early hours of May 28, Pflimlin saw President René Coty at the Élysée. He offered his resignation, conditional upon de Gaulle having a clear majority in the Assembly. Later in the day, in Colombey, de Gaulle received General André Dulac, an envoy sent by Salan. They talked about "resurrection". De Gaulle was as enigmatic as ever. He said that he wanted to be called to power by popular demand, rather than installed by putsch. But the message he sent back to Algiers with Dulac was approving: "Tell Salan that what he has done, and is going to do, is for the good of France."

A huge demonstration set out in the afternoon on the traditional *voie royale* of the left from place de la Nation to République. "Soustelle to the scaffold!" they chanted. "De Gaulle au musée!" But no one was willing to take to the barricades in defence of the Fourth Republic. That night, Coty arranged a secret meeting for de Gaulle with the Speakers of the Senate and the Assembly. It was again held at Saint-Cloud. The general laid down his terms. They were onerous, nakedly revealing his contempt for the constitution and for parliament. He was to be excused a personal appearance in front of the Assembly when it voted for or against his nomination as prime minister. A new constitution was to be submitted to a referendum. The Assembly was to be prorogued for a year, during which time he would govern by special decree.

André Le Troquer, the Speaker of the Assembly, "vain, pompous and of questionable morals", and, more to the point, an anti-Gaullist Socialist, would have none of it. De Gaulle bade him a menacing adieu – he had no alternative, he said, "but to leave you to have things out with the paratroops and go back into retirement, with grief as my companion" – and returned to Colombey. Coty had lost all belief in the Republic of which he was first citizen. He no longer had the stomach to haggle with the parties for yet another government. He determined to call on the only person whose "incomparable moral authority" could save the country. Preparations for "resurrection" continued in Algiers and Toulouse. How far de Gaulle connived with this was not clear: the general had a genius for obfuscation. Some of the conspirators, notably Salan and General Jouhaud, were to claim that de Gaulle had agreed that the operation should go ahead at 1 a.m. on May 30, and that it was cancelled only after it was known that Coty had called de Gaulle to the Élysée. This was in 1962, and by then they had good reason to paint de Gaulle as sly and devious: they had rebelled against him over Algerian independence, and were on trial for their lives. What seems certain is that, had de Gaulle not been accepted by the Assembly, then paratroops would have arrived in Paris in short order with his tacit blessing to install him. The Socialists were the key. Auriol, Mollet and other party grandees drove out to Colombey on May 30, where de Gaulle delighted them and flattered them, reassuring them that his government would remain responsible to the Assembly. The general returned to Paris to charm the other party and faction leaders on May 31, the unspoken menace of red berets and leopard camouflage behind him. The next day, he was voted into power by 320 votes against 224. It was no triumph, but it was enough.

De Gaulle flew to Algiers on June 4, on a Caravelle, the airliner that symbolised the renascent brilliance of French industry. He shook hands with Salan and Soustelle on landing. That evening, he stood on the balcony of the GG in front of an enraptured crowd, and stretched his great arms upwards into a V. "Je vous ai compris," he said, and perhaps he had, but not in the way they thought.

The wind was with him, and he sailed fast. A new constitution was drafted over the summer. He explained it lucidly to a crowd of 150,000 Parisians in the place de la République; he spoke for 25 minutes without notes, for it followed the reforms he had first suggested in a speech at Bayeux in 1946, and he knew its provisions by heart. It retained two chambers, and ministerial responsibility, but the executive was greatly strengthened at the expense of parliament. The president was given strong powers. He appointed the prime minister, and he had broad if imperfectly defined primacy in foreign policy, defence and fundamental political issues. It was a throwback to monarchy, transforming de Gaulle into "King Charles XI", or so Sartre complained. "I do not believe in God," the philosopher wrote, "but if in this plebiscite I had the duty of choosing between him and the present incumbent, I would vote for God. He is more modest."

But the electorate approved of it by 80 per cent in the referendum in September, and parliamentary elections in December gave a big majority to the Union pour la Nouvelle République (UNR), the reconstituted Gaullist party. At the end of the year, de Gaulle was elected president of the new Fifth Republic. He was 68.

It was less easy to bid Algeria goodbye. Yet de Gaulle had immense advantages over the men of the Fourth Republic whom he so despised. The constitution was custommade to facilitate a settlement on his terms. He enjoyed undreamt of executive power. His party dominated the Assembly. His prime minister was the loyal Michel Debré. He was riding, too, at least at first, on a wave of popular goodwill. No one knew his policy on Algeria, because he had none. What emerged was so serpentine, so subject to fits and starts and reversals, that its purpose perhaps eluded its creator himself. The empire had never much interested him. Ambitious fellow officers had sought out colonial postings before the war. De Gaulle, exceptionally, chose to stay in metropolitan France, a brief stint in the Levant apart. Despite his assurance to the *pied noirs* that he "understood" them, he was never committed to *l'Algérie française*. He used the phrase only once – on June 6, 1958 – and even then made sure that it did not appear in his collected speeches. Typical of his style was his declaration a few months later: "Long live Algeria with France, long live France with Algeria!" That, of course, can mean everything, or nothing. These early months were his best chance, a time to bang the heads of ultras and *fellagha* together, and to impose a compromise settlement: the war was largely won, and momentum and prestige were on his side. He squandered them. He left the *pieds noirs* untouched and, while the Muslim moderates may already have been so alienated by torture and reprisals that it was no longer possible to separate them from the terrorists, the first offer he made to the FLN was cackhanded.

A year later, in September 1959, he tried again. He went on television to say that Algeria's future lay in "self-determination". A referendum would offer its people three choices: "francisisation", secession, or self-government in association with France. The vote would take place four years after a ceasefire, which he again invited the FLN to negotiate. The FLN issued another humiliating rejection. This was, nonetheless, his first public mention of possible independence – even if he used the pejorative "secession" – and it alarmed the *pieds noirs*. They smelled betrayal. Lagaillarde and Joseph Ortiz, the *patron* of the Bar du Forum, a *colon* hothouse, were the prime conspirators.

On January 24 1960, ultras began building barricades. Many were territorial soldiers, in uniform and carrying weapons. Gun battles broke out when the police tried to clear the streets. Two dozen were killed, and scores injured, most of them police. French were killing French for the first time. Worryingly, too, paratroops fraternised with ultras. Civil war and revolution seemed ever closer until de Gaulle addressed the nation on television on the evening of January 29. He wore his uniform, with the two general's stars, the familiar figure of the Liberation, and he spoke with genius. He was pitiless with the rebels – "coupables, usurpateurs, conspirateurs" – and he ordered the army, as soldier and head of state, to obey him. His conclusion was mesmerising, an intimate, affectionate appeal to France: "Mon cher et vieux pays, nous voici donc ensemble . . ." (Well now, my dear old country, here we are, together again, facing a stern trial . . .). The pay-off line was stern: "I expect the support of all, no matter what may happen." After a week, wearing his medals and camouflage, with a sub-machine gun slung on his chest, Lagaillarde climbed over the great barricade in the rue Charles-Péguy, and got into his wife's car for a final appearance on the balcony of the Bar du Forum. "Pour Lagaillarde!" the faithful cried. "Pour l'Algérie française! Hip, hip, hurrah!" It was not the end of rebellion.

Another year slid by. De Gaulle made a "tour of the messes" in Algeria to reassure the army that it would not be humiliated. He used a new phrase now, an "Algerian Algeria linked to France". In June, he secretly met a group of FLN dissidents in Paris. Negotiations with the FLN itself opened at Melun, but broke down. Terror and counter-terror continued. More stories of torture appeared in the French and international press, as young conscripts returned after their military service.

In December 1960, de Gaulle paid his final visit to Algeria. He was mobbed by angry chanting *pieds noirs*, and by Muslims waving FLN flags. He walked into the hostile crowds, with his characteristic courage, but they persuaded him that compromise was impossible, and that independence was inevitable. A referendum he called on the principle of self-determination in January 1961 showed, as he suspected, that the French in France wanted rid of Algeria. Three-quarters of those voting in the *métropole* approved. He opened secret negotiations with the FLN.

The army sniffed a sell-out. Foreign Legion paratroops moved in small groups through Algiers at 2 a.m. on April 22. By dawn, the city awoke to find strongpoints and the radio station controlled by the men in camouflage. The *putschistes* appeared on the famous Forum balcony, four of the country's most senior generals including Salan. The conspirators planned a march on Paris. Eighteen hundred paratroops had gathered in the forest of Orléans, and a further 400 at Rambouillet.

De Gaulle went on television in the evening of April 23, to speak of the nation "defied", shaken, its prestige debased, its role in Africa "compromised". And by whom? "Hélas! Hélas!" he said. "By men whose duty, honour and raison d'être it is to serve and to obey." He was again in uniform, and in masterful mood. He spoke contemptuously of "ce quarteron de généraux en retraite", this little quartet of retired generals. "In the name of France," he said, "I order that all means, I repeat all means, be used to block every avenue to those men . . . I forbid every Frenchman, and above all every soldier, to carry out any of their orders." He ended this bravura performance with a call to arms: "Françaises, Français! Aidez-moi!"

Across France and Algeria the conscripts listened to the speech on their radios. Cries of "Vive de Gaulle!" were heard in the barracks in Algiers. The putsch was done for. The Foreign Legion paratroops, the elite heart of the revolt, stylish to the last, dynamited their barracks at Zeralda and marched off to be disbanded, defiant to the last, singing Piaf's "Je ne regrette rien."

De Gaulle reopened negotiations with the FLN. The putsch had, however, revealed his hand to them. The first talks were held at Evian in May 1961. By July, they had failed. The FLN were holding out for total capitulation.

Ultra gunmen of the OAS traded atrocities with the FLN, and both sides killed their own. The young French officers of the SAS saw the schools they had built burnt down and the Muslims who worked with them on village improvement schemes with their throats slit. The anti-war liberals in the *métropole*, they noted, ever on the *qui vive* for French misdeeds, were silent when the outrage was Arab.

Indeed, Sartre and others justified Muslim terrorism. Frantz Fanon, a black psychiatrist from Martinique, and a persuasive and powerful writer, elevated terrorism beyond a simple response to repression. "At the level of individuals, violence is a cleansing force," he said. "It frees the native from his inferiority complex and from his despair and inaction. It makes him fearless and restores his self-respect." Sartre, in particular, was enchanted. The Third World, he said, "found itself" in Fanon and "spoke through his voice".

The OAS began a bloody campaign in mainland France: a desperate, foolish move that merely bolstered the public desire to be rid of Algeria at any price. Attempts were made on de Gaulle's life. On September 8, 1961, a bitter young colonel, Jean-Marie Bastien-Thiry, attacked the general's Citroën with explosive and napalm at Pont-sur-Seine as he was being driven home to Colombey. The explosive dated from the Resistance and was degraded. Car and passenger survived. The police were targets for both OAS and Algerian terrorists. Sixteen were killed and 45 wounded in two summer months.

Thousands of Algerians – men, children and women in veils – congregated round the Opéra Métro station as it grew dark on October 4, 1961. They had come to protest against a new police curfew that banned them from the Paris streets after 8.30 p.m. They swept down the avenues in great numbers, cascading through the traffic, terrifying shoppers coming out of the Galeries Lafayette, "gloomy, forbidding figures", the women giving their ululating cries, half shrill bird, half wounded beast.

The chief of police was Maurice Papon, later to become notorious when his record as a Vichy official was revisited. He decided to control the demonstration with his city police – the ordinary *agents* in kepis and cloaks – rather than call on the hard-nosed riot professionals of the CRS. The police panicked; demonstrators were clubbed and thrown to drown in the Seine. The official death toll was put at 200.

In the shambolic OAS assault on Paris, the editor-in-chief of *Le Figaro* was bombed twice. *France Soir* was *plastiqué*, too, attacks that merely hardened press condemnation. The big new drugstore on the Champs-Élysées was bombed, and a machine-gunner raked the front of the Communist Party headquarters. They tried to bomb Sartre's apartment on the rue Bonaparte, but they chose the wrong floor. One of a clutch of bombs that exploded on February 7 was intended for André Malraux; he was away, and it disfigured and half-blinded a four-year-old girl. The following day, a leftist demonstration was called at the Bastille. Ten thousand attended, a small turnout, but the police were nervous and charged at the Charonne Métro station. Eight died, and a crowd now estimated at half a million followed the coffins to Père-Lachaise for the funeral. "My God!" Simone de Beauvoir wrote in her diary. "How I hate the French!"

Negotiations continued at Evian, and killings in Algiers. De Gaulle conceded everything: even the Sahara oil and gas, which France had fought so hard to keep, was to go. On March 26, 1962, a strike and demonstration by *pieds noirs* in Algiers led to the fusillade of the rue d'Isly, in which 80 were killed. In April, 90 per cent voted in favour of the accords in the referendum. Algeria was to become independent in July. The *pieds noirs* fled.

The ferry *Ville de Marseille* sailed at midday, with a typical cargo, her decks packed tight with émigrés. A woman sobbed her husband's name – "Marcel, Marcel" –

as if it might bring him back. He was a petty official, and she did not know whether the OAS or the FLN had abducted him. Her *fatma* (nanny) had warned her the day before that she had been told to slit the throats of her children, so she fled with them, on the boat. A boy sobbed as he looked on to the white walls of the cemetery of Saint-Eugène, where both his parents lay, killed by an FLN bomb four years before.

It was over. A million Algerian French left for France. The Algerian political elite came back, from prison or from exile in Tunis. Strangely, though, very few of the 400,000 Algerians in France returned. Perhaps they sensed the unpleasantnesses – renewed civil war, assassinations, torture – to come.

13

The General

The government had begun to offer free passage from Algeria in May 1962. By July, all but a handful had gone. The battered and beggared masses who stumbled off the boats in Toulon and Marseille, with no more than a few pitiful suitcases to show for three generations of toil, were nonetheless absorbed into France with stunning ease. If one had to be expelled from house and home, at least 1962 was the year to do it. The economy expanded by 6.8 per cent, a record. OAS violence had its last hurrah on August 22. As de Gaulle's black DS passed through the village of Petit-Clamart, the indefatigable Colonel Bastien-Thiry returned to riddle it with machine-gun fire. The bullets were so close that they passed behind the general's head and in front of his wife. Had either ducked, they would have died. Both remained erect and unperturbed. "Bad shots," the general murmured. Madame de Gaulle, after checking that the chickens she had packed in the boot were undamaged, remarked that, though it would have been sad for her son-in-law if they had died, "for the general and myself, it would have been a fine ending". As to the colonel, he was caught and – though other military rebels were reprieved – was shot.

It is ironic that the revival of France, for which de Gaulle took such credit, was based on things he scorned. Its roots, deep and hardy, were laid by the Fourth Republic. It was carried through by the bourgeoisie, by businessmen and cadres of great quality, whose motive was profit. The general approved of neither. He despised money: "My greatest adversary, that of France, has never ceased to be the power of money." This carried through into an acid view of the middle class. "I have never been bourgeois," he said. "The bourgeoisie is wealth – the sense of having it, or the desire to acquire it. My family and myself have always been poor . . . I have never felt linked to the interests of this class."

De Gaulle is difficult to typecast in terms of class, for he was driven by destiny, and he had the eccentricity which goes with such singularity of purpose. But in his family life, with his wife Yvonne, and in La Boisserie, their comfortable little manor house in Colombey, with its sombre brown paint and heavy furniture, where he spent his evenings reading to the clicking of her knitting needles, they lived by the old rituals of a bourgeois couple of honourable breeding and no great means.

He read Corneille, Racine and Chateaubriand – and Sagan, one of the few tastes he shared with Mitterrand – and described himself as a "Catholic by geography and tradition". Mme de Gaulle, "Tante Yvonne", was austere and a prude, known to intervene only to prevent him from having divorced men as ministers, and perhaps to persuade him to revive a 300-year-old law that opened landlords to the confiscation of their property if its was used for prostitution. Their daughter Anne died of Down's syndrome at 20 in 1948; he loved her very dearly, and set up a foundation for handicapped children, to which he gave much of the money from his memoirs. He had, so Harold Macmillan claimed, "all the rigidity of a poker with none of its occasional warmth"; but he had intense emotions, for Anne, for France, and he was very conscious of serving an ambition higher than himself. It gave him great personal courage, and stage presence, but it made him disdainful of those who pursued wealth and personal ambition. His qualities were soldierly, and he knew and cared little for economics, though his lofty dismissal of them – "l'intendance suivra", the baggage train will bring up the rear – was probably apocryphal. But he chose his ministers well.

Young talent could rise under the old man. Giscard, a secretary of state at 33, was the youngest finance minister of the century: too young, too sharp, too ambitious to be anyone's lackey. It was a major blow when he launched a splinter centrist party, the Fédération Nationale des Républicains Indépendants. "Are you Gaullist?" *Paris Match* asked him in 1967. "I have retained the lesson of General de Gaulle," he replied. "I am French." Another youngster tipped for the top that year was Jacques Chirac, entrusted with youth employment at the age of 35, an *énarque*, like Giscard, and a fireball of energy, hurtling in his Peugeot 403 at 180 kph twice a week to and from his fiefdom in the Corrèze.

The boom was strong and sure. Growth climbed an average of 5.8 per cent a year. Germany managed only 4.9 per cent, and Britain – whose output France overtook – a miserable 2.9 per cent. In 1965, the reserves reached $5 billion, a cushion plumper than any but the Bundesbank's. It was easy to strangle initiative with high taxes, inflated social security costs, rampant bureaucracy, over-regulation and protectionism. Freed by talented ministers from these bugbears, relishing lower corporate taxes and increased depreciation allowances, French industry modernised and became highly competitive on world markets. Mergers were encouraged. The steel industry was focussed around three firms; CII was created in computers, and the nationalised aviation industry was combined into SNIAS.

A shopping revolution sparked off by the Breton store-builder Édouard Leclerc gained speed when Carrefour opened the first hypermarket at Sainte-Geneviève-des-Bois in 1963. Within six years, there were 253 hypermarkets in the Paris suburbs alone. Agricultural production climbed steadily, though the number of farmworkers, and the amount of land farmed, continued to fall. The baby boom helped the makers of toys, prams, refrigerators and washing machines. The proportion of exports almost doubled, a sure sign that French companies were becoming more competitive.

Many young people were changing their vision, taking their leave of their milieu. Less than a quarter of homes had a refrigerator in 1960. In a decade, that shot up to 85 per cent. The same number now had a television set, providing the mass audience so brilliantly exploited by de Gaulle. Seventy per cent of homes had baths or showers, and half had central heating, unthinkable luxuries a few years before. As late as 1954, a third of homes had no running water; within a decade half had washing machines. The telephone, under the dead hand of state control, was another matter. In 1969 only 28 per cent of households had one, and there was a 16-month waiting list for a line. Fashion turned egalitarian. Dresses and skirts lost out to trousers and blouses. The key year was 1971, when skirt production fell by three million, and, with perfect symmetry, trouser making advanced by the same figure.

New housing was built at record pace, with vast new estates of high-rise flats. They were modern enough, in terms of plumbing and electrics, but some were already descending into soulless vertical slums, stripped of the familiar comfort of local meeting places, corner cafés, bakeries, grocers' shops: "hospitals for long-term maladies", Jean-Luc Godard called them in his bleak film *Alphaville*.

By 1972, there were more than 2,000 kilometres of motorway, and by 1974 70 per cent of households had a car. French engineers were masters of front-wheel drive and diesel. The car was a source of status and national pride. It was also a means of death. The road toll, grievous enough at 9,900 in 1962, reached 15,100 in 1970. Camus was dead on the road; so, overtaking on a wet road outside Saint-Tropez, was Françoise Dorléac, sister of Catherine Deneuve, whose red hair and freckles had charmed audiences at the premiere of *Les Demoiselles de Rochefort* a few months earlier. Despite this appalling record, a 90 kph speed limit on main roads was not brought in until 1972, and it was two years later before a 130 kph limit was brought in for motorways. Safety belts became compulsory in 1973.

Cars and exotic holidays replaced excursions by bicycle and the fortnight on a crowded beach. Skiing, the vacation sport of an elite 1 per cent in 1964, soon reached 17 per cent, to the benefit of the likes of Les Arcs and La Plagne. Gilbert Trigano, a veteran of the Communist Resistance, launched Club Med with great marketing savvy. Money was replaced by beads, giving the illusion of freedom from bourgeois consumerism, and the patch of shingle on the Norman or Breton coast became a gleaming expanse of southern sand. Vacations were longer, too, with four weeks' paid holiday from 1963. *Résidences secondaires*, holiday homes, began their long climb.

Tiercé betting was the most profitable public enterprise in the country. It exploded in 1962 with the 3-franc, 3-horse wager. Turnover rose from 1 billion to 6 billion francs, eight times more than total cinema takings, and it was producing 19,000 franc millionaires a year by 1973. Only *pétanque* could match the speed and geographic penetration of its growth. In team sports, France won the Grand Slam in the Five Nations rugby in 1968.

Prosperity and bustle sucked in immigrants. During *les trente glorieuses* France's foreign population doubled, from 1.7 million in 1946 to 3.4 million in 1975, and by then Arabs and Africans made up almost 40 per cent of the total. It had been assumed that they would return home after earning money, but growing numbers began to bring their wives and families to France. The feminisation, and hence growth and permanence, of a non-Christian foreign population was not yet a political issue of any real significance, but it had surfaced.

Prosperity enabled Gaullism fully to flower. Impoverished, the country would have had less truck with grandeur. The essentials of Gaullism – the strong president with his *chasse privée*, his "reserved domain" of great questions of state, the taste for referendums and tinkering with electoral processes, the powerful executive and often timid legislative, the mistrust of Anglo-Saxons, the prickly notions of status and independence – survive to this day. Its architect is a living force. He turned defence, foreign policy and critical issues like Algeria into presidential prerogatives. The constitution did not specify this – the sharing of executive power between president and prime minister was badly defined, and remains so – but he made it so.

Debré was known as Fidel Castrato – a commentator asked: "Does he exist?" – so powerful was his master. The prime minister wanted to dissolve parliament after the Evian accords in 1962, to produce a new Assembly for new issues. Instead, though the issue had not been debated in parliament, de Gaulle replaced Debré with the banker Georges Pompidou, a former adviser, who had never sat in an elective assembly. His government got only a narrow majority in parliament. Cartoonists showed him as a valet, always with a feather duster in hand. Cabinet meetings saw no lively exchange of views. "Funeral wakes with one difference," a minister described them. "The corpse speaks." No smoking was allowed, and no asides. De Gaulle was even-handed in those he annoyed: conservatives over Algeria, Socialists with economic liberalism, liberals with anti-Americanism.

Gaullism did well among old-fashioned conservatives – in the west and east, with women, Catholics and the elderly – but it had a populism that took votes from across the divide. The general held plebiscite to be an important fountain of democracy. One result was his passion for holding referendums; eventually, he was to try the electorate's patience with these once too often. Another was his distinction between *la nation profonde* and the *régime*. In its contempt for parties, its admiration for heroic leadership and plebiscitary democracy, Gaullism had a passing resemblance to Bonapartism. He called parties elites, clans, castes, with their own clientele and interests: but, though he thought of his own as a *rassemblement*, it in fact had its Gaullist barons and fiefdoms, and slid easily enough into *Chiraquerie*.

The last president to be elected by universal suffrage was Louis-Napoléon in 1848. He had gone on to abolish the Republic, and Republicans had feared a directly elected head of state ever since. They were naturally suspicious when de Gaulle raised the issue and, as a further provocation, put it to the test directly by a referendum, even though his own constitution required that such a constitutional reform first be debated by parliament. De Gaulle, of course, turned the referendum into a test of faith in himself, threatening to resign if he was defeated. The reform scraped through; then, when the first popular presidential election was held, in 1965, he failed to win outright, and was forced into a run-off with François Mitterrand, whom he beat but did not overwhelm. Mitterrand, the Fourth Republic's most sinuous careerist, had no such inhibitions. He famously described the Fifth Republic as "a permanent coup d'état", but had no qualms about vying to become its head of state.

De Gaulle's temperament, his "certain idea of France", and the underpinning of prosperity made him redouble his search for grandeur. "France is not really herself except in the front rank," he said. "France cannot be France without greatness . . ."

Though he had denounced the Treaty of Rome in 1957 – it was the achievement of the Fourth Republic – he saw rare opportunities once he was in power. With admirable economy of words – "Italy is not serious . . . the English console themselves for their decline by saying they share in American hegemony . . . Germany has had her backbone broken" – the general stated that Europe was the chance for France to become "what she has ceased to be since Waterloo: the first in the world". He thought of France as the "third international reality", the "only one at the moment, apart from the Americans and Russians, to have an ambition for the nation".

On January 14, 1963, sweeping the trial of Salan off the front pages, de Gaulle dealt the Anglo-Saxons a dramatic double drubbing. He announced that he would veto British membership of the EEC, and he turned down an offer by President Kennedy to provide the French with Polaris missiles as part of a multilateral NATO force. He did so because he mistrusted them both. Britain would always follow America – Churchill had told him as much – while Europe had "become an American protectorate without realising it".

He thought that Europe could become the "most powerful, prosperous and influential political, economic, cultural and military grouping in the world". Its individual countries had, of course, been all of those things in the past: now he saw its future as a bloc free of American domination. But he thought supranationality to be a dangerous illusion. Who would die for the European Commission? Or who for NATO? So France was to be brought out of NATO's integrated command structure. Ironically, his view of the Europe of Nations coincided with that for which the British were roundly criticised. It was, as Macmillan said, a "Europe à l'anglaise, but without the English." Great importance was placed on an independent French nuclear deterrent. The first atom bomb, for which the credit must go to the Fourth Republic, was exploded in 1960. He was dissatisfied, and at once pressed for a thermonuclear bomb.

He did not trust the Americans to risk their own annihilation to protect Western Europe from the Soviets. Never in "their entire history", he said, had they put their "existence in the balance for an engagement abroad". The expeditionary forces they did send were no more than a fraction of their capability, "even if", he added with breathtaking condescension, "they fought hard". This was niggardly – and vacuous, for history had never tested America in such a way – and the truth of the matter lay more in his prickly sense of grandeur. It was, he said, "intolerable that a great state should confide its destiny to the decision and action of another state, however friendly it may be". In fact, the French deterrent in the 1960s was so weak that it is doubtful it caused Washington or Moscow many sleepless nights.

The French Mediterranean fleet had been withdrawn from NATO in 1959, and the Americans were forbidden to put nuclear weapons on French soil. The aggravation continued. In 1964, de Gaulle recognised the government of communist China. He visited Cambodia in 1966, and, in a speech in the sports stadium at Phnom Penh, demanded that the Americans withdraw from the region. The same year, France pulled out of NATO, whilst remaining in the Atlantic Alliance, and all foreign troops were required to leave French soil. When President Lyndon Johnson was told, he asked whether all the American dead from the two wars buried in France would have to go too. As the NATO nations left their French headquarters, the British military band played "Charlie is my darling", to cock a snook at the deliberately absent de Gaulle. A few months later, to rub in his independence, he visited Russia.

None of this caused real harm, or indeed much good. Grandeur tends to be in the eye of the beholder. Relations with West Germany – a country he would happily have seen dismembered in 1945 – were more positive. He asked Chancellor Adenauer to stay at Colombey in September 1958, a singular honour extended to no other foreign leader. In 1962, the two leaders attended mass in Reims Cathedral. The special relationship lost some warmth when the Bundestag insisted on a reaffirmation of German loyalty to NATO being included in a new treaty with France, and Adenauer was replaced by Ludwig Erhard, a less ardent Francophile.

A policy of *Eurafrique* was pursued, with much aid and goodwill poured into Africa, where French interests were directly managed from the Élysée by the president's adviser, Jacques Foccart. This became a lasting strand in French foreign policy. So has de Gaulle's insistence that the Revolution gave France "latent moral capital". He toured South America and Mexico, and then precipitated a real crisis on a visit to Canada. His trip, to Expo 67, drew cheering crowds of French Canadians as he progressed from Quebec to Montreal. Here, he became a parody of himself. Overcome by the size of the crowd perhaps, or by his festering dislike of Anglo-Saxons, or by vengeance for Montcalm's defeat by the British on the heights of Quebec in 1759, but certainly overcome – he roared to the world from a balcony: "Vive Montreal! Vive le Québec! Vive le Québec libre! Vive le Canada français! Vive la France!" Anglophone Canadians, many of whom had died on the beaches of Dieppe and Normandy, had been in fact much more sympathetic to de Gaulle's Free French than the largely Pétainist *Québécois*. Ottawa, outraged, had him bundled out of the country within hours.

Little of his foreign policy brought rewards. But it certainly got France noticed. "Our country has suddenly become one of the principal actors in a play where before she had only a walk-on part," he said with pride.

France was losing its edge in painting – the art market was starting to slip away to New York and London, and she was producing fewer artists of her own – but it remained a cultural titan. A long drought in Nobel science prizes was broken in 1965, when André Lwoff, François Jacob and Jacques Monod, friends from the Institut Pasteur, were honoured for their research in genetics.

The *France* was launched at Saint-Nazaire by Madame de Gaulle in 1960. A crowd of more than a million watched the most beautiful of ships, the very perfection of the ocean liner, created at the very moment when the jet age wrecked its market. The same beauty marked the Mirage fighter-bomber that brought the *force de frappe* to reality.

In 1960, Camus was dead at 46 in a banal crash when his car hit a plane tree on the RN5. "It is not my role to transform the world or men," he said of himself with hallmark modesty. "I do not have virtue or insight enough for that. But it is perhaps to serve some of the values without which existence is worthless, even in a transformed world, without which a man, even a new man, should earn no respect." There was compensation for this savage loss. As Hollywood reeled under the assault of television, the French cinema burst with brilliance. The concept of the director as *auteur*, as the creative source or author of his films, was developed in Jacques Donoil-Valcroze's monthly magazine *Cahiers du cinéma*. The critics who wrote for it moved on to make their own films. Three overlapping generations of the finest film-makers graced the cinema over the decade. Jean Renoir, whom the *nouvelle vague* directors recognised as one of the original *auteurs*, made *Le Caporal épinglé* in 1962. Jacques Tati, whose career stumbled as wildly as his heroic Monsieur Hulot between fame and bankruptcy, released his satire *Playtime*, and Robert Bresson made his haunting *Une Femme douce* in 1969. The young directors themselves produced an outpouring of films whimsical, charming, tragic and gripping.

Their work was marked by the use of natural light thanks to new super-fast film, hand-held cameras, and by unusual angles and close-ups, the use of freeze frames, and Godard's jump cuts, where frames were cut from the middle of a sequence to show film as a contrivance and give the unsettling effect of watching the passage of time.

It was marked, too, by the rarest quality. Alain Resnais's *Hiroshima mon amour* was a near-perfect combination of story and form; the script, by Marguerite Duras, told of a brief affair between a French actress and a Japanese architect in Hiroshima, and the pain of her wartime love for a German soldier. Truffaut's *Les Quatre cents coups* remains one of the best studies of youth ever made. Jean-Luc Godard's masterpiece, *À bout de souffle*, tells of the final days of a Hollywood B-movie-besotted hoodlum, played by Jan-Paul Belmondo, who had murdered a policeman.

The story in Godard's *Deux ou trois choses que je sais d'elle* was banal enough, of a housewife who is a part-time prostitute, but it was thick with images, peppered with references to Marx, Wittgenstein, Braudel and structuralism, a thinking film from a different planet to Hollywood. There were other directors and other films – Éric Rohmer's *Ma nuit chez Maud,* Louis Malle's *Zazie dans le métro*, Jacques Demy's *Les Parapluies de Cherbourg* – for this was a cascade of talent.

It did not last. Television wounded the cinema. In 1964, people watched the little screen for an average of 57 minutes. By 1970 that had climbed to 115 minutes. Some serials and childrens' and current affairs programmes had panache and skill. News, though, was tame, and subservient to authority. The ministry of information kept a close eye on it and programmes that upset it were suppressed. ORTF, as the state-owned broadcaster was renamed in 1964, was an *entreprise nationale* – even if it accepted its first TV commercial, for Boursin cheese, in 1968 – and it showed.

The irresistible Astérix led the charge of the *bandes dessinées* (strip cartoons) an art dominated by the brilliance of French draughtsmanship and humour. *Charlie Hebdo* kept the old anarchist vein of satire alive and kicking; and new titles like *l'Écho des savanes* joined with the first BD annual festival in 1973 to give French comics an unrivalled edge. In detective novels, another field the Americans had once had largely to themselves, the *néo-polar* flourished.

Paris remained at the heart of the thinking man's universe. Claude Lévi-Strauss, appointed to the chair of social anthropology at the Collège de France in 1959, soon published *La Pensée sauvage*. This was a phenomenon, an anthropological international bestseller, drawing on his time in the backwoods of Brazil and Cuba, and his study of myths from around the world. He thought of myth as "a kind of collective dream", an "instrument of darkness" that might reveal the universal structures that underlie human experience.

Lévi-Strauss personified the dash and élan in French thought, going far beyond anthropology, into psychology, literary criticism, history, and even architecture; he had a knack for controversy, and for appearing anti-elitist, claiming that writing was the privilege of a powerful caste for whom "its principal function" was to "enslave and destroy". For him there was no difference between the "primitive" and the "modern" mind. He described geology, Marx and Freud as the "three mistresses" that influenced him. This enthusiasm for Marx and Freud was a common strain in French thought. Jacques Lacan, famous for his seminar at the École Normale Supérieure, was a guru and Freudian psychoanalyst. Sartre's huge *Critique de la raison dialectique* appeared in 1960. Where once he had called Marxism the "unsurpassable horizon of our times", he now allowed that it had "come to a halt" in Stalin's ice age, but Sartre maintained that historic inevitability was far from lost, and that Marxism was ideally suited to an anti-imperialist, Third-Worldly and leftist age of violent class struggle.

The philosopher Michel Foucault succeeded Sartre as the leading intellectual *provocateur*; his work *Les Mots et les choses* had sold 100,000 copies by 1967. He was the star pupil of Louis Althusser, the frail Communist philosopher, who championed Marxism as an "unassailable and unavoidable" science, before a tragic descent into madness and murder. Foucault was stridently anti-Vietnam, pro-gay liberation, pro-drugs, pro-counter culture, and studiously outrageous: he argued that, but for rape and sex with children, there should be no restraint on behaviour. Social attitudes, he said, are manipulated by those in power. They first define categories like madness, sickness, sexuality and criminality; then they use this to identify and punish "deviants". The bourgeois humanist has had his day; liberalism, he said, was a fake, a mere instrument of class power and social privilege. After the events of 1968, he had the chair of philosophy at the new experimental University of Vincennes, where students with no baccalaureate were accepted to read courses on cinema and semiotics in an atmosphere "like a noisy beehive".

Jacques Derrida developed his views on language and his theory of deconstruction, in which words are always inexact and "truth is plural". "There is nothing outside the text," he said, and the written word is always superior to spoken language. His meaning was often obscure – "Once again, deconstruction, if there is such a thing, takes place as the experience of the impossible" – and he attracted as much mockery as admiration.

Wit and a warm individuality spared Roland Barthes this fate, though his position had much in common with Derrida's. For him, the author's intentions are irrelevant in interpreting his text. Meanings differ from one reader to the next, so that no author can predict what his work will mean to others. The pattern carries through to Alain Robbe-Grillet's *Pour un nouveau roman* (1963), in which his aim was to trash the bourgeois novel by wiping out character, narrative and plot. Writing and structure were more important than meaning. Philippe Sellers and Jean-Marie Le Clézio abetted him, but readers remained obstinately fond of novels with a plot and a purpose.

The president, so energetic at the start, began to drift. In November1966, at his half-yearly press conference at the Élysée, he said: We have nothing dramatic to say today. In contrast to the past, France is not living any drama at present." That showed a certain hubris, a mocking of fate. The following year, when a journalist mentioned "après Gaullism", the general said tetchily that life "après de Gaulle" could begin tonight or tomorrow or in ten or even fifteen years time. A major strike brought Paris to a standstill: "Down with Pompidou!" the slogans said, and "No Government by Decree!", for this was not a strike about money, but about politics.

In 1968 the communist Tet offensive unrolled in South Vietnam, giving Gaullist anti-Americanism an agreeable sense of Schadenfreude. Jean-Claude Killy won three gold medals in the Winter Olympics. But there was a whiff of boredom in the air. "La France s'ennuie," *Le Monde* observed in March. In Germany, a gunman shot a left-wing student, Rudi Dutschke, and student rioting broke out. Pompidou caught some of his master's smugness. That could not happen here, he said, because France had "no opposition capable of overthrowing us, much less capable of replacing us". De Gaulle himself complained of lethargy. "This no longer amuses me much," he told an aide in April. "There is no longer anything difficult or heroic to do."

He was about to get a wake-up call.

Interregnum

Old revolutionary habits die hard. When government was felt to be too high-handed, people expressed themselves as they always had when they wanted authority to sit up and take notice. They went down into the street.

The sacking of the director of the Cinémathèque Française, the film institute, was a reminder of this early in 1968. Here, amid a collection of more than 50,000 films of every genre and quality, Henri Langlois indulged a passion that had started with a home projector in his bathroom in the Thirties. He collided with André Malraux, whose culture ministry funded the institute. Scourge of left and right, ex-Communist Gaullist, aesthete, swashbuckler, Malraux was for the most part a brilliant minister. His *blanchissage* campaign cleaned Paris of its soot and pigeon droppings. He restored the Marais and the wondrous place des Vosges. But when Truffaut, Godard and Renoir marched arm in arm in support of Langlois, Malraux had to back down.

Students took an angry part in the protests. There were more of them than ever before, and they were restless. The baby boom, and the increase in the school-leaving age from 14 to 16 in 1959, had virtually doubled the number of secondary schoolchildren. This great wave had now passed on to flood the universities, which it had never been easier to enter. The number of students had shot up from 174,000 to 514,000 over the past ten years. More did not, of course, mean better. Entrance was automatic for anyone with a *bac*, the school-leaving exam; survival at university was another matter, though, with nine out of ten medical students failing to get through their second-year exams. Initial enthusiasm was often dulled, by barrack-like and desperately overcrowded concrete campuses. The number of university teachers had rocketed from 8,000 to 40,500, many young, inadequately trained, easily unionised, and hostile to the old guard, or third-rate teachers drafted in from schools who floundered at a higher level.

Ordinary degrees were devalued on the job market. The *grandes écoles*, however, retained all their former status. The oldest, Ponts et Chaussées in 1747, and the École des Mines in 1783, were founded to provide engineers in royalist times. The Revolution had closed the universities, as hotbeds of reaction and clericalism, but it was kind to the schools. The École Polytechnique was created to add to the pool of administrators and officers, and the École Normale Supérieure was set up in 1794 to train the brightest professors in literature, philosophy and the sciences. New disciplines and specialities were added. By 1968, there were hundreds of *grandes écoles* – 230 engineering schools alone, some dependent directly on the ministries of defence, industry and agriculture – training more than 100,000 students as chemists, agronomists, architects, aircraft designers, mathematicians. There were elites within elites. At the apex was the École Nationale d'Administration, the tiny, post-war foundation whose *énarques* dominated the very top posts in public life, while the 400 students whom the École des Hautes Études Commerciales took on each year were expected to rise to the highest echelons in business and finance. The rigorous *classes préparatoires* needed to get into them ensured that no more than 2 or 3 per cent of entrants came from blue-collar backgrounds. *La prépa* could take two or three years, at great expense, with no guarantee of a place at the end of it. The prospects were glittering enough for parents to make the sacrifice willingly. The schools had the best teachers, the best researchers, libraries and laboratories, and the best pupil-staff ratios, and no university degree matched the allure of their diplomas.

The student mass was thus hugely expanded, but the cream stayed where it was, and the skim below it felt aggrieved and inferior. Coming back from abroad, Raymond Aron was shocked by the dinginess even of the flagship university, the Sorbonne, where security of tenure had bred an idle and elitist *mandarinisme* among the professors. Aron had one colleague who had not published a paper for 20 years. Others started the year with 150 students at their lectures, and ended it with none. The best students, Aron observed, "contrived to take their exams and graduate without ever setting foot in the place".

By 1968, the Sorbonne had 130,000 students. The old Left Bank buildings could not cope with the numbers, and they spilled over into the suburbs. Twelve thousand in arts and human sciences were housed on a muddy concrete campus in Nanterre, a miserable place, ill-served by transport, cafés, bistros and cinemas, it was known as the "anthill of the psychologists", with a large sociology faculty, taught by an inadequate number of left-wing professors so enamoured of Marcuse's ideas that a sociology degree was described by some as a "certificate in anarchy". It was boasted that these were the key disciplines of the future, and leftist students feared that the techniques of social manipulation they studied – group dynamics, mass psychodrama, workforce incentives – would be used by management to exploit the masses.

Trouble broke out at the inauguration of the campus swimming pool in January 1968. It was a proud moment for Pierre Grappin, the dean of Nanterre. He was a former Resistance hero, and a liberal-minded progressive who had allowed the 300 or 400 extremist students to hold meetings and proselytise on campus. They formed little "groupuscules", some devoted to Mao, others to Trotsky, Castro and Che Guevera. As the ceremony began, some 60 students appeared, led by Daniel Cohn-Bendit, a 22-year-old sociology student, the son of wealthy Franco-German Jews, carrot-haired, gap-toothed, with "the heavenly blue eyes and suspect candour of a nursery favourite". The students interrupted the speeches, with jokes and ironies. "Dany le Rouge" then ridiculed a book Grappin had written on youth: it was "600 pages of rubbish" which "didn't even mention sex problems".

Sociology students began to boycott their exams, and produced a pamphlet entitled "Why do we need sociologists?", drawing the irresistible counter-question, "Why indeed?", from right-wing groups. The teaching staff split over the student demand for a lecture hall to be given to them to hold permanent political debates. The students short-circuited the debate. Hundreds of them occupied a large lecture hall on April 2. A manifesto was issued. It called for "outright rejection of the Capitalist Technocratic University", and for solidarity with the working class.

In the poisoned atmosphere, rumours were spread that Grappin had drawn up a blacklist of troublemakers, which he would use to make sure they did badly in their exams. He denied this vehemently. The extremists, armed with crowbars, smashed up the administrative block anyway. Grappin called in the police, suspended classes and closed the faculty. He also started disciplinary procedures against Cohn-Bendit and seven others, asking the rector of the Sorbonne, Paul Roche, to have them examined by the university council with a view to excluding them. This gave Cohn-Bendit and his friends a larger stage to strut on. At midday on May 3, he began to harangue students in the central courtyard of the Sorbonne. An hour later, reinforcements arrived on scooters and motorbikes from Nanterre, wearing crash helmets, which were to become the uniform of the revolt. Right-wing extremists of the Occident group got to hear that some leftists from Nanterre were in the courtyard, and prepared to fight them.

Worried, Roche asked the police to clear the courtyard. This violated the 700-year-old tradition of the university as a place of sanctuary. Liberal opinion was further outraged when students were beaten with batons and hustled off in police vans. By 7 p.m., around a thousand students had massed on the boulevard Saint-Michel. The first fights with police broke out. Tear gas was used. Some of the arrested *enragés* were given short prison terms. The revolt now had martyrs.

On May 6, a crowd of over 20,000 gathered in the place Denfert-Rochereau, chanting sarcastically "We are a groupuscule," and demanding, "Free our comrades." As they marched towards the Sorbonne, they ran into a police cordon on the rue Saint-Jacques. A running battle took place on the boulevard Saint-Germain, as marchers hurled metal grilles and paving stones at police who charged and tear-gassed them. More than 300 police were injured, but it was the beatings they gave to the youngsters that caught the eye on the television news.

Ten thousand angry souls – schoolboys, workers and hooligans were mixed in with the students – congregated on the evening of May 10. They confronted the police lines. A full-scale battle was soon raging. The streets were rapidly stripped of their cobblestones. The Paris *pavés* were small enough to be hurled hard, by hand or by sling, and they were dangerous, able to inflict skull and facial fractures. The first barricades to go up in Paris since the liberation appeared on the rue Gay-Lussac. A passing labourer showed the students how to use a pneumatic drill – he was fondly remembered as the first worker to support the student cause – and tarmac on the road was broken to reveal fresh supplies of cobblestones below. The CRS riot police laid down a barrage of tear gas and attacked with long batons and riot shields. They stormed the first barricade, but the students had put up five more within 500 yards. They enjoyed strength in depth. As well as crash helmets, many wore goggles, masks and scarves soaked in baking powder against the gas.

Amid the crack of grenade launchers, the thump of exploding gas grenades, and the whump and crackle of burning cars, the crew of a Radio Luxembourg radio car tried to negotiate between the chief of police, Maurice Grimaud, and the student leaders. Fighting continued through the night. Police repression swung public sympathy towards the students. At 1 a.m., a reporter noted that "thousands" were helping to build barricades, "women, workers, bystanders, people in pyjamas, human chains to carry rock, wood, iron". By morning, 367 people had been injured, and 460 arrested. As troop carriers moved in to clear the barricades, they were booed and hissed.

On May 13, a great mass of people with banderoles and red flags marched to the Bastille. It was a nostalgic sight, not seen since 1936, *la vieille tradition rouge* in full cry; and, for the government, dangerous, because Communist and Socialist union leaders, at each others' throats a few days before, were marching arm-in-arm to hear demands for a general strike. In Rouen, a group of young workers from the Renault-Cléon plant went onto the streets to fraternise with the students. "Les étudiants avec les ouvriers", the headlines bellowed. That, if true, would be lethal indeed for the regime.

A great wave of collective memory – racing back through the Commune, 1848 and 1830 to 1789 – washed through the country. The defiant students, chanting "Nous sommes chez nous" as they battled to regain the ancient academic heart of the Left Bank, touched a historic chord. They marketed themselves with brilliance. Students from the lithographic department of the École des Beaux-Arts set up an *atelier populaire*, from which streamed posters created by sloganeers and artists of the highest quality. "It is forbidden to forbid", "I take my Desires for Reality, because I believe in the Reality of Desires", "Be Reasonable, Demand the Impossible": these dreamlike phrases gave a sweet innocence and idealism to the masked and crash-helmeted rioters. They had wit: "The general will against the will of the general." And they could be brutally dismissive: the bourgeois press sketched as a poison bottle, with the legend "Do not swallow". A thuggish image of their enemy fixed the CRS in the public mind: beneath an inhuman head, all curved helmet, goggles, gas mask, shield and baton was the simple legend: "CRS=SS". It was nonsense, of course. The life of any student insane enough to riot in front of the real SS would have been snuffed out in a trice. But it had panache – as a piece of agitprop, it was close to perfection – and it swept the public along for the moment.

Men of letters formed *comités de contestation*. Sartre urged the students on to revolution, and a few hours later they took over the Odéon national theatre. Jean-Louis Barrault, the grand actor-manager at the Odéon, and Madeleine Renaud, the theatre's most renowned actress, at first welcomed them. The mutual love-in did not last long. The students took no notice when Barrault asked them to stop smoking; they painted "ex-Odéon" on the safety curtain and the walls, and turned the stage into a *tribune libre* where speakers ranted on in relays. They broke into the costume store, and dressed up. Their numbers swelled to several thousand. The theatre was delivered over to "veritable destruction, vandalism pure and simple". Barrault complained, as he retreated to his room to read Rabelais.

The students had great presence as they looked after their own Boul' Mich' heartland. The Irish writer Peter Lennon saw a van with a full load of CRS in it meekly waiting instructions from the student who was directing traffic round the debris of the barricades on the boulevard. Lennon marvelled that the grandeur of France had been brought "to an absolute standstill by a bunch of children". The question adult France asked itself of the students, he said, was: "Did they know the Secret of Life – the one we all fumbled in growing up?" Groups of students debated happily with curious bourgeois families from the *beaux quartiers*, who prudently came by foot, lest their cars end up in a barricade. "The adult world came panting humbly after the students, but neither generation knew precisely what was going on."

De Gaulle, dismissing the students as kids and jokers, "ces gamins, ces rigolos", had gone on an official visit to Romania on May 14. He left France "awash with folly", it was said, governed by Georges Pompidou, Daniel Cohn-Bendit and Georges Séguy, the Communist union leader. Pompidou, seeking a balance between repression and concession, withdrew the police from the Sorbonne. Its courtyard became a "gigantic revolutionary drugstore", with stalls peddling pamphlets by Stalinists, Maoists, anarchists and three varieties of Trotskyites. The walls were plastered with posters and inscriptions. "Religion is the last mystification," it said on the door of the chapel, and, less elegantly: "We want somewhere to piss, not to pray."

Rooms were allocated to committees and study groups. *Assemblées générales* were held every night in the giant amphitheatre, seating 5,000. News of the first factory occupation, when workers seized the Sud Aviation plant at Nantes, locking managers in their offices, reached the Sorbonne late at night on May 14, to scenes of "indescribable enthusiasm . . . delirious cheering". Students regarded each new occupation – Nouvelles Messageries de Presse in Paris, Kléber Colombes at Caudebec, Dresser-Dujardin at Le Havre, Renault at Boulogne-Billancourt – as evidence that "the battle had really been joined".

With hindsight, May 17 was the critical day. The Renault plant at Billancourt was occupied by 4,000 strikers, who slept on air beds and first-aid stretchers. A delegation of 1,500 students set out from the Sorbonne in the late afternoon to join them. They marched under a single banner, hastily prepared by some Maoists: "The strong hands of the working class must now take over the torch from the fragile hands of the students." They sang revolutionary songs as they went, such as "Le Jeune Garde" and "Zimmerwald". It was dark when they arrived at the plant, where the strikers had locked themselves in behind the gates. A truck with a loudspeaker barred their way. An official from the CGT Communist union was aboard it. He was icily correct: "We appreciate your solidarity. But please no provocations. Don't go near the gates . . . Go home soon. It's cold . . ." No student was allowed inside the plant. The Communists did not want their militants to be ideologically contaminated. It was past midnight. The student crowd thinned, and then disappeared.

The strikes continued. Industry in Paris, Lyon and Normandy virtually halted. Coal production came to a halt. Red flags floated over the factories at Flins and the great shipyards at Saint-Nazaire. Buses, the Métro, trains, even taxis stopped running. Garbage built up in the streets. Air traffic controllers at Orly came out, as did ORTF television. Garages ran out of petrol and diesel. Food supplies were short. Workers in the Berliet factory rearranged the sign over the works to read "Liberté". Bank withdrawals were limited to 500 francs as the money supply dwindled. Undertakers went on strike. "Now is not a good time to die," it was observed.

Cohn-Bendit left on a visit to Berlin. When the interior ministry announced that he would not be allowed to return, students and *lycéens* marched on the Assembly and the Senate. Their placards – "We are all German Jews" – were as gifted as ever. Fighting with police lasted into the early hours.

De Gaulle returned and he broadcast to the nation on May 24. It was a flop: he sounded tired, vague – "yes to reform, no to *chienlit*", the last an antiquated word for havoc – and out of touch. But Pompidou grasped that the essential task was to deal with the unions: do that, and the student riots would die away. He met with representatives from the unions and the employers on May 25. After two days and nights of talks, an outline agreement with concessions on pay and hours was reached. The union rank and file promptly rejected these "protocols of Grenelle".

Smelling blood, François Mitterrand offered on May 28 to form a provisional government. Mendès-France claimed that all regimes of the Gaullist genre "are finished brusquely by one incident, one crisis". De Gaulle was in despair that evening. "What can I do?" he asked his adviser Jacques Foccart. "Enemies reappear and destroy everything. The country is disintegrating and I can do nothing about it. How can one stop it if it is what its people want to do?"

The next morning, he told Pompidou that he was putting off the day's cabinet meeting because he was tired and wanted to go to Colombey. At 11 a.m., he left the Élysée by a side door. An abdication seemed imminent. But he did not appear in Colombey. He disappeared. He was flown by helicopter to Baden-Baden, where the French forces in Germany were commanded by General Massu, who had backed his return to power ten years before. He spoke to Massu for 90 minutes; he also saw his son-in-law, General de Boissieu, who commanded an armoured division at Mulhouse. Reassured that the army would fulfil its duty to combat interior subversion, he flew home, to Colombey and wrote a short speech for delivery on May 30.

As he began to speak in Paris the next day, tens of thousands of people began assembling at the place de la Concorde, not now with red flags, but tricolours. They were Gaullists. "I shall not resign," the general said. "I shall not change the prime minister ... The Republic will not abdicate ..." By 6 p.m., the crowd had spilled from Concorde into the rue de Rivoli, the rue Royale, the boulevards, and then – "like a gigantic river defying nature" – it flowed uphill, up the Champs-Élysées to the Étoile, almost a million strong, with all the senators and deputies of the majority, and Debré and Malraux and Mauriac, the faithful trinity, at its heart.

The revolution that never was had ended. It lacked momentum because it lacked a common purpose. The Nanterre *enragés* professed their profound shame that they were not workers, whom, worse still, they felt they were being trained to enslave. As sociology and psychology graduates, they would become personnel and work-study managers, "psycho-technicians" whose task was to lobotomise the proletariat. These *fils de papa* were servile in their adoration of the heroic proles. "Your struggles are more radical than ours," the Nanterre manifesto said. "The form of your struggle offers to us, students, the model of a truly socialist activity." It was a statement of love – "We must destroy everything, newspapers, habits, that isolates us from each other . . . there must be a joining together of faculties and the occupied factories" – but it was unrequited love. The PCF disliked almost every quality the students possessed: they were anarchic, argumentative, individualistic, erratic, free-thinking and impossible to control.

Ultimately, there was no revolution because no one came up with a compelling reason to have one. "Down with the Gaullist government of unemployment and poverty", the students chanted. But France was more prosperous than ever before. Wages were rising by 5 per cent a year; car ownership had doubled, and the number of television sets quintupled, in a decade. Workers complained of *les cadences* – the intense rhythms of the production line – but jobs were so plentiful that foreign workers were brought in to fill them. The union leaders, inspired by cash, not ideology, cynically used the students to get what they wanted from a rattled government. The minimum wage up by a third, an immediate 7 per cent wage increase, with half pay for time spent on strike.

And the students? Theirs was not a real war. The Czech students in the Prague Spring that same May were celebrating a brief victory against a dictatorship whose reality would soon be re-established by Soviet tanks. The Americans demonstrating on their campuses feared being drafted to a war whose body count was being swollen by the Tet offensive. A single killing by the police might have tipped Paris over the brink. It would have covered the ludicrous notion that Gaullist France was fascist with a fig-leaf of reality. Miraculously, there was none until the very end, when a passer-by was hit by shrapnel from a stun grenade.

And yet there was a splendour to the students, with their outpouring of verve and imagination. Theirs was a thinking country, with some of the brightest young minds at work in May '68, and it showed. But the movement was also irrelevant. That is why it evaporated so swiftly. A final gesture was made in July. A huge poster showed a flock of sheep and the legend: "Retour à la normale". It was the last hurrah of revolutionary France.

Within a few days, the damaged Saint-Germain drugstore was selling replica paving stones made of rubber. It cost 150 million francs to clear up the city. Some of it was spent replacing the *pavés* from the streets round the Sorbonne with tarmac, thus removing the supply of ammunition. The students were tossed a few crumbs; the Sorbonne was broken up into smaller units, and some of the dust was blown off the mandarins, who no longer held their chairs for life.

The legislative elections held in June saw a Gaullist landslide. For the first time ever one party had an absolute majority. But de Gaulle had enjoyed his final moment of history. The last months were lean. He replaced Pompidou with Maurice Couve de Murville, the former foreign minister. Pompidou had come out of de Gaulle's shadow as a formidable figure in his own right. He had been decisive where de Gaulle had wobbled in May – "de Gaulle no longer exists", Pompidou had remarked, "he is dead, there is nothing left" – and it was his persistence with the unions that had saved his ungrateful ex-master.

He had not long to wait for the tables to turn. In February 1969, de Gaulle announced that he was holding a new referendum. The people were to be asked to approve modest proposals for Senate reform and to reduce the capital's administrative stranglehold on the regions. The fifth referendum of the Fifth Republic proved fatal. There was no need to go to the country, and even less to turn it into a vote of confidence. On April 10, 1969, however, de Gaulle went on television to say that he would resign if the referendum failed. This was a foolish challenge on a minor issue to a tired electorate. Three weeks later, on a sparse turnout, the noes registered a narrow victory, and de Gaulle went at once. It was a petulant, and petty farewell, a rerun of 1946. But he had a fine grandeur, too. He was stamped deep with courage and devotion to the destiny of France, whose history since his wounding at Verdun he embodied. It is a measure of the selflessness of this extraordinary man that, after more than ten years' residence in the Élysée, his baggage and that of his wife were removed from the Élysée to Colombey in a single van.

Pompidou changed style more than content. He was sleekly plump and gregarious, with a jolly sense of mockery, at ease with good food, film stars and *le tout Paris*. He enjoyed power, and he had the self-confidence and solidity that comes from spinning a lofty career from a lowly start. He was one of those ambitious Auvergnats, like Laval, who made their way by talent and a dash of luck, his parents primary school teachers of peasant stock in the Cantal. He was a brilliant schoolboy and excelled as a *normalien*. Politicians often regret the writer or artist they claim pines within them. Pompidou did, too, but his talent was real. His taste for the modern in art and architecture – "the juxtaposition of violent lyricism and mathematical coolness" – gave birth to Richard Rogers and Renzo Piano's brutally original Pompidou Centre, its pipework and heating ducts exposed on the exterior like offal on a butcher's slab. A novella Pompidou wrote on May '68 revealed a satirist's eye in its student anti-hero, Girondas, elected to the board of his *lycée* on the strength of his cowboy shirts and blue jeans.

Young Pompidou had taught literature in Marseille before the war. He fought briefly as a sub-lieutenant before returning to teaching at the smart Lycée Henri IV in Paris. His luck lay in catching de Gaulle's eye in 1944, when he joined the general's staff, before carving out a career as an administrator and banker with Rothschild Frères. His place was in the middle. "If it means weighing the need for movement and change", he said of himself, "with the need to avoid destroying everything in an old country which has amassed a lot of intellectual, moral and material goods, then, yes, I am in the centre." Instinctively, he avoided confrontation, and was happy to fine-tune his Gaullist inheritance. His sacking had freed him of any personal loyalty to his former chief. De Gaulle himself avoided any meddling. He never visited Paris again, apart from an incognito appearance at a christening, and soon enough, the old colossus was gone. He was writing the second volume of his memoirs when, on November 9, he sat down after dinner to play patience, and died suddenly.

On only one major issue, the veto on British membership of the EEC, did Pompidou break with him. France was a fully fledged nuclear power by now, the first H-bomb having been tested on Muroroa atoll in the Pacific, but he was a pragmatist, and he realised that de Gaulle's vision of a France ploughing its own furrow in world affairs was make-believe. "France is a Western country," he said when he went to Moscow, "and intends to remain so without restriction."

Pompidou continued the regional reform that had cost de Gaulle his head in the referendum. Michel Rocard had called on Paris to "decolonise the provinces", and this had resonance, not least because Rocard was a Socialist, and the left had a Jacobin and centralising tradition. Powers were taken from the departments, for the first time since their creation in 1790, and handed to regional assemblies. Big economic programmes also benefited the regions. Pompidou chose the emblem of Concorde for his election campaign, and the construction of the supersonic jet poured money into Toulouse. To the south, the great new oil refinery at Fos lifted the Marseille region.

This was the high-water mark of the boom. Pompidou's grand ambition, much helped by his glamorous young finance minister, Valéry Giscard d'Estaing, lay in French industry and its ability to compete in world markets. Encouragement was given to so-called "national champions" to act as magnets in particular industries: Thomson-Brandt in electronics, Schneider and CGE in mechanical and electrical systems. The first section of the RER rapid-transit railway leapfrogged Paris to the front of urban transport systems; Airbus-Industrie, the consortium that was to keep Europe in the commercial big-jet market, was created and work on the Airbus A300B project began; SNECMA and General Electric cooperated to make big progress in civilian nuclear reactors; and Pompidou himself, at the wheel of a Renault, inaugurated the final stretch of the A6 Lille-Marseille motorway. But the number of miners and farmworkers was falling rapidly with increased mechanisation; inflation was high; and the boom was sucking in immigrants in unprecedented numbers. Two new political parties were founded. François Mitterrand achieved the fusion of the non-Communist left in the Parti Socialiste, which did much better than predicted in the legislative elections of 1973. Jean-Marie Le Pen, whom we last met in Algiers, founded the far-right Front National. Immigration was the new party's major concern. By 1974, there were 3.8 million foreign immigrants in France, 7 per cent of the total population, and 14 per cent of the Paris conurbation. Some were European – they included 750,000 Portuguese and 570,000 Spaniards and Italians – but the largest single group were 900,000 Algerians. The fact that two out of every three French women from 20 to 30, the prime child-bearing age, went out to work, where immigrant wives tended to lead fecund lives at home, meant that immigrants outbred natives. The ex-Poujadist Le Pen had found himself a promising new career.

Pompidou was ill from the end of 1972. His succession was not clear. Jacques Chaban-Delmas was his first prime minister, mayor of Bordeaux, a charmer, a great rugger player and *résistant*, a Gaullist baron and brigadier-general at 29, but too liberal for the cautious president, and much too popular. His approval rating topped Pompidou's own. Such lese-majesty has proved a capital offence throughout the Fifth Republic; it had cost Pompidou his own head, and it cost Chaban his in 1972. A scandal orchestrated by a jealous rival was often the means of such a downfall. Valéry Giscard d'Estaing made a point – a special point? – of stressing how the fight against tax fraud had Chaban's personal blessing. *Le Canard enchaîné* then published Chaban's tax declaration, showing that the prime minister had paid no income tax from 1966 to 1969. Only Giscard's finance ministry could have leaked the details to the satirical weekly.

Chaban's tax declaration was perfectly proper, but his reputation was sullied. The next revelation concerned Jacques Chirac, Chaban's young minister responsible for relations with parliament. It was found that he had bought himself a château in the Corrèze which had been reclassified as a "historic monument" shortly afterwards, thus enabling the new owner to restore it at the expense of the state. The new premier was Pierre Messmer, a colonial and military expert, a believer in law and order, too obviously conservative – he kept Paris streets visibly flooded with police – to have serious presidential expectations. Giscard did. He was astute, popular and ambitious, with a ruthless streak the hapless Chaban had already felt.

Pompidou, exhausted, puffy with drugs, worked to the end, dying in Paris on April 2, 1974. He did much to change the city. Some of what he did may not have been improvements, notably the expressway on the bank of the Seine that bears his name and, the black slab of the Montmartre tower; but at least the latter's ugliness ensured that he had other skyscrapers sympathetically tucked away at La Défense, and the city became far easier to navigate. He had the great city market transferred to Rungis, and its old site at Les Halles renovated. It is, though, the Pompidou

Centre, the striking if fragile arts multi-centre, that is the best-known memorial for a man who gave France the quietest five years since the Twenties.

The disloyalties, expediencies and bad blood that flowed from the struggle to replace Pompidou haunt France still. The three principals in the 1974 presidential election – Valéry Giscard d'Estaing, François Mitterrand, Jacques Chirac – were to rule the country for 30 years.

For once, the broad left had a single candidate. Mitterrand had reinvented himself once more and had signed an accord for a common programme with the Communists. Pompidou had left no Gaullist dauphin, but behind the empty throne a pair of kingmakers busied themselves. Marie-France Garaud was a lawyer from Poitiers, a dominatrix who seized on any weakness in a man to bend him to her will. She spun her webs with Pierre Juillet, a man who kept himself in the shadows or on his sheep farm in the Limousin, as ruthless as her in keeping Gaullism alive and the left dead. The natural successor was Jacques Chaban-Delmas, the former prime minister, but, for the Garaud-Juillet axis, he was a dangerous liberal whose reedy voice and tax affairs might lose him the campaign.

Their eye alighted on Valéry Giscard d'Estaing. He was a brilliant man – graduating second in his year as a *polytechnicien*, and third as an *énarque*, he was arguably the cleverest young man in France – and well aware of it. "Elite" was stamped through his lofty figure like a stick of seaside rock. He was born in Koblenz in 1922, where his father, an *inspecteur des finances* from a wealthy, conservative and Catholic family from the Auvergne, was serving with the French occupation authorities. Giscard was brought up in the XVIe arrondissement in Paris, and in the Auvergne.

He was a whisker more *haut bourgeois* than *aristo*, despite his familiarity with *beaux quartiers* and châteaux, and his marriage into the plutocratic Schneider steel dynasty. His own family had improved its standing by adopting "d'Estaing" in 1922. This was quite commonplace. Since the nineteenth century, some 15,000 French families have paid to change their name by deed poll to include the nobiliary particle "de". Their names were revealed in the *Dictionary of Vanities* published in 1972, but rarely arouse much comment. With Giscard, however, it was noticed. His virtues had an unfortunate knack of drifting into vices in the public eye. His cleverness mutated into too clever by half, his lofty patrician figure became remote and condescending, and his splendid rolling name, far from conjuring romantic images of a Norman crusader, was thought mere snobbery. He strove to be modest and modern – he listed his likes as Mozart, Maupassant and forget-me-nots, his dislikes as long words, tobacco smoke, and wearing jackets – but only the striving was noticed.

He got, in short, under some people's skin. This was, perhaps, nature's revenge for a career that was flawless in every respect: a Croix de Guerre as a young wartime officer, a slot in the prime minister's private cabinet at 28, a deputy for his Pétainist grandfather's old seat in the Puy-de-Dôme at 30, and de Gaulle's finance minister a month before his 36th birthday. He was at finance for nine years, basking in the final glow of the *trente glorieuses*, hugely self-confident, stylish, good on television, and awesome in debate, able to speak intelligibly and at length without notes on complex monetary matters in the chamber. He lacked only one necessity for the Élysée, a mass political party, and Garaud-Juillet were preparing to loan him the Gaullists.

They were not particularly fond of him; but then Giscard was always a man more admired than loved. Their own affection was reserved for Jacques Chirac. People warmed to Chirac. Pompidou had treated him as his political son and heir; and when his mentor had died, Chirac said that he had the "feeling of being an orphan", and wept publicly at the memorial mass.

Chirac was a Paris banker's son, of mettle enough to have a teenage affair with the left, selling *l'Huma* on the streets before reverting to his roots and progressing to *énarque* status, via a stint at summer school at Harvard, earning himself a HoJo certificate in ice-cream making. Pompidou took the young man into his secretariat before sending him off to get a parliamentary seat in the Corrèze. His patron progressed him through the ministerial ranks, from agriculture, where he defended French interests with ferocious aplomb, to industry, where his energy got him the tag of *le bulldozer*, and then to interior.

Garaud-Juillet planned for him to be the Gaullist candidate in 1976. Pompidou died too soon. At 41, Chirac was too young to be *présidentiable*. Giscard passed muster at 48. The kingmakers whispered in his ear. Chirac was organising the election at interior, and secret RG reports on the state of public opinion passed over his desk. They showed that Chaban would lose to Mitterrand. Chirac decided to jump ship. "Chirac is a falcon placed on the gloved fist of Marie-France," Chaban wrote later of the duo. "From time to time, Juillet slips the chain so Chirac flies for an hour. And kills." In the first round, Chaban got a meagre 15 per cent to Giscard's 33 per cent and Mitterrand's 43 per cent. Giscard had Mitterrand floundering in their televised debates, tossing him questions on international finance that were beyond the ken of his drab and ageing opponent. Yet he scraped home with a bare 50.81 per cent in the second. The electorate had not warmed to him. Chirac's reward was the Hôtel Matignon: he became prime minister.

Luck was against Giscard. The oil price rise after the 1973 Yom Kippur War in the Middle East brought the *trente glorieuses* to a brutal end. There were some last hurrahs: the *boulevard péripherique*, the RER rapid-transit line, and Roissy Charles de Gaulle airport were inaugurated in Paris; a huge programme for new nuclear power stations was begun; and French rail engineers beat the world speed record. But growth was killed off by *la crise*. The industrial world as a whole was affected, and France was unquestionably fortunate to have so financially literate a president in office. But it did not show.

Unemployment rose from 200,000 to the unheard-of level of one million in November 1975, and then on to more than two million. The talk was of closures, lay-offs and bankruptcies across the board. As Chirac's government tried to spend its way out of recession with a huge government deficit, inflation surged to 15.2 per cent in 1974.

When time and finance were still with him, Giscard tried to forge a *septennat* of reform. His natural supporters were not the classic right. They were, Roger Chinaud, his party secretary, said, "the new generation", who had no time for social hierarchies and compartments, and rejected the "fetishism of etiquette". Such people sounded fine and modern, but they made up a rather thin constituency. His aim, Giscard said, was an "advanced liberal society". But this cost money, and the tax base was shrinking, and had more pressing demands on it, in unemployment benefit, restructuring funds, and industrial bail-outs. He set out in style, nonetheless. The voting age was reduced from 21 to 18. Gaullist control over television and radio was removed, at least in theory, by breaking up ORTF, the state broadcasting corporation; though, since the heads of the seven new agencies were government-appointed, their independence remained suspect. A risk was taken by appointing Marcel Jullian as head of the second TV channel, Antenne 2: when it became clear that he would remain his own man, lively and critical, he was soon replaced by a pen-pusher. Comprehensive schools were brought in at secondary level, as were measures to slowly lower retirement age to 60. The last execution in France was held in Baumettes prison in Marseille in 1977, when Hamida Djandoubi was decapitated for rape and torture.

It was in the onset of the permissive society that France was most changed. Partly, this was Giscard's intention, but much that happened was due to a more general shift to the self-centred, uncensored lifestyle that was common to the new West. *Cohabitation juvénile*, once known as "living in sin" but now called "trial marriage", was spreading rapidly, while the rate of premarital conception went from one child in five to one in four. Civil law was reformed in 1972 to give illegitimate children the same rights as legitimate. Divorce rates accelerated. The 1920 law against abortion was flouted. Catholic opponents were mocked as *lapinistes*, the rabbit clan. The Neuwirth law of December 1967 legalised the sale of contraceptives, and the number of women on the pill quadrupled in three years.

In 1974 Giscard's health minister, Simone Veil, introduced a law legalising abortion. Nine-tenths of the deputies were men, and she had to undergo a 32-hour marathon to get it through the Assembly. At the end, exhausted and victorious only through Communist and Socialist votes, she dissolved in tears. Veil and her family had been in Auschwitz and Bergen-Belsen, and her critics asked how a survivor of the German death camps could thus dispose of the right to live of the unborn child. The Catholic pressure group, Laissez-les-vivres, warned that Europe was committing "demographic suicide", a perceptive remark that was almost entirely ignored. The abortion rate settled at around 180,000 a year.

The French still thought of themselves as overwhelmingly Christian, but only a minority translated this into practice. Regular church-goers had fallen to 17 per cent by 1972. The Church suffered some self-inflicted wounds. The Second Vatican Council had stripped much of the grandeur and mystery from services. The liturgy was to be in French. Family occasions, like the ancient and binding rite of first communion, were stripped of their significance. Triumphal hymns were quietened, and incense and rich trappings and vestments disappeared. Priests dressed down. The Virgin, the saints and angels and rosaries, and even the devil, were ignored. Priests called for the "declergification" of religion and espoused pacifist causes. A poll showed that 59 per cent thought that, through trying too hard to adapt to secular trends, "the Church is no longer the Church". The vacuum was filled by charismatics, and by the "integrist" Monsignor Lefebvre, who opened a traditionalist seminary at Ecône in Switzerland. At home, the seminaries withered, and existing clergy were leaving in numbers, often to get married. At the same time, the number of non-Christians was multiplying. As well as the Muslim millions, French Jewry had swollen with the arrival of 140,000 Sephardic Jews from North Africa.

Mainstream politicians rarely spoke of religion or demographics; and they never discussed the two together, despite the obvious long-term social and cultural implications. That, disdainfully, they left to Jean-Marie Le Pen. At first, Giscard personified the laid-back new style. He invited dustmen to breakfast at the Élysée. He ate with ordinary mortals – a truck driver, a picture framer, a gamekeeper and, as a barb, with a couple in Garaud's home town of Poitiers – and toured the Paris *bidonvilles* (shanty towns). He played the accordion. He visited Lyon prison, and shook hands with the inmates. He wore cardigans and shirt sleeves, and he allowed himself to be photographed in red swimming trunks. He had the "Marseillaise" slowed down and softened to make it less martial. But the monarchical streak in him was always present, and it came to predominate. He insisted on being served first in the presence of state guests at official banquets, and for all his accordion-playing, man-of-the-people act, his favourite dish betrayed him. It was scrambled eggs, true, a classless dish, but with truffles. His vanity showed in his dealings with his prime minister. Chirac was ordered to walk three steps behind his master on formal occasions.

It did not inhibit him that he had denounced de Gaulle's "solitary exercise" of power. He did the same. He had his close friend Michel Poniatowski appointed interior minister, to keep an eye on Chirac, and to build up Giscard's own political base, so that he could be re-elected in 1981 without Gaullist help. He had sent 12 *lettres directives* to Chirac by 1976, telling him in detail what he was to do, and he called 52 special councils to direct specific parts of the government agenda. That was four times more than Pompidou. He also telephoned ministers directly, bypassing his prime minister.

He reshuffled the government in 1976. Chirac was not consulted; it was presented to him as a fait accompli. At Whitsun, he invited Chirac and his wife to the presidential retreat on the coast at Brégançon, a dramatic spot looking out at

Hyères and its wondrous islands. The prime minister looked forward to a heart-to-heart with the president. Instead, he found that Giscard had also invited his ski instructor, and meaningful chats were not on his agenda. The two men reviewed the fleet at a naval exercise. Giscard gave a television interview, disdaining Chirac, who was so angry that, as he tried to conceal his rage by staring out to sea, he found that he had the binoculars the wrong way round.

The cabinet assembled at the Élysée on August 25, 1976, after the summer break. Giscard regaled them with an account of his trip to Gabon, where he had enjoyed big game hunting laid on by his friend, the dictator Omar Bongo.

He then turned to Chirac: "Prime Minister, I believe you have something to say?"

"Mr President," Chirac replied. "I have the honour to present you with the resignation of my government." Prime ministers of the Fifth Republic – Pompidou, Chaban – had been sacked before. Never had one resigned. Soon enough, Giscard would find, the ill-treated squire would ruin his master.

A few days later, Chirac had Sunday lunch with Marie-France Garaud at Pierre Juillet's farmhouse in the Creuse. He was to revive Gaullism by founding a new mass party, with its own band of militants, given fire in its belly by Chirac's own energy. He launched it at a great rally in Paris in December 1976. He called it the Rassemblement Pour la République (RPR); Giscard responded to this lese-majesty by constructing a new coalition, the Union pour la Démocratie Française. As is the nature of a grand and poisonous feud, it did not benefit the protagonists. Instead, it was the making of François Mitterrand.

Giscard damaged himself by deciding that Paris, its workers largely decanted into the suburbs, was now conservative enough to be forgiven for 1871, and allowed to have its own mayor. Garaud–Juillet spotted the potential. Paris offered their man the perfect platform to go with his new party: grandeur, patronage, exposure, funds, and the chance to humiliate Giscard. D'Ornano, Giscard's candidate, was plump and rosy, a Norman aristocrat and a countryman. Chirac was Parisian born and bred, a presser of flesh, a whirlwind sweeping through streets and television studios. It was no contest. Seven months to the day after quitting the Matignon, Chirac moved into the Hôtel de Ville.

Though not a Gaullist, Giscard was skilled at upsetting the Americans. He gave Leonid Brezhnev, the car-mad Soviet leader, a red sports model. He signed arms deals with Nicaragua. He was pro-Arab and pro-Islamic, a stance imposed in part by necessity. France was dependent on oil for 75 per cent of its energy needs, and most of that oil came from the Middle East. Michel Jobert, the foreign minister, toured Iraq, Libya and Saudi Arabia in 1974, selling arms for oil. A nuclear reactor went to Iraq in 1975, for "peaceful purposes"; the Israelis, unimpressed, bombed it. Giscard welcomed Ayatollah Khomeini, Iran's Yankee-baiting cleric, to set up his headquarters-in-exile at Neauphle-le-Château in 1978, returning him to Tehran in 1979 in an Air France jet. He refused to join the boycott of the Moscow Olympics after the Soviet invasion of Afghanistan. Relations with Germany were happier. Giscard got on well with Chancellor Schmidt. They spoke in English, without interpreters, and lunched together at a favourite restaurant, *Au Boeuf* at Blaesheim in Alsace. The pair secured agreement for the European Monetary System in 1978; they introduced the six-month rotating chairmanship of the Council of Ministers, and they brought in direct elections to the European Parliament.

Troubles broke out in Corsica and Brittany, but the luminaries of the left glowed less brightly after the implosion of May '68. They had taken a further battering when Alexander Solzhenitsyn's masterwork, the *Gulag Archipelago*, made its first appearance in the West in Paris on December 28, 1973. It was proof positive that communist bestiality was the equal of fascism in all but statistics: and here, in the numbers of victims, in the size of camps, and in the length of time they operated, it was very much worse. In his *Barbarism with a Human Face*, Bernard-Henri Lévy, the leader of the New Philosophers, famously blessed by the gods with looks, brains and money, traced Stalinism and its evils back to socialism itself, attacking French leftists who had never really broken with it for good measure. François Furet and other historians challenged the most sacred cow of all, the Revolution, for producing the Jacobin dictatorship and the Terror. Even Michel Foucault questioned the idea of revolution in general, at least as a single cataclysmic event. He rejected Marxist class struggle and historical evolution – he thought of linear narrative as the "history of victors" – and focussed on marginal groups, like prisoners and homosexuals.

The new thinkers had a public presence on television programmes like *Apostrophes*, and France still paid handsome attention to ideas. But some of the zest had gone. In the cinema, too, the old mastery was slipping, though the emergence of Gerard Depardieu in 1977 showed that the well of talent was not yet dry. The singer Jacques Brel had died and his replacement in French affections was Jean-Philippe Smet, whose style was as bogus-American as Johnny Hallyday, his stage name, and the heavily chromed and monster-finned Detroit cars his publicity agents had him drive.

In crime, at least, the old flair burned steadily. In the "break-in of the century", the *gentlemen-cambrioleurs* of Nice relieved the Société Générale bank in the city of 60 million francs-worth of gold jewelry, gems and cash. The gang of twenty men who dug a tunnel from the municipal sewers into the bank in July 1976 were led by Albert Spaggiari. The crime was committed "without guns, without violence, without hate". Spaggiari was caught, but escaped from a window of the Palais de Justice in Nice onto the back of a waiting motorcycle, eventually to reappear on a ranch in Argentina. Jacques Mesrine, then public enemy no. 1, was also to make a dramatic escape from his lawyer's office; he, however, having given press interviews whilst on the run – "Le folklore et le champagne, c'est fini", the infinitely quotable Mesrine said, "il ne reste plus que la guerre" – was shot dead by police in central Paris.

The desperate search for oil underpinned the imaginative fraud of the century. The head of Elf, the state-owned oil company which politicians came to regard as a sort of private piggy bank, signed a 400 million franc contract giving it one year's exclusive use of project Delta, a revolutionary method of detecting oil deposits so secret that no one at Elf was allowed to inspect it. The system used an airborne black box, developed by a Belgian engineer, Count Alain de Villegas. The results, he claimed, were promising enough for a further 300 million francs to wing its way to a Swiss bank account. Alas, it eventually turned out that the count was a fantasist, his black box no more than a random assemblage of dials and wires, the oil deposits non-existent, and the money had gone. Where? Had any found its way to political parties? Why were the perpetrators not in court? It was as well for Giscard, who was one of those gulled, that the full story did not emerge until after he had left office. Other *affaires* did, however, and there were too many for comfort.

Political murders of Judge Renaud, Jean de Broglie, labour minister Robert Boulin, and Joseph Fontanet, former minister of health and education were carried out by assassins who are still unknown. De Broglie was murdered in December 1976 as he left the residence of a notorious swindler. This was a man of substance: a prince, a deputy, a signatory of the Evian accords that had ended the Algerian war, a co-founder with Giscard of the Républicains Indépendants. *Le Canard enchaîné* revealed in 1980 that, despite denials by Michel Poniatowski, the police knew that a contract was out to kill de Broglie, but the surveillance kept on him was lifted shortly before the murder. There was talk that the dead man was linked to the Catholic group Opus Dei, and to an 800 million franc scam involving Spanish export credits, and to the trafficking of 140 million francs in fake treasury bonds in Gabon; some of the money was said to have gone to French political parties.

Most damaging to Giscard was his link with Jean-Bédel Bokassa dictator of the Central African Republic. Giscard went on safari in his dusty and malnourished realm. He allowed himself to be called Bokassa's friend, and he let the French taxpayer foot much of the bill in 1977 when the deranged tyrant crowned himself Emperor Bokassa I in Napoleonic pastiche. When the emperor's vices became too well known – there was talk of human body parts stored in the imperial refrigerators – Giscard casually had him removed by coup d'état, as the year before he had intervened in Africa by sending French troops to Zaire to crush a left-wing rebellion against the dictator Mobutu. His adviser on African affairs, René Journiac, was credited with this, though the maestro of French intervention was Jacques Foccart, the shadowy figure who ran French Africa like a "virtual empire" from his Paris apartment, a grey parrot on his desk, a manipulator of coups and regimes, at whose funeral in 1997 eight African heads of state and government paid their respects.

Bokassa was removed from power in September 1979. A month later, *Le Canard enchaîné* said that Giscard had received 1 million francs' worth of diamonds from the dictator when he was finance minister in 1973.

The explanations Giscard gave were slow and scanty and half-hearted. They hung heavily in the air in the lengthy run-up to the 1981 presidential elections.

Workers in banking, insurance and steel came out on strike. A further steep rise in the oil price was provoked by the crisis in Iran, when Ayatollah Khomeini overthrew the Shah. The sharp mind of Chirac's replacement as premier, Raymond Barre, belied his portly and reassuring figure. He was a first-rate economist, and he remained his own finance minister. His deep budget cuts earned him much unpopularity as unemployment rose, but his policies were more effective than Chirac's inflation-stoking attempts at reflation. France came through *la crise* at least as well as West Germany, and very much better than Britain. But the country had become so used to a 5 per cent growth rate that a fall to 1 per cent seemed a disaster. In truth, given the world climate, it was a fine achievement. Neither Barre nor Giscard got the credit they deserved. Eight months before the election, Giscard had a 61 to 39 lead over Mitterrand in opinion polls, but it was a shakier one than it seemed.

Written off as a two-time failure, Mitterrand's faith in himself was undented. "What do they know of my destiny?" he confided in his diary. "Is it the destiny of the Seine to water Paris, or to flow on to the sea?" The ambivalence was revealing. So, too, was the way that, even when writing for himself, he concealed the vapidity of his thought beneath a surface grandeur.

These qualities made him brilliant in electoral tactics. Though the union of the left had collapsed, Mitterrand continued with its language. "We believe there is a class struggle," he intoned. "We consider that the class that leads the struggle is the business bourgeoisie that governs today." This was nonsense. He believed no such thing, and his own businessmen-friends were to profiteer wildly from his presidency; but it helped him to be sure of sweeping up the Communist vote. Other voters, of course, were frightened at the prospect of the left coming to power. Mitterrand took advice on how best to reassure them from Jacques Séguéla, an advertising man. The candidate had his teeth capped. He wore natty suits. He was projected as the safe elder statesman, and a victory for the left as no more than "alternance", the comforting word used to describe the changing of the seasons.

Mitterrand dined with Chirac, at the home of his devotee Édith Cresson, and dripped poison in the mayor's ear. A Mitterrand victory might prove more providential; a further seven years of Giscard rule would kill Chirac's career stone dead. True, the left's programme committed it to bringing in proportional representation, damaging to Chirac's Gaullists. It was promised that whatever Mitterrand might say in public, the electoral system would not be changed if he won.

Giscard and Mitterrand emerged comfortably enough as the two winners from the ten first-round candidates. But the diamonds hung heavily on Giscard between the two rounds. When he tried to intimidate Mitterrand during their televised debate with a question on currency exchange rates, Mitterrand merely smiled, and then had his aides leak it to the press that he thought about asking Giscard the going rate for diamonds, but had held back from respect for his office. A fresh *affaire* centred on Maurice Papon, Giscard's budget minister. In 1942 he had been the official reponsible for Jewish questions at the regional prefecture in Bordeaux. Papon's career had flourished after the war; having served Vichy, he moved on to work for Socialist governments under the Fourth Republic, and for the Fifth as de Gaulle's head of the Paris police. "There are no crises of conscience", Papon once wrote, "when one obeys the orders of the French state."

Michel Slitinsky, a Jew whose sister had been deported by Papon, contacted *Le Canard enchaîné*. It ran the story at the most sensitive time of the campaign, just before the second round. "PAPON, AIDE DE CAMPS", it splashed.

The deepest hurt, though, was done by Chirac. Georges Marchais, the losing Communist, was swift to urge his supporters to vote Mitterrand in the run-off. Chirac was vindictively slow in suggesting that his Gaullists back Giscard. Mitterrand rubbed Giscard's patrician nose in Chirac's criticisms of him – he quoted Chirac ten times during their televised debate – and Chirac said nothing. It was decisive. Mitterrand won 51.7 per cent of the vote.

Giscard gave a final address on television. He told the director that, after he had said his "au revoir", the camera should remain fixed on his empty chair as the "Marseillaise" played. It was a final vanity, to suggest that France was orphaned, and to fix the idea of *bonheur perdu*, of paradise lost.

15

The Inheritance Man

The left celebrated its victory with the rapture of a second Liberation. A love-in was held at the Bastille, with songs and wine and roses and kisses. Daniel Barenboim conducted Beethoven's Ninth. Mitterrand made a pilgrimage to the Panthéon. He had red roses in his hand – the rose in a clenched fist was the symbol of his party, and the title of one of his books – and he placed a single flower on each of three tombs. The heroes of the Republic whom he thus honoured were Victor Schoelcher, emancipator of slaves a century before, the Socialist martyr Jean Jaurès, and Jean Moulin. De Gaulle had interred Moulin in the Panthéon in 1964, but Mitterrand now laid claim to him for the left. His visit appeared intimate and solitary. It was caught by cameras tucked away behind the pillars, however, and shared with millions of television viewers. It was a scene of manufactured spontaneity. But most, like the cineaste Serge Moati, saw it as intended, as the "solitude of a man swept along by the weight of history".

Mitterrand's early days had a historic, Popular Front aura. The government, under Pierre Mauroy, the firebrand mayor of Lille, was retro in feel and policy. It had four Communist ministers, and it pursued Mitterrand's campaign theme of "a clean break with capitalism" with wet-behind-the-ears idealism. Holidays and shorter hours, the legends of 1936, were revisited. The working week was cut to 39 hours, with an eventual commitment to 35, and a fifth week was added to paid holidays. An amnesty for illegal immigrants was declared.

A new ministry for women's affairs was set up. Independent radio and television stations were permitted. Mayors and the regions were given greater powers. Jack Lang, a lawyer turned experimental theatre director, was appointed culture minister. He subsidised the arts with a doubled budget, and launched the annual *fête de la musique*, a sort of national music party, to celebrate the summer solstice.

Déjà vu was strongest with the "Auroux laws", the starry-eyed 1981 employment reforms. Trade unions were strengthened. The minimum wage was increased by 10 per cent, despite the cut in hours. The retirement age was lowered to 60. Family allowances, housing subsidies and pensions went up by a heady 25 to 30 per cent. Income tax was revamped in favour of the lower paid.

Sweeping nationalisations saw the state in control of 13 of the largest 20 companies in the country. The proportion of the workforce directly reliant on the state doubled, with a further 140,000 recruited for the public sector, many in cultural projects. In theory, the higher wages would stimulate greater consumer spending, creating more jobs as production rose to meet demand. This had not worked in 1936. It was less likely to succeed in 1981. The planned economies of the Soviet bloc were visibly beginning to implode. The Western world was meeting the crisis with privatisations and cuts in public spending. This, critics mindful of Stalinist Russia warned mournfully, was "socialism in one country". A third of the ministerial team, however, were teachers ignorant of the facts of economic life. Mitterrand's France grandly ignored the rest of the world. The world – or its money markets – did not ignore him. Almost $20 billion poured out of France in May. The financial credibility Barre had laboured to win in four years of austerity was squandered in a fortnight.

A whiff of vengeance went with these early enthusiasms. Old enemies were not forgotten. The rich were punished with a new luxury tax on expense accounts, yachts and up-market hotels, a 20 per cent increase in death duties, and a wealth tax, which caught some 170,000 families. This brought little in – 4 billion francs a year from the *impôt sur les grandes fortunes*, a piffling amount in total tax terms – but they were visible scalpings. So were the nationalisations. The new finance minister, Jacques Delors, thought 51 per cent state ownership enough. Mitterrand insisted on 100 per cent. "Jew under the Germans," the head of Rothschild's said as his bank was taken from him a second time. "Capitalist under Mitterrand."

The mixture of good and ill will was reflected in Mitterrand himself. He was the most complex of presidents – ambiguous, fluid, an adventurer. His great virtues – courage, charm, intellect, patience, a deep and unfussy sense of French grandeur and civilisation – were matched by vices that, as is their wont, became more pronounced as he aged in power. He was full of paradox. He created a great Socialist Party, and smothered the Communists in fraternal embrace; he was loyal to Europe, and to the Atlantic alliance, but he slid into vindictive and petty scheming on lesser issues. He was committed to human rights, but ordered illegal phone taps, hiding behind a smokescreen of *secret défense*. He attacked the Gaullist Republic as a "permanent coup d'état", but he enjoyed it for longer than any. He despised money – "money which kills," he railed, "money which rots right through the conscience of men" – but close friends and colleagues were tainted by corruption.

So much of French life had flowed through him that he seemed to mirror it. Jean Lacouture titled his biography of him *Mitterrand: une histoire de Français*, as if it were the story not of one man, but of all the French. He understood them, and grasped their subtleties. They, for their part, recognised something of themselves in him, and forgave him much.

He was born at Jarnac in the rolling brandy country of the Charente in 1916. In upbringing, at least, he was of the right. His father was in the vinegar trade; one brother became an air force general, another a leading businessmen. He studied politics and law in Paris, painting himself as a shy provincial in knickerbockers and white socks, with a love of the theatre and ice skating. There was more to him than that. A press photographer caught him at an Action Française demonstration, protesting at the over-subscription of Jews in medical schools.

Serving as a sergeant in an infantry regiment in 1940, he was wounded, captured and escaped. He worked for the Vichy government, reclassifying prisoners of war, meeting Pétain, and winning a Vichy award. This, he claimed, provided perfect cover for him when he became a *résistant*. His role and courage in the Resistance cannot be faulted – he risked his life on dangerous missions to England and North Africa and back to France – but some of the ambivalence that clung to occupied France attached itself to him, too.

He set himself up as deputy for the Nievre after the war. In 1947, he became the youngest minister since 1870, responsible for veterans and war victims. The Fourth Republic, and its "adhésion/trahison" (adhesion–treason), suited a man who travelled light. He moved well, "the tango dancer", they called him, or "the Florentine". *Elle* magazine selected him as one of the ten most handsome men in France. Albert Camus and Jacques Chaban-Delmas kept him company. He was a minister eleven times, latterly as justice minister in Guy Mollet's government in 1956, at the time General Massu's paras were let loose in Algiers. He considered de Gaulle's new regime to be illegal, and refused to attend the general's investiture.

The "Observatory affair" in 1959 almost finished him. As *plastiqueurs* went on the rampage in Paris, Mitterrand was warned by Robert Pesquet, a former yoghurt salesman, of plans to assassinate him. Driving home in the early hours, he sensed he was being followed, braked and took cover in the Observatory gardens. His car was raked with gunshots. As Mitterrand told of his narrow escape, Pesquet popped up to claim that it was a carefully rehearsed fake, staged by Mitterrand to win sympathy and votes. At worst, Mitterrand was a fraud, at best a dupe. Efforts were made to strip him of parliamentary immunity. When he rose to defend himself, he was supported only by Communists and four Socialists.

It marked him. "He was terribly treated by the right in the Sixties," Pierre Mauroy noted, "He had to survive their diatribes and mockery, and he has never forgotten it." Patience, and foresight, saved him. He realised that de Gaulle would last, and he rebalanced on the left, as a moderate Socialist. He did not like the Communists – their policies, he had earlier said, were "dictated by Russian imperialism" – but he needed them. Already armed with his own party, he invented the "union of the left". Before, there had just been de Gaulle and the Communists, with nothing solid in between.

He was, too, a brilliant showman. Mauroy, his first prime minister, had grown up in Lille in the great leftist tradition of the northern mills and mines. "Mitterrand isn't like that at all," he acknowledged. "He came to socialism when he was over fifty. He intellectualised his way there. It took him ten years of hard reading." Yet he played the part to perfection. Mauroy recalled a performance at an obscure demonstration in Alsace. "There was this figure in a big black hat and scarf, just like Léon Blum," he said. "Blum's widow could have thought it her husband. Under the hat was François Mitterrand."

Blum had failed to beat recession, and so, for much the same reasons, did Mitterrand. Unemployment neared two million, and went on increasing at 60,000 a month. A fifth of those under 25 had no work. The new consumer spending sucked in imports, with a balance of payments crisis. Investor confidence weakened. Inflation accelerated.

There was panic selling on the Bourse, where the main index fell by 30 per cent. The franc was devalued in October 1981. Delors asked for a "pause" in reforms. By June 1982, a policy reversal was clearly needed. Prices and wages were frozen. The franc underwent a second, panicky devaluation. Welfare spending was cut by taking 300,000 off unemployment benefit. The trade deficit ballooned to 11 billion francs a month. Senior figures such as Michel Rocard and Pierre Bérégovoy urged that the franc be taken out of the Exchange Rate Mechanism.

Mitterrand vacillated. "People say I am hesitating," he claimed. "No, I am reflecting. France will be grateful to me for that." He thought of replacing Mauroy with Delors. Mauroy knew that the president was listening to rivals – "we called them the *visiteurs du soir* [the night visitors]", he said, – but he and the ERM hung on. Delors, whose skill prevented a worse crisis, was obliged to raise interest rates to a record 20 per cent. The franc was devalued again.

This final humiliation induced a sea change. Delors slashed public spending, and increased taxes and health service charges. Real spending power went into reverse. Growth slowed to 1 per cent. But inflation was brought down to the EEC average, the huge foreign-trade deficit was slashed, and Mitterrand discovered the error of his ways.

"Anyone", he had once thundered, "who does not accept the rupture with capitalist society cannot, I say, be a member of the Socialist Party." The quasi-Marxist now accepted the virtues of the free market. It was a stupefying volte face. "The French are beginning to understand," he said in January 1984. "It is the firm that creates wealth, it is the firm that creates employment."

It was revealing that he said "beginning" to understand. Private firms had, after all, underpinned the *trente glorieuses*. Yet suspicion and hostility were still very much alive. As late as 1981, it was thought proper for the state to seize and manage key companies. And it was of course Mitterrand himself who was slow to understand wealth creation.

State intervention was seen as a natural part of industry. It was a striking example of the "French exception". *L'état* in French has more resonance than *le pays*. Right as much as left agree on its primacy. "For a Frenchman," Chirac has said, "the notion of the public good is inseparable from that of the state." The idea of *l'état providence*, the state as the fount of milk and honey, pre-dated the welfare state. State-owned concerns, and the semi-public Société d'Économie Mixte, were a common tradition. De Gaulle had nationalised with gusto from 1944, returning to it to establish Elf in 1963. The French, too, had a better record than any in running them.

The high-speed TGV line to Lyon was inaugurated in 1981. This made it possible for someone in La Défense, on the western outskirts of Paris, to book and pay for a TGV ticket on a Minitel videotext screen attached to his telephone. He could then make an RER rapid-transit journey under the city to the mainline station, and from there race in comfort to Lyon in a smidgen over two hours. Nowhere else had so brilliant a train and transit system, nor so simple and ubiquitous a service provider as Minitel. All this pioneering brilliance was the fruit of state enterprise. Some projects, the TGV, or EDF's nuclear power programme, needed pockets too deep for private enterprise. But Minitel was an inspired individual creation, by the telecoms department of the PTT, once a byword for Soviet-style sloth.

It could take three years to get a new phone line when Gérard Théry became boss of PTT. By 1981, he was installing 1.5 million lines a year. The waiting list vanished. He introduced Minitel, which connected users to a huge range of individual service providers. Up to 1997, Minitel generated more electronic trade inside France than the internet was attracting worldwide. Théry was ahead of his time, too, in giving away some six million Minitels. Cellphone operators were later to copy him in boosting network usage by distributing free mobiles.

Cars, mixing advanced engineering and design with consumer tastes, seem stony ground for *dirigisme*. Yet Régie Renault, confiscated from Louis Renault by the state in 1944, was run on competitive and commercial lines. Its plant at Billancourt was the first in Europe to use automation in 1946. Pierre Dreyfus, its outstanding chairman, was set on making cars every family could afford. The 4CV was followed by the hugely successful Dauphine. Though Renault made heavy losses in the early 1980s, it was restored to health by another gifted technocrat, Georges Besse, murdered by terrorists in 1986.

In aerospace, where the individual genius of Marcel Dassault created the strongly selling Mirage and Mystère fighters, the elegant but loss-making Concorde exposed the perils of projects led by politics and prestige. But without state support for French-led Airbus, the Americans would have had the big jet market to themselves. With it, Toulouse was able eventually to outsell Boeing. French Ariane rockets kept Europe in space, too, winning a major share of world satellite launches.

The Mitterrand nationalisations, however, were ideological, ill-planned and damaging. "I was carried away with our victory," he later admitted. "We were intoxicated." The state had no reason to take over 36 private banks, nor leading industrials in a hodgepodge of sectors – electrical goods, glass, aluminium, chemicals and electronics. Delors and the industry minister, Pierre Dreyfus, well-placed to judge as the former Renault boss, had little stomach for the programme. It was a doctrinaire decision, playing on deep suspicions of profit and private enterprise.

France had world-class entrepreneurs, like Édouard Leclerc, the extraordinary Breton grocer who broke price-fixing. They were not universally admired. Leclerc was a young Jesuit seminarist when he felt called to challenge the high prices retailers maintained after the war. He opened a shop in 1949 in his home town, Landerneau near Brest, selling chocolate and biscuits at big discounts. Rivals tried to destroy him by getting wholesalers to black him.

He complained to the government, which confirmed that fixed prices and refusal to supply were illegal. Others rallied to his crusade. Centres E Leclerc spread to Grenoble, and then to Paris. By 1960, 60 stores were members of his association. No member could have more than two stores, and each signed a "moral contract" promising to keep margins low. Leclerc fought the pharmacists, and sold cheap petrol in defiance of state price-fixing. "Maybe my work has been close to religion," he told the writer John Ardagh. "I admire Christ for chasing the tradesmen from the Temple."

Competitors like Carrefour, founded by a shopkeeper from Annecy in 1960, copied him as the *supermarché* swelled into the *hypermarché*, and French retailers challenged the Americans. Though the *petit épicier* was almost killed off, new shops set up in multi-boutique arcades to sell designer clothes and specialist goods in the shadow of the giants.

The potential of the leisure industry in its many forms was realised. The French were early in most fields. Lacoste's crocodile sportswear, Gilbert Trigano's Club Med resorts and Bombard's blow-up boats were all pioneers. In winter sports, Laurent Bois-Vives transformed Rossignol from an old family workshop near Grenoble into the world's biggest ski maker, with factories in five countries and over a fifth of a rapidly expanding global market.

Fine minds, artistic and scientific, remained at work. The virologist Luc Montagnier at the Institut Pasteur isolated the HIV virus that caused AIDS in 1983. In engineering, a treaty was signed with Britain in 1986 to build the Channel Tunnel, eventually to expose the benighted islanders to the glories of the TGV.

The shell of the abattoir at La Villette was transformed into the Cité des Sciences, a showcase for technology matched by the wondrous conversion of the old Orsay railway station into a haven for nineteenth-century arts. Pierre Boulez composed Répons, the high point of his work at IRCAM, the music research laboratory at the Pompidou Centre. Claude Simon won the Nobel Prize in Literature with rich and sensuous novels like *Le Vent* (The Wind) and *La Route des Flandres* (The Flanders Road). Bertrand Tavernier exemplified the old school of French cinema in his graceful *Un dimanche à la campagne* (A Sunday in the Country). Louis Malle was filming *Au revoir les enfants*, his autobiographical masterpiece, set in a Catholic boarding school during the Occupation.

For all that, and Jack Lang's energy, it was a leanish crop by local standards. Fittingly, the great cult film was Luc Besson's *Le Grand Bleu*, on an extreme diver, half-man, half-dolphin, shot in the rapturous depths of the sea. It was in extreme sports that the French excelled.

French sailors were emerging as masters of long-distance single-handed races, the sea-going equivalent of the "raids" for cars and motorbikes like the Paris-Dakar. Éric Tabarly became a national hero when he won the transatlantic race in 1964, taking 13 days off Francis Chichester's original 40-day record. A French stranglehold saw them win eight of the first 11 races. In 2000, Francis Joyon made the first crossing in under ten days.

The public took to the old dash and courage, enduring in an age of carbon fibre and satellite navigation, on an unrelenting sea that swallowed heroes of the stature of Tabarly and Alain Colas. Races like the Route du Rhum were reminders of the islands France still possessed, from the Caribbean to the Pacific. Even in the wastes of the Southern Ocean, crews hurtled by the lonely French island of Kerguelen on the westerly gales.

Sponsors loved it, the postal service so much that it raced its own yacht *La Poste* around the world with a crew of eight postmen. So, too, did the booming boat and marina business. The number of French-registered boats, hardly 60,000 in the 1960s, had climbed to the half-million mark when Mitterrand took office, and reached 800,000 by the end of the century.

Climbing, on the edge of skill and endurance, produced a lesser known but brilliant generation. In the summer of 1985, Christophe Profit climbed the north faces of the Matterhorn and the Eiger, and the Linceul face of the Jorasses in a single day of rock and ice and exposure. In a dazzling 42 hours in the winter of 1987, he tackled the two great north faces, and rounded off with the Croz spur of the Jorasses.

Some muttered at record-breaking, more so when climbers took to paragliding off the summit to save time on the descent. But the "speed climber" Marc Batard, a short, slender figure racing up ice walls on the points of his titanium crampons, in a one piece black climbing outfit, sucking black coffee from a bladder sewn into his climbing suit, had a classic purity of line and style. In 1990, he climbed and descended Everest in 22 hours 29 minutes, without oxygen, a record that still stood 15 years later.

As in sailing, women made their mark. Catherine Destivelle was the first woman to climb a Grade 8a+ route, in 1986. Her elegant rock climbing, and her mental toughness on routes like her winter solo on the Eiger – "The fact that I'm three months pregnant doesn't change anything," she said as she prepared to solo the Old Man of Hoy, a ferocious Orkney seastack – made her perhaps the world's finest woman climber. Chantal Maudit had climbed five 8,000-metre peaks before she died on Dhaulagiri.

Pierre Tardivel excelled in extreme skiing, the new sport of going down precipitous slopes, dropping 3,000 metres on skis from the south summit of Everest. Four million went skiing in more orthodox fashion each year. The country was more *sportif* than ever. Tennis, once elite, was played by more than a million. It threw up a new star as it shed its old persona, the dreadlocked Yannick Noah, Roland-Garros champion in 1983, and a sign of the sporting heights that immigrants would reach.

As the Marxist ardour cooled, the Communists pulled out of the government in 1984, a spent force. The extreme right now made the running. Le Pen's Front National won 11 per cent of the vote in the European elections of June 1984. It thrived on fear of crime and immigration. The two were mixed in an explosive emotional cocktail, made the more potent by the 250 per cent rise in the crime rate over the past decade. SOS-Racisme responded to Le Pen's taunts with mass rallies. The classic right was recovering its nerve, too. Plans by education minister Alain Savary to increase state control over private schools brought a million demonstrators onto the Paris streets in June. The reforms were dropped. The prime minister went in July.

Laurent Fabius, the new man, was in utter contrast to the hearty Mauroy. He was young, suave, metropolitan, the youngest premier for over a century, an undeniable product of privilege. The son of a leading Paris antique dealer, he grew up eating family meals under a de La Tour that now hangs in the National Gallery in Washington. He was a *normalien*, and an *énarque* to boot. He caught the presidential eye early. As budget minister in the high-rolling days, he had watched money pour into lame duck companies, *canards boiteux*, in steel and shipbuilding. Now, as premier, he was to inflict rigour, and close enterprises he had subsidised a few months before.

Prominent among these were the steelworks at Trith-Saint-Léger, near Lille, in Mauroy country. It was a holy place of the left, with a marble monument to the victims of accidents, "To the Dead from Labour". The old premier had it expensively modernised as a symbol of regeneration. Now Trith became martyr to the great U-turn. Mauroy mourned it at party headquarters in Lille, amid mementoes of his dead dreams: posters promoting "École Laïque", the failed attempt to bring private schools to heel, "Une Press Libre", the abortive campaign against press monopoly, and "Entreprises Publiques Pour Réussir", the failed takeovers. The Dunkirk shipyards went. The Nord and the Pas-de-Calais were losing 40,000 people a year. It was better to look for work in the southern sunbelt than in the rainy rustbelt of the north.

Terrorism was a constant reprise, largely in Paris. Then across the world, explosives sank the *Rainbow Warrior* in Auckland harbour in 1985, killing a crew member. The Greenpeace ship was on its way to protest against French nuclear tests in the Pacific. The bombers were caught and found to be French agents. Fabius survived, his authority compromised; the defence minister, Charles Hernu, reluctantly resigned. The president's responsibility remained murky.

Fabius steadied the economy, but with conservative policies. Mitterrand introduced proportional representation, to contain damage in the 1986 parliamentary elections and encourage fracture on the right. The classic right duly won, its inner tensions exacerbated. Le Pen was confirmed as a fixture at the extreme. A Socialist president with a right-wing National Assembly was uncharted waters. Raymond Barre found it unthinkable. Chirac, though, was amenable. Mitterrand was ready for "cohabitation" to become a fundamental constitutional doctrine.

Chirac was the new prime minister in 1986. In sheer speed, he was a match for Alain Prost, reigning Formula 1 champion. Ideas, speeches, handshakes and ruffled air marked his passing like exhaust plumes. His pace was close to the limits of adhesion, for time was against him. Cohabitation worked well enough for Mitterrand. He was happy to give Chirac his head on domestic issues, where unpopular issues lurked. He reserved diplomacy for himself, refusing to accept Chirac's nominees for the foreign and defence ministries, insisting that neutral "technicians" be appointed. Here, he acted as the lofty guardian of French interests in the world, safely above the swill of party politics.

For Chirac, though, the 1988 presidential elections loomed too soon. His policies had only two years to bite: long enough for the initial pain to be felt, but not for the fruits to be tasted. His majority was small; he was in a hurry, and he had to muscle measures through. He set about privatising, with Édouard Balladur, the cool technocrat who had overseen the road tunnel beneath Mont Blanc, in charge of the economy. Mitterrand publicly criticised the plan to sell off 65 companies, but baulked at creating a crisis by rejecting it. The wealth tax was abolished. The Quillot housing law of 1982, which favoured tenants, was repealed. Aid to ailing behemoths was stopped. Normed shipbuilders went to the wall, with 6,900 jobs lost.

Electricity and transport workers came out on strike. Students suspected that planned reforms were intended to bring selectivity to university entrance. A day of nationwide demonstrations saw them in bloody clashes with the police. The reform was dropped and the education minister sacked. There was more terrorism, and the stock market crash in October threatened the privatisations.

Mitterrand, by contrast, was without stress. His concern was simply that the right repeat the fratricide of 1981. The auguries were excellent. Raymond Barre was to run against Chirac. Barre was the more dangerous for Mitterrand to meet in the second round. He was more *présidentiable*; he had kept out of party infighting, he was round and cuddly – "Barzi the Bear" – and he understood economics. He could dent Mitterrand's gravitas.

But these very qualities made his survival in the first round unlikely. Chirac smelled of burning rubber even when he was standing still. Barre was a tortoise, refusing any publicity machine. He operated from a modest pair of rooms on the boulevard Saint-Germain. Chirac flitted between the Right Bank town hall as mayor, and the Left Bank premier's residence. The odds favoured Chirac.

The National Front, further dividing the right, was another Mitterrand asset. It was not all skinheads, street battlers and the damned. Bruno Mégret, Le Pen's campaign director, was the *grande école* and Berkeley educated son of a state councillor. The party played classical music at rallies – Beethoven, not Wagner – and held dinner jacketed soirées in the Bois de Boulogne. The ground swell it fed on, particularly the influx of Muslims, was deep and angry. And Le Pen, with his promises to send home "Ghanaian prostitutes and Tamil drug pushers", and his attacks on the "Babelisation" of society, knew how to exploit it.

So, indeed, it transpired. Le Pen got 14 per cent in the first round. Chirac beat Barre. In a few hours between the two rounds, on the edge of the biggest test of his political life, Chirac had three French hostages freed in Lebanon, their aircraft conveniently touching down in Paris for him to greet it live during the evening television news. In the Pacific, he ordered force to be used to free captives of Kanak rebels in New Caledonia, and had a secret agent convicted over the *Rainbow Warrior* returned to France, despite an agreement with New Zealand to detain her on a French atoll.

It was a supercharged performance, but it was not enough. Mitterrand was brilliant at exuding the dignity of France whilst maintaining a common, but not too common touch. By comparison, Chirac seemed Jumping Jacques Flash made flesh. Mitterrand was home at a canter. He called parliamentary elections. The left won, if with a smaller than expected majority. Michel Rocard, his one-time Socialist rival, became prime minister. Mitterrand seemed to have reinvented himself and his authority.

He had not. Rather, he made a virtue of vapidity. His catchphrase was "ni-ni". Neither, nor. There should be "neither new privatisations, nor renationalisations": the issue was a "sterile quarrel". The 3,000-word essay on economic policy he wrote for his campaign had just two concrete proposals: he would increase spending on education and bring back the wealth tax. Drift was installed as a principle. Some took this flux to be a part of his philosophy. "Mitterrand considers that everything is double, true and untrue," Fabius said. "Life is a dialectic to him. You have to understand that. He is ambivalent - but not ambiguous." It was, perhaps, no coincidence that he had spent the previous Christmas in Egypt, looking at the Sphinx.

France marked time. Mitterrand toyed with Rocard. He received student protesters at the Élysée in 1990, and then sent them off to the education minister with orders from himself. The prime minister was not consulted. In 1991, Rocard was dropped.

He was replaced by the sharp-tongued Édith Cresson. The Élysée was already well feminised. Enough young mothers worked there for a crèche to be opened for their children in a converted stable block. Cresson and the "techno-blonde" Élisabeth Guigou were said to form an elite presidential guard; Anne Lauvergnon was a close adviser, outspoken, sexily dressed and the author of a social history of French brothels. A woman prime minister was an important symbol, the historian Michelle Perrot noted, but why had Mitterrand chosen one? "Is it a masculine-feminine reflection in his thought? Or because Édith Cresson is loyal? Or because it irritates Rocard?" All of the above perhaps. The results were certainly disastrous. By the time she was replaced by Bérégovoy less than a year later, Cresson had become the least-admired premier of modern times.

The hapless Bérégovoy lasted for 11 scandal-ridden months before he was overwhelmed by the landslide victory of the right in the parliamentary elections in March 1993. He shot himself with his bodyguard's pistol by a canal in Nevers at the end of April. He was buried in the town on May Day. Mitterrand was at the funeral; "Béré" was one of his oldest loyalists. He lashed a system which allowed "the honour and life of a man to be thrown to the dogs". By "dogs" he meant the newspapers and the magistrate who had pursued Bérégovoy over a million-franc interest-free loan. It came from the late Roger-Patrice Pelat, a Mitterrand intimate, one of the half-dozen or so people, outside his immediate family circle, with whom the president used the familiar *tu*. Pelat was suspected of insider share dealing in a state-owned company.

The ferocity of the attack failed to hide Mitterrand's rejection of Bérégovoy, who had eaten alone in the National Assembly after his defeat, on boiled eggs and water, and tranquillisers, humiliated by his fall from the Hôtel Matignon to a poke-hole office in the Assembly whose number he could not remember. Above all, those who met him said, he was hurt and confused that Mitterrand would not return his phone calls. The president turned his back on another colleague in need. In a scandal over the use of blood contaminated with the HIV virus, he left Fabius to fight his corner alone.

His own present was bleak. He was effectively neutered at home. His new government was led by the courteous and competent Edouard Balladur, whom the cartoonists dubbed "His Sufficiency" and respectfully pictured in powdered wig being carried in a sedan chair. His own nicknames, once affectionate ("Tonton", uncle) or coolly respectful ("the Sphinx") or admiring ("God"), gave way to "Conchita", the Spanish maid fussing round the table of her conservative master.

Balladur resumed the privatisations, and quietly maintained the recovery. Foreign affairs were left to Mitterrand, but his ability to nurture his priorities – closer European unity, the implementation of Maastricht, the preservation of the Paris–Bonn axis, which his close relations with Helmut Kohl had done much to foster – was much reduced.

He was a dying man. "Seven years is too much," he had said a few weeks before he became president. "Fourteen years is even more so . . ." But he went on to the bitter end. His monuments multiplied. A crystal pyramid in the courtyard of the Louvre, a national library, a new opera house, a City of Music and a spectacular Grande Arche celebrated his presidency. Paris future could hardly ignore its Mitterrand past.

But what was that past? "Mitterrandism functions in a hole of memory," a biographer wrote. "He does not preserve the past." He was, indeed, at great pains to conceal it. At the last gasp of his presidency, in 1995, he signed a secret agreement over the handling of his presidential papers. In a protocol, the French national archives signed away its rights to the papers for a period of 60 years. Access could be granted only by his trustee, Mme Bertinotti, a socialist militant and academic whom he had brought to the Élysée. Further, the archives had no oversight to ensure that state papers were not transferred into his personal archives. He had granted his *droit moral*, his moral rights, in these to his illegitimate daughter Mazarine Pingeot. It was deeply disturbing for the papers of a public man to be so privately guarded, and by members of the Association des Amis de l'Institut

François Mitterrand, to which both Mme Bertinotti and Mlle Pingeot belonged. Its founding president, Roland Dumas, stated that the Mitterrand archives "will not be open to people who ask 'What spicy stories can I find?'"

Open archives would, as Dumas well knew, be searched for details of his own and the president's conduct in Elf and other scandals examined by magistrates. The total of alleged slush funds at Elf reached 305 million francs. These were not "spicy stories". They touched on a corrosive indifference to legality at the heart of a great nation.

A former foreign minister and head of the constitutional council, Dumas was the highest profile figure to be prosecuted in the Elf affair. His conviction for receiving misappropriated public funds was cleared on appeal. His mistress Christine Deviers-Joncour, whose book on the affair was titled "The Whore of the Republic", served a prison term for receiving millions of francs in bribes. Elf's former head, Loïk Le Floch-Pringent, a golfing partner of Mitterrand, claimed in court that the president had agreed to fund his 5 million franc divorce settlement from secret funds. He was sentenced to five years. It was also alleged that Mitterrand had ordered $15 million to be paid to Helmut Kohl's Christian Democrat party from the "commissions" paid out by Elf in 1992 after it bought the Leuna oil refinery and petrol stations in the former East Germany. A French-Tunisian intermediary for Elf, André Guelfi, also known as "Dédé la Sardine", said that both the French president and the German chancellor were aware of the payments.

Mitterrand's patronage of the businessman Bernard Tapie was another cause for concern. The charismatic Tapie, president of Olympique de Marseille football club, and owner of *Phocéa*, a yacht with a 14-metre-long drawing room, was appointed minister for urban affairs in 1993. By 1997, he had received three prison sentences for fraud and suborning witnesses. The president's 1988 re-election campaign enjoyed a 24 million franc donation from Urba, a major building consultancy set up by the Socialists. It siphoned money from public works contracts into party funds. A contractor on the tunnel under Marseille harbour, for example, gave a backhander of 5.7 million francs. The policeman who investigated Urba, Antoine Gaudino, described it as "the party's back office, created to collect money through a system of bribery and corruption organised on a national scale". Mitterrand announced a grand amnesty for those under investigation for financial misdemeanours after the election. It applied to all elected representatives, including himself. It was, he said, part of his victory celebrations.

He also violated the privacy of hundreds of personalities by ordering their phones to be tapped. This was carried out by a special unit at the Élysée. Its object, so Mitterrand claimed, was to "fight terrorism". In fact, it spent much of its time ensuring that Mitterrand's affair with Anne Pingeot, and the existence of his daughter Mazarine, remained secret. Many of the thousands of notes of tapped conversations bore the word "Seen" in Mitterrand's hand. It was, as Giscard said, a "repugnant" encroachment on civil liberties. A few weeks before Mitterrand's death, in January 1996, it was Giscard who visited him to express his concern over the presidential papers. The elite as a whole, however, self-serving and self-protective, ignored the matter.

Mitterrand's great achievement was to educate the French to the idea and practice of alternance. He calmed the divide between them. He protected the interests and good name of France abroad. He was sensitive to the past. He held that the wounds of Vichy should be bound up. The wreath he sent to Pétain's tomb on Armistice Day 1992 was an act of political courage; so, it might be said, was his promotion of Jews to important posts during his presidency.

He ruled France for longer than anyone since Napoleon III, though it is with de Gaulle, off whose inheritance he lived, that he most begs comparison. It is not flattering. For all his virtues, he corroded public life, and he let the nation drift. Ni-ni . . .

The general built no monuments to himself. Mitterrand erected many, the Bastille Opéra among them. Bits fell off it, and scenery collapsed. Like him, it was prey to vainglory.

16

Fin de Siècle

The right bathed itself again in bad blood in the race to succeed Mitterrand. This was Chirac's third and realistically final chance to win a prize for which he had hungered all his adult life. The man most likely to deny it him was Édouard Balladur, once his own loyal lieutenant, now the suave and smooth prime minister.

The early signs were ominous. Some of Chirac's bright young men went over to "cher Édouard". But Chirac left no hand unshaken and no back unslapped. His campaigning was ferocious, and he controlled Paris and the country's most powerful party. Slowly, the gloss came off his rival. He was too soft, too Balla-mou, wags said, not Balla-dur. A lamb wetted his jacket, and farmers chortled at his discomfort. Bad weather forced his helicopter to land. A passing motorist gave him a lift, and he sent her a well-publicised bunch of roses. Alas, the press discovered that she was related to a Balladur aide, who had telephoned to ask her to pick him up. His gravitas was undermined by chuckles, whilst Chirac sprayed promises like a firehose.

The first round of a two-round contest invited protest, of course, but its scale in 1995 was startling. Millions voted for a Stalinist and a Trotskyite, and one in five for Le Pen and an ultra-nationalist. Chirac squeezed past Balladur. The beaten man urged his supporters to rally to Chirac, with a grace the latter had not extended to Giscard in 1981. They did so in enough numbers to give Chirac a comfortable passage against the left's Lionel Jospin in the run-off.

Chirac was a machine politician, a vote-winner more than a vote-user, brilliant in the pursuit of power, less accomplished when he had it. He was prone to waver when he met resistance. Chirac liked to be liked. It was soon clear that he would not deliver on his promise to heal "la fracture sociale", choosing the clever, hard-line technocrat Alain Juppé as prime minister. His brief was to slash the budget deficit to meet the entry criteria for the euro, not to help *les exclus*. Juppé planned to reduce benefits, and to trim the railway network. It hurt. He ran into a paralysing three-week strike, with two million on the streets. It was the worst unrest since 1968. The country was plunged into *morosité*, sullen and moody.

The new president had learnt from the old, now dead. Chirac let the sourness flood over the prime minister, whilst he busied himself with defence, ending military service, and integrating France more closely in Europe. He dealt sensibly with the post-Cold War world. Relations with Washington improved. The nuclear test site at Mururoa was run down.

Then, ever itchy, Chirac called early parliamentary elections in 1997. He was, he said, "acting in the name of Europe". The plan was to catch the left unprepared, and to give Juppé a clear mandate for the austerity dictated by the Maastricht criteria. It was entirely unnecessary. The right controlled the Assembly and Senate, and 19 of the 22 regions.

All this was thrown away. Chirac was not the campaigner now, Juppé was, and the right was out of sorts, with Gaullist barons growling for his head. The Socialists sensed a prize, and snapped out of their torpor, tossing the voters a sackful of carrots: a 35-

hour week without pay cuts, mass job creation, greater job security, a coalition of Greens and Reds. Juppé said he would unveil his programme after the vote. What horrors must he have in store, voters fretted, if he dare not declare it now.

First round success by the National Front compounded the disaster. Juppé resigned, aware that the 76 surviving NF candidates would wreck the right's chances in the second round. Chirac found himself marooned in a five-year cohabitation with Jospin. The euro, the cause of the disaster, limped through the 1998 referendum anyway.

Jospin, said to resemble a "provincial Swedish curate", was livelier than he looked. By the end of the Mitterrand era his career had been in tatters, his seat lost and his marriage broken. A new wife spruced up his shambling, corduroyed figure, and his luck changed. He became premier just as Juppé's austerity measures bore fruit. Unemployment fell and output recovered strongly, despite the 35-hour week. Jospin sold off more state assets in his first 18 months than Juppé had in two years. He soaked in the reflected glory of French triumph in the 1988 World Cup, with Brazil beaten 3-0 in the final in Paris.

His interior minister resigned over his soft approach to separatists in Corsica. The assassination of the island's prefect was followed by the killing of François Santini, a former separatist who had denounced Corsica's culture of gangsterism. Overall, his record was strong, however, and he was ahead of Chirac in the run-up to the 2002 presidential campaign. A record number of candidates were standing, 16 of them. Le Pen was in form, belting out his anti-immigrant, anti-EU message at meetings pungent with sausage, tobacco, beer, red wine and tricolours. Chirac, for once, and Jospin were as insipid as their slogans – respectively "for a united France" and "for France and the French to be united" – but the only real race seemed to be between them, with Chirac making up ground fast, helped by revelations of Jospin's secret Trotskyite past, and his tactless description of the president as "tired" and "past it".

Then came the first round. It was, as Fabius said, "a political cataclysm". Three million voted for Trotskyites, with their 1930s-sounding party names, Lutte Ouvrière, Ligue Communiste Révolutionnaire, Parti des Travailleurs. Well over a million backed Jean Saint-Josse, the hunting, shooting and fishing candidate of the splendidly titled Chasse, Pêche, Nature, Traditions movement. He outperformed the remnant of the once mighty French Communist Party.

The great blows, though, were struck in the middle. Chirac and Jospin mustered little more than a third of the vote combined, a historic low in an election whose low turnout broke another dismal record. Worse, Jospin was beaten into second place by the Front National's 73-year-old warhorse. The run-off was between Chirac and Le Pen.

It was a torrid affair, marked by verbal brickbats and big anti-Le Pen rallies. "Confronted with hatred and intolerance," Chirac said, "no deals, no compromises, no debates are possible." Le Pen flung back insults. Chirac, he said, was "the godfather of the clans who are bleeding this country dry. He stinks of corruption. He is dripping with dirty money." A Chirac victory was a racing certainty. The first round losers, Trotskyites included, urged their supporters to vote for him. So did Daniel Cohn-Bendit, the carrot-topped firebrand from the May Days, who begged his fellow Greens to "say No to the Chopper, to Hatred, to Intolerance, to Racism, to Anti-semitism, to Cancer . . . it spells Chirac!" It was a summary of Le Pen's platform: the "chopper" was the guillotine, whose return he advocated.

After the lowest score ever recorded by an incumbent in the first round, Chirac now registered a historic high, of 82 per cent. It made him beholden to left as well as right for victory, and it did not heal the first-round wound.

Ten million votes from 41 million registered voters was a shocking joint tally for an incumbent president and prime minister. It was, an observer wrote, "the vengeance of the people". Something was seriously amiss.

A fear of loss of identity showed in a brittle resentment of foreign influence. France had wielded immense influence on others, the English language included. Yet words were solemnly invented under the aegis of the Commissariat Général de la Langue Française to substitute for anglicisms: "capitaux fébriles" for "hot money", "navire-citerne" for "tanker" and, more happily, "balladeur" for "Walkman". A summit of 37 francophone countries in Quebec was told gloomily that it had slipped to tenth place in world rankings, spoken by "only" 200 million people. The headline in a Paris paper boded ill: "Le Sommet du French-speaking".

French is a glory – with English, it is the only language spoken on every continent – and its rude good health matters to the world. It no longer echoed in the arts and thought as it had. The country had 3,000 literary prizes on offer; it gave unparalleled support to festivals and exhibitions of every sort, but playwrights and poets and novelists of world class were gone. Directors like Jean-Pierre Jeunet kept French brilliance in the cinema alive, with *La Cité des Enfants perdus* (The City of Lost Children), a dark and carnivalesque fairy tale, and the fantasy *Le fabuleux destin d'Amélie Poulain*. But the market share of French films had slid from half to a third.

Worse, the *clercs*, the thinkers, were silent. Great issues were stirring – France and a federal Europe, France and Islam, France and Vichy, corruption, crime, immigration – that affected national identity and that needed a moral compass. "Le Pen poses good questions," Laurent Fabius noted, "and offers bad solutions." But who offered good ones? Malraux and Sartre were long departed. Foucault, the heir to Sartre's magisterium, wrote of the death of "le grand intellectuel"; he, and Barthes and Fernand Braudel and Lacan, were all soon gone. There was television debate, of course, with polished pundits like Bernard-Henri Lévy and Emmanuel Todd, but these were not the *maîtres à penser* of old. The French were ill at ease, and no great voice was there to guide them.

Disillusion with politicians was rampant. The "années fric", the years of easy money, still darkened the landscape. France was ranked 25th by Transparency International in order of ethical cleanliness. Only Italy and Greece ranked lower in

Western nations. Misdoings that elsewhere would have sunk a career without trace were often met with a wry smile. To investigate them was thought un-French. "I've never understood these immense cases which drag on for ever," a tribunal president told Eva Joly, the Oslo-born magistrate who investigated Elf. "I imagine you chose fraud because you're Norwegian and Protestant."

Humble taxpayers were tempted to follow their leaders and cheat. A champions' league of tax evaders, headed by taxi drivers who failed to declare 52 per cent of their earnings, also included lawyers, vets, chemists and restaurateurs. Charities reported that their actual receipts were a tenth of the amount that "donors" claimed in relief on their tax returns. "Most Frenchman defraud with a clear conscience," observed Henri Emmanuelli, a former budget minister. "They see it as self-defence."

Small wonder, when the grandest in town halls across the land, in Nice, Lyon, Grenoble, Cannes, were implicated. In Paris, multiple allegations – corporate kickbacks, fictitious jobs for party workers, rigged electoral lists – accompanied Chirac's long tenure in power. His chosen heir, Alain Juppé, was temporarily barred from holding public office. A helicopter was chartered to search the Himalayas for a vacationing judge to block proceedings into a payment made to the wife of Jean Tiberi, his successor as mayor.

Chirac was granted virtual immunity from testifying whilst president following a controversial Constitutional Council decision. He dismissed all allegations with a single magnificent word: "Abracadabrantesque!" The constant allegations of abuse and the intimate detail – free holidays, free apartments, free food and wine, even 700,000 francs worth of free gardening work – nonetheless gave the Fifth Republic a whiff of the Third. They were a reminder, too, of the absence of Justice from the Revolutionary pantheon, and of the tendency for the law to be the servant of the great, and not their master. "The French judiciary, since Napoleon," as Robert Badinter, lawyer and former justice minister, put it, "was installed in a culture of reverence, if not obedience, towards the political powers of the day."

The morality of civic obedience resonates most with Vichy. The past, too, troubled French self-esteem. The Occupation years were exhumed as part of the "devoir de mémoire" (duty to remember). Crimes committed under Vichy seemed to have run their legal course in 1964, when the 20-year time limit for prosecutions was reached. A charge of crimes against humanity had no limit, but it was expected to apply only to Germans. French complicity stirred little interest. When Marcel Ophül's moving film on the fate of Jews in France, *Le Chagrin et la Pitié* came out in 1972, French television rejected it. But slowly, the "national amnesia" eroded. A key moment was the publication in *L'Express* in 1978 of an interview with Louis Darquier de Pellepoix, living under a false name in Spain. He was Vichy's commissioner for Jewish questions. He was dying, and anxious that the Vichy police commissioner René Bousquet and not he himself should bear the blame for Jewish deportations, on which the spotlight now turned.

Prosecutions proved complex and divisive. The first to be accused was Jean Leguay, the police official who directed the Vél' d'Hiv' round-up. He died of cancer in 1989, ten years after being accused, still untried. The trial of Klaus Barbie, the Gestapo "butcher of Lyon", plucked back from Bolivia, was hugely publicised. Bousquet was shot dead at his Paris home in 1993 before his case was heard; the assassin was not an idealist or the relative of a victim, but an exhibitionist, known for running onto the pitch during football internationals, who held a press conference to announce his crime.

Maurice Papon, a prefect under de Gaulle, budget minister under Giscard, did not go on trial until 1997, when he was 88. He was sentenced to ten years for his role in the deportation of Jews whilst a young official in Bordeaux. The trial lasted six months, the longest criminal trial in French history; the jury rejected the prosecution's demand for a lengthier sentence, and it seemed typical of the national ambivalence to the case that, when Papon fled from France shortly before his appeal was heard, he should have been found in a Swiss hotel sheltering under the name of a Resistance veteran who bore him no ill will.

To re-examine the darkest side of collaboration was wholly justified. In 1995, Chirac became the first president to admit the "inescapable guilt" of Vichy leaders in the deportations. Nonetheless, looking at the past is a delicate business. "Voir n'est pas savoir," to repeat Alain Finkielkraut's exquisite phrase, "To see is not to understand." Vichy was the creature of the armistice. It is from the armistice – the failure, as it were, to surrender – that complicity flows. It is this that distinguishes France from the rest of occupied Europe, whose experiences, partly in consequence, were mostly much worse. 75 per cent of the pre-war Jewish population in Holland perished, 60 per cent in Belgium, 50 per cent in Norway, and 26 per cent in France. *Crimes d'obéissance* were peculiar to French officials, not through any moral quirk, but because only in France was there a government to obey.

Such subtlety was lost in a long-drawn out historical onslaught. The past reached out its clammy embrace to Mitterrand and his post-war links with Vichy officials, to the Communist leader Georges Marchais, with his wartime stint in Germany, to Jacques-Yves Cousteau, whose first underwater film was screened at a German-sponsored film festival. A 13-man commission of historians and sporting figures even looked at the politics of wartime sportsmen. The Occupation was transformed from an age of heroes into a wasteland of wretches. In reality, of course, it had both, but, at a distance of 60 years, de-Vichyfication still picked at the nation's self-image. "The obsession with this part of the past", wrote Henry Rousso, author of *Vichy, un passé qui ne passe pas*, "is a substitute for the urgencies of the present. Or, worse still, a refusal of the future."

The future was seen as a time of troubles. European integration, long a touchstone, aroused new and defensive worries of Anglo-Saxon liberalism, job insecurity, an influx of low-paid foreigners like the famous "Polish plumber" who would snatch work in everything from ski instructing to architecture. The feeling combined with opposition to Turkish entry to the EU. France, many thought, already had problems enough with the large, poor and Muslim countries facing it across the Mediterranean. Unemployment and sluggish growth remained running sores.

These fears were meat and drink to Le Pen, an embarrassment to others. The countries of the north, he said, the "non-black world", were rich and had ageing populations. They faced a Third World of five billion, who were young and dynamic. This demographic problem led to immigration, whose consequence, if nothing was done, would be "the submersion of our country, our people, our civilisation . . ." For good measure, he linked crime to immigrants, and corruption to the classic political class. National identity, he said, was being whittled away by the foreigners within France, and by the ever-increasing powers of the European Union.

How many immigrants were already in France – and how many, in the post 9/11 world of Islamic terrorism, were Muslim – was not known. Figures up to five million were bandied about, but it was taboo in a secular republic to collect racial and religious statistics. "Our ancestors the Gauls", in theory at least, applied to Algerians and Malians as well as the white *Français de souche*, born and bred. To distinguish between them, it was feared, would lead to "communautarisme" on Anglo-Saxon lines. Chirac firmly put down suggestions of "positive discrimination". All French people were equal before the law, he said; France did not recognise ethnic minorities, and "to appoint people because of their origins is not acceptable".

In reality, as the *petits blancs* among Le Pen's supporters who lived on crime- and drug-ridden estates well knew, many immigrant areas had already become virtual ghettoes. These were not shanty towns, but high-rise buildings that had become filthy and overcrowded, disfigured by violent graffiti – "Fuck la police" – with AIDS, tuberculosis and a rampant drugs culture. "Little by little," a priest said of one estate, "everyone feels caught up in this return to a savage state." The satellite dishes that peppered them were tuned to African and Maghreb stations. When Algeria played France at football in Paris in 2001, the "beurs", the second-generation immigrants from North Africa, whistled the "Marseillaise" and invaded the pitch carrying Algerian flags. In the ghettoes, the French were the foreigners: "babtou" to Africans, "gaori" and "gouère" to Arabs, "roum" to gypsies.

France had no race riots on the scale of American or British cities. But seven hundred districts round the country were classified as "sensitive". There was a constant low-level war of attrition with the police, with ambushes, hurled paving stones, Molotov cocktails, and shots. A poll in 2003 found that 49 per cent of those questioned felt they were "often" at risk of crime. It was a shockingly high figure.

Le Pen, stridently, blamed the immigrants. As noisily, and in larger numbers, the organisers of "anti-racist" demonstrations blamed the French. As wartime shame was re-attributed, so the post-Vichy generation found itself accused of "racism". The young, backed by fashionable actresses and media stars, had found a new stick with which to beat their parents.

The ghosts of the Algerian war were summonsed. "For some, the Algerian war isn't over yet," Tahar Ben Jelloun wrote in *Hospitalité française*. "The presence on French territory of a little less than one million Algerian immigrants arouses their nostalgic hatred." It was an astonishing attack. Few of the 400,000 Algerians present in France in 1962 had returned home. They had stayed on, to be joined by fresh hundreds of thousands of their countrymen. This was not the behaviour of an abused people.

Something profound, however, had gone missing from Alger la Blanche, the European city that tumbled down steep hills to the sea in white terraces. Its creators, the French, had disappeared. Hardly a Christian, or a Jew, remained in Saint Augustine's homeland. The few who remained risked butchery, like the seven French Trappists kidnapped and murdered in 1996. In Algeria, its oil and gas money squandered, abusive of human rights, tens of thousands had died in grisly night massacres. Add the tension between Arab and Berber, and Algeria indeed seemed "racist".

Against this, the French had a long history of assimilating immigrants. None seemed more native than Yves Montand, Charles Aznavour or Simone Signoret. Yet they were born Ivo Livi, Chahnour Aznavourian and Simone-Henriette Kaminker. Might it not be that the problem was the Algerians, not the French? The question was not as black and white as that, of course, as General Paul Aussaresses's shocking memoir on the workaday use of torture in Algiers made all too clear. But "racism" was an insidious and catch-all concept that added to a melancholy and self-excoriatory mood at a time when the subsuming of the nation state into Europe, and the decline of traditional faith – the number of priests being ordained in France, a thousand a year in the 1950s, slumped to a hundred, whilst the number of mosques accelerated – were already straining old identity.

It was easy to posture. When it was claimed that Muslims were excluded from the mainstream – no deputies, no prefects, leading businessmen, TV newsreaders, only national football players – the National Assembly reacted "firmly". It draped 14 portraits of black and brown Frenchwomen across its façade. Easiest of all was to ignore the issues themselves on the ground that Le Pen had raised them. He was unsavoury, crude and demagogic: so, therefore, was any discussion of these questions.

The April shock waves were subsiding by June 2002. Chirac called and won parliamentary elections. Jean-Pierre Raffarin became prime minister, a portly and amiable man from the Charente, with a rugger player's squashed nose and a lived-in face. He had his advantages: he did Chirac's bidding, he took the day-to-day blows, he was expendable, and he was not Nicolas Sarkozy.

In a reprise of old rivalries, Sarkozy did not endear himself to the president by being easily the most popular politician on the right. "The obstacle to change in France is a lack of political courage," he said in unspoken criticism of Chirac. As interior minister, he had the nerve to install thousands of new speed cameras, risking protest from the country's heavy-footed motorists, but winning them over by cutting road deaths.

Dashing, decisive, the son of an aristocratic Hungarian, with his striking wife Cécilia, Sarkozy was the coming man, and it hurt. "The Europe of 25 will force us to rethink what the central core should be," he said of the EU. That was taken to mean that he thought Franco-German primacy had had its day. In Gaullist eyes, it was near heresy. Too popular at interior, Chirac moved him to finance. When Juppé had to stand down as president of the UMP, Chirac's party, in 2004, Sarkozy replaced him. It gave him a springboard for his 2007 presidential bid. State subsidies have replaced donations in party funding, so Sarkozy had a scandal-free treasure chest for his campaign, and a ready-made think tank from which to winkle out the hapless Juppé's advisers.

The tough line Sarkozy took on crime and terrorism – he boosted the numbers of prison places by a fifth – was followed by his successor, Dominique de Villepin, who as foreign minister was the symbol of troubled relations with Washington. He followed a policy of zero tolerance for radical Islam. A close eye was kept on radicals. The courts overturned a decision to expel Abdelkader Bouziane, an Algerian cleric in Lyon, who preached the stoning of women. De Villepin changed the law and the imam was on the next aircraft out. Chirac himself described the wearing of the Islamic scarf as a "sort of aggression". A strict prohibition was applied to all visible religious symbols, including the crucifix and yarmulke. At the same time, efforts were made to whittle away at the alienation of the Muslim community. It was given an official voice in the CFCM, the French Council for the Muslim Faith, led by the rector of the Paris mosque. Imams have been offered courses in French and French law and civics; three quarters of the country's 1,200 clerics were not French, and a third spoke no French. The rejection of the EU constitution in the 2005 referendum showed mistrust of the elite to be as strong as ever. In the short term, it led to de Villepin replacing Raffarin, and Sarkozy's reappearance as interior minister. Long-term though, it revealed a nation troubled by a sense of its fragility in the face of Muslim stridency, harsh Anglo-Saxon working practices, and of the "Polish plumbers" whom the EU would allow to steal French jobs.

The economy laboured under a heavy burden of regulation and taxes. Over a quarter of the workforce were public sector employees, a proportion matched only in Scandinavia. Government spending was 53 per cent of GDP, compared with an OECD average of 38 per cent. The finance ministry employed almost 180,000 people, with two distinct organisations, one to assess tax, and one to collect. The education ministry continued to employ 960,000, regardless of a fall in school numbers. The defence ministry sported a junior minister with his own department to deal with the dwindling number of war veterans.

Public sector unions fought tooth and nail to preserve the feathers in their bedding. Their pensions, for example, were based on the final six months of salary. Such generosity was demographically unsustainable. Gas and electricity faced difficult privatisations, due to their huge unfunded pension obligations. The health service was enviable. Hospital waiting lists were short, family doctors made home visits at weekends, and most bills were covered by the state or cooperative insurance. But it cost almost 10 per cent of GDP.

Not only unions resented reform. Forty per cent of deputies were themselves on leave from the civil service. They, too, had a vested interest in undoing any minister who took them on. Strikes were so commonplace that in 2005 French surgeons decided to hold their protest against low pay and long hours at a holiday camp on the other side of the Channel. "We have so many strikes in France," one explained, "that we thought we would get more press coverage in France if we went into exile in England."

That was the rub. The French "social model", hugely expensive and restrictive, was no longer creating jobs and growth nor paying its way. Painful surgery was needed to restore health, but the country refused to submit to a knife wielded by a political class, mired in scandal and plump with perks, in whom it had lost its confidence. It expressed itself with a brutal "Non" to the 2005 referendum on the EU constitution.

The "Non" was partly a rejection of "Anglo-Saxon liberalism", the cruel world of mass sackings, factory closures and unbridled competition, that nonetheless, some quietly noted, was delivering lower unemployment, higher growth and greater job creation than the French model. The result was also a humiliation for the elite, who almost to a man had urged the electors to vote "Oui". The Socialists were split down the middle, with Laurent Fabius disciplined for his temerity in leading the "Non" campaign. For Chirac, it was a personal disaster. He was forced to sack Raffarin, bringing in Dominique de Villepin as prime minister, though the non-elected ex-diplomat was a perfect example of the very elite whose nose the voters had just bloodied; worse, the president had to accept the recall of his bête-noir rival, Sarkozy, to the interior ministry.

But the vote was also, in a broader sense, a condemnation of the Mitterrand and Chirac years. The "Non", the "child of fear and despair", the historian Nicolas Baverez wrote in *Le Monde*, marked the onset of the "death of Gaullist France, corrupted by François Mitterrand and then ruined by Jacques Chirac". These were terrible words, but they had a ring of truth.

A change of generations was due. "Sarko" and "Ségo", Nicolas Sarkozy and the Socialist Ségolène Royal, younger and with fresh ideas, were the darlings of right and left. At grass-roots level, at least, the old guard viewed Royal as facile and inexperienced, whist ill-feeling between Sarkozy and de Villepin was manifest, and the Clearstream affair, with false allegations of foreign bank accounts, was the equal to any of the right's old blood feuds.

Both promised to break with the past – "rupture" was Sarkozy's favorite word – and both attacked old party taboos. Whether they had the stomach to push through painful reforms – to grasp all those nettles Chirac said he would in 1995, but left largely untouched – remained to be seen.

Chirac's "calamitous *fin de règne*", as *Le Monde* put it, gave that task special urgency. Riots broke out in October 2005 after two teenagers electrocuted themselves while running away from the police at Clichy-sous-Bois. It was such a pretty name for a place that, like the 93 postcode for Seine-Saint-Denis, gained such a bad reputation for violent youths in hooded tops that the council appealed for photographers to shoot "Clichy sans cliché". The petrol bombings and attacks on les *keufs* (the police) spread to other predominantly immigrant *banlieues*, and continued, night after night, for three weeks. Ten thousand cars were torched, and over three hundred schools and post offices attacked, with 4,400 arrests.

The man who had predicted such troubles was quick to plaster up reminders. "Immigration, explosion of the *banlieues*," his posters proclaimed. "Le Pen told you so!" Indeed he had, and his talk of a "migratory invasion" and the "submerging" of the native population of France no longer shocked. "Now people on the left, in the center, on the right, use the same language," Le Pen crowed. "But voters prefer the original to the copy."

Sarkozy, at least, was aware of how mainstream politicians had avoided unpleasant truths. "It is not by hiding one's head in the sand," his website proclaimed, "that we will help the French resolve their fears." For 25 years, socio-Gaullism and an antiquated socialism had held sway. "France," François Bayrou declared, "has never been properly dé-Marxisé." The left nourished its belief that efficiency was injustice and profits immoral. Amid the deep mistrust of flexibility and change – Chirac himself said that liberalism was a greater threat than communism – what reform occurred was done by stealth. "Reform in our country," said Michel Camdessus, former IMF director, "still moves forward with its face masked."

The outside world was held to blame for problems. Barely a third of the French agreed that the free market was the best if imperfect system on offer – this, compared to two-thirds of Germans. Such hostility was astonishing in the world's fifth richest country, which had at least its fair share of world-class companies, and which was itself no slouch at globalisation. French companies were the world's third biggest source of cross-border takeovers, and the second largest investors in the United States, where 600,000 Americans owed their jobs directly or indirectly to French enterprises.

Just how hard old habits die was clear in March 2006. The ingrained resistance to change in the job market joined forces with the old revolutionary itch to resort to the street, throwing up the biggest mass demonstrations since 1968. Somewhere between one and three million people marched, from all five main unions – train drivers, postmen, electricity workers, civil servants, teachers – and large numbers of students, united in opposition to the CPE, the *contrat première embauche* (first job contract).This would have allowed employers to hire under 26-year-olds for two years, with the possibility of making them redundant before full job protection began. It was a modest enough measure, if clumsily introduced, intended to help, in particular, the ill-qualified youngsters from the *banlieue*. Those who protested most were often the least directly affected. They feared it as the thin end of an ultra-liberal wedge, an "institutionalized insecurity" that would "victimise the young". The students imagined themselves to be the heirs of '68. They borrowed its slogans – "beneath the cobblestones, the beach!" – and tactics, and its clashes with the police.

But this was no revolution. The students were not out to shock their parents, to break with the old, as in Red Dany's day. They wanted to imitate them, to cling to the old world of jobs for life. "May '68 was an offensive movement, with a positive vision of the future," said Cohn-Bendit himself, now a Green Euro-politician. "Today's protests are based on the defensive, the fear of insecurity and change." The street won.

Over the twentieth century, the French achieved perhaps the finest quality of life in the world. That is why so many foreigners wish to live there; the squalor of a *banlieu* estate is preferable to a hut in Mali, and the *douceur* of a Brittany village, as the Bretons have found to their chagrin, is more enjoyable for the British second-home owner than the rat race in his own overcrowded island. There is more to it than French wit and *savoir vivre* (a term, like *douceur*, untranslatable in English), or the soft blue of a lavender field, the lonely vastness of the Auvergne, a secret courtyard in Paris.

It is the ensemble of a great nation. Its genius, displayed in every art and across the sciences, has enlivened the world. So has its intellect, wisdom, taste and humanity. World-leading companies are found across the board: L'Oréal in cosmetics, insurers AXA, Michelin tyres, LVMH in luxury goods. International trade accounts for 25 per cent of GDP, the same as Germany and double the American rate.

Yet something in the soul, a fine wildness, has given way. Half the young wish to join the civil service: why join the persecuted entrepreneur when you can do the persecuting, sometimes for as little as 32 hours a week, with a safe pension to come? The dynamic young – the type that had created the *trente glorieuses* – set themselves up abroad. People no longer take to the streets in the battle of ideas, as in storm-tossed 1871 or 1936 or 1968, but to defend *les avantages acquis*.

There is a loss of self-confidence, an uncertainty, a modesty that is unbecoming and unwarranted. France has become too hard on itself, too correct, too concerned of what others might think. It is too fretful about its own past, and too diffident of the past of others. Sarkozy won a clear mandate for reform in the 2007 election, though Royal and the left spoke menacingly of his "path of brutality", and he needs a steady nerve to see it through.

The young Alexis de Tocqueville described the French as the "most brilliant and dangerous nation . . . an object of admiration, hatred, pity or terror but never indifference." That is why they so profoundly influenced Europe, with the infectious brilliance of their ideas and style; now, perhaps, they are tending to the sclerotic, hidebound, dull. And that is dangerous, too. Europe past is inconceivable, drab and forlorn without the French exception. As it undergoes its own identity crisis, Europe future needs the genius of a lively France more keenly than ever. A nation that remains *pas comme les autres*, its pride intact.

Bibliography

AMOUROUX, Henri. *La Vie des Français sous l'Occupation*. Paris: Fayard, 1961.

ARDAGH, John. *France Today*. London: Penguin Books, 1988.

ARON, Raymond. *France, the New Republic*. New York: Oceana Publications, 1960.

ARON, Raymond. *La Révolution introuvable: réflexions sur les événements de mai*. Paris: Fayard, 1968.

BEAUFRE, André. *Le Drame de 1940*. Paris: Plon, 1965.

BEEVOR, Antony and Artemis Cooper. *Paris after the Liberation 1944–1949*. New York: Doubleday, 1995.

BERNIER, Olivier. *Fireworks at Dusk: Paris in the Thirties*. Boston: Little, Brown and Company, 1993.

BERSTEIN, Serge. *La France de l'expansion: la République gaullienne (1958–1969)*. Seuil: 1989.

BERSTEIN, Serge and Jean-Pierre Rioux. *La France de l'expansion, l'apogée Pompidou (1969–1974)*. Paris: Seuil, 1995.

BLOCH, Marc. *L'Étrange Défaite*. Paris: Albin Michel, 1957.

BLUM, Léon. *À l'échelle humaine*. Paris: Gallimard, 1945.

BODIN, Louis and Jean Touchard. *Front populaire 1936*. Paris: Armand Colin, 1961.

BORNE, Dominique. *Histoire de la société française depuis 1945*. Paris: Armand Colin, 1998.

BOUSSEL, Patrice. *L'Affaire Dreyfus et la presse*. Paris: Armand Colin, 1960.

BREDIN, Jean-Denis. *L'Affaire*. Paris: Julliard, 1983.

BROGAN, D.W. *The French Nation: from Napoleon to Pétain, 1814–1940*. New York: Harper, 1957.

BURY, John Patrick Tuer. *France 1814–1940*. London: Methuen, 1949.

CHASTENET, Jacques. *Histoire de la IIIe République* (seven volumes). Paris: Hachette, 1952–1963.

CLEMENCEAU, Georges. *Grandeurs et misères d'une victoire*. Paris: Plon, 1930.

COLTON, Joel. *Léon Blum: Humanist in Politics*. New York: Knopf, 1966.

CRONIN, Vincent. *Paris on the Eve 1900–1914*. London: Harper Collins, 1989.

CRONIN, Vincent. *Paris, City of Light, 1919–1939*. London: Harper Collins, 1994.

DALLOZ, Jacques. *La France de la Libération, 1944–1946*. Paris: PUF, 1983.

DULONG, Claude. *La Vie quotidienne à l'Élysée au temps de Charles de Gaulle*. Paris: Hachette, 1974.

DUPEUX, Georges. *La Société française, 1789–1970*. Paris: Armand Colin, 1972.

DUROSELLE, Jean-Baptiste. *La Décadence, 1932–1939*. Paris: Imprimerie nationale, 1979.

DUTOURD, Jean. *Les Taxis de la Marne*. Paris: Gallimard, 1956.

FENBY, Jonathan. *On the Brink*. London: Little, Brown & Company, 1998.

FRANÇOIS-PONCET, André. *De Versailles à Potsdam, la France et le problème allemand contemporain*. Paris: Flammarion, 1948.

FREARS, J. R. *France in the Giscard Presidency*. London: Allen & Unwin, 1981.

GAULLE, Charles DE. *Le Fil de l'épée*. Nancy-Paris-Strasbourg: Berger-Levrault, 1932.

GAULLE, Charles DE. *Vers l'armée de métier*. Nancy-Paris-Strasbourg: Berger-Levrault, 1934.

GAULLE, Charles DE. *Mémoires de guerre*. Paris: Plon, 1954, vol. I: *L'Appel 1940–1942*; vol. II: *L'Unité 1942-1944*; vol. III: *Le Salut 1944–1946*.

GIDE, André. *Journal 1889–1949*. Paris: Gallimard, 1950.

GILDEA, Robert. *France since 1945*. Oxford: Oxford University Press, 1996.

GILDEA, Robert. *Marianne in Chains*. London: Macmillan, 2002.

GOUTARD, Adolphe. *1940: la guerre des occasions perdues*. Paris: Hachette, 1940.

HORNE, Alistair. *The Terrible Year the Paris Commune 1871*. London: Macmillan, 1971.

HORNE, Alistair. *The French Army and Politics 1870–1970*. London: Macmillan, 1984.

HORNE, Alistair. *A Savage War of Peace Algeria, 1945–1962*. London: Macmillan, 1997.

JACKSON, Julian. *The Politics of Depression in France 1932–1936*. Cambridge: Cambridge University Press, 1982.

JACKSON, Julian. *The Popular Front 1934–1938*. Cambridge: Cambridge University Press, 1988.

JACKSON, Julian. *La France sous l'Occupation 1940–1944*. Paris: Flammarion, 2004.

JOHNSON, R.W. *The long March of the French Left*. London: Macmillan, 1981.

LACOUTURE, Jean. *De Gaulle 2. Le politique 1944–1959*. Paris: Seuil, 1985.

MACLEAN, Mairi. *The Mitterrand Years–Legacy and Evaluation*. Basingstoke: Macmillan, 1998.

MAYEUR, Jean-Marie. *La Vie politique sous la IIIe République*. Paris: Seuil, 1984.

MICHEL, Henri. *Histoire de la Résistance, 1940–1944*. Paris: PUF, 1950.

MOLLIER, Jean-Yves and Jocelyne Georges. *La Plus Longue des Républiques 1870–1940*. Paris: Fayard, 1994.

OUSBY, Ian. *Occupation: The Ordeals of France 1940–1944*. London: John Mumay, 1997.

RAYMOND, Robert. *Histoire de Vichy*. Paris: Fayard, 1954.

RAYMOND, Robert. *Histoire de la Libération de la France*. Paris: Fayard, 1959.

RIOUX, Jean-Pierre. *La IVe République*. Paris: Seuil, 1980.

SAINT-EXUPÉRY, Antoine DE. *Pilote de guerre*. Paris: Gallimard, 1942.

SAUVY, Alfred. *Histoire économique de la France entre les deux guerres*. Paris: Fayard, 1965.

SHIRER, William Lawrence. *The Collapse of the Third Republic, an Inquiry into the Fall of France*. London: Heinemann, 1970.

SPEARS, Sir Edward Louis. *Assignment to Catastrophe*. London: Heinemann, 1954, two volumes.

SPEARS, Sir Edward Louis. *Two Men who saved France: Pétain and de Gaulle*. London: Eyrea & Spottiswoode, 1966.

THOMSON, David. *Democracy in France, the Third Republic*. Oxford: Oxford University Press, 1946.

THOMSON, David. *Two Frenchmen: Pierre Laval and Charles de Gaulle*. London: Gresset Press, 1951.

TOUCHARD, Jean. *Le Gaullisme 1940–1969*. Paris: Seuil, 1978.

TUCHMAN, Barbara. *The Guns of August*. New York: Macmillan, 1962.

ZELDIN, Theodore. *France 1848–1945*. Oxford: Clarendon Press, 1973, two volumes.

Acknowledgments

There are many people to whom thanks are due for their help in the creation of this book, in particular the Getty Archive researchers Ali Khoja and Jennifer Jeffries who helped source and collate unpublished photographs at Getty as well as Mia Stewart Wilson and Mary Pease in France.

We would especially like to thank the British Ambassador Sir John and Lady Holmes in Paris, and Monsieur and Madame Christian Pol Roger Épernay, for their support and enthusiasm for this project; our thanks also to the photographers, archivists, curators and individuals who were so generous with their time, including: Guy McLeod, Airbus, Toulouse; Simon Dominic Fisher, Keystone Paris; Simone Olivetti, ECPA, Ministère de la Défense, France; Monsieur Pierre de Longuemar, Association pour L'Histoire de Paribas; Suzanne Tise-Isore, Paris; Hamish Crooks, Magnum; and Mme Ornella Volta, Archive Eric Satie.

We would also like to pay a special tribute to Paul Welti, book designer extraordinaire, for his discerning eye and for always going the extra mile.

Photo Credits

AFP Agence France Presse, AC Archives Charmet, AFES Archives de la Fondation Erik Satie, AV Collection Annette Vaillant France, BAL Bridgeman Art Library, BET Bettmann, COR Corbis, GI Getty Images, GIR Giraudon, HD Hulton-Deutsch Collection, KAP Keystone Agence Photos, MP Magnum Photos, P12 Photos12.com, RV Roger-Viollet, RGA Ronald Grant Archive, TLP Time Life Pictures

t top, m middle, b bottom, l left, r right

1t GI;1 2ndt GI; 1 3rdt French photographer (20th century), Musée de Montmartre, Paris, AC/BAL; 1 3rdb GI; 1 2ndb P12/Collection Cinéma; 1 b GI; 2 AFP/GI; 4 Private Collection, Paris; 7 Horace Abrahams/GI; 8b HD/COR; 9 Alinari Archives/COR; 10t Lege Bergeran/GI; 10–11b P12/Oasis; 11t HD/COR; 12t GI; 12b HD/COR; 13–14 GI; 15 Faissat/ Archives Larouse, Paris/GIR/BAL; 16–17 GI; 18t Branger/GI; 18b GI; 19 GI; 20b French photographer (20th century)/Private Collection, AC/BAL; 21 RV/GI; 22 Alfred Natanson/Private Collection, AC/BAL; 23tl Alvin Langdon Coburn/GI; 23tr Daniel-Henry Kahnweiler, Private Collection, AC/BAL; 23bl Private Collection, GIR/BAL; 23b 2ndl French photographer (19th century)/ AV, AC/BAL; 23b 2ndr French photographer (20th century)/AV, AC/BAL; 23br French photographer (20th century)/ Private Collection, AC/BAL; 24 P12/Keystone Pressedienst; 105 Collection RV/GI; 106 Archives Municipales d'Épernay (Marne); 107 Branger/RV/GI; 108tl GI; 108tr GI; 108b COR; 109 Edmund Joaillier/GI; 110bl GI; 110tr French photographer (20th century)/ Private Collection, AC/BAL; 111 Branger/RV/GI; 112tl BET/COR; 112b HD/COR; 113 HD/COR; 114 P. Delbo/GI; 115 Harlingue/RV/GI; 116 French photographer (19th century)/Private Collection, AC/ BAL; 117 Parisbas, Paris; 118 Jacques Moreau/Archives Larousse/GIR/BAL; 119 Branger/RV/GI; 120t Collection RV/GI; 120b ECPAD; 121 ECPAD; 122–123 GI; 124 GI; 125 Collection RV/GI; 126 ECPAD; 128 French Photographer (20th century)/Bibliothèque Littéraire Jacques Doucet Paris, AC /BAL; 129 P12/Oasis, 130tl AFES; 130b René Clair/AFES; 131 AFES; 132 COR; 133 P12/Oasis; 134–135 Private Collection, Paris; 136–137 GI; 138 RV/GI; 139 KAP; 140–141 P12/Collection Cinéma; 142 GI; 143t RV/GI; 143b Jacqueline Masselin Catenos, Paris; 144 Private Collection, Paris; 225 Herbert List/MP; 226 GI; 227 Lucien Aigner/COR; 228 KAP; 229 GI; 230 French Photographer (20th century)/Bibliothèque Nationale, Paris, AC /BAL; 231 P12/Hachedé; 232 Bundesarchiv Koblenz; 233 GI; 234t GI; 234b KAP; 235 BET/COR; 236–237 BET/COR; 238t Bibliothèque Historique de la Ville de Paris/USHMM; 238b KAP; 239 Alinari/RV/GI; 240 BET/COR; 241 KAP; 242t and b KAP; 243 P12/Hachedé; 244–245 AFP/GI; 246–247 AFP/GI; 248 Lester Hajenina/USHMM, courtesy of National Archives; 249 AFP/GI; 250 KAP; 251 L'Illustration; 252 BET/COR; 253 Private Collection Épernay; 254 Collection RV/GI; 255 KAP; 256 GI; 257 AFP/GI; 258t David Seymour/MP; 258b KAP; 259 Charles Hewitt/GI; 260 AFP/GI; 261 GI; 262bl P12/Luc Fournol; 262mt GI; 262m 2nd t GI; 262m 3rd t Enzo Graffeo/GI; 262mb P12/Collection Cinéma; 263 Luc Fournol; 264 Yale Joel/TLP/GI; 345 Reg Lancaster/GI; 346 Henri Cartier-Bresson/MP; 347 Henri Cartier-Bresson/MP; 348t KAP; 348b AFP/GI; 349 KAP; 350t AFP/GI; 350b AFP/GI; 351 ECPAD; 352 Erich Lessing/MP; 353 Loomis Dean/TLP/GI; 354–355 Nicolas Tikhomiroff/MP; 356t KAP; 356b KAP; 357 ECPAD; 358t P12/Collection Cinéma; 358b Walter Daran/TLP/GI; 359 GI; 360t KAP; 360b KAP; 361 Bruno Barbey/MP; 362 AFP/GI; 363 GI; 364l Henri Cartier-Bresson/MP; 364r ESA/AFP/GI; 365 Jean Gaumy/MP; 366t Luc Fournol; 366b GI; 367 René Burri/MP; 368t Jean Gaumy/MP; 368b Jean Gaumy/MP; 369 Henri Cartier-Bresson/MP; 370 Patrick Zachmann/MP; 371br AFP/GI; 372tr Inge Morath/MP; 372tm Ferdinando Scianna/MP; 372b Martine Franck/MP; 373 AFP/GI; 374tl Collection RV/GIM; 374bl Elliott Erwitt/MP; 374mr Jean Gaumy/MP; 374 Bruno Barbey/MP; 375 Bruno Barbey/MP; 376tl KAP; 376b Georges Bendrihem/AFP/GI; 377 Michel Clement/AFP/GI; 378t Patrick Kovarik/AFP/GI; 378b Pierre Verdy/AFP/GI; 379 Marcel Mochet/AFP/GI; 380–381 AFP/GI; 382t Gabriel Bouys/AFP/GI; 382b Pascal Rondeau/AFP/GI; 383 Marcel Mochet/AFP/GI; 384 Patrick Hertzog/AFP/GI; 465 Guy Le Querrec/MP; 466l Thomas Coex/AFP/GI; 467 Patrick Zachmann/MP; 468tl Abbas/MP; 468ml Derrick Ceyrak/AFP/GI; 468bl Gérard Julien/AFP/GI; 469 Paolo Pellegrin/MP; 470t Jean-Pierre Muller/AFP/GI; 470bl Boris Horvat/AFP/GI; 470br Carl De Keyzer/MP; 471 André Durand/AFP/GI; 472 Eric Cabanis/AFP/GI; 473 exm company/H. Goussé/AIRBUS S.A.S. 2005; 474–475 Chad Ehlers /Stone/GIM; 476tl RGA; 476b RGA; 477 Vince Bucci/GI; 478 l Robyn Beck/AFP/GI; 478r Bertrand Guay/AFP/GI; 479l François Guillot/AFP/GI; 479r Guy Le Querrec/MP; 479b Guy Le Querrec/MP; 480 Henri Cartier-Bresson/MP

Index

*The Renault-Elf team in
the 1985 Tour de France*

UNWELCOME ARRIVALS

Illegal immigration created crises as chronic poverty, conflicts, political instability and corruption drew people from African and Middle Eastern dictatorships into Europe. Some passed through France to Sangatte (right) on the Channel coast, in the hope of getting on a ferry or freight train headed for Britain. Many illegal immigrants were difficult to budge. Some, like these Africans (below), defied deportation orders by seeking well-publicised shelter in a Paris church.

RIGHT TURN

Jean-Marie Le Pen (middle left), here training in the gym at his house in Saint-Cloud, won both admirers for and protesters against (top left) his National Front party by exploiting the fears raised by mass immigration. Muslims (bottom left) raised tensions in 2004, by demonstrating against the ban on the Islamic headscarf in state schools. It was disturbing that newcomers should demand the overthrow of the century-old republican tenet of secular schooling. Disturbing, too, that immigration, far from boosting the economy, should lead to drab enclaves (right) with high unemployment rates.

HOME PRODUCE

French farmers dumped tons of cauliflowers (facing page) in Saint-Malo in 2004 to vent their anger against foreign imports. They also bombarded a McDonald's in Marseille (below left) with apples, retaliating against American agricultural sanctions, which in turn had been sparked by an EU ban on American beef. José Bové, farmer, longtime protester and champion of Roquefort cheese (right), spent three weeks in gaol in 1999 after burning a McDonald's in the Aveyron. He became a hero of France's anti-globablisation movement, also deeply suspicious of the arrival of Disney Europe outside Paris (below right).

UP IN THE AIR

The Millau Viaduct soars for a mile-and-a-half across the mists of the Tarn Gorge (left). The world's tallest bridge, its highest pillar taller than the Eiffel Tower, it was completed in 2004 to the designs of Norman Foster, evidence that the French retain their engineering genius. Without the Airbus programme, French inspired and led, Europe would have abandoned the market for large passenger aircraft to the United States. By 2005, Airbus was outselling Boeing, and outbuilding the 747 with its own super-large, if problematic, 555-passenger capacity A380 (right, at Toulouse).

ETERNAL FRANCE

*A brace of baguettes,
a duo of demoiselles,
and the promise of a fine
vintage to come: eternal
France, here in the
vineyards of St Emilion*

Directors kept the brilliance alive in the cinema, though the market share of French films was sliding. Jean-Pierre Jeunet's fantasy Amélie *(opposite)* (Le fabuleux destin d'Amélie Poulain) *was nominated as best foreign-language film at the 2002 Academy Awards in Hollywood.* To Be and to Have (Être et avoir) *(right) showed a one-room, one-teacher country school in* la France profonde. *The beauty and passion of Isabelle Adjani (below, with Vincent Perez) was caught in the historical melodrama* La Reine Margot.

(Above, from left to right) Jean-Benoit Dunckel of the duo Air at the
Hollywood Bowl in September 2004; the singer M at the Paris
Omnisports, November 2004; Kool Shen of the rap group NTM; the
singer Patricia Kaas.